CONFRONTING HOMOPHOBIA IN EUROPE

Homophobia exists in many different forms across Europe. Member States offer uneven levels of legal protection for lesbian and gay rights; at the same time the social meanings and practices relating to homosexuality are culturally distinct and intersect in complex ways with gender, class and ethnicity in different national contexts.

The essays in this volume illustrate the findings of a European project on homophobia and fundamental rights in which sociologists and legal experts have analysed the position in four Member States: Italy, Slovenia, Hungary and the UK.

The first part of the book investigates the sociological dimensions of homophobia through qualitative methods involving both heterosexual and self-defined lesbian and gay respondents, including those in ethnic communities. The aim is to understand how homophobia and homosexuality are defined and experienced in the everyday life of participants.

The second part is devoted to a legal analysis of how homophobia is reproduced 'in law' and how it is confronted 'with law'. The analysis examines statute and case law; 'soft law'; administrative practices; the discussion of bills within parliamentary committees; and decisions of public authorities. Among the areas discussed are 'hate crimes' and 'hate speech'; education at all levels; free movement, immigration and asylum; and cross-border reproductive services.

Confronting Homophobia in Europe

Social and Legal Perspectives

Edited by

Luca Trappolin

Alessandro Gasparini

and

Robert Wintemute

·HART·
PUBLISHING

OXFORD AND PORTLAND, OREGON
2012

Published in the United Kingdom by Hart Publishing Ltd
16C Worcester Place, Oxford, OX1 2JW
Telephone: +44 (0)1865 517530
Fax: +44 (0)1865 510710
E-mail: mail@hartpub.co.uk
Website: http://www.hartpub.co.uk

Published in North America (US and Canada) by
Hart Publishing
c/o International Specialized Book Services
920 NE 58th Avenue, Suite 300
Portland, OR 97213–3786
USA
Tel: +1 503 287 3093 or toll-free: (1) 800 944 6190
Fax: +1 503 280 8832
E-mail: orders@isbs.com
Website: http://www.isbs.com

British Library Cataloguing in Publication Data

Data Available

ISBN: 978-1-84946-275-4

Typeset by Columns Design XML Ltd, Reading
Printed and bound in Great Britain by
Page Bros (Norwich) Ltd

This publication has been co-funded by the European Union's Fundamental
Rights and Citizenship Programme.

Foreword

GUSTAVO GUIZZARDI

We could approach this volume from this standpoint: a social group feels discriminated against and reacts to the phenomenon of debasement it suffers. Depicting itself as an 'active minority' (Melucci 1996), such group exposes and counteracts the negativity imposed on it by society. Study and analysis are, in this way, combined with the issue of agency. It is therefore useful to detect at least some of the elements of such connection.

One of the main goals of anti-homophobic policies is protection at institutional level through juridical norms which remove negativity, confront discrimination, punish the people causing it and defend minorities' rights. Here we have the neo-liberal framework of fundamental rights and universal citizenship equality. The formulation, apparently simple and unquestionable, is actually complex and articulated. The legislative factor, be it of *common* or *civil* law, represents a necessary objective to be achieved, but it may reveal itself as insufficient. Such a factor is necessary in order to remove from the juridical system provisions—both evident and hidden, both written and applied—which produce actual discrimination and debasement; it is also necessary in order to legitimise and implement positive actions driven by legislation. Such distinction between homophobia *in law* and opposing homophobia *with law* is depicted in the analyses of the juridical chapters in the second part of the book, which deal with issues connected with the differences among juridical and institutional systems in the European Union. The aim is ambitious: to overcome existing diversities at State level, from a supranational standpoint, typical of the building process of the EU.

Once realised, as in the case of the United Kingdom, analysis and action concerning legal rules appear important, as they give force to and legitimise the voice of groups and individuals (Putnam 2000); give the opportunity to come out of the closet and of the situation of discrimination; legitimise objective and subjective positions seeking recognition (Honneth 1992). From thereon, however, structural and cultural latent phenomena come to light, revealing how they are deeper and more persistent than the basically 'enlightened' and partly elitist action, which is a substantial part of the legislative institutional dimension.

At this level, intersectionalities and resistances reveal themselves as deeply rooted and profound and they show how long-term analyses and actions are necessary.

The first point concerns the culture of heterosexuality and the relationship between heterosexuality and homosexuality which is not symmetric. The subjects questioned in the sociological case studies of the first part of the book clearly recognise this point, but at the same time they prove that they experience it in different ways, depending on which one of the two positions they place themselves in.

Heterosexuals, at first sight, prove to be open-minded, liberal and modern: from their point of view, there is and there should be no discrimination, because it has no reason to exist. Lesbians and gays, on the other hand, declare discrimination and denounce it openly. The denial of a conflict by a dominant group, while such conflict is perceived and exposed by the homosexual group, de-legitimises the very possibility of a voice for the discriminated group. The latter, from the point of view of the dominant culture, has no reason to complain, since the problem does not exist. Victimisation, when denounced, may appear incongruous and be downgraded as an improper complaint. We could ask ourselves whether this could be a possible unintentional effect of legislative interventions, and whether there may be a connection with the spread at national and European level of wider attitudes of tolerance. In other words, the spread of an ideology of equal dignity and protection of rights may contain, together with surely positive aspects, a paradoxical one: the paternalistic solution, by the dominant group, of granting fictitious recognition to marginalised groups, hiding, and hence denying, real inequalities behind the veil of political correctness. This makes more sense the more the causes of discrimination are labelled as pathologies, considered as occurrences to be fought and extirpated (and this is the positive aspect), but to be kept on the margins of a system that continues to be valid in its substantial structure.

Lesbians and gays oppose this solution, bringing to light their everyday experience, recalling the symbolic violence—often subtle but relevant—they suffer, as well as actual acts of violence, perhaps less widespread but certainly occurring. Inconsistency between the opinions of the hegemonic group and the everyday practices of its members seems then a general phenomenon, which van Dijk (1991) would define as 'implicit racism'.

At this point, the situation becomes more complicated for different reasons. The simplest reason is that there are, at a structural level, collective dimensions occurring, making the situation much less dynamic. Collective factors can be found in the secondary socialisation system, that is, school; in the creation of collective representations, that is, media; in the codification of interpretive systems, that is, religion. These factors can work in active ways, for example keeping and nurturing aversions, stereotypes and prejudices; or in passive ways, through censorship and silencing. Interactions with the peer group, depicted as crucial for individuals subjected to implicit or explicit degradation ceremonies, appear as specific places of operative intersections between institutional and everyday life, and reveal the deep, even if not always explicit, conflict existing within the institutional system.

But the deepest aspects of the domination of the hegemonic group are found on two levels. One is institutional, that is the family; the other pertains to the reciprocal collocation of groups (heterosexuals and homosexuals), which are considered as placed in a binary dimension, although the context is much more complex and articulated.

'The family' is one of the obstacles to the processes of transformation described in the book, as it contradicts a privatisation of the conflict, showing the limits of the reassuring neoliberal solution, which does not judge behaviour in the private sphere, as long as it does not spread into the public sphere and question its shared foundations. At family level, as a matter of fact, gender articulations seem important but secondary features, instead the basic aspect remains in the dual differentiation of sex (Bimbi 2009; Di Cori 2000). This is, in essence, the core of the contradiction exposed by the claim for, and the legally-recognised possibility of, creating lesbian and gay families, even with children.

There are many possible motivations in defence or in denial of such families. As regards denial, there is the issue of the 'nature' of the heterosexual composition of the family, which reifies institution of the family, de-historicises it and confines it to a sort of 'naturalised nature', preventing any kind of solution to the conflict. Another argument for denial is the appeal for the 'tradition' of the family, although it takes into account the historical and social variations in the family's formation. The conservative content remains, even if covered by a subtle pluralistic gloss, because the potential change is deferred to an unforeseeable and distant future, while the superiority of the dominant institutional system ('our tradition') is stated at the expense of other possible 'traditions'.

Those who advocate homosexual and homoparental families also use the issue of the 'nature' of the family, but they do so from a different basis, that is, the right to form a family. This is a normative interpretation of 'nature', which favours the institution over the specific features of its members. A second argument is the challenge to the sexual basis of the family, replaced by a more modern element, that is, reciprocal love. This is surely a point of opposition to the hegemonic culture, but it is not anti-traditional, as it maintains the stability of family and it does not deny its continuity. The perpetuation of new life inside lesbian and gay families is, as a matter of fact, achievable through techniques which have become 'natural', as they are culturally available, even if not equally widespread and accessible in every country.

So, the argumentative strategy of subordinate groups goes through different dimensions; it tries to demolish from the inside the system of legitimation of the hegemonic group, accepting its structure and, at the same time, changing its application.

Nevertheless, even in postmodern complexity, social stratifications of intersectionality are steadily at work. Differences are elements of intervention, among them the difference pertaining to ethnic communities is important, but others could be brought to light. On the surface, it appears that according to some immigrant groups (see chapter six), homosexuality and even more, homoparental families, are a Western disease, a feature of total decay of the acceptable rules of behaviour, of 'immorality'. In this case, the group perceives itself as an absolute 'Other', it reifies its own interpretive system and its own rules of conduct, together with the Western ones. Is this the 'clash of civilisations', seen from the other side? This question remains open. Certainly, the research on homophobia inside ethnic communities brings to the surface more general tensions connected to their integration in the societies they live in. We could, for example, suppose that migrants and Western people questioned in the research give different meanings to the concept of family. Whereas the Western debate refers to the nuclear family, interpretations emerging from ethnic communities refer to the extended family, which not only maintains strong parental bonding, but also specific duties, centralised authority and diffused social control. So the conflict does not rise from the family founded on sexual diversity anymore, but from the family reduced to the couple. This is the main element of opposition between ethnic communities and Western culture, since the nuclear family is by far the most widespread one and then it stands as an actual alternative. In other words, family represents an area of problematic tensions motivated by the trans-nationality of ethnic families' experiences.

The second point showing the deep rootedness of the heterosexual hegemony is the heterosexual-homosexual distinction. We know that, at the theoretical level, this distinction is very weak, above all because it detects in sexuality the cornerstone of a classification which is fundamental. Nonetheless, it seems to be useful but at the same time fragile, to be maintained, but at the same time overcome. Why this ambivalence? In my opinion we could answer by placing such distinction in a particular historical situation of the struggles for recognition (Honneth 1992). The basic tension is between group and subject, between the collective and the individual dimension.

The point of arrival of these struggles is the reciprocal recognition, among autonomous subjects, of the value of everyone within an accepted plurality of values, of the possibility, collectively recognised, of responsibly pursuing a quality of life that is considered worthy. So sexuality disappears as a basic and discriminating characteristic, as it is absorbed by a wider exchange of reciprocal esteem inside a plurality of possible options. The starting point is the collective classification of individuals by putting them inside a group, which is given a value (in our case a negative value, above all, perceived as negative by the group itself), regardless of the personal value given to any single member. This is what Max Weber defined as status allocation. The intermediate point is the need to act as a group, and to accept being identified as a group, moreover to underscore such belonging, even at the cost of reducing the individualising feature, which tends to affirm the autonomy of the subject. At the macro level, as a matter of fact, we are assisting in a continuous cultural conflict in which various groups try to affirm their way of life as worthy of value and to transform into recognition what is experienced as reciprocal solidarity within the group. The processual instrumentality is visible, and so is its contingent necessity. It is worth underlining how the situation is provisional, and how it will end not with the 'victorious affirmation' of the instances of the group, but rather with the dissolution of the group itself, caused by its dynamic and inner purposes.

Legislative action, in this intermediate phase, confirms its own importance and fully shows its own meaning. The cultural aim, which is probably more important and certainly more long-lasting, reveals the difficulties of the path. The provisional feature is one of these, together with the need for some action, for example stressing the differences between the dominated and dominant group, in order to get attention and visibility. The contradiction between the tactical goal and strategic aims of the minority group causes strong tensions within it. However, it is also possible that the binary model, at least in the medium term, ends up being a regulatory practice confirmed by the hegemony of the heterosexual group. This is a practice which creates coherent and stable identities at the normative level in order to maintain culturally understandable notions of identity, at the expense of an actual process of personification, as Judith Butler puts it with regard to the concept of 'metaphysics of substance' (1990).

A question about the structural aspect remains: how do institutions, for example the family and the law, act within a pluralistic and globalised society, where not only different cultures but also diverse institutional systems—connected in different ways to the whole social system—live together and confront each other? This question may become the subject of future research.

Contents

Contents

List of Contributors

TAMÁS DOMBOS is a Junior Research Fellow at the Center for Policy Studies at Central European University (Hungary).

ALESSANDRO GASPARINI is a Research Fellow and Contract Professor of Private Comparative Law at the University of Bologna.

SILVIA GORINI is a lawyer (Bologna Bar Association) and co-founder of CESD (European Center of Discrimination Studies).

GUSTAVO GUIZZARDI is a Senior Full Professor at the Faculty of Political Sciences at the University of Padova.

ŽIVA HUMER is a Research Fellow at the Peace Institute (Slovenia).

NEŽA KOGOVŠEK ŠALAMON is a Research Fellow at the Peace Institute and PhD candidate at the Faculty of Law at the University of Ljubljana.

ROMAN KUHAR is an Assistant Professor in the Department of Sociology at the University of Ljubljana and a researcher at the Peace Institute (Slovenia).

CATHY LA TORRE is a lawyer (Bologna Bar Association) and co-founder of CESD (European Center of Discrimination Studies).

SIMON MALJEVAC is a director of the Slovenian LGBT non-governmental organisation Legebitra.

GYÖRGY MÉSZÁROS is Assistant Professor at the Faculty of Education and Psychology of the Eötvös Loránd University, Budapest.

TATIANA MOTTERLE is a PhD student at the Doctoral School of Social Sciences at the University of Padova.

ESZTER POLGÁRI is lecturer and special project officer at the Legal Studies Department at the Central European University (Hungary).

MONICA RUSSO holds a PhD on topics related to women and migration studies, and is a co-founder of CESD (European Center of Discrimination Studies).

JUDIT TAKÁCS is Scientific Deputy Director at the Institute of Sociology at the Hungarian Academy of Sciences.

List of Contributors

TAMÁS P TÓTH is a Junior Research Fellow at the Institute of Sociology at the Hungarian Academy of Sciences.

LUCA TRAPPOLIN is an Assistant Professor of Sociology at the Faculty of Political Sciences at the University of Padova.

ROBERT WINTEMUTE is a Professor of Human Rights Law in the School of Law, King's College London.

ANDREW KAM-TUCK YIP is an Associate Professor and Reader in Sociology at the University of Nottingham.

Table of Cases

European Court of Human Rights

Court of Justice of the European Union

Hungary

Italy

Slovenia

United Kingdom

United States

Table of Legislation

International Conventions

European Union

Treaties(and Instruments with Same Status)

Directives

France

Hungary

Italy

Slovenia

United Kingdom

Statutes

Statutory Instruments

United States

1

Introduction

LUCA TRAPPOLIN AND ALESSANDRO GASPARINI

How can we widen our understanding of homophobia? This is the main question this volume seeks to answer. It presents the findings of a comparative research study on homophobia and fundamental rights in four European countries, where discrimination and hostility against lesbian and gay people have different quantitative and qualitative features. The analysis included in this book was derived from the project *Citizens in Diversity: A Four Nation Study on Homophobia and Fundamental Rights*, which was co-funded by the European Union within the Fundamental Rights and Citizenship programme (Directorate-General Justice, Freedom and Security) for the years 2010–11.

The project involved sociologists and legal experts from Italy, Slovenia, Hungary and the United Kingdom with the aim of better understanding homophobia and discrimination against lesbians and gays at the national level, and promoting their fundamental rights in the European context. The Department of Sociology at the University of Padova (Italy) coordinated the activities in the four countries. The partners in the project were the Municipality of Venice (Italy), the European Study Centre on Discrimination (*Centro Europeo Studi sulla Discriminazione*) in Bologna (Italy), the Peace Institute in Ljubljana (Slovenia), the Institute of Sociology of the Hungarian Academy of Sciences in Budapest, and the School of Sociology and Social Policy at the University of Nottingham (UK).

Considered as a whole, the chapters of this book pursue the aim of widening the understanding of homophobia by investigating three analytical dimensions:

(i) the cultural and institutional definitions of homophobia and, more broadly, discrimination and hostility against lesbian and gay people, which are embedded in social representations of women and men of different social groups (self-defined heterosexuals, self-defined lesbians and gays, members of ethnic minorities), as well as in the legal systems of the involved Member States;

(ii) the actual experiences of such phenomena in the everyday lives of women and men of different social groups (self-defined heterosexuals, self-defined lesbians and gays, members of ethnic minorities) and in cases in national courts;

1

(iii) the strategies of resistance to homophobia and discrimination which come to light in the social practices of women and men of different social groups, and the strategies of opposition which can be seen in the legal system and/or derive from its operation.

Overviews of the investigation of these three dimensions are presented in chapter two for the sociological analysis, and in chapter seven for the legal analysis, while more comprehensive information about the results of the research are included in the chapters devoted to the sociological and legal analysis of each country. In the next few pages of this Introduction, we shall briefly contextualise our approach within the international sociological debate on homophobia and the legal discussion on the protection of lesbian and gay rights. At the same time, we will provide some information about the specificities of the diverse national contexts.

1. Exposing and Opposing Homophobia in Society

Until the 1960s, in Western societies, hostility towards homosexuality was not understood as a problem to be combated or opposed, or even to be publicly discussed. Homosexuality—rather than the negative social reaction to it—was itself perceived as the problem to be confronted. Then, something happened. Lesbian and gay people began to come out of their closets, to organise themselves as a social movement—which now has a worldwide dimension (Adam, Duyvendak and Krouwel 1999)—and to challenge the shared beliefs, social practices and institutional mechanisms which support their subordination. The public emergence of distinct lesbian and gay voices occurred at different times and took diverse forms in the four countries involved in the research: it is deeply rooted in the social history of the UK (Greenberg 1988; Weeks 1979), but did not begin until the early 1970s in Italy (Nardi 1998; Trappolin 2004), and some 15 years later in Slovenia and Hungary (Kuhar and Takács 2007; Long 1999; see also chapters four and five in this volume). Despite its different national paths, lesbian and gay mobilisation has been crucial in all countries in turning the definition of the problem related to homosexuality upside down.

The concept of homophobia played a significant role within these revolutionary changes. The idea that distress over homosexuality is unwarranted and socially damaging emerged in the late 1960s and the early 1970s, as the result of the criticism some psychologists and psychiatrists expressed about the medicalisation of homosexuality, and its consequent interpretation as a mental disorder. As George Weinberg wrote in the first page of his seminal book *Society and the Healthy Homosexual* (1972): 'I would never consider a patient healthy unless he had overcome his prejudice against homosexuality.' His famous definition of homophobia as 'the dread of being in close quarters with homosexuals' came from an interpretation of anti-homosexual hostility as a prejudice, that is, an unfounded judgment or a misconception about the ways homosexuals lead their lives. In order to understand this fear, Weinberg proposed investigating the psychological motives and intra-psychic conflicts which sustain it.

Discomfort about this approach arose soon after its formulation, and by the late 1970s, the need for a 'better understanding' of homophobia became relevant for social scientists, although in different ways (Sears 1997).

From the point of view of psychological research, after Weinberg's work the main problem was that the appropriation of the concept of homophobia by non-professionals—as well as the concept's easy use by professionals—reduced its scientific clarity. Homophobia became an 'umbrella under which all negative responses towards homosexuals have been grouped' (Roderick et al 1998: 80). To maintain the scientific usefulness of the concept, the main response by researchers has been to restrict it to a specific dimension of a broader phenomenon called 'homonegativism'. Homonegativism has been framed in multidimensional terms as the 'entire domain or catalogue of anti-gay responses' (Hudson and Ricketts 1980: 358), and homophobia has been operationalised as the emotional or affective dimension of it, that is, the experience of fear, disgust, anger and discomfort in dealing with lesbian and gay people.

From the point of view of sociological research, the discomfort arising from Weinberg's definition of homophobia has been more radical. Because it is mainly focused on individuals, it fails to properly consider the structural nature of hostility against homosexuality and homosexual people. Homophobia, it is argued, is not a dysfunctional and pathological attitude which derives from intra-psychic conflicts. It is rather a feature of the very mechanism of social reproduction which constructs homosexuality as a disadvantaged identity— through attitudes, behaviours, practices, symbols and policies—and preserves the dominant position of (heterosexual) men in defining masculinity and the subordinate status of women (Britton 1990; Kimmel 2005; Hamilton 2007). Accordingly, sociologists developed new conceptual tools—some are listed in chapter two—which framed hostility against lesbians and gays in collective and structural terms. Nevertheless, the deployment of the term homophobia has never been completely replaced by alternative terms owing to its popularity and communicative power.

In considering the sociological research as a whole, we can identify two main approaches to studying the societal dimension of homophobia. The first approach is to study the degree of diffusion of bad attitudes and stereotypes towards homosexuality and homosexual people among representative samples of the general population, on the basis of the hypothesis that 'the treatment of a group is affected by the attitudes held by others about that group' (Loftus 2001: 763). International surveys carried out by European institutes of research follow this assumption and provide quantitative data permitting a comparison of the situation in different countries. As an example, data from the Eurobarometer surveys allow us to compare Italy, Hungary, Slovenia and the UK in relation to three subject areas. The first is the social visibility of lesbian and gay people and their integration into heterosexual networks (European Commission 2009). In the UK, the percentage of interviewees who state that they have lesbian or gay friends or acquaintances is 56%, hardly similar to the percentage of Italian interviewees (32%), and not at all similar to the percentages of Slovenians (17%) and Hungarians (11%). The second area of comparison is the social acknowledgment of the fact that lesbian and gay people are discriminated against (European Commission 2009). Anti-homosexual discrimination reaches the highest level of social visibility in EU Member States in Italy (61% of Italian interviewees consider this discrimination to be very or fairly widespread in their country), whereas the UK is one of the countries where anti-homosexual discrimination is considered less widespread (40% consider this discrimination very or fairly widespread). Hungary and Slovenia rank in the middle of EU countries, and nearly half of the Hungarian and Slovenian samples consider discrimination against lesbian and gay people as an emerging problem in their societies, because they believe that it is more widespread than it was five years before. The third area of comparison is the pervasiveness of negative attitudes towards lesbians and gays. In the UK (European Commission 2008), interviewees did not commonly express any aversion to having lesbian or gay neighbours: 80% said they would be comfortable with that situation. In contrast, such aversion is more common in Slovenia, where only 62% of interviewees expressed the same attitude, in Italy (44%) and above all in Hungary (35%). Although less generally accepted, responses are similar to the question of having a lesbian or gay man in the highest elected position in the country (European Commission 2009): 58% of the British sample would fully accept this hypothetical situation, whereas only 36% of Slovenians, 27% of Italians and 17% of Hungarians would do so.

A second approach in the sociological analysis of anti-homosexual hostility comes from the qualitative studies on the circulation of discourses on homophobia, and the social effects produced by their deployment in order to stigmatise circumstances, social groups or cultures. This approach does not give the word homophobia a particular meaning. Rather, it investigates homophobia as a 'discursive resource for individuals and collectivities to … respond to discrimination against gay men and lesbians' (Bryant and Vidal-Ortiz 2008: 387–88).

To borrow Adam's argument (1998: 183), discursive analysis of homophobia has two interrelated aims: (i) to identify how discourse produces subjectivity; and (ii) to identify how already constituted actors deploy discourses, adopting some specific frameworks and discrediting others. Both aims can be properly achieved only if the analysis considers the ways in which society reproduces the hegemony of heterosexuality.

With regard to the first aim (how discourses produce subjectivity), examples can be found in the work of scholars such as Mason, Tomsen, Stanko and Curry. Mason (2002) carried out in-depth interviews with lesbian women in order to understand the ways in which their awareness and experiences of 'heterosexed violence' construct a system of knowledge which sustains their subordination through an ongoing self-surveillance over their bodies and manners and the self-limitation of social spaces. On the other hand, analysis of antiviolence projects which involve the police (Stanko and Curry 1997), as well as analysis of criminal trials and expert discourses on homophobic hate crimes (Tomsen 2006), show how the protection of victims through a criminological approach reinforces the (heterosexual) expectation that lesbians and gays have to be 'responsible' and 'normal'.

Examples of research inspired by the second aim identified by Adam (how social actors deploy discourses) include ethnographic studies of the deployment of homophobic language in schools (Pascoe 2007), and of the accusation of 'being homophobic' among members of multicultural lesbian and gay communities (Vidal-Ortiz 2008), together with qualitative studies which investigate the ways in which lesbian and gay activists frame the problem of violence against them (Jenness and Broad 1994). Considered as a whole, this body of literature shows us that discourses about homophobia can also be investigated as powerful tools in the preservation of the dominant social positions of the ones who deploy them. As Guzmán puts it (2006: 4):

> Attribution of homophobia, a technology of homosexual selfhood, is implicated in the maintenance of racial distinctions as it is used in the description of Latinos and other people of colour in a manner that is not commensurate with the actual incidence of homophobia in those communities as opposed to white communities.

The sociological analysis presented in the first part of this volume interprets homophobia as a structural feature of European societies, which reminds lesbians and gays 'what' they are—that is subordinated and vulnerable social actors—although it does not automatically dictate 'who' they are, that is, how they embody and react to this structural oppression.

On one hand, the comparison between different European countries, the inclusion of ethnic minorities in the comparative design (see chapter six), and the focus on everyday life, certainly help in achieving a better understanding of homophobia, whose shapes and effects depend on cultural and institutional elements of the social context of life, as well as on individual circumstances. On the other hand, the comparison between the experiences and views of members of the hegemonic social group (self-defined heterosexual women and men), and the experiences and views of self-defined lesbian and gay participants, allows us to sharpen the mechanism of symbolic violence (see Bourdieu 1998), which helps to sustain homophobia through the normalisation of homosexuality.

2. Recognising and Combating Homophobia in and with the Law

To discuss homophobia in relation to the legal system can be more difficult than one might think. This is because the relationship between homophobia and law has two aspects: one internal and one external. On one hand, the word 'homophobia' (or 'homophobic'), which is rarely if ever found in a legal text (a statute or regulation), can be used to describe laws and judicial decisions which themselves create unfair discrimination based on sexual orientation. On the other hand, homophobia defines a social phenomenon external to law, which law recognises as a violation of fundamental rights, and seeks to prevent and fight with specific provisions. When we use the term 'homophobia' with reference to a legal system, we intend to combine both aspects. We will analyse how the presence or absence of legal rules creates discrimination against people because of their sexual orientation, that is, the law itself is both an example and a cause of the social phenomenon of homophobia (by 'recognising homophobia in law'). We will also examine the ways in which national legal systems react to the social phenomenon of homophobia ('combating homophobia with law').

The four countries included in the study are all EU Member States, but their legal, historical, religious and linguistic-cultural differences permit potentially interesting comparisons. Italy, Slovenia and Hungary have civil law systems, whereas the UK has a common law system. Slovenia and Hungary are 'post-communist' societies, whereas Italy and UK have been 'always capitalist' since 1945. Italy, Slovenia and Hungary have Roman Catholic majorities, whereas the UK has a Protestant majority. Finally, each country represents a different family of languages: Romance (Italy), Slavic (Slovenia), Uralic (Hungary) and Germanic (the UK). Such different countries display some of the main social and legal diversities of the EU, and appear to be a useful sample of the present situation in national legislation with respect to the fight against discrimination based on sexual orientation.

In order to compare the results of this research (see chapter twelve for the result of this comparison), it has been necessary to look at those systems with the 'glasses of the comparatist'. This means that every system must be analysed from the point of view of an external and impartial observer, without assuming that concepts belonging to one national system are common and shared. Only from this perspective can it be understood why, even under legal systems such that of the UK, where the legislation on lesbian, gay, bisexual and transgender (LGBT) rights is certainly much more complete and coherent, the social situation is not very different to countries—such as Italy—where no laws have been passed.

This study also attempts to contribute to comparative legal studies on protection against discrimination based on sexual orientation, studies which are in their initial stages. Because of its interdisciplinary dimension, which includes criminal law, administrative law, private law, immigration law, family law, EU law and international human rights law, there are few academic studies that deal with this subject from a truly comparative perspective. Many articles can be found at the national level which concern the recognition of same-sex couples in national law and other aspects of the fight against discrimination based on sexual orientation. However, few authors go beyond this limited dimension and examine the problem as a systemic lack of protection of fundamental rights that is, they do not consider the problem from the perspective of recognising the existence of homophobia in the law itself.

Only at the end of the 1990s, when academics began to systematically include the demands of gay men and lesbian women for liberation and emancipation in the context of universal human rights did the new frame of reference replace the preceding approach: consideration of universal rights met the locally-defined struggle for civil rights, moving the legal discourse to a constitutional and fundamental rights level that every legal system must now deal with. In recent years, authors and activists have begun to use the phrase 'sexual rights', which incudes the right of all persons to express their sexual orientation, with due regard for the well-being and rights of others, without fear of persecution, denial of liberty, or social interference.

From this perspective, the first step in the debate has been to define the object of protection: is it an identity, a form of behaviour, a status or a manifestation of one's private life? Sexual orientation can be understood as a personal and private matter that does not have public relevance. As a consequence of this assumption, homosexuals cannot be identified as a social group or a minority to protect, it being sufficient, from the point of view of the legislator, to grant respect only for one's private life. This debate encounters national differences concerning ways of protecting minority rights, such as by creating ad hoc, special or exceptional legislation, especially in the field of criminal law. Secondly, even after agreeing with the autonomous dimension of sexual orientation as an expression of personality, in either private or public places, many disputes have arisen over the terms to use in granting the defined protection, which involve issues of accuracy as well as resistance to definition and compartmentalisation. Lying behind these worries about the use of language to define people is often a refusal to recognise non-approved sexual practices and identities, or to develop, by using new terms in the law, new cultural values and systems of meaning for a society that is not yet able to accept a concept of 'citizenship in diversity'.

This debate at the international level has had different consequences at the national level, which vary from country to country, especially within the EU. From this point of view, the UK has certainly had the most developed and comprehensive academic debate, which, together with a favourable political situation, has supported the endorsement of laws that give full protection to the rights of lesbians and gays. In other countries such as Slovenia and Hungary, even though legal scholars have little interest in sexual rights, the legislator has nonetheless chosen to adopt significant legal reforms. Finally, in some cases such as in Italy, the debate on sexual rights is at a very early stage and faces strong social, cultural and political resistance, including in academic debate.

In this context, the most significant contribution at the European level to the academic and institutional debate has been the comparative studies conducted by the Fundamental Rights Agency (FRA) of the EU, which constitute a crucial starting point for the analysis of institutional and social homophobia.

Taking into account the lines of research pursued by the FRA, and seeking to broaden the horizons of the study, the legal research team chose to analyse four areas of national legal systems legislation: on hate crime and hate speech, on education at all levels, on free movement, immigration and asylum, and on cross-border reproductive services, considering them, as will be explained in chapter seven, possible areas for action or further study by EU institutions. To do so, in some cases the legal analysis has had to put to one side some debates that are still open at the national level, and try to consider the particular topic from a purely legal perspective. For example, it must be recalled that the right to parenthood through assisted reproduction is the subject of a heated discussion among movements and associations for gay and lesbian rights: socially, a clear distinction between donor insemination and surrogate maternity has been made. The former is accepted as a legitimate means of realising the right to parenthood, while there is no agreement regarding the latter, which is seen as conflicting with women's rights. From the legal point of view, if a national system recognises a right to parenthood or a right to procreate, the question moves to the person, man or woman, who wishes to enjoy this right independently from his/her sexual orientation, and the ways in which this right can be exercised.

For the above reasons, we described the main aspects of national legislation, in the context of the general framework of each national legal system, and the legislation's efficacy, formal contradictions and impact on civil society, demonstrated through case law. Our studies reveal how public institutions (including legislatures and courts) can often be resistent to change, and to providing real and effective protection against discrimination. Furthermore, in countries where there is a lack of legislation securing LGBT rights, the possibility of challenging the maintenance of particular practices or stereotypes is greatly undermined. In these situations influenced by social actors, governments and other public institutions are often reluctant to offer systematic and coordinated solutions, either through specific statutes or through administrative regulations.

The gap between social homophobia in Europe, and the legal response to homophobia in Europe, can be better appreciated if we cast our minds back to an apparently distant, in time and space, social and legal reality: the racial segregation in the USA that formally ended less than 50 years ago. In justifying the doctrine of 'separate but equal', the Supreme Court of the USA,[1] in 1896, used words that remain worryingly apt regarding homophobia in Europe in 2011:

---

[1] *Homer A Plessy v Ferguson*, 163 US 537 (1896).

Legislation is powerless to eradicate racial instincts or to abolish distinctions based on physical differences, and the attempt to do so can only result in accentuating the differences of the present situation. If the civil and political rights of both races be equal, one cannot be inferior to the other civilly or politically. If one race be inferior to the other socially, the Constitution of the United States cannot put them on the same plane.

PART I

EXPOSING AND OPPOSING
HOMOPHOBIA
IN SOCIETY

2

Introduction to the Sociological Case Studies

ROMAN KUHAR, JUDIT TAKÁCS AND ANDREW KAM-TUCK YIP

This Part consists of five chapters; this introductory chapter and a further four chapters, each based on a sociological case study carried out in one of the four countries covered by the project. Although recognising the legal, historical, socio-cultural and political specificities of these countries in relation to the issues of sexual equality, homosexuality and homophobia—and this is reflected in each study's research design—these case studies collectively aim to produce a more nuanced understanding of homophobia.

Since the authors of these chapters conceptualise homophobia as a multi-faceted and multi-layered phenomenon, they have sought to explore it from the standpoints of heterosexual women and men as well as lesbians and gays, attempting to examine how this term itself is perceived, contested, and used in an everyday context. By giving voices to both the heterosexual majority and the lesbian and gay minority in this respect, the authors hope to illustrate convergences and divergences across sexual orientation, and promote a better understanding of homophobia within the European context.

Of course, understanding is only one side of the story. As the title of our book suggests, equipped with nuanced understandings, the authors also want to confront homophobia through the lens of the lived experiences of the lesbians and gay men who opened their hearts to them. They have examined the diverse strategies lesbians and gay men developed to manage and resist homophobia in various aspects of life. More specifically, the authors locate this exploration within two broad empirical contexts—education (see chapters three, four and five) and ethnic minority communities (see chapter six)—in order to demonstrate the 'lived' nature of this contestation.

These four case studies operated within the qualitative paradigm, using focus groups and individual interviews as the primary data collection tools. In total, 32 focus groups and 55 individual interviews were conducted between March 2010 and January 2011. Two hundred and five individuals participated in the research, comprising 68 heterosexual women, 28 heterosexual men, 32 lesbians, 71 gay men, and six transexuals. Each of the following chapters provides a more detailed methodological account.

All four studies followed the same three thematic frames, applied to focus groups and interviews, although the UK case study differs from the others in its specific focus on ethnic minorities. The first area of investigation relates to different definitions, interpretations and understandings of homophobia. We wanted to explore how respondents understand the concept of homophobia and how their interpretations can be applied to possible resistance towards homophobia in diverse contexts. We were also interested in the familiarity of this concept in each national context and in representations of lesbians and gays at the national level or—in the UK—at the level of different ethnic communities.

The second thematic field addresses the critical issue of homosexuality and education. We were interested in both the experiences of lesbians and gays with homophobia in school settings, and the suggestions of students of educational studies and trainee teachers on possible strategies to prevent homophobia in schools. We investigated how and where homosexuality is/should be addressed in the school setting and the potential for going beyond the currently heteronormative nature of school curricula.

Our third field of investigation tackles the role of the law in combating homophobia. We focused on respondents' awareness and expectations of equality legislation (where such legislation is in operation). We tried to investigate how the existing legislative framework in the national contexts provides the ground for overcoming homophobia.

Following the focus group and individual interviewing procedures, a standard topic guide was applied with open-ended questions around the main research themes. All potential participants were provided with an explanation of the study, and willing participants provided written informed consent. All interviews were conducted by experienced interviewers. Each respondent was given an assumed name. The interviews were tape-recorded, transcribed verbatim and then transformed into national code books.

Methodologically, the study is based on the tradition of Critical Discourse Analysis (CDA), which aims at understanding the discursive practices as those which construct the social reality and individuals as social subjects (see Fairclough, 1992; Fairclough and Ruth, 1997). It also helps to investigate power relations and consequent inequalities within given social structures. As such CDA is never non-political as it implies a form of intervention in social practice and social relations. It is directed against social exclusion, through sexism, racism, homophobia and so on. In other words, CDA is aiming at the disclosure and explanation of ideological power relations behind the discourse and implicit elements of the text.

Drawing all these four chapters together, four broad unifying themes could be identified as common traits of the comparison: (1) the uses and limitations of 'homophobia' as a concept; (2) the persistence of heterosexuality as an organising principle of social life; (3) the power of the 'child protection' or 'child welfare' discourse in militating against sex and relationship education in schools and recognition of same-sex parenting and family life; and (4) the necessity of strategies to confront homophobia engaging with local specificities.

With regard to the understanding of homophobia as a concept, the case studies were conceptually designed to examine homophobia on various levels. Taking their cue from scholars such as Gregory Herek, the authors conceptualised homophobia as not only individual behaviour and acts against lesbians and gays, but also as a cultural ideology that simultaneously stigmatises homosexuality and elevates heterosexuality, as well as institutional and community practices which accentuate the glare of heterosexual lifestyles, making invisible and silencing—however implicitly—lesbians and gays.

As the findings show, the majority of respondents were familiar with the concept of homophobia. Although no clear line can be drawn between lesbians and gay men, and heterosexual respondents in their views of homophobia, the latter tended more often to resort to the interpretation of homophobia as a personal trait of individuals who see homosexuality as abnormal or as an illness. From their standpoint, homophobia implies the fear of lesbians and gays. It can be explained as an emotional reaction to something unknown, a reaction to the threat that lesbian and gay people pose to these individuals. In that sense, homophobia is stripped of its structural elements, because its focus is on the individual's views and attitudes. Lesbians and gays, on the other hand, more often interpreted homophobia outside of its classical psychological definition as a fear of homosexuals. In this context, homophobia was seen as a form of violence or as a discriminatory attitude or act, against homosexuals. Drawing on their own experiences, they see homophobia as an organising principle of social life, which reflects and is connected to broader socio-economic, cultural and political contexts. In their opinion, the traditional definition of homophobia as an individualised cognitive and affective state (that is irrational fear or disgust) is not sufficiently comprehensive in capturing the levels that transcends the individual. Therefore, the invisibility, silence, and at times physical violence that lesbians and gays experience are more than simply outcomes of discriminatory acts by individuals; they are also consequences of social and cultural norms and values that explicitly and implicitly construct homosexuality as the 'other': to be distanced, managed, or even suppressed. Confronting homophobia, then, becomes not only the reformation of individual minds, but also the transformation of social and political structures and practices, so that silence could be broken, invisibility dispelled, and violence stopped.

Whether one thinks that homophobia is still a useful concept in such endeavours—and adopt variant concepts such as 'homonegativity', 'heterosexim' or 'heteronormativity'—is one that academics will continue to debate. On a policy and practice level, however, such commitment could not be over-emphasised. If we apply the results from the focus groups to the classical functionalist analysis of homophobia (see Herek 1984), the non-experiential functions of homophobia, the symbolic (peer pressure, ideology, world views) and the defensive functions (internalised homophobia, repressed homosexuality) seem to gain special importance. Furthermore, the research findings show that knowledge about the social conditions of lesbians and gays is most often not mediated through educational institutions (homosexuality being a rarely-addressed topic in school curricula), but rather through often stereotypical cultural representations, including representations and homophobic language use (such as homophobic jokes) reflecting a culture of homophobic social exclusions. The latter includes different 'disciplinary systems' (Kimmel 2005) which especially enables men to preserve their social privileges and power positions.

In relation to the above, all four case studies also highlight the powerful and entrenched nature of heterosexuality as the primary organising principle of social life. Evoking the concept of 'heteronormativity', the authors incontrovertibly demonstrate cultural, religious, and social values and practices that legitimise and perpetuate heterosexuality as the norm; namely, the referential framework for life. Heteronormativity underpins the structural context within which the inter-actional order is suspended. It is a powerful context, because it is everywhere, yet not explicit at all times. It defines, and it delimits.

Many lesbians and gay men in all the case studies reported the challenge of swimming against this current. While legal recourse could be helpful in some cases where discriminatory acts were committed against them, lesbians and gays found it much more challenging and energy-sapping to toe the heterosexist line, in order to benefit from qualified and fragile tolerance. The lack of actual experiences of interacting with lesbian and gay people led some heterosexual respondents to suggest—and perhaps to pretend—greater social visibility of lesbians and gays as a way to greater tolerance. However, as the respondents believe, these images should be normalised to the extent that they do not in any way shock, provoke or interrupt the 'normal life' of society. In other words, while tolerance might be found in some social relations and spaces, there was always a string attached: do not rock the boat; be gay, but do not be too loud or too obvious, or this fragile tolerance might be withdrawn. Tolerance and 'propriety', therefore, are inextricably linked.

Additionally, individualised notions of homosexuality, focusing on specific features of individuals to be kept private, which dominated all focus group sessions with heterosexuals, also seemed to foster the notion at least in some respondents, that social acceptance of lesbian and gay people is in inverse proportion to their social visibility. In this context, social acceptance was inter-preted as being tolerated, and equal rights claims were often overshadowed by the convenient application of a 'don't ask—don't tell—don't bother' strategy. For some respondents, the presence of openly lesbian and gay people on the streets, seen as an act of invading public space with the most public form of coming out, constituted an unnecessary extreme or even provocation, reinforcing the view that homosexuality is a private matter and should be kept that way. In this context normal behaviour was equated with keeping the expression of sexual preferences mostly hidden, creating a new division between 'extreme activists' and ordinary people, replacing the conventional heterosexual–homosexual divide.

In that sense homosexuality was seen as a private matter, which means that even the 'normalised' expressions of homosexual feelings and lifestyles should stay mostly hidden. The latter was not suggested solely by heterosexual respondents, but also by some of the lesbian and gay respondents themselves. All of them argued for human rights of sexual minorities, but they conditioned it by the normalisation of homosexuality. In that sense the classical division between heterosexuals and homosexuals was extended to a new one: good gays versus dirty queers. Here we can see how old binary oppositions are being reconstructed: one is invited into the 'power position club' (we will tolerate you), but has to succumb to the heteronormativity of the club and distance him or herself from 'the Others' (the dirty queers) who are casting a shadow on 'Us' (good, normalised gays and lesbians).

But what exactly does normalisation entail? On the surface the respondents' answers include requests for proper dressing, non-exposition of naked skin (in Pride parades) and the like, but the real content behind these expectations is actually gender conformity. Men should act like men and women should act like women. In this interpretation effeminate men and butch women as well as transsexual and transgender persons, represent the source (and the excuse for) homophobic stands. In other words: homophobia does not start with sexual orientation, it starts with gender.

In parallel with the heteronormative 'corrections' of lesbians and gays are the interpretations of which acts can be classified as homophobic. As the studies have shown, some participants apply the label of homophobia only to those acts which are intentionally harmful. Some ways of thinking and acting are rationalised as not being homophobic when participants consider them as common in the context of their everyday life.

The third unifying theme that unites all the case studies is the power of the 'child protection' and 'child welfare' discourse in militating against sex and relationship education in schools and recognition of same-sex parenting and family. Through the perspectives of heterosexual and lesbian and gay participants, we uncovered the recognition of the expansion of the ripple of tolerance in all four countries studied, albeit to differing extents—with the UK being the most tolerant and Italy, the least—in this respect. However, a closer inspection reveals that the level of tolerance for homosexuality decreases when the 'child protection' or 'child welfare' discourse is evoked. This is clearly demonstrated in the Italian, Slovenian and Hungarian case studies whose heterosexual participants were high school or university students of educational studies and trainee teachers. There was unanimous agreement among all these respondents that homosexuality and homophobia should be included in school curricula and should be discussed in schools. According to the respondents, the purpose of such discussions is in combating homophobia; preventing stereotypical representations of lesbians and gays; and creating a culture of inclusion and tolerance. However, none of the trainee teacher respondents considered the possibility that lesbian and gay topics could be brought to school by one or more of their students coming out as lesbian or gay: when they were asked what they would do in such a situation, after an initial reaction of astonishment ('this possibility has never occurred to me!'), they started to consider it as a realistic option for which they should be better prepared, even if it did not seem to be part of their professional training. This points to a serious lack in the teacher training programmes that hardly provides guidelines, or helps to develop skills and competence on how to tackle sensitive issues related to ethnic, religious or sexual minorities in their future teaching practice.

Students also stressed that lesbians and gays are 'just like anyone else' and should be presented as normal. One of the best ways to do that is through an example: normality can become visible if pupils (and their parents) can interact with lesbian and gay individuals in classrooms. Although it is possible for such an approach to have a positive effect, lesbians and gays are again created as an 'object of observation', which has to meet certain higher standards in order to be constituted as normal and consequently accepted. The underlying expectation from the lesbian or gay guests is not only to inform pupils about homosexuality, but rather to have a positive effect on their 'heads and minds' about homosexuality. In other words: these guests should be likeable ... which means should be 'normal', just like anyone else. The less one can see his/her homosexuality, the better. Furthermore such an approach creates lesbians and gays as the only source of truth about their 'special situation', which cannot be accessed from outside.

The well-meant approach which creates lesbians and gays as a 'special category' to be tolerated and included, can be seen most explicitly in the responses of those students who believed that homosexuality (and other Otherness) should be dealt with in (one) special workshop, as a one-off discussion, and should not be addressed throughout the curricula. However, the majority of respondents believed that the topic should be addressed whenever appropriate throughout the school curicula.

There was a wide interpretation of what is the appropriate context to discuss homosexuality. For some, the most appropriate context is within sex education. This position was challenged by those who believed that a discussion of homosexuality also includes a debate on lesbian and gay families, which cannot be placed into such a context. This issue turned out to be another breaking point, especially for Italian students, who framed the best interest of the child as an insurmountable limitation in the definition of normality of lesbians and gays. In other words: if lesbians and gay men pretend to have children in their own families, that is seen as trespassing on the gender matrix and as such is undesirable. This interpretation, however, was not so typical of Slovenian and Hungarian education students.

For most of the respondents in the study, the question of how to deal with homosexuality and homophobia in schools was something they had not thought about before. While they did mention that homosexuality (rarely) comes up as a topic of their studies, the majority reported not being at all equipped to discuss these topics in classrooms. It seems that training programs hardly provide any guidelines on how to tackle such sensitive questions. Some respondents also pointed out that homosexuality should be explicitly mentioned in the official curricula in order to avoid possible protests from the parents. Students of education believed that homosexuality and related topics should be addressed, but within a heteronormative framework, which suggests tolerance, but keeps the power relationship unquestioned. Homosexual issues should be presented, but in a 'neutral' way, that is avoiding the suspicion of pursuing 'gay propaganda' or being 'too provocative'; homosexuality must be included but not in a way which would deconstruct the hetero-homo binary opposition and decentralise hetero-sexuality as the main organising principle. It is evident that there was much fear about the 'promotion' of homosexuality that might disrupt the 'normal' psycho-logical, emotional and social development of the child.

Although the British case study focused on ethnic minority communities generally, such concerns were also explicitly articulated whenever the educational context was mentioned. Indeed, the findings suggest that this discourse also underlined many heterosexual participants' attitude towards same-sex parenting and family, citing the welfare of the child to justify their objection. This illustrates a focal point that efforts to confront homophobia need to focus, in order to extend the acceptance of lesbian and gay rights.

The fourth and final unifying theme that the case studies have identified is that the effort to confront homophobia is a multi-faceted endeavour that must engage with local specificities. As this Part of the book shows, the four countries covered by the project occupy different positions in terms of legislative development in relation to sexual equality. This, at least partly, influences the socio-cultural context. While we are not suggesting a unidirectional relationship between legislative progress and attitudinal or social change, we do acknowledge the empowering and liberating potential of the law in enabling subordinated indi-viduals and groups to step out of the darkness of the margin, and embrace the mainstream. This is clearly illustrated in the findings. Most of our respondents knew and acknowledged the advantages provided by the existing legislative framework in their countries. However, for example, Hungarian lesbian respond-ents who had or wanted to have children expressed their dissatisfaction with the Hungarian legislation and interpreted the lack of equality in the field of family law as a violation of children's rights. On the other hand, some respondents did not want to register their partnership even in those countries where it was a legally available option because it would have meant an 'official coming-out' which they wanted to avoid.

For quite a few lesbian and gay respondents secrecy was still a very important element in maintaining their social integrity and helping them to avoid being stigmatised. At the same time, it was also acknowledged that secrecy can have serious negative consequences, including stress from information management and leading a double life. Lesbian and gay participants demonstrated acute awareness of local, national and international socio-cultural and political contexts, within which they navigated their lives and constructed resources to confront homophobia in meaningful ways. Nonetheless, while there is evidence of organised and confident efforts among lesbian and gay participants to confront homophobia in various aspects of life, we have also uncovered voices of fear and resignation. These are voices of lesbians and gays who were far from confronting and resisting homophobia, for they did not have the social, cultural, political and emotional capital to do so. Among our respondents, when considering practical ways to combat homophobia, the dominant feeling often seemed to be one of incapacity and powerlessness.

However, resignation cannot be always interpreted as a sign of fear and low social capital. As shown in Slovenian case study, resignation in terms of withdrawal from a homophobic situation can be understood as a proactive behaviour. It contributes to one's personal protection and represents a strategy of actively managing stigma. On an everyday basis, resignation is a strenuous attempt to manage the weight of heteronormativity, often in silence and invisibility. This strategy is meant to offer, however tentatively, a 'safe' space, free from stigma (being lesbian or gay is bad, sinful, disgusting, etc) as well as from totalising categorisation (you are nothing but a lesbian or a gay man), which in effect perpetuated shame and stigma, rather than encouraged the living of holistic and proud lives. Indeed, as Poon and Ho (2008) and Pile and Keith (1997) have reminded us, resistance takes a myriad of forms, with some being institutionalised, visible and political; while others are personal and even invisible.

On the whole, the findings of these four case studies continue to remind us of the uneven and convoluted trajectory of sexual rights acquisition across Europe and within each of its Member States.

3

One Step Beyond: Researching Homophobia in Italian Society

LUCA TRAPPOLIN AND TATIANA MOTTERLE*

1. Introduction

The use of the term 'homophobia' is consolidated at international level, in the social sciences and in the public debate, when reference is made to discrimination, ostracism and violence against lesbians and gays. Social scientists are aware of its problematic connotations. They emphasise the inadequacy of the original formulation of the concept and its vagueness due to the increasing use of the word in everyday speech. Nevertheless, 'homophobia' used by both researchers and activists may be connected to a desire to give an interpretation to the phenomena in question, to explain them by focusing also on the systems of definition of reality and the institutional practices which present heterosexuality as the unquestioned norm in relations between men, between women, and between men and women. As regards these aspects, the Italian context is quite different from the international one.

In order to shed light on this discrepancy, we begin this chapter by examining how homophobia is discussed and studied at the national level. Then we develop the analysis of our case study, which is aimed at widening the understanding of homophobia which is revealed by Italian research. So far, research on victimisation—much less developed than research on anti-homosexual stereotypes, as we shall see—has clarified some phenomena, from the most striking to the more ordinary ones, but has not sought those elements which help or hinder our attempts at interpreting some experiences as discrimination. At the same time, the perspective of heterosexual subjects has been examined by applying quantitative methods based on standardised questions. These allowed us to record some opinions—and possible changes in those opinions in time and

* This chapter is the result of mutual collaboration between the authors. The Sections 1–6 were written by Luca Trappolin, and sections 7 and 8 by Tatiana Motterle. Section 9 (Concluding Remarks) was written by both.

space—regarding questions connected to homophobia and, to a lesser extent, the activation of behaviour which reproduces or is in contrast to it. The aim of this research was to intercept signals of a cultural change in an anti-discriminatory direction, and to reveal the persistence of its opposite. In both cases, the role of heterosexual subjects in discrimination against homosexuals is exclusively considered as a position in terms of acceptance or refusal of requests for citizenship from lesbian and gay communities. The qualifying aspect of these positions—the conditions of acceptance and refusal—were not questioned.

Our approach involves the above mentioned 'grey' areas, in the certainty that this will take us one step beyond in the study of homophobia and discrimination against lesbians and gays. The central questions of our analysis are: What are the conditions for a heterosexual point of view in recognising discrimination against lesbians and gays? What are the assumptions which may allow lesbians and gays to feel as if they were victims and express their suffering socially? To what extent are these assumptions conditioned by the hegemony of the heterosexual point of view? These questions focus on the relationship between the viewpoint of heterosexuals on discrimination—how they empirically see it and through what frameworks they understand it—and what comes to the surface from narrations by lesbians and gays.

Our approach is based on the concept of symbolic violence (Bourdieu 1998). Following it also implies studying homophobia as a *discourse* that produces the system of knowledge justifying it (Mason 2002), in which some subjects are considered vulnerable because of their subordinate social position. Since these knowledge systems reflect and in some ways reproduce heterosexual power, we start our analysis from the narrations of the hegemonic group (sections 5 and 6). Analysis of the stories and narratives of lesbians and gays will identify the ways in which the above hegemony is supported or challenged (sections 7 and 8).

2. The Public Debate on Homophobia in Italian Society

The topic of the everyday life of lesbians and gays and their requests for recognition have been present in the national debate for over a decade, although they have received only discontinuous interest in the mass media and marginal involvement from the political establishment. Discussion of the causes of victimisation of lesbians and gays, and the spread of the concept of homophobia, regardless of its definition, have been less well rooted.

We consider an exemplary selection of 998 articles devoted to homosexuality published between 1998 and 2005 in *Il Corriere della Sera*, the most widespread

Italian daily newspaper.[1] Lesbian and gay ostracism and discrimination stand out predominantly in descriptive articles, in which the possible causes are not singled out or treated in depth. In this period of time, references to elements of the cultural and institutional system of Italian society are basically limited to the debate on the 2000 World Gay Pride event in Rome, and to the recognition of lesbian and gay couples in the second half of 2005, following the law allowing homosexual marriage in Spain. The use of the word 'homophobia' in these discussions is, in terms of quantity, negligible: it occurs in 12 out of 998 selected articles.

In recent years we have seen a greater articulation of the discussion on homosexuality, which has allowed us to focus more on the structural dimension of discrimination and violent acts, promoting the use of the word 'homophobia'. On one hand, this change has been facilitated by the debate which developed in 2007 and especially in 2009 about the presentation of bills aimed at introducing specific measures in the penal code to punish discrimination against homosexuals (see Gasparini et al chapter eight in this volume). On the other hand, this was promoted by the capacity of lesbian and gay organisations to impose the topic of fighting against discrimination in the political agenda of some large urban centres such as Rome, Turin, Bologna and Naples, facilitating the implementation of specific actions (Gusmano and Bertone 2011).

3. Homophobia and Social Sciences in Italy

A review of social sciences in Italy shows important changes in research, although we are still far from the levels reached in other Western countries. Until recently, the creation of knowledge on the various phenomena ascribable to the concept of homophobia focused on the diffusion of negative stereotypes among the Italian people. The (few) opinion surveys which are relevant to our case are researches which have mainly included homosexuality in the area of more general topics, such as changes in the values of young people or changes in values throughout Italian society. These studies are interesting, because they also consider: (a) the representation of Italian society as discriminatory for lesbians and gays; (b) the legitimisation of homosexuality by interviewees; and (c) the interviewees willingness to recognise lesbian and gay families. Even with the necessary caution, mainly due to sample diversity, we can identify the characteristics of population trends on such topics. We find that: (a) those who were consulted definitely

---

[1] Articles were collected and analysed in the context of wider research entitled 'Citizenship and Cultural Pluralism', coordinated by Franca Bimbi for the Department of Sociology, University of Padova, financed by the Italian Ministry of Education, University and Research (MIUR) over the period 2004–2006 (see Trappolin 2011a).

acknowledged some discrimination dynamics in their social contexts; (b) inter-viewees mainly declared their estrangement from traditional stereotypes; and (c) acceptance of lesbian and gay lifestyles and recognition of their experiences of family-life are far from being widespread, especially when referring to parent-hood.

Let us consider, for example, the surveys on youth carried out from 1983 by the IARD research institute (Altieri and Faccioli 2002; Zanutto 2007). Results show that, in the 20 years between the first survey and the latest one available, a large majority of young people (88.2% in 1983; 83% in 2004) believed that Italian society stigmatises homosexual *experiences*, that is, sexual acts between same-sex partners. Research on a sample of students from the Friuli Venezia Giulia region carried out in 2006 (Trappolin 2007) indicates that the perception of discrimina-tion against lesbians and gays turns out to be milder when related to its practical effects. In fact, if we change the object of the question and replace homosexual *experience* with homosexual *people* ('Italian society discriminates against homo-sexuals') the perception of discrimination fades (61.6% in agreement), and even becomes uncertain (48% in agreement) when the question is about the presumed 'higher exposure to violence of lesbians and gays'.

At the same time, the IARD research shows an increase in the percentage of those who believe that homosexual *experiences* are acceptable: from 36.7% in 1983 to 46.2% in 2004. These data reveal that opinions on homosexuality have progressively become polarised, resulting in the creation of two almost equivalent blocks of acceptance and refusal. This division among young people is encoun-tered throughout the national population. Surveys on samples of all ages show that the percentage of interviewees who consider homosexuality 'a form of love like heterosexuality' reached 49.9% in 2003 (Eurispes 2003) and 52.5% in 2008 (Eurispes 2009).

Moving to the topic of negative stereotypes of homosexuality, the above mentioned research in Friuli Venezia Giulia shows how the stereotypes persist among young people, mainly boys. In the first place, the idea that homosexuality is a disease was considered plausible by almost one-third of the boys (28.3%), a percentage which falls to 12.2% in girls. A similar result was reported 10 years earlier by an Italian work on affectivity and sexuality among young people between the ages of 18 and 30 (Buzzi 1998).[2] Secondly, a remarkable percentage of boys declared they had feelings of hate (22.4%) and repulsion (12.1%) towards gay men. The same boys did not declare this type of emotional reaction about lesbians. Moreover, these feelings were not expressed by the girls interviewed, whether the object of the questions were gay men or lesbians.

Research carried out so far also shows a division in reference samples on the question of giving recognition to lesbian and gay couples. Among young people,

---

[2] According to this research, about one-third of men interviewed did not deny that homosexuality is a disease (Buzzi 1998: 60).

the percentage who believed such couples should enjoy the same rights as heterosexual couples reached 47.1% in 1997 (Buzzi 1998) and 41.9% in a regional survey of 2006 (Trappolin 2007).[3] A more recent nationwide survey of the entire Italian population (Eurispes 2009) indicated that legal recognition of cohabitation between people of the same sex was accepted by 58.9% of those interviewed.

Conversely, the above divisions disappear when we consider access to adoption for lesbians and gay men. In a nationwide survey of the moral pluralism of the Italians, carried out in 2000, only 14% supported this right (Cappello and Gasperoni 2003). Nearly 10 years later, those in favour of adoption by lesbians and gays was estimated to be 19% (Eurispes 2009). Access to adoption by lesbians and gays is a problematic topic also for young people, although to a lesser extent: in Friuli Venezia Giulia, only one-third of interviewees (32.3%) approved it (Trappolin 2007).

3.1. New Research Approaches

Anti-homosexual discrimination has only recently received definite interest in Italian research, and researchers have also started to study the dynamics and modalities of lesbian and gay victimisation. One example is the recent involvement of two important national institutions, the Italian Institute of Statistics (ISTAT) and the Office for the Elimination of Racial Discrimination (UNAR) at the Department for Equal Opportunities of the Presidency of the Council of Ministers. In 2009 ISTAT started the first pilot survey on gender, sexual orientation and ethnic origin discrimination to hear opinions of the population about homosexuals and to collect data about their victimisation. UNAR started a similar project in four regions in Southern Italy in 2011. Unfortunately, no data is available at the time of writing.

This new interest in victimisation is mainly due to the lesbian and gay organisations which have stimulated and often directly promoted—with national and international funds—surveys on the experience of lesbians and gay men. In the first Italian research, which was carried out on a sample of 2,000 lesbians and gays at the end of the 1980s, about one interviewee out of four reported that he/she had been a victim of violence, aggression or blackmail, mainly by strangers, in the experience of gay men, and by acquaintances, in the case of lesbians (ISPES 1991: 93).[4] A study carried out 10 years later on a sample of 500 members of the lesbian and gay community of Turin showed a considerable increase in the acknowledgement of victimisation: half the interviewed gay men and one-third of the lesbians declared that they had suffered from aggression or

---

[3] On these subjects, see data in Barbagli and Colombo (2007: 306–12).

[4] Reported cases of aggression mainly refer to isolated instances, although it is necessary to recall that the sample was predominantly (85%) made up of gay men.

abuse (Saraceno 2003: 191–92).[5] Arcigay—the best-known Italian non-governmental organisation in this field—directly interviewed 4,690 men and 2,084 women in 2004, and found that 20% of lesbians and gays declared they had been insulted because of their sexual orientation in the previous year (Lelleri et al 2005).

More recently, lesbian and gay organisations have focused their attention on victimisation in specific contexts, such as in the school and workplace. In 2001 the Lesbian Subjectivity Group of Milan collected 691 questionnaires from Italian lesbian women. 25.5% of the interviewees (with a peak of 41.5% for women under the age of 20) had suffered discrimination at school, especially in the form of derision and ostracism (Sonego, Podio, Benedetti et al 2005). In April 2011, sponsored by the Ministry of Labour, Arcigay started the first nationwide research on discrimination against lesbian and gay workers.

Bullying originating from homophobia was also studied for the first time by Arcigay in 2006 (Lelleri 2007). The aim was to understand how students support or prevent acts of bullying against schoolmates who are—or are thought to be—lesbian or gay. In 2010, funds made available by the Ministry of Labour and Social Policies allowed Arcigay to focus more sharply on these phenomena, placing side by side a survey on school populations and a collection of lesbian and gay victimisation stories at school (Prati 2010). The results of these two surveys clearly reveal a situation in which being insulted, derided, ostracised or physically attacked are all present in a system which is not perceived as discriminatory by schoolmates and teachers.

4. Methodology of the Italian Case Study

The project 'Citizens in Diversity: A Four-Nation Study on Homophobia and Fundamental Rights' took into account the perspectives of both heterosexuals and homosexuals to analyse representations and experiences of discrimination, following the example of the most recent Italian research.

In the period March 2010 to January 2011, the research group created eight focus groups—four composed of self-defined heterosexuals, two with self-defined gay men and two with self-defined lesbians—and collected 28 individual interviews. In total, 72 subjects were involved: 26 heterosexual women, 10 heterosexual men, 13 lesbians and 23 gay men. The choice to be only interviewed, to take part only in the focus groups, or to be involved in both, depended on candidates' availability. As a general rule, the research group asked everyone if they were available for interviews and focus groups; the interviews included

[5] In this case, the presence of lesbians in the sample had more balance. The greater victimisation of gay men is due to their higher exposure to aggression in contexts assigned to sexual encounters.

in-depth stories of experiences of victimisation, and the focus groups covered aspects of the collective definition of various types of discrimination and strategies of resistance. Those who did not wish to take part in the focus groups were also interviewed on subjects debated collectively.

The lesbian and gay group was composed of women and men living in the Veneto region. The women were between the ages of 19 and 46, and the men between 17 and 65. Nine out of 13 of the lesbian women were involved in both interviews and focus groups, two were only interviewed, and two only took part in a focus group. Only one of the 23 gay men took part in the focus group after he had been interviewed, 15 took part only in focus groups within a Catholic gay network, and seven were only interviewed.

The heterosexual group was composed of students from schools and universities in the Veneto region, aged between 17 and 35. Nine of them were high school students (five boys and four girls), 19 were university students registered in courses related to education, human sciences or psychology (three male and 16 female) and eight were PhD students in Educational Sciences (two men and six women). The nine high school students were only interviewed, all the others only took part in the focus groups. In-depth interviews with high school students mainly took into account their opinions and experiences of homosexuality and victimisation of lesbians and gays, leaving out their views on citizenship.[6]

5. Heterosexual Understanding of Homophobia: Homophobia as a Pathology

The research group used the term 'homophobia' explicitly to start discussions in focus groups and introduce narrations from the people interviewed. Participants were first asked to give an abstract definition of the concept of homophobia from their own sources of knowledge. The same concept was later given a more operative definition by also considering the school context as the site of possible prevention strategies. Lastly, participants were asked to think about different concepts of discrimination, in order to reveal types of hostility which appear to be less discriminatory or even justifiable.

Not surprisingly, during the research we learnt that heterosexual respondents do not use the term homophobia in their standard language, but this does not mean that they were completely unaware of its 'practical' meaning. All our heterosexual students considered the term as socially charged with a strongly negative and stigmatising meaning, apart from their specific suggested definitions, which were not only concerned with sexual orientation. Being accused of homophobia, and accusing someone of it, were seen as categorisations which can

---

[6] Interviews were recorded by Sara Cavallaro.

drastically and negatively affect the reputation of individuals involved. This aspect is exemplified by the dialogue between Alessandra and Daniela, both 20 years old:[7]

> *Daniela*: In my opinion, if someone says 'Yes, I'm homophobic', then whatever they say, it's pretty clear that you belong to that category, meaning that you think this or that. So, if someone says 'No, I'm not homophobic, but I think this or that', it's because you pay more attention to what they're saying.

> *Alessandra*: If a person tells you 'I don't like homosexuals' and you go 'Ah, you're homophobic!' I think the distance increases, categorising people like that doesn't make sense …. I think … well, that homophobia is a complex thing. Then, honestly, if I have to speak about individual people I'd rather not say 'That one is homophobic', because it's like saying that's the only thing he or she is … But the person himself or herself, well, they have different nuances.

The accusation of homophobia was thus considered a label denoting some sort of *abjection* which is socially generated by the delegitimisation of traditional stereo-types against homosexuality. Subjects who are so labelled become people whose opinions put them outside the admissible. There is no possibility of dialogue or confrontation with them. Therefore, homophobia—which is a *certain* kind of discrimination against homosexuals, as we shall see later—becomes a description from which our participants wanted to distance themselves. As a consequence, homophobia was seen as a problem which always concerns *others*. It happens through social dynamics and categorisations which do not involve our hetero-sexual participants, unless they are simply observers. Apparently, placing them-selves outside the observed situation was the only way they could talk about it.

But what are the characteristics of this abjection? What are the conditions in which discrimination against homosexuals becomes absolutely condemned? And what are the phenomena and definitions which are not included? The latter question is central to our analysis, because interpreting homophobia as abjection does not mean that *all* requests for protection, safety and inclusion coming from lesbian and gay people are understood. As Sonia, a 21-year-old student, told us:

> Just because a word (homophobia) was used by him (a gay), it doesn't mean that it's proper to use it.

In the prevailing interpretation, homophobia was perceived as an individual or social *pathology*. From this point of view, it corresponds to an inadequate reading, 'dysfunctional' we could say, of social reality, of which some subjects or some social groups are the victims. This interpretation does not have nuances in the definition of the problem, but develops two different approaches regarding prevention strategies in schools (see next section).

---

[7] Pseudonyms are used throughout.

Discussions among participants also revealed some signs of a structural interpretation other than the main one. According to this interpretation, homophobia was defined as the product of the culture and dynamics on which the reproduction of society is based. This was the point of view of a small minority of participants; it was generally strongly opposed, so that it could not develop further.

Homophobia as a pathology uses a model of explanation which recalls the formulation of the concept suggested by Weinberg (1972). In the first place, participants defined this concept in multi-dimensional terms: it has emotional, cognitive and behavioural dimensions. Secondly, the definition of homophobia was applied only to cases of hostility against lesbians and gays which include all three dimensions. This second aspect has important consequences, because it allowed our participants not to apply the label of homophobia—which, we must recall, is equivalent to an abjection, condemned in the most absolute way—to some relational difficulties, ways of thinking and acting which they attributed to themselves or which they considered common in their context of life. The first consequence is that not feeling at ease in the presence of gay men or lesbians or thinking in stereotypes, were not considered types of homophobia, unless they translate into hostile behaviour. In these cases, our participants at most talked about 'homophobic tendencies' which have no predetermined link—for example, in terms of structural sources—with 'true' homophobia. The second consequence is that the dimension of behaviour—although essential in this interpretation—ended up by being the most contradictory and misinterpreted. Condemning a certain hostile or discriminating kind of behaviour against lesbians and gays was not based on the consequences it produces, but on the motivations supporting it. The rhetorical strategy supporting this interpretation was insistence on *intentionality*: it is homophobia only if its empirical manifestation translates into a precise will to harm. The episode told to us by Paolo (35 years old) in a focus group was strongly rejected as an appropriate example of homophobia, because of the structural reading it offers which does not consider the element of intentionality:

> For example, I know people who, I'm 100% sure, are intellectually against any form of discrimination against homosexuals, but who every now and then make jokes about them. Once, I was having dinner with a friend and pointed this out to him, I don't remember his comment, it was something like 'But what are you? Faggots?' A very silly joke. I made him notice this and he even said he was sorry. It's something automatic, a joke.

The emotional dimension corresponds essentially to a fear of lesbian and gay people and a disgust for homosexual desire or sexual intercourse between people of the same sex. Hate as an emotion was mentioned only marginally, in this way differing from scientific literature (see Sears 1997) and public discourse. Participants described fear, disgust and hate as unrestrained and ungovernable states of mind. In other words, it is thought that those who feel them cannot avoid feeling them. The incapacity to overcome such feelings qualifies the hostility they produce as irrational, even from the point of view of the very subjects who express it. Accordingly, homophobia cannot have a raison d'être, nor a rationality within the logic which rules social life. Above all, the emotional sphere is of pre-eminent importance in the definition of homophobia. It defines a smaller field of application of the concept, because condemnation of discrimination against homosexuals is significant only in cases in which those who commit it have negative feelings about homosexuality and lesbians and gay men.

The cognitive dimension concerns what Herek (2004) defined as 'sexual prejudice', which is a negative attitude towards lesbians and gays and their lifestyle. Exactly as in Weinberg's wording (1972), this dimension is considered the cause of homophobia.[8] Such prejudices were described by our respondents as the effect of discrediting categorisation. These are particularly widespread in certain social contexts, the most frequently mentioned being the group of male peers. The most interesting fact is that this discussion followed a thread which did not require participants to talk explicitly about the content of prejudices or the stereotypes from which they derive. It is discrediting categorisation for the simple reason that it presumes a difference between homosexual and hetero-sexual people in their respective attitudes and lifestyles. The reason which makes any prejudice unacceptable is the idea that diversity in sexual desire may cause a difference in the ways lesbians and gay men live their lives.

From the point of view of our participants, those who agree with this assumption show that they do not know the 'real situation' of lesbians and gay men, except at a merely stereotypical level. Thus, homophobia was mainly explained as a type of ignorance to be condemned, in the same way that there is conviction that degrading categorisation has lost the social legitimisation it had in the past—although it is still fuelled even at institutional level by the Vatican's opinion on the subject. As Ambra, an 18-year-old student told us:

> There certainly are commonplaces, but I think nowadays it's possible to have an opinion on the subject through reading and politics.

In the rhetoric of ignorance, the target of prejudice—that is the object of fear, contempt and hate—is the *stranger*, the person who does not belong to the prevailing group and who therefore cannot take reality for granted as the group interprets it. In this context, homophobia may be explained by the same processes of exclusion which sociological thinking has put at the centre of the metaphor of stranger, defined as the one who lives in the social space of a group but is not an original member of it (Simmel, 1908; Schütz, 1971–73). It is no accident that, during discussions, hostility against lesbian and gay people was often associated with hostility against migrants.

---

[8] 'This phobia in operation is a prejudice, which means that we can widen our understand-ing of it by considering the phobia from the point of view of its being a prejudice' (Weinberg 1972: 8).

But what is the 'truth' about lesbians and gays, a truth hidden by prejudices which presumes that they are 'different'? In other words: why are prejudices considered inadmissible? The answers converged on the idea of normalisation of homosexuality, or that lesbians and gays are 'normal'. This representation of normality is diametrically opposed to prejudice, because it breaks the link between the sphere of homosexual desire and the lifestyle of subjects who socially live out this desire as an identity. The private sphere of desire, in this sense, becomes the only (symbolic) space in which the difference between heterosexuals and homosexuals is admissible. Thus, refusing stereotypes means not making the mistake of reducing lesbians and gays to their simple homosexual desire: this desire must not be interpreted as an independent variable from which all other aspects of identity derive. The dialogue of Carla (35 years old), Emanuela (24) and Lara (22) shows awareness of the mechanism at the base of this definition of homophobia:

> *Carla*: This thing about homosexuality, homophobia, I see as really connected to the sexual act. For us, at least for me, when we speak about a homosexual or a lesbian couple, our minds immediately go to the sexual act. But when I see a male–female couple, it's not as if I think right away about their sexual relationship. I think about their relationship, but from the human, affective aspect, and others.
>
> *Emanuela*: Don't you think that with a homosexual couple?
>
> *Carla*: I imagine … the sexual act immediately comes to mind. I mean, it enters my head something that maybe doesn't come to mind with other couples.
>
> *Lara*: I feel that way too.

In the discussions, the idea of 'normal' lesbians and gays mainly concerned two aspects. The first was the self-positioning of lesbians and gays within their proper gender: being gay or lesbian does not mean having doubts about the existence of differences—even though socially constructed—among male and female attitudes and styles. As a consequence, the stereotype of the effeminate gay man and butch woman was clearly rejected. The second aspect concerned the self-collocation, in a constant way, within the polarisation between homosexuality and heterosexuality: lesbians and gays never change their idea about their sexual orientation and, above all, they do not have sexual and affective relationships with the other sex. Our participants took for granted the existence of a lesbian/gay minority, defined as a specific group of subjects who are separate from the majority and whose members recognise that they belong to the same collective identity. The discursive construction of this minority mainly occurred through a process which we may define as 'racialisation', in which sexual orientation depends on biological factors which are present in the subject since birth. The idea of there being *natural-born* lesbians or gays, in the same way as there are *natural-born* heterosexuals, was strong as soon as the discussion included the idea that talking about homosexuality to children leads them to develop homosexual orientations. This idea was completely rejected and considered not grounded—in some cases even irrational—because of this essentialist approach to homosexuality. The opinion of Fabiana (33 years old) on this topic was largely shared:

> Then, there's the question of sex drive. If you're heterosexual ... I've never been attracted by a woman, and I suppose it's the same for homosexuals. Even if children want to copy them they only go so far, because at some point biology acts. The sex drive cannot be controlled.

The explanation of homophobia in terms of ignorance was supported by a precise concept of the victim's subjectivity which tends to exclude from full protection all expressions of homosexual desire which do not conform to it. Both in the focus groups and in the interviews, a clear distinction between 'real homosexuals' and 'fake homosexuals' was frequently stressed. The first category falls within the normalisation criteria used to explain the inadmissibility of prejudices; the second is recognisable because 'fake homosexuals' are not *gender-conventional* and do not define their identity in a permanent way. For example, let us consider the views of Daniela (20 years old):

> There are some of them who have the gay stereotype and this way of showing themselves ... as if they took the stereotype of the excessively pretty girl and amplified it to maximum level. So I wonder if some of these boys, who call themselves gay and have this appearance, maybe do it just to be at the centre of attention and show they're different.

The interesting point is that this distinction conditioned the criteria used to define discrimination against homosexuals. Lesbians and gays who disobey normalisation codes were accused of bearing part of the responsibility for the victimisation they suffer, because they do not fight against the prejudices that cause it.

In view of its characteristics, the discursive mechanism which allowed the framework of pathology to develop is based on identifying the problem and negating any structural dimension among the causes determining it. This mechanism uses some of the strategies we have already identified, such as insistence on the themes of intentionality of the offence and normalisation of homosexuality, or the denial of the system of shared beliefs—which Herek (2004) calls sexual stigma—to support prejudices against homosexuals and thus homophobia. The same rational can be found in the way our participants interpreted the relationship between homophobia and the construction of masculinity in the peer group. The predominant idea was that prejudices against homosexuals are widespread among young people and change into hostile behaviour especially within a group, ie within a context where the surveillance over the exhibition of one's masculinity is more powerful. This opinion envisages the existence of a link between homophobia and processes of gender construction. However, the structuring function of the discipline that makes the hegemony of a specific model of masculinity effective was limited to the group of peers. In other words, despising everything that could lead to a suspicion of homosexuality or ascribed to female subordination was read as a ritual necessity which is abandoned once adult life is reached. The participants in the focus group rejected and marginalised the (few and weak) attempts to explain homophobia as an effect of the social dynamics which cause the differentiation in men and women's social fates. For example, the suggestion by Paolo (36 years old) to trace homophobia back to the institution-alisation of the heterosexual family was not even taken into account by other participants in the focus group:

> I see the imposition of a heteronormative ideal at school from another aspect: we draw a family composed of a man and a woman. I think it would be better to say clearly right from the beginning that families aren't just heterosexual.

5.1. The Fight against Homophobia and the Limitations of Social Integration of Lesbians and Gays

As already noted, our research aimed at contextualising the topic of contrast to discrimination against homosexuals mainly within the school context, and we selected the focus group participants from the educational and psychological disciplines. The discussion about prevention strategies in schools aroused great embarrassment and perplexity, both because of general unpreparedness of our participants and the difficulties they mentioned. The latter were the level of maturity of the students in the younger classes; the persistence of sexual taboos among parents and teachers; and the diffusion of stereotypes against homosexu-als on the part of parents, teachers and above all peers. However, the need to consider homosexuality in school activities was unanimously recognised on the basis that not talking about it would increase the spread of stereotyping.

Two strategies of intervention, not mutually exclusive, emerged from the discussion. On one hand, they strengthened the framework of the pathology we identified. In particular, the idea of normalisation generated strong expectations of coming out: only if lesbian and gay normality becomes visible—even and above all in the eyes of those who have prejudices against such people—is it possible to prevent discrimination and homophobia. On the other hand, the strategies showed the limitations of the prevailing framework on the integration of lesbians and gay men.

The first strategy to prevent homophobia and discrimination against homo-sexuals consisted of the promotion of the 'normality' of lesbian/gay lifestyles. This is an approach which reflects an assimilationist logic. It overlooks the presence of diversity in the dimension of desire and emphasises common convergence towards the same cultural orientation. From this point of view, educational activities with pupils should focus on the sphere of affectivity (lesbians and gays build affection relationships in the same way as heterosexual people) and on the possession of those social desirable requirements on which success and respect are based. Let us consider, for example, the dialogue between Fabiana (33 years old) and Maria Luisa (22):

Fabiana: You can focus on all the characteristics which shape that person. You have to teach children that a person is homosexual but a person, with whom you play and have fun, who is intelligent, who does sports. That is, you go to the positive aspects. I mean, you could avoid focusing too much on homosexuality, but focus on the whole person and then see the rest too …. They may have a different sexual orientation but that's not what identifies the person.

Maria Luisa: What comes to my mind is that, throughout history, there have been a lot of really great, brilliant people who were homosexuals. You can show this too, have a historical excursus about it.

Participants based this approach on the spread of 'correct information', which can prevent prejudices and stereotypes causing hostility against lesbians and gays. On one hand, the information is scientific, considered objective and neutral as regards value judgments; it should also be considered necessary in teachers' training. On the other hand, correct information comes from lesbians and gay men themselves, from their everyday life stories. One consequence is their direct involvement in school activities as 'self-experts'. This strengthened the 'racialising' approach of the representation of the lesbian/gay community, whose members are seen as the only repository of the truth about themselves, truth which is hardly accessible from the outside.

Whatever the available information, the strategy of promoting lesbian/gay normality came up against the insurmountable limitation of the complementarity of the sexes: that is, against the assumption that the difference between men and women is the pivotal principle on which the reproduction of society is based. This assumption made our participants rule out the possibility of recognising that lesbians and gays can have parental functions: disregarding their parental expectations was not considered an indicator of discrimination or homophobia. The normality approach was thus conditioned by a structural element related to the construction of gender which must also be obeyed by lesbians and gays. As Federico (34 years old), Marta (22) and Fabiana (33) stated (when talking about the refusal to recognise lesbian/gay access to adoption):

Federico: This limitation I feel means I have some … homophobia? That is, does it somehow mean that I'm homophobic, too? Or … how shall I put it? Is it a limitation comprehensible because I can't imagine these children with a couple of male parents?

Marta: I don't think this is homophobia.

Fabiana: Nor do I.

The second strategy to prevent homophobia in schools was promotion of the principle of respect of diversity through the use of national laws and international agreements which formalise this principle. As Manuela (24 years old) said:

In my opinion, we should talk not so much on the subject of homosexuality, as on the subject of democracy and tolerance which, theoretically, are part of our nation.

In this case, the approach is not strictly assimilationist, because it includes a diversity which must be respected, although this is limited to the intimate sphere. Nevertheless, the principle which protects such diversity does not originate fundamental rights which must be defended independently of circumstances. Rather, respect for lesbians and gay men was discussed as a goal to be pursued through negotiation with parents and colleagues, the result of which may cause the suggested initiatives to be abandoned. In the words of Carla (35 years old):

> You can't have an idea, something axiomatic, already written, predetermined, that's the rule. You must consider class, you must consider environment, age, context.

Above all, the defence of this principle appeared subordinate to the defence of another principle which was considered more important: the defence of 'the child's best interests' to grow up within a functional family environment, headed by a man and a woman. Also in this case, therefore, the topic of complementarity of men and women was imposed as an insurmountable limitation in the definition of normality of lesbians and gays.

6. Empirical Dimensions of Homophobia from the Heterosexual Standpoint

What sources did heterosexual people use to interpret homophobia and discrimination against homosexuals? What episodes or situations were mentioned to support their point of view? The focus groups and individual interviews revealed three main sources of knowledge: (1) mass media; (2) lesbian/gay organisations; (3) everyday life experiences.

Considering these sources together, there are two significant points. The first is that what is known about homosexuality and the social conditions of lesbians/ gays does not come from school curricula or university teaching. All our participants stated that they had never received information on these topics at school or university. The second remarkable point is that the sources of knowledge to which our heterosexual participants have access drove them to consider almost exclusively the victimisation experiences of gay men which generally—but not always—occur in interactions with other boys or men. This male bias of discrimination against homosexuals minimises the specificity of the ways in which lesbians experience discrimination. In fact, the episodes of lesbian victimisation we heard may be viewed as female versions of typically male phenomena. Consistent with the logic of the pathological interpretation of anti-homosexual discrimination discussed in the previous section, is the fact that this male bias—together with the disciplinary mechanism which calls for the exhibition of 'proper' masculinity—is an aspect that our heterosexual participants took for granted and did not stop to think about. We can, for example, consider the words by Federica (21 years old):

> I've always felt these things we're talking about, I mean it's obvious that a boy in general, my brothers for example, don't like homosexuals. It's logical: it's because you're a *recchione* (faggot), as we say where I come from.

Mass media are a source of knowledge especially for high school students, who referred to the news far more often than university students. This source provides information about socially legitimate interpretations of discrimination against homosexuals, that is types of victimisation which are unmistakably recognised as such. Episodes were quoted which refer to physical attacks suffered mainly by lesbian or gay couples, carried out in public places. These episodically come to the general attention because of reports by the victims and the consequent intervention of institutions.

Lesbian/gay organisations represent a source of knowledge for those (few) participants in the focus groups who were part of social volunteering or political activism networks, which also include homosexual organisations which try to generalise their protest.

Most participants relied on everyday life experiences as their main source of knowledge about discrimination against homosexuals. This gives access to two kinds of sources: the standpoint of victims and of those who are defined as perpetrators. The first concerns experiences described by lesbians or gay men who are part of the more or less extensive network of friends (acquaintances, work colleagues, and so on) or episodes which involved people in this network and which our participants knew about indirectly. The types of victimisation reported in interviews and focus groups were related mainly to two specific aspects connected with homophobia: loss of one's job or expulsion from social contexts resulting from coming-out or revelation of homosexuality; a condition of isolation as a consequence of keeping one's homosexual orientation secret. The definition of the situation and recognition of discrimination are mainly linked to the victim's point of view and how he or she describes the experience to friends. Obviously, our participants considered this definition of the situation plausible: it corresponds to the interpretation codes through which they give the world a meaning. It is remarkable that episodes which create real 'degradation ceremonies' (Garfinkel 1955) against lesbians and gays in school contexts of all types were almost non-existent among the phenomena which came to the attention of our respondents. We mean here, for example, offensive writing, often anonymous, or widespread rumours which have the effect of completely undermining the basis of the identity that the targetted person has built up and uses in their social context. Massimo, a 16-year-old student, is one of the very few interviewees who was sensitive to this kind of systematic discrimination which, however, is regularly present and emphasised in research on homophobic bullying (see Lelleri et al 2005; Prati 2010):

> I know a girl from another school, who is a wonderful person and is homosexual. They wrote things on the school walls about her … such terribly offensive words could really

destroy a person's school life. [*Interviewer*: What?] For example, they wrote she was a whore and that there was no place for lesbians at school.

The second source of knowledge related to everyday life—which we call the standpoint of the perpetrators—consists of the behaviour and opinions of friends and acquaintances which our participants condemned as examples of discrimination against lesbians and gays. In this case, the definition of the situation originates in the observers, who refer to an interpretation system which does not correspond to that of the subjects they are observing. The episodes our participants mentioned as examples of discrimination can be grouped into three main categories: (1) avoidance of lesbian/gay people and censorship on the topic of homosexuality; (2) derision and insults against lesbians/gays; and (3) condemnation of male behaviour which fails to comply with gender expectations through the use of terms, metaphors and phrases which hint at homosexuality.

Avoidance behaviour consists of the refusal to share the same space or come into contact with lesbian/gay people, real or presumed. As an example, the following is a discussion among four female students (Daniela, 20 years old, Gaia 24, Sonia and Federica both 21) during a focus group:

Daniela: I've got a friend who happened to share a flat with two homosexual boys. He's really frightened and thinks they might do something to him.

Gaia: I've also heard about people who would rather not share a flat with a homosexual.

Sonia: I've got a friend too, she studies in [name of the city], and when she learnt that the person she would be living with was a lesbian, she refused to go there and is now a commuter rather than living with her.

Federica: I know other people too of my own generation, who don't want to have anything to do with homosexuals. They don't like the idea of having a homosexual neighbour, they wouldn't want to stay with homosexuals, they don't want to live in their houses.

This first category also contains behaviour which not only avoids lesbians and gays, but also the topic of homosexuality in general. More specifically, homosexuality is not a topic to be talked about and to be exposed to by taking a position. If the protagonists of these strategies of avoidance are other young people, what was condemned by our participants is the refusal to speak about homosexuality outside the peer group and thus out of the usual language range, as explained in the words of Sonia (21 years old):

I give private lessons to a young girl in the second year of secondary school. Once a month at school they talk about a different topic, of various types, at a social level. They also talked about homosexuality. They started from a story they had read in class, and then they all had to write about the pros and cons of homosexuality. And then they discussed them …. The girl told me some people refused to talk about it, because for them it was a topic in itself … 'No, it's absolutely disgusting'. And they didn't talk about it.

When these avoidance strategies involve older people, they concern the refusal to consider homosexuality as an option, or even mentioning it in the educational relationship between teachers and students or parents and children. An example of this censorship is offered by Emanuela, a 24-year-old student:

> I see parents, even friends, who maybe have smaller children, who are scared by the simple fact that there might be an occasion to talk about homosexuality with their children. They say 'Ah, my son becoming a homosexual ... better not to speak about that'. Or something like that.

The second category of discrimination concerns the different ways in which lesbians and gays are derided, offended, humiliated and degraded in face-to-face relations involving them, or in discussions among heterosexuals, who intentionally refer to the topic. Our interviewees, who are still at high school, are those who mainly noticed this kind of discrimination. Their attention focused on peer relationships, as can be seen in the examples reported by Massimo (16 years old) and Carlo (17) in their interviews:

> For example, there's a boy who is officially homosexual, and even though our school is easy-going about things like this, there are still people who insult him, and, well, when he bumped into someone I happened to hear the other one say 'Fucking faggot' between his teeth ... yes, so, well, these kinds of things.

> I know some people who say 'I would kill gays, all of them'.

The third and last category of reported discrimination concerns the use of metaphors of homosexuality to stigmatise behaviour or styles of self-expression which do not follow social expectations of masculinity. The interpretative frame of discrimination was used here to denounce both the spread of negative stereotypes of homosexuality and discrimination based on strict duality in the construction of male identity. This divides the depiction of victimisation into two levels. On the first level, the subjects who are considered victims were children or teenagers who show a 'lack of masculinity', independently of their sexual orientation, for example, weakness or few qualities or prerogatives of the hegemonic model of masculinity. At a more general level, the circulation of such labelling practices was thought to be harmful, because it contributes to the creation of a disqualifying situation which penalises teenagers who are starting to conceive an idea of themselves as being gay.

These examples took into account different interaction contexts among peers, adults and teenagers, or among adults. Nevertheless, different stigmatisation episodes were not evaluated in the same way. Those involving their peers—mentioned mainly by younger interviewees—seemed less serious, regardless of the age of the participant talking about them. The words of Alessia (17 years old) are typical:

> It's always a playful situation, in which they make a dig at gays or make jokes, let's say. At that moment, if it was just a joke and it wasn't offensive, we let it pass.

On the other hand, stigmatisation by adults—primary school teachers or parents—towards their male pupils or children, seemed to be more serious and was thus a more important example of discrimination. The words of Claudia, aged 36, are especially illustrative of this:

> So many times at the nursery two children, after playing together, two boys would kiss and straight away a teacher, one of the older ones, would intervene. She would say 'No, no, young boys can't kiss', implying intentions that the children did not have.

Understanding this kind of discrimination was quite problematic, because involvement in this type of behaviour is not directly connected with contempt towards homosexuality, nor to the intention to denigrate lesbians and gays with terms used as epithets (see previous section). The fact that the use of homophobic language cannot be linked simply to hostility against lesbians and gays has been emphasised in various ethnographic researches on the construction of masculinity in young people (see Pascoe 2007; Plummer 1999). Nevertheless, there is a remarkable distinction between the interpretation proposed by researchers and the one suggested by our heterosexual respondents. Whereas the latter explained homophobic language as a ritual practice confined within male peer groups, the former link it to the gendered dimension of homophobia, that is, to those disciplinary systems among boys and men which allow them to protect their social positions of privilege (Kimmel 2005).

7. Lesbian and Gay Sources of Knowledge on Homophobia

As seen in the previous section, our heterosexual respondents consider homophobia, and more generally anti-homosexual hostility, understandable only as intentional mistreatment against lesbian/gay people motivated by 'pathological' misrecognition of their normality, which is the idea that 'they are like us and they trust what we trust'. The episodes they considered as proper examples of anti-homosexual hostility are consistent with this interpretation. Lesbians' and gays' narratives reveal a different standpoint to that of heterosexuals. In this section, we analyse this difference at two levels: the position of subjects in relation to the issues in question, and the sources from which lesbians and gays develop their knowledge on the same issues.

While heterosexual respondents talked about discrimination and homophobia from an external point of view, our lesbian/gay respondents clearly perceived themselves as directly involved in the matter—as victims of homophobia and discrimination—regardless of their direct personal experience. In fact, most them had never been involved in episodes consistent with the kind of homophobia our heterosexual participants understand as *abjection*—for example, deliberate physical aggression[9]—and homosexuals themselves also interpret this abjection as a particularly serious form of anti-homosexual hostility. Nonetheless, all lesbians and gays represented themselves as potential victims of such episodes, as a consequence of the victimisation involving other homosexuals as well as other forms of discrimination encountered in everyday life. From this point of view, 'violence does not have to be experienced to have repercussions' (Mason 2002: 79) because 'it is the knowledge that violence embodies—knowledge of pain, fear, danger, disorder and the like—that oppresses individuals' (Mason 2002: 135). The words of Stefania (38 years old) help us understand this aspect:

> When I found myself in this condition [that of being a lesbian] … from that moment I started to think 'I may be a victim of homophobia, prejudice, and so on in the future, just because of what I have found out about myself and what life will bring me, for example, having a partner'. So at that moment I realized even more how serious that is.

This excerpt tells us about the power of subjectification of anti-homosexual hostility, that is, how the knowledge of such hostility shapes lesbian and gay people's perception of their identity. In other words, identifying oneself as gay or lesbian automatically implies knowing that one may be a victim of any act of discrimination committed against other homosexuals. Previously Stefania, as a heterosexual woman, knew what homophobia was. She was well-informed about it through the media but, as a consequence of her self-discovery, she found herself 'on the other side', with a different awareness of her own position in the social context.

We now review the sources of knowledge through which lesbians and gays came to know about homophobia, that is through the media and everyday direct and indirect experiences, the latter being the main source of knowledge.

Some of our respondents recalled episodes reported by the media as examples of homophobia and discrimination. In particular, they referred to recent acts of anti-homosexual physical violence in Italian urban areas such as Rome and Padova. They commonly mentioned violent attacks as evidence of the existence of serious anti-homosexual hostility in Italy. However, unlike heterosexual participants, they also interpreted news reports as the institutional dimension of homophobia. For example, they referred to the Italian political debate over homophobic discrimination and derogatory public declarations by representatives of the government and the Church. Another considerable difference compared with heterosexuals is that the mass media were mentioned not only as sources of information but also as being responsible for discrimination, mainly because of their stereotypical representation of homosexuals. Again, in this case,

---

[9] Being attacked was not a widely shared experience among our participants, as only two gay men had experienced it.

our lesbian and gay participants stressed the institutional aspect of discrimination against them by referring to the system of shared beliefs, which is basically denied by heterosexual respondents (see above, section 5):

> it must be acknowledged that we homosexuals can have love relationships too, that we aren't as the media sometimes describe us ..., as depraved, incapable of having long-lasting love affairs. (Javier, 43 years old)

The main sources of knowledge about discrimination were everyday life experiences, both direct and indirect. They encompassed many episodes, ranging from having artificial insemination therapy refused because the gynaecologist only supports a 'family parented by a man and a woman' (Vittoria, aged 27), to having a friend who committed suicide because he could no longer bear a double life (as a gay and a Catholic). However, we focus on the most widely shared experiences of direct discrimination, which do not include physical assaults.

First, being, for example, pointed out or jeered at when engaging in public displays of affection with one's partner was described as a typical everyday experience. The perpetrators may even be police officers charging the couple with obscene behaviour, a lesbian participant told us.

A second kind of experience concerned facing various problems in the workplace or in other life settings as a result of being publicly out as, or being found to be (or believed to be) homosexual. Having problems with parents, relatives and friends after coming out also emerged as a common experience. Clara (38, lesbian) summed up most of these troubles and their different nuances:

> Only really few people treat me exactly as they treat other female friends with boyfriends. Most people, maybe due to ... I would say due to their discretion? I don't know ... they never ask questions using the plural form, they only ask me 'What did you do last weekend?' But, for example, if I answer 'My partner and I went to ... ' I always notice a kind of embarrassment. That's the discrimination I live with basically. ... A really good friend of mine has a very difficult family situation, precisely due to her homosexuality ... One day you explode, you tell your parents because you can't help it any more, and they ...actually trash your room and kick you out of the house. That was their first reaction, then for the first year they asked her to avoid any kind of contact with women and with that [homosexual] world, as 'Maybe, you know, if you keep away from that you could be cured'.

Many respondents told us about being (directly and indirectly) offended, called names, threatened, or attacked for being—or being presumed to be—homosexual.

> No, I had no idea about myself [as a gay man] but the context was very ... my peer group was very harsh with me, the boys above all .... When I was a kid, from 11 to 14, they used to be very hostile to me, they used to make fun of me, mock me, and that was very hard for me actually .... I suppose I have a certain kind of voice, of movements ... so that even without opening my mouth I've always been labelled, due to the simple fact that I exist. It's always been like that. (Fabio, 30 years old)

Fabio's words lead us to the question of gender non-conformity, which emerged from our research more as a 'gay problem', that is, always connected to male experiences. We can understand this as a kind of unintentional visibility: you just cannot control it or can only control it with great effort. Fabio learned by direct and indirect experience that being effeminate or not conforming to masculine gender standards (which may take on specific forms in different contexts) could result in being discriminated against as homosexual, independently of his actual sexual orientation. Regardless of the difficulty of the task, people try to manage this unintentional visibility by constant control over their body and manners, and this is another example of the power of subjectification of anti-homosexual hostility.

The intertwining of gender non-conformity and anti-homosexual discrimination was very clear for most our lesbian/gay participants, and for the heterosexual ones. But the former framed it more as a structural dimension of homophobia. In this sense, homophobia is understood as a phenomenon shaped by gender and by heterosexual and masculine hegemonic discourses (Jenness and Broad 1994; Tomsen and Mason 2001; Tomsen 2006). While gender non-conformity was mostly regarded as a male problem, our lesbian respondents told us about a peculiar kind of discrimination, which only affects women and is also understood as a problem connected with gender non-conformity (Tomsen and Mason 2001): men's curiosity about lesbian sex and their suspicion that lesbians are just 'women who haven't found the right man yet'.

> At my workplace, a pair of female friends know about me and a colleague who I suppose he's mainly interested out of curiosity … that very male curiosity, you know, that morbid curiosity which I can't stand at all, kind of 'Do lesbians like penetration? Are you really sure you don't like it with men? Maybe your husband disappointed you', so these kind of levels, really … You feel helpless, you give answers but you don't know how to … (Viviana, 45 years old)

Lastly, knowledge of anti-homosexual discrimination among our lesbian/gay respondents was mainly revealed by a constant perception of a generalised, subtle 'feeling in the air', sometimes manifest and explicit, sometimes not, so that it is difficult to notice it even if you are gay or a lesbian. This category contains many examples, such as the use of words related to homosexuality in order to offend; jokes involving homosexuality; the avoidance of homosexual issues at school and in public; the lack of national laws on same-sex marriage and adoption as well as against homophobic discrimination; and prejudice and discrimination in the national political debate, including public homophobic declaration by politicians. This issue is another good example of the peculiar viewpoint of our homosexual respondents, who, unlike heterosexuals, clearly reckoned on a structural dimension of anti-homosexual hostility.

Going back to the typical heterosexual interpretation of anti-homosexual hostility as a 'male issue', some of our respondents explicitly shared this opinion, particularly as regards its physical expression:

And [homophobia] it's much stronger against men than girls, for example, even one of my classmates defined himself as gay and he had many more problems than me, because in the collective imagination two girls anyway ... On one hand, the idea of two girls together is arousing, on the other hand, we got used to seeing two girls walking hand in hand, staying together at night, sleeping together. There's much more violence towards men and that's definitely homophobia, no doubt about it. (Elena, 19 years old)

However, some of our lesbian respondents—unlike heterosexuals—questioned this perception, mainly recalling the argument of lesbian 'invisibility' which is connected with gender expectations about body and manners. It may be that they were more likely to take into account the intertwining between homophobia and gender structure because of their particular external position with respect to the heterosexist system which produce such intertwining. In other words, from the lesbian perspective it may be easier to criticise—and contrast—the 'male gaze', one of the most powerful constituents of the heterosexist system which regulates the meanings of sexuality and the ways of expressing it. This hypothesis is confirmed if we consider the consequences of lesbian invisibility. On one hand, some gay men told us that lesbians are less likely to face victimisation because of their social invisibility:

I know lesbian couples who are terrified that people might know about them, and that surprises me since, as a man, I can't see any big prejudice against female homosexuality, honestly. However, it apparently exists, since many women have such fears. (Valerio, 52 years old)

On the other hand, some lesbians highlighted the risk of downplaying the homophobic dimension of violence against women, as Stefania (38) told us:

In Italy, they often talk about homosexuals as men .... But many lesbian women have been raped, that's a fact.

8. Homosexual Interpretation of Homophobia: Challenging the Heterosexual Framework

How did lesbian and gay respondents explain the anti-homosexual hostility they face and talk about? The pathological and structural interpretations of homophobia—which we first introduced in the analysis of heterosexual narratives and discussions—were both visible and coexisting.

According to the pathological interpretation, we found that a number of respondents were not comfortable with the word 'homophobia', as they think it has a very negative meaning, so they usually adopt it to describe physical—or severe psychological—violence. Their understanding of homophobia also recalls Weinberg's approach, held by heterosexual participants. They distinguished occurrences on the basis of emotional, cognitive and behavioural elements and recognised the existence of 'true' homophobia when such elements are all discernible at the same time.

> [Talking about people who are embarrassed about her lesbianism]

> They've never been in touch with such a thing, they don't know how to manage it, so I think it's a form of … I don't know, maybe ignorance. But people who do it just to be mean are … at least, until now I only saw one of them, personally. You see, they act that way because it [her homosexuality] bothers them, they don't want to know …. So, homophobia in my opinion … [laughing], it makes me think about something more … physical violence, something. It seems to me to be too big a word. Anyway, if you look up homophobia in the dictionary … I don't know … it's so—inverted commas—subtle, no direct insults, no despicable words, no violence … personally it's almost hard for me to define [those embarrassed people] as homophobes. (Clara, 38 year old)

The framework of homophobia as pathology was even more manifest when we reached the issue of ignorance and prejudice. Almost all our homosexual respondents stated that discrimination and homophobia are consequences of ignorance and, hence, fear of the 'unknown' (see above, section 5), implying—sometimes explicitly—that knowledge and visibility of homosexual realities would bring about a real change and would undermine homophobia. Consequently, some of our respondents stated that coming out is a duty for lesbians and gays and that it is more effective when it shows their 'normality'. Also, like our heterosexual participants, some stated that closeting and 'wrong' visibility are one of the causes of anti-homosexual hostility. Some respondents told us that a certain kind of public expression of homosexuality, particularly during Pride parades, are excessive and aggressive, and may transmit a biased representation of homosexuality.

> [Heterosexuals] have stereotypes because they don't know, they've never met any homosexual people and so they grow up with the stereotype of Gay Pride, like 'These guys only think about partying' … Many people who call themselves homophobes—there are people who do that—are not homophobic that much in my opinion, I think it's only because you thrust the thing on them in the wrong way. I mean, you have to find the right way to tell them about it. (Maria, 25 years old)

However, the very issue of normality was questioned by other respondents, who explicitly described it as a more or less shared narrative among lesbians and gays which derives from an embodiment of the heterosexual standpoint. In this case, we can see how the pathological framework of homophobia does not prevent its structural dimension from being recognised as such by lesbian/gay respondents:

> I've heard about this theory—bits of it are true—that new trends are now appearing among homosexuals, that there are good gays, that is the ones who are integrated, who are well-dressed, and then there are less good gays. (Dorotea, 32 years old)

> There's very often homophobia among homosexuals, who say homosexuals shouldn't wear wigs or high heels if they want to. (Valerio, 52 years old)

These excerpts not only challenge the heterosexual gaze about normalisation. They also reveal the awareness of how heterosexual symbolic violence works: by denouncing homophobia as a social problem without querying the actual basis of the hegemony of the group which produces it. So, although the pathological framework and its various facets have been internalised by part of our lesbian/gay respondents, the framework itself was also often challenged.

First of all, the interpretation of homophobia as a structural phenomenon was widely shared and it explicitly blamed institutions like the Church and the Italian Government as actual perpetrators, particularly due to their stubborn defence of the heterosexual family as the only just and natural form of kinship. Lesbians and gays shared the idea that anti-homosexual hostility does not involve only deliberate physical aggression, which is what heterosexual participants framed as *abjection*. Their understanding encompassed various occurrences: experiencing embarrassment among people who know that a certain woman is a lesbian, getting nasty glances when walking hand-in-hand with the partner, growing up without having homosexual love patterns to refer to, not being able legally to get married or adopt children—in short, the 'feeling in the air' mentioned above. As well as Weinberg's definition of homophobia (1972), lesbians and gays identified another kind of intolerance, corresponding to every situation and event which betrays the general opinion that being homosexual is wrong or not normal. There was no shared opinion about what to name it: some called it homophobia, some preferred the word discrimination. What was shared is the meaning of this intolerance, which was thought to be as damaging as 'true' homophobia. Such an assessment mirrors the interpretation of homophobia as heterosexism, defined by Herek as 'an ideological system that denies, denigrates, and stigmatizes any non-heterosexual form of behaviour, identity, relationship, or community' (1990: 316; see also Morin and Garfinkle 1978).

This structural framework emerged in implicit and explicit terms as a subtle process which shapes lesbians' and gays' perception of their own homosexuality, their personal safety and, hence, their visibility management. Clara (a 38-year-old lesbian) and Carlo (a 34-year-old gay man) gave us examples of the awareness of this process:

> When I'm walking down the street with my partner, I must be careful ... I might want to hug her and I can't, I have to remember that ... I would say that's a form of homophobia, too.

> I feel clearly discriminated against in the workplace, even if nothing has happened until now, precisely because I've never said anything, but the fact that I'm not saying anything is absolutely ... Maybe I'm too cautious, but I don't think so. This is a form of discrimination, maybe self-inflicted, but anyway it comes from the outside. ... You could say it's indirect discrimination.

The general opinion of our respondents was that even seemingly trivial occurrences are to be condemned because they remind you of 'what' you are in the

45

social context (Mason 2002). They were perceived as part of a continuum which links them with more violent and explicitly anti-homosexual acts:

> That's homophobia in my opinion, and it can take the shape of trivial attitudes, gossip, despicable jokes, that kind of vulgarity, that is, it goes from verbal vulgarity to the vulgarity of living, since there are various degrees and the more you go on, the worse it gets, and the more you get hurt. (Linda, 46 years old)

Lastly, as regards the issue of ignorance and prejudice as the main cause of homophobia and discrimination, the homosexual point of view adds some critical elements. Lesbians and gay men also detected specific categories of people who are supposedly more likely to be anti-homosexual (that is, members of the political right wing, conservative Catholics, the armed forces), but the most commonly shared idea was that ignorance and prejudice characterise Italian society as a whole, at an institutional and social level.

8.1. Opposing Homophobia: Resisting Strategies

Considering the ways in which our homosexual participants attempt to describe homophobia, we focus on two examples: education and daily visibility management.

As already noted, the majority of respondents believe that anti-homosexual hostility is a consequence of ignorance and prejudice, so that they believe school plays a key role in fighting this problem in various ways: by implementing hypothetical anti-discrimination laws, giving (potential and actual) lesbian and gay children the opportunity to accept and develop their sexual identity easily, and teaching children in general that homosexuality exists and that it is part of the social world.

A peculiar, specific viewpoint of homosexuals also emerged with regard to schools, since we talked to gay men who are directly involved in the educational system.[10] In any case, regardless of their jobs, most respondents again recalled the structural argument that school—as an institution—is also understood as a context where structural anti-homosexual hostility takes place. This explains why, according to our participants, the subject of homosexuality is never or seldom treated in the classroom, is not included in the official curricula, and often arouses resistance among teachers and parents.

A very significant difference compared with heterosexuals—and one consistent with the structural framework—is the opinion that dealing with the subject is the duty of all teachers, both heterosexual and homosexual, as forming open-minded children is a fundamental aim of their work. This also calls into question the issue of visibility and coming-out as an educational practice, which is definitely not

---

[10] Among our homosexual respondents there were four secondary school teachers, two university professors (all gay men) and one lesbian student of Educational Sciences.

consistent with the experience of the gay teachers and professors we involved. In their opinion, being gay may make them more aware about anti-homosexual behaviour among young people, but what they do as educators with respect to homosexuality problems is simply part of their job. The best way to educate and create open-mindedness among their students is simply to be a role model for them, which means always being ready to answer all their questions, paying attention to what they say about homosexuality, and trying create greater awareness by reasoning and class discussions. Our experienced teachers stated that they always intervene when they are present at anti-homosexual events among students and often talk about homosexuality in class, but they have never came out, because it may be dangerous—that is, they could face discrimination in the workplace—or irrelevant. They presumed that their colleagues and students probably know about their homosexuality and they never pretend to be heterosexual, but they do not want the fact to be explicit.

> In the case of a direct question, such as 'Do you have a girlfriend?', it depends on the situations you want to create and who you are dealing with. If you're dealing with a gay boy or a lesbian girl, for example, it would be better if you told the truth, as at that moment you are an example .... You are like the mirror of a possible future .... So you have a few seconds to reflect and make a decision. Which is not always the same one, that's what I mean. Your decision may be affected by the fact ... that you think that's a particular situation, so you don't say anything because you could lose the authority you need ... or for teaching reasons. (Vincenzo, 45 years old)

Vincenzo summed up how visibility management is complicated once it is put into practice, not only in educational contexts. Visibility is a contradictory issue. Although if it was often depicted as a means of 'curing' individual and social homophobia, when it comes to our respondents' everyday lives, being 'out of the closet' is not easy. Narratives of visibility and the closet—fuelled by scholarly and popular literature and homosexual identity politics (see Sedgwick 1990; Adam, Duyvendak and Krouwel 1999; Seidman, Meeks and Traschen 1999; Guzmán, 2006; Trappolin 2004; 2011b)—are deeply rooted in shared knowledge about homosexuality and also shaped our respondents' understanding of their identity as lesbian and gay people. Being 'out' is mainly understood as a duty and a liberating practice. However, everyday practices also show how passing and visibility are shaped by various aspects, some of which were mentioned by our respondents. In particular, they told us that passing is not only a managing strategy to avoid discrimination, as we saw above, but also a way of resisting external definitions of individual identity. Being 'out' as a gay or a lesbian may result in being wholly defined by the stereotypical understanding of such a particular part of one's identity:

> Usually I don't come out to people, not because I think they would reject me as a person ... I don't think that would happen. What I would really hate is that they would define me using patterns of homosexuality which don't fit me, patterns they learn by

watching Big Brother or American sit-coms. I'd be seriously pissed off if that happened, because I'm not like that. (Flavio, 44 years old)

The principle of public visibility was also deconstructed through strong opposition to understanding homosexuals as a victimised minority or even as a minority at all. The exchange between Clara (38 years old), Linda (46) and Giulia (44) exemplifies this point:

[Talking about the hypothesis of specific legal protection for homosexuals]

Clara: I don't want that!

Linda: I don't want to be a minorities minority.

Giulia: The fact that there's a minority already bothers me enough.

Clara: Honestly, I think it's like self-ghettoisation once again. 'Please, think of me as a poor lesbian, desperate because everyone is down on me', no, I don't want that.

This kind of thinking challenges the framework of compulsory visibility by criticising the minority paradigm as it is understood by heterosexual respondents and by part of the lesbian, gay, bisexual and transgender (LGBT) movement. This challenge did not question the 'pride' of being gay or lesbian. What some of our homosexual respondents feared was the risk of losing control over the meaning of their actions as gays or lesbians, the risk of being trapped in situations over which they have no control by the very anti-homophobic strategies that emphasise their social vulnerability.

9. Concluding Remarks

This research shows that the inclusion of lesbians and gays in social life by contrasting anti-homosexual hostility is not only a concern for lesbians and gays. The heterosexual students we questioned were convinced that fighting this kind of discrimination is part of their future jobs as educators. Although they complained that they do not have the professional skills to face this task properly, they clearly had the cultural competence to detect and recognise some social dynamics which lead to unequal treatment of lesbians and gays between peers and, more generally, in Italian society.

Nevertheless, our case study also shows that the aim of creating a sense of citizenship through the involvement of institutions such as school and the law is subject to the interpretation of homophobia and anti-homosexual discrimination as a pathology. This master framework—which arises from the hegemony of the heterosexual definition of reality—was shared by our lesbian and gay participants, particularly as regards the principle of their normalisation and understanding ignorance as the cause of hostility against them. But at the same time, lesbians and gays themselves questioned it by attacking its basic tenet, such as the refusal to admit the existence of a structural link between the 'true' and condemnable homophobia—the intentional mistreatment and hostility against homosexual people motivated by fear, disgust or hate—and other forms of 'unintentional discrimination' or institutional misrecognition.

Comparisons between heterosexual and lesbian/gay discourses allow us to associate the fight against homophobia with several social processes. On one hand, the popularity of the pathological interpretation of homophobia among heterosexual students reflects the success of lesbian and gay mobilisation in achieving some cultural changes in society. Within this interpretation, the views we recorded from lesbian and gay participants receive full recognition by heterosexual students, although the support of the latter is far from being promoted by national institutions.

On the other hand, the existence of an alternative and more structural framework among lesbians and gays points to an expression of suffering which is not, and perhaps cannot be, legitimised by heterosexual students. As Lucia, a 23-year-old student, told us:

Sometimes homosexual boys perceive discrimination when it is not actually there.

In this case, our research detects a field of symbolic conflict which is difficult to address by anti-discrimination laws or policies. This is both because of the problematic interpretation of the kind of phenomena to be tackled, and also because the laws can themselves be questioned as sources of (unexpected) discomfort by the very people they should help.

4

Integrated, but Not Too Much: Homophobia and Homosexuality in Slovenia

ROMAN KUHAR, ŽIVA HUMER AND SIMON MALJEVAC

1. Introduction

'Welcome to the second most homophobic country in the world!' This is how a participant from Slovenia greeted her fellow participants in the international seminar on intimate citizenship organised in Ljubljana in 2005. Astonished looks on the faces of the researchers and activists quickly turned to smiles, as the speaker explained her unusual greeting: 'The second, because we all believe our own countries to be the most homophobic countries in the world.'

Although such an impression may be understandable from the position of those fighting against various forms of homophobia daily, it certainly does not stand up to empirical scrutiny. In the existing research on homophobia, homo-negativity and social distance towards homosexuals, Slovenia ranks in the middle of European countries.

A study on homonegativity in Europe (Štulhofer and Rimac 2009) places Slovenia on the margin of the medium-homonegative group of countries, which consists mainly of Western European countries. Similar conclusions were reached by research on the relationship between social acceptance of lesbians and gays and satisfaction with democracy in 26 European societies (Takács and Szalma 2011). Slovenia is in the middle group between Western European countries, expressing the highest levels of satisfaction with democracy and of tolerance towards lesbians and gays and having a legal institution regulating same-sex partnerships and/or families, and Eastern European countries with a low level of satisfaction with democracy. 'The Rainbow Index' introduced by the international non-governmental organisation ILGA-Europe, which only looks at legal institutions for lesbian, gay, bisexual and transgender (LGBT) citizens (and does not take into consideration the quality of the institutions) ranked Slovenia as the fourteenth among 50 European countries.[1]

The findings of the Slovenian Public Opinion Survey show that in the 1990s, about half the respondents in Slovenia did not want to have a homosexual as their neighbour, but in 2005 the proportion fell to 35% (Toš, Malnar et al 2005) and to 34% in 2008 (Toš et al 2008). The 2008 Eurobarometer included a question about how comfortable respondents would feel if a homosexual person was their neighbour, on a scale from 1 (very uncomfortable) to 10 (totally comfortable), and Slovenia's score was 7.5, whereas the European average was 7.9.[2]

Although there is no research available on how many people in Slovenia are familiar with the meaning of the word 'homophobia', we can be fairly certain that in the last decade the word has become part of everyday vocabulary. This is partly due to reports in the media about various homophobic incidents in Slovenia, as well as the organised lesbian and gay movement, which was established in Slovenia as early as 1984. Although the movement started at the time of the communist political system (Slovenia decriminalised homosexuality in 1976, when it was still part of Yugoslavia) and is therefore the oldest organised lesbian and gay movement in Eastern Europe, the authorities did not oppose the movement openly. In 1986 the movement articulated its first political demands, which included the introduction of homosexuality as a topic in the school curriculum (Kuhar 2001a; Lešnik 2006; Mencin Čeplak and Kuhar 2010).

Homophobia has been more frequently mentioned since the second half of the 1990s. The point at which homophobia entered 'public awareness' can rather arbitrarily be located at the beginning of the new millennium. To be exact, in 2001 a homophobic incident occurred (a security guard prohibited two gay men from entering a bar in the centre of Ljubljana because of their sexual orientation) which led to the first Slovenian Pride parade being organised. Most media reports about both the event and the Pride parade focused on the question of homophobia in Slovenian society, and some reports specifically emphasised 'homophobia' as a new word entering public discourse (Kuhar 2001b).

In spite of a seemingly higher acceptance and a higher level of (at least professed) tolerance towards the lesbian and gay community in Slovenia, a change in the functioning of homophobia can be perceived. We could speak of 'the new homophobia', which is a reflection of wider changes in the operation of prejudices and stereotypes and a consequence of shifts in the operation of violence and discrimination against various social groups (Rener 2008; Rener 2009; Smith 1997; Ule 2005; Švab and Kuhar 2005).

---

[1] Rainbow Europe Country Index (2011), available at www.ilga-europe.org/home/publications/reports_and_other_materials/rainbow_map_and_index_2011.

[2] European Commission. 2008, Special Eurobarometer 296, *Discrimination in the European Union: Perceptions, Experiences and Attitudes*, available at www.ec.europa.eu/social/BlobServlet?docId=769&langId=en.

Rener (2009: 115) stresses three fundamental changes in the operation of stereotypes and prejudices. First, there has been a shift from the discourse of prejudice towards political correctness. Modern prejudices and stereotypes are much more covert and subtle when compared with traditional ones. Open physical violence has been replaced by ignorance and distance. Although homophobia is not an acceptable way of functioning and public expression (the culture of political correctness simply no longer allows it), numerous events reveal broad agreement with the discriminatory statements of those who, despite everything, 'dare to say things out loud'. The more political correctness attempts to silence intolerant voices, the more attention the voices which dare to cross the line receive. They very frequently include certain Members of the Slovenian Parliament who use intolerant standpoints for political gain—their potential voters recognise them as the ones who 'dare' to say what the majority supposedly think. This is exactly what made the debate on the new Family Code between autumn 2009 and summer 2011 a fertile ground for many such transgressions of political correctness.[3]

The second shift, addressed by Rener, is the change in targets. 'New' groups are being established as the targets of prejudice, stereotyping, violence and discrimination (for example, people who are overweight, smokers, lesbians and gays and so on), adding to the 'old' groups suffering prejudice (for example, women, Roma people, migrants and so on). The victims of prejudice and stereotyping are the social groups which have the role of scapegoat for a range of social problems. The debate on the new Family Code was a very good illustration of such scapegoating. One of the most frequent arguments against the adoption of the new Code was criticism of the government for wasting its time on an insignificant social minority, at a time when many employees are being made redundant due to the economic and social crisis.

The third shift in the functioning of stereotypes and prejudices in our time is the change in mechanisms. Overt violence and hatred of the old days is now transformed into less obvious, symbolic, 'cultivated' violence, which tends towards its own general acceptance. Such violence, Rener (2009) asserts, is 'slippery and elusive, which makes it all the more difficult to identify and resist'.

In addition, the level of homophobic violence clearly demonstrates the inconsistency between standpoints, opinions and values, and actual everyday practices. A research on the everyday life of lesbians and gays in Slovenia (443 respondents),[4] for instance, showed that 53% of the responding lesbians and gays had

---

[3] In the autumn of 2009, the Ministry of Labour, Family and Social Affairs prepared a new version of the Family Code (to replace the 35-year-old existing act) for public debate. The new Code stipulates legal equality for heterosexual and homosexual partnerships, including the right to adopt children, which was still a legislative option during the time when focus groups were held. The Ministry later introduced a 'compromised' version of the Family Code, allowing same-sex partners only second-parent adoption. For more on that, see Kogovšek in this volume.

[4] In the sample 66% of respondents were men and 34% were women.

experienced violence because of their sexual orientation. The most frequent forms of violence are psychological (91%), physical (24%) and sexual (6%),[5] with most violence taking place in public, that is, in public places (Švab and Kuhar 2005). Similar conclusions were reached by research carried out by the non-governmental organisation Legebitra in 2008 (221 respondents).[6] The most frequent forms of violence are insults (80%), ignorance or intentional exclusion from social circles (35%) and threats with physical violence (32%)[7] (Kuhar and Magić 2008).

'The new homophobia', Smith writes (1997), actually pretends to be tolerant towards lesbians and gays, as it promises the integration of homosexual identities within social frameworks—but only in as much as they assimilate into the existing heterosexist society. Or, as Rener says (2008: 25): "'The different" are still okay as long as they remain invisible and silent; when they show up and start talking, they become irritating, and if they were to become—god forbid—better than us in anything whatsoever, it would become unbearable.' Being different is thus acceptable, provided that it remains within the existing and, most of all, unchanged frameworks of functioning. This is clearly supported by the use of the linguistic term 'different' (Slovenian: *različen*) in the Slovenian cultural environment. 'The different' are all those who are unlike 'us'. There is therefore some degree of tolerance towards 'the different', but the position of power in relation to which the different are to be construed as such—that is, as 'different' from 'us'—must be preserved. The use of the term 'diversity' (Slovenian: *različnost*), which extends difference over the whole of society (everybody is different, nobody is the norm), is consequently very rare in debates on the inclusion/exclusion of various social groups, including lesbians and gays.

The above-mentioned shifts and discrepancies between views and practice in Slovenia have also been noted in the research which was part of the project 'Citizens in Diversity: A Four-Nation Study on Homophobia and Fundamental Rights'. Between May and November 2010, four focus groups with lesbians and gays were held, with 12 men and eight women participating. The youngest respondent was 18 years old, the oldest 38, and the average age was 28.6 years. Fourteen respondents lived in large towns (Ljubljana or Maribor), five in villages, and one did not answer the question about place of residence. As regards education, one respondent had primary school education and was attending secondary school, 11 had secondary school education (six were studying), five had university education, one had college education, one held an MA and one a PhD. Four more focus groups and two individual interviews were carried out

---

[5] The percentages add up to more than 100% due to the multiple response question. It means that some respondents have experienced more than one type of violence.

[6] In the sample 44% of respondents identified themselves as gay men, 29% as lesbians, 21% as bisexuals, 5% as queer; the remaining 1% refused to identify themselves.

[7] The percentages add up to more than 100% due to the multiple response question. It means that some respondents have experienced more than one type of violence.

with students at the Department of Educational Studies, University of Ljubljana—with 16 female and four male students participating. Their average age was 22.3 years, the youngest was 19 years old, the oldest 27. Eight respondents lived in Ljubljana, five lived in smaller towns, and seven lived in villages. All had secondary education, and most of them had finished high school.[8]

Selected results are presented in the following three sections. The first section addresses understanding of the concept of homophobia; in the second homosexuality and homophobia are placed in the context of the educational process in primary and secondary schools (it was for this reason that we carried out focus groups with students of educational studies) and the third describes the strategies lesbians and gays use to respond to homophobia.

In order to understand the context, it is important to point out that the focus groups were carried out during the period of public debates on the new Family Code. Consequently, respondents set the various issues examined during the focus groups in the context of these debates. The focus groups with the students of educational studies also underwent a certain amount of group pressure when individuals answered specific questions, especially the question on the right of same-sex couples to adopt children. Only one of the students took an explicitly negative view of such adoption, while the others primarily gave 'politically correct' answers, dictated to some degree by 'group pressure'. This does support Rener's thesis about the fundamental shift in prejudices and stereotypes in the direction of political correctness. In addition, the students' groups expressed a mainly normative and uniform position in understanding homophobia and homosexuality: unanimous rejection of homophobia and normative acceptance of homosexuality—all within the context of the culture of political correctness. Nevertheless, on the basis of the focus groups with students of educational studies, we can conclude that the topics related to homosexuality and homophobia remain marginalised, are considered infrequently and certainly not in any depth since, as some of the respondents pointed out, they began thinking about these issues only when they had been faced with the questions. Here, we should not overlook the systemic level, where such topics are absent. That is, the respondents reported not receiving (enough) information and knowledge about the topics during their university (as well as primary and secondary school) education.

In contrast, as expected, the focus groups with lesbians and gays were much more contextualised, founded on personal experience and on more or less reflected attitudes, and they were also completely removed from the principled (dis)agreement with and moral evaluation of the topics associated with homosexuality, education and homophobia.

---

[8] To preserve respondents' anonymity, assumed names are used throughout. The number next to a name indicates the respondent's age. Colloquial language has been standardised, but the meaning and its different nuances have been preserved.

2. Defining and Expressing Homophobia and Homosexuality

As a rule, homophobia is no longer understood according to Weinberg's classical view as a fear similar to claustrophobia, agoraphobia and other such phobias—which means a *physical* fear of being close to homosexuals. Nowadays, homophobia in everyday discourse primarily means general disapproval of homosexuality. It comprises various negative connotations, from hatred to condemnation, violence and discrimination against lesbians and gays (Kuhar 2009). Herek (2004) understands it as a cultural ideology which preserves the stigma by denying and demeaning any non-heterosexual forms of behaviour, identity or community. It is incorporated in institutions, language and legislation, through which it is expressed and maintained. However, Kuhar does think that Weinberg's classical concept of homophobia still exists and that it remains an important part of the culture of fear of homosexuals. This is immediately obvious from the structure of jokes about homosexuality, which:

> Repeatedly express fear of a physical contact with homosexuals (as in the classic example of a bar of soap falling on the floor in the area where men are having a shower, which leads on to the supposedly comical situation of a man bending over to reach for the soap and thus risking anal penetration from an imaginary homosexual, who seems to be always present and preying upon such situations under the showers). (Kuhar 2006: 546)

Weinberg's (1972) concept of homophobia as fear of homosexuals was quite frequently expressed in both students' and lesbian and gay focus groups, although fear was not necessarily understood as 'physical'; rather, it signified a view of homosexuality as an abnormality, illness or something which threatens us. Most of the explanations and interpretations of homophobia may thus be placed in Herek's (1986, 1987, 1991, 2004) functionalist account of homophobic behaviour, primarily in its experiential–schematic function. It gives homophobia meaning though a person's past negative or positive experiences with lesbians and gays or—to broaden the definition slightly—through the absence of such experiences. The debate on the school system in the students' focus groups kept returning to the dilemma about how to convince parents that the topic of homosexuality and related issues are an integral part of the topics that school needs to cover. The respondents emphasised the very aspect of personal experience—children should meet a lesbian or a gay man. Needless to say, such a position can be problematic if it does not include simultaneous changes in the social climate. It is also questionable whether a homosexual person should be exposed as 'an object in the shop window' for others to realise that lesbians and gays can have positive characteristics.

2.1. The Meanings of Homophobia

All the participants in the focus groups were familiar with the term 'homophobia'. Some of them had heard it in secondary school (most frequently in sociology classes), others during their tertiary education, but the majority reported becoming familiar with the term through the media, chiefly through reports on homophobic violence or debates on legislative changes (for example, same-sex marriages).

We encountered three interpretations of homophobia: (1) homophobia as a consequence of seeing homosexuality as an abnormality or illness—in this context, homophobia implies fear of lesbians and gays or a threat posed by them; (2) homophobia as fear of any kind of diversity; (3) homophobia as a form of violence or as a strategy to discriminate against homosexuals.

Lesbians and gays most frequently associated homophobia with discrimination, violence and prejudice against the homosexual population. They described it as a form of violence or a strategy to discriminate against lesbians and gays. Some respondents in the educational studies students' focus group also related homophobia to violence, although that was not the dominant view. More often they understood homophobia as an emotional response to something unknown which manifests itself in the form of hate speech. One of the respondents stressed that there is a lot of homophobia in Slovenian society (most participants agreed) and that it is encouraged precisely by the normative prohibition of the expression of homophobic standpoints. A subtle expression of homophobia can, as a result, be even more pronounced and even more dangerous.

> I see homophobia as an emotional repose to something different, that is, something you don't know. These emotions manifest themselves in the form of hate speech or other forms of violence. But I do think that homophobia is perhaps increasingly present in a hidden, covert way. Well, publicly, too, of course, but perhaps precisely because of the imperative of 'let's accept difference' it is more hidden. (Andrej, 24, student)

Most of the respondents emphasised ignorance, and prejudice—which, they believe, also stems from ignorance—as the reasons for homophobia. One convenient solution which they offered was—not surprisingly—the experience of getting to know a homosexual person.

> The main reason is certain prejudices. Perhaps not having the experience of being in contact with same-sex orientation, too. I see that at work, I work with adolescents, who have to face the fact of me being gay. Sooner or later they find out, because I don't hide it from them. … They'll provoke you: 'Have you got a girlfriend?' [I reply:] 'No, I've got a boyfriend' … And then a mass of prejudices emerges. From that I can conclude that their position is often homophobic. 'Oh, God, no, keep a long way from me, because otherwise you'll rape me.' Or rubbish like that. Then it takes some time for the prejudices to be suspended. They see you're a human being like everyone else, and they can talk to you normally. (Alex, 37, gay)

In public discourse, terms like discrimination, violence and homophobia often appear together, sometimes even interchangeably. So what is the relationship between discrimination, violence and homophobia? Most respondents in the focus groups thought that the three things are interrelated, while emphasising two important points: (1) According to some, homophobia can lead to discrimination and violence, but homophobia itself is not the same as discrimination and violence. An individual can express homophobic views, without discriminating against or being violent towards homosexuals. (2) The other group of respondents thought that any kind of homophobia necessarily also means discrimination. Homophobia therefore turns out to be a hyponym of discrimination.

> I don't distinguish between discrimination and violence. For me, any kind of discrimination is violence. If someone treats me differently merely on the basis of a personal circumstance, I see that as violence against me. (Marija, 29, lesbian)

The above-mentioned polarisation became even clearer when respondents were placed in the hypothetical situation of seemingly mutually exclusive rights: the right to free speech, and the right to non-discrimination on the basis of sexual orientation. We asked whether opposing homosexuality, homosexual marriage or Pride parades can in itself be described as homophobic. The first group argued that such opposition is not homophobia, but only an expression of disagreement. However, the second group thought that such opposition can definitely be labelled homophobic, since it implies a denial of human rights.

The first group tried to support its position by establishing a distinction between 'standpoints' and 'homophobia as an emotional position'. The respondents argued that standpoints were about expressing one's personal opinion, whereas homophobia was an emotional response to homosexuality. Some of them added that the main difference lies in the manner in which a standpoint is expressed, starting from the belief that everybody has a right to their own opinion. They attempted to define the difference at the point of personal opinion. If people are sufficiently open-minded, if they can listen to other people's opinions and are ready to change their opinions if they realise they are unacceptable, intolerant and homophobic, then, some educational studies students think, this is not a case of homophobia. Here, one of the respondents added the remark on the public–private relationship. If a person with an opinion tries to influence others publicly and bring them round 'to their cause', then we can no longer speak of a personal opinion (for example, disagreement about same-sex marriages) but of an instance of a homophobic act.

> As long as you keep your opinion to yourself and have your own beliefs [we cannot speak of homophobia]. But when you start talking about it publicly and refuse [lesbians and gays] certain rights ... then you're already entering the space of their rights. (Martin, 27, student)

Further discussions about Pride parades and same-sex marriages revealed that the students of educational studies do not perceive granting or respecting human rights as something unconditional; rather, they impose at least three conditions. They do not have the classical conditional structure (if → then), but they do reveal the unreflected tolerance position which preserves the relationship between 'them' and 'us', and the condition for 'them' being granted human rights is, essentially, 'their' integration with 'us'. In other words, the relationship between heterosexuality and homosexuality is not solved through seeing the binary relationship as problematic, but rather through the integration of homo-sexuality in the heteronormative matrix, which leaves the foundation of the binary relationship unaffected.

The students in our sample listed three aspects that the lesbian and gay community should reflect upon in order to achieve social integration and respect for human rights more easily: (1) numerousness; (2) normalisation; and (3) a drive towards privacy.

Numerousness is related to the belief that only a clear idea of the numbers of lesbians and gays can contribute to the community being granted human rights. In this view, the numerousness of the group would warrant and legitimise calls for human rights. In this interpretation, rights are not understood as something enjoyed by an individual, but primarily by a (large) group. Interestingly, the students did not mention the need for lesbians and gays to 'come out' in order to make the minority visible, but rather the need of society to realise the size of the lesbian and gay minority.

> Perhaps we don't have the sense of [homosexuality] being so widespread either. [Only if people became aware] that there are so many such people [lesbians and gays], [they would think] they deserve the same treatment, the same rights ... (Valentina, 21, student)

The second condition, normalisation, was most clearly expressed during the debate about Pride parades. Some students of educational studies thought that Pride parades prevent the homosexual community from normalising itself. Pride parades excite intolerance towards lesbians and gays and preclude them from full assertion of human rights. Also, since some respondents deemed Pride parades to be a kind of 'excessive exposure', the violence they provoke seems to be their own fault. Such political actions were, accordingly, not understood as a human right, and respect for those could only follow 'normalisation' of the community.

> [Pride parades are] ... a way of calling attention to yourself as well as some kind of promotion, but in a very strange way. I think the approach to pride parades is wrong, because they often turn out to be a sort of circus. And that leads to various instances of intolerance—I think the approach to these parades is wrong. (Neja, 22, student)

Normalisation is also related to the third 'condition' for human rights: the drive towards privacy. Exposure in the public space as a form of political activism is understood as a deviation from heteronormative patterns of behaviour and functioning. Some respondents consequently suggested a withdrawal into pri-vacy, believing that invisibility would lead to less violence and, presumably, to a greater respect for human rights. Interestingly enough, the third 'condition for human rights' (invisibility) is somewhat contradicted by the argument about numerousness. However, the respondents did not realise this inconsistency in their interpretations.

> Not such a bang, loads of people in the street, loads of ornaments, everybody half naked … It's all presented as something really horrible, something horribly different from the majority [of people], which—after all—homosexuality is not. Perhaps not all homosexuals like showing off, and I think those who are perhaps not so provocative then acquire a bad reputation because of that. (Neja, 22, student)

'Conditioning' human rights through numerousness, but especially through normalisation and the drive towards privacy in the focus groups, revealed the most obvious sign of the (unreflected) heteronormative context that the respondents came from. They did argue for the human rights of lesbians and gays and do think that homosexuality is something completely ordinary and normal (the whole trouble, of course, lies in the word 'normality'), but they conditioned it all by normalisation of homosexuality. At this point, a parallel may be drawn with similar conclusions in cultural studies, which find that lesbians and gays ever more frequently appear in the products of popular culture. That is, they are no longer the butt of jokes as they used to be; rather, they are becoming ordinary, 'everyday people'—under certain conditions, among which normalisation is the prevailing one (see Seidman 2002: 133). In other words, normalisation actually means integration through invisibility and the preservation of the heteronormative status quo (Mason 2002).

In the lesbian and gay focus groups, such restrictions were not mentioned and human rights were not conditioned by any kind of normalisation. In fact, the majority of lesbians and gays (due to the period in which the focus groups were carried out) discussed the need for homosexual couples to be put on an equal legal footing with heterosexual ones. Consequently, they believe, the symbolic position of lesbians and gays in society would improve. To what extent this could be understood as the normalisation of homosexuality or the embodiment of heteronormativity is a matter of interpretation and a topic of numerous debates within LGBT/queer studies (see Warner 2001; Kuhar 2010).

2.2. Homophobia in Public Discourse

When discussing how homophobia is understood in public discourse, the respondents in all the focus groups frequently referred to homophobia as it appears in media discourse. That is, they called particular attention to the media, which often uncritically report homophobic incidents (for example, homophobic speeches in Parliament). Homophobia in public, the respondents claim, manifests itself as hate speech, appearing in the light of a spectacle. The respondents, for instance, mentioned the case of the physical attack on the LGBT café Cafe

Open in Ljubljana, which political parties from both political sides strongly condemned, but about which there was no subsequent in-depth discussion.[9] Moreover, those who condemned violence simultaneously encouraged it with their homophobic statements. As a result, the respondents emphasised the need for greater higher responsiveness by the media—not only in terms of their functioning along the lines of political correctness, but also in terms of more critical responsiveness.

> When the Cafe Open was attacked, there was lots to read about it, it was on the front pages of all the newspapers. People talked about it a lot, there's no denying that. But some kind of notoriety and spectacle was created around it. Political parties condemned the attack fiercely, but we never reached the next level—how to deal with the core of the problem. (Andrej, 24, student)

In addition to the media as the key point of the channelling of homophobia in the public space, our respondents also focused on politicians, who create public discourse from their position of power. Respondents mostly called attention to the problem that Rener (2009) terms the shift from the discourse of prejudice towards political correctness. This means that sexism, racism and other 'isms' are no longer acceptable in the public space, but their substance remains unchanged. In fact, homophobia has not disappeared from the public space, but it is either not perceived as hate speech or is hidden under supposedly politically correct speech and the right to free speech. Our respondents, however, stressed that the hate speech accompanying the parliamentary debate about the new Family Code originated from positions of power and, as such, it had a huge communicative value, particularly in quantity. With the help of the media, politicians' countless homophobic statements and examples of hate speech reached a very large audience, which not only gave them added impetus but also provided them with legitimacy, since the discourse of public figures—for example, politicians—was not sanctioned. The communicative value of such excesses in public is the legitimacy of homophobic statements, which encourages the reproduction of homophobia in the public space.

> I find it sad that people who make such [homophobic] statements represent us in Parliament. It's sad to hear someone say that homosexuality is a disease and that they should seek treatment. When the whole of Slovenia sees or reads such a statement … then people who know next to nothing about it, in certain rural areas where there is no education about it, then they cling to that and stick to it, and it's very hard to do away with it or change these peoples' opinions in any way. (Dorinda, 24, student)

We conclude that respondents perceive Slovenian society as homophobic. This was a unanimous conclusion in the focus groups. Both the student and lesbians/

---

[9] On 25 June 2009, there was an attack on the LGBT café Cafe Open, during which a gay activist was physically injured. In the following days, the police found three perpetrators of the attack, who were convicted of public incitement to hatred and violence, and sentenced to five to seven months in prison.

gay focus groups most frequently linked homophobia to age and place of residence. Many of them stated that older people and those living in rural areas are more conservative, less open and liberal, and find it hard to accept different patterns of living, which also makes them more homophobic. Respondents seem reductively to imagine older people as a homogenous group in which there are no differences between individuals and where conservatism is the binding principle, whereas the young are stereotypically seen as more open, finding it easier to accept social diversity. Age is often interrelated with religion, and the focus groups believe that the latter is directly linked to place of residence. They identify dichotomous urban-rural relationships as another factor affecting homophobia. Rural areas are presented as backward-looking, as areas where people are not highly educated, which makes them more traditional in their beliefs and world views. Instead, urban areas are believed to be spaces of openness and acceptance of diversity.

3. Building Citizenship through Education

Nadja (30): I spoke to a teacher who said: 'I'll never accept these people [homosexuals]. Never! There's a boy in my class who can draw beautifully and he only plays with girls. I know I can't treat him differently, but I cannot accept this.'

Marko (38): I think it'd be fair for her to tell the child's parents, and let them decide whether they'll keep him in her class or send him somewhere else. It would be fair if she told them that she's incapable of accepting him. Let her say to them: 'I don't accept that. That's my weakness. Put him where they can love him more.'

Marija (29): Perhaps the parents won't understand. It might be nothing but a stereotype, perhaps the child is not gay at all. If they send him somewhere else, he'll lose his social circle, because the teacher can't accept homosexuality. Then everyone might start doing the same thing. The next time we organise a pride parade, a hundred police officers will say: 'I can't accept it, I won't protect them.' It would be like going to the dentist and hearing him say: 'My moral principles don't allow me to treat a gay.' You need to stick to certain things, so you try and solve them. Full stop.

[A lesbian and gay focus group debate on professional standards and the right to exclusion]

In the last five years, there has been some research in Slovenia on the various aspects of homosexuality and homophobic violence in schools. In the most general terms, the results show that homosexuality is not a frequent topic of discussion at school (Švab and Kuhar 2005; Maljevac and Magić 2009), that school is not a safe place for same-sex-oriented students (Kuhar and Magić 2008; Maljevac and Magić 2009) and that the official curriculum systematically leaves the discussion of homosexuality out of its educational aims, although there are certain points which could lead to that discussion. These are mostly related to the issues of the differences among people in society and discussion of the concept of tolerance (Komidar and Mandeljc 2009).

The accounts provided by the students of educational studies and lesbians and gays in the focus groups support the findings of the above research. We confirm the finding that 'homosexuality as a topic of discussion during school instruction … appears sporadically, unsystematically and probably with quite some restraint, since talking about it is still interpreted as promotion, not education' (Maljevac and Magić 2009: 100). Some respondents reported having homosexuality presented to them as something negative during the process of education, with students themselves occasionally reacting to such interpretations of homosexuality.

> During sex education at secondary school, one lesson was devoted to that. A nurse from the gynaecological clinic came and told us that homosexuality was an illness and absolutely disgusting. Then a classmate, whose cousin was gay and who was naturally highly protective, criticised her and so the whole lesson took the form of a quarrel. (Orlando, 22, gay)

Arthur Lipkin (1999) finds that a simple inclusion of homosexuality as a topic in school curricula does not suffice. Nor is a simple discussion or a mere remark about the topic sufficient, since—as Orlando's story illustrates—students (as well as teachers) are not willing to quietly accept information that contradicts their own beliefs. For that reason, Lipkin advocates *transformative interactive education*, the aim of which is 'to raise a person's moral judgment to include respect for the dignity and rights of all'. That can be achieved by first establishing cognitive dissonance in the individual, which points to 'the inadequacy of his or her reasoning to resolve a moral conflict' (Lipkin 1999: 231–34).

3.1. When and How to Talk about Homosexuality

On the basis of the interviews and focus groups carried out, we conclude that students of educational studies have no dilemma about whether to include the issue of homosexuality in school curricula; their only concern is how and when to talk about it. Some respondents showed a certain degree of unease, since they tend to reduce homosexuality to a mere question of sexual behaviour. They thought the topic was only appropriate for discussion at secondary (not primary) school, and they—mostly implicitly—supported their view by equating homosexuality with sexuality or sex education. All the social aspects of homosexuality (partnerships, families, and so on) were left out of their interpretation.

> Frankly, they don't talk about it at primary school. I also think they should introduce [the topic] in the eighth or ninth grades when students already understand what it's all about. There's no point in doing it earlier, as they don't know anything about sexuality anyway, and there's really no point. But at secondary school, I think, this is exactly

what's missing. They teach you about sexuality, safer sex and what have you, but there's not a single word about homosexuality. (Sara, 23, student)

Those who reduced homosexuality to a mere question of sexuality placed the topic in secondary school education, but the majority did think it should be brought up earlier (especially if there are children coming from same-sex families in the class), but 'in an appropriate way'. This very fear ('in an appropriate way') yet again conceals the explicit reduction of homosexuality to a sexual relationship between two people of the same gender. That is, no participant thought of heterosexuality as a problem, as a topic to be introduced as soon as possible, but 'in an appropriate way'. Some of them attempted to solve the dilemma by suggesting a more general discussion about 'differences', without first focusing on homosexuality.

> I think [homosexuality] needs to be discussed, but not with such young children—but the sooner the better. Because children already form certain opinions between the ages of one and seven or eight, which I think are pretty strong. So I believe we should start talking about it earlier. Not so much about gays and lesbians, but more generally about differences. (Martina, 21, student)

The view quoted above is a good reflection of the standpoints other respondents also expressed: homosexuality should be addressed *covertly*. In particular, for younger children, it should be placed in the context of broader topics (differences) and the issue itself should not be mentioned explicitly. However, such a debate on differences does not make a problem of the self-evidence of the established norm, in relation to which differences can only start to be constituted. Homosexuality is therefore treated as something which must be tolerated, but it retains the status of difference and marginality.

Whereas some respondents interpreted homosexuality primarily through sexuality, the students of educational studies focus groups repeatedly revealed a 'humanistic aspect', that is, *the normalisation of homosexuality*, which constructed homosexuals as 'different', but still 'human beings'—and therefore worthy of being talked about at school.

> [Blacks] have a different skin colour, but underneath they are the same as you and me. And it's the same with them [homosexuals]. They behave a little differently, but under the skin they are the same as us, they have two arms, two legs, a brain, a head, they have everything. (Sara, 23, student)

The 'humanistic aspect' was also often related to the need for 'empirical evidence'. When discussing what to do if parents protested against the debate on homosexuality at school, some respondents thought it would be best to invite a homosexual couple or a homosexual to a school meeting with parents. Parents would thus be able to see 'empirical evidence', on which the humanistic position on homosexuals would be founded. In other words, parents could finally realise that there is nothing wrong with homosexuals, that 'under the skin they are the same as us'.

They [students] should meet a family or a gay willing to talk to them. They'd socialise, say, for a couple of hours, and then they'd see that he's a pretty cool person. [...] And then children could also tell their parents if they saw they had a totally different opinion: 'Look, I met one today, and he was so nice, I think there's nothing wrong with him.' (Maja, 21, student)

I'd like to see as much of that as possible—let children see, meet someone who's gay or lesbian. Let them see they're just people, that they're pretty normal and okay and funny and amusing and all that ... (Martina, 21, student)

The 'normalisation' of homosexuality through 'empirical evidence' was the leitmotif of most of the debates about homosexuality and the school space. Although we maintain that there is a humanistic perspective in the background of the quoted responses, suggesting the acceptance of lesbians and gays regardless of their difference, this aspect is also interrelated with the simultaneous expectation that the image of homosexuals as 'empirical evidence' will be acceptable, likeable, amusing. Hence, homosexuals need to be 'so cool', 'okay', 'funny' and 'amusing'—only then are they constructed as 'normal' and acceptable. But, as Lipkin emphasises (1999: 233), an anti-homophobic project that depends on 'repackaging' the gay image is either utopian or cynical, since it implicitly expects homosexuals to meet certain higher standards—and that is a precondition for the establishment of tolerance. But such tolerance is basically flawed.

Besides, simple, one-off contacts with members of certain groups do not lead to a simple elimination of intolerance; if those contacts are involuntary and forced, they may even increase the feeling of resentment in the group where such feeling is already strong. Although such contacts can contribute to greater integration and acceptance (respondents were right in claiming that the latter is based on the realisation that the 'other' is not essentially different from us), they may also turn to the opposite: contacts do not necessarily lead to realisation of the similarities between 'us' and 'them'. If making contact only reinforces the notion of difference still further, it may lead to even stronger prejudices against the social minority (Lipkin, 1999: 236–37).

Thus, the respondents in our research understood the introduction of homosexuality into school curricula as something which might encourage a higher level of tolerance towards and acceptance of homosexuals and, in particular, might help those who are themselves same-sex-oriented. Yet the future educationalists did not generally question the heteronormativity of the school space; they mostly saw homosexuality as something that needs to be 'attached' to the existing system. This, for instance, is shown in the idea they expressed that, at least once a year or every four years, a workshop on homosexuality should be organised.

I think it would be right for students at least once every four years ... so that each generation has one lecture on the topic. ... It doesn't have to be one hour of talking about it non-stop, five, ten minutes are enough to stimulate students' thinking. (Sara, 23, student)

Takács (2006) finds that the described approach (a one-off discussion) is the dominant model in addressing homosexuality in Europe, which creates the impression that it is a marginal, controversial issue or a problem requiring a solution.

The opposite approach—spreading the topic over different learning areas—was primarily supported by respondents who were more familiar with the topic (for example, students who attended the course in lesbian and gay studies), because they, like Takács (2006), thought that focusing on one single workshop might actually constitute discrimination. The students of educational studies also emphasised that inserting the topic in the curriculum is crucial for a widespread discussion of homosexuality.

All participants agreed that homosexuality needs to be discussed in school and, similarly, they were unanimous about the need to react to homophobic insults. Although they mentioned various ways of reacting to someone using the word 'faggot' as an insult, some of their answers were characterised by attempts to use the reaction in order to prove that the person addressed as a faggot is not in fact a 'faggot' at all. It means that they would, first and foremost, try to prove the incorrect usage of the word, and only then would they question insulting someone on the basis of that person's actual—or even imaginary—sexual orientation.

Despite identification of the need to react to homophobic insults, some of the respondents still thought that they did not have any practical knowledge and actually do not know how to react in such a situation. Most of the participants also thought that they had not received enough information about homosexuality to be able to talk about it at secondary or primary school. The students who attended the optional course in lesbian and gay studies were, as expected, more familiar with and more sensitive to the issues. They were also the only ones who thought they could talk independently about the topic to students. According to Kuhar (2009), the importance of lesbian and gay studies—either as specific optional subjects or subjects forming part of larger study areas—did not therefore lie merely in the production of knowledge in the area, but mainly in their dissemination.

> The future teachers who have access to gay and lesbian studies at university are definitely more sensitive not only to the issue of homophobic exclusion from society, but to all sorts of discrimination. At the same time they are more able to identify the places in the curriculum that allow for a discussion about homosexuality, which they are also professionally prepared for. It is only then that a discussion about homosexuality in the spirit of the respect for human rights, with a simultaneous concern for the principles of criticality, plurality and objectivity, is encouraged. (Kuhar 2009: 44)

The students of educational studies thought it is necessary to talk about homosexuality 'in a neutral way'. The topic needs to be dealt with like any other, it needs to be approached from a distance—not too positively or too negatively—

or, as one respondent said, students need to be made aware of it, and then it should not be talked about too much, unless a problem arises.

> It needs to be talked about neutrally—say, the teacher should be careful not to talk too negatively or too positively. … It's right for them to say it's something normal, but it's also right to say that there are people who don't agree with that, and people who do it. (Lili, 22, student)

> You say good and bad things [about homosexuality], not only good or only bad things. (Valentina, 21, student)

It is not quite clear what the 'good' or 'bad' sides of homosexuality are, though. Tanja Rener did examine the issue, asking her university students on a course in lesbian and gay studies how they would approach the topic of homosexuality in schools. Some of the responses were similar to Valentina's above. Rener argues that such views rest on the belief that homosexuality is a moral issue, that is, that homosexuality is morally controversial. But if morally controversial issues are to be defined according to the epistemic criterion (Rener 2009: 112), which states that morally controversial questions are those about which we have opposing viewpoints, which do not oppose publicly available knowledge, the standards of truth and the criteria of the verification process, then homosexuality cannot be placed among them. To support her thesis, Rener cites the epistemic criterion for the issue of 'consensual sexual practice', which she sees as including 'pleasure, emotions, affection, reproduction, mutual support, sexual satisfaction, ecstasy, intimacy and mutual communication' (Rener 2009: 113). She finds that the only thing distinguishing homosexuality from heterosexuality is biological reproduction (not even other forms of economic, social, cultural and emotional reproduction). Yet we cannot take biological reproduction to be an 'essential constitutive element of sexual practice', since that would make all other non-reproductive sexual practices just as morally illegitimate, which makes no sense. It is this very point that reveals the answer to the dilemma about how to talk about homosexuality in schools (Rener 2009: 112–14).

Kovač Šebart and Krek (2009) reach a similar conclusion when emphasising that education in public schools should prevent teachers from forcing on students views about issues on which different groups have different opinions. But they distinguish between two groups of topics. The first consists of questions which are empirically impossible to answer (for example, the existence of God). The teacher's task here is to present different views about the question and allow a plurality of views. The second group comprises questions which are directly related to the respect for human rights and dignity, where the question of an individual's identity surely belongs. Here, people may also differ in their views, in spite of empirical facts. It is therefore the teacher's task to set a clear boundary between acceptable and unacceptable behaviour—unacceptable behaviour being actions which are intolerant and do not respect human rights (Rener 2009: 95–96).

3.2. Coming Out at School

A similar 'humanistic approach'—which some argued for, regarding the need for discussion about homosexuality in schools and which on one hand, anticipates the 'likeability' of homosexuals and, on the other, puts them in a position where their rights can only be recognised if they turn out to be 'normal' and 'there is nothing wrong with them'—was used by some respondents as a response to the coming out of a homosexual student. The extract quoted below clearly shows how the 'we–they' boundary would be established, together with a simultaneous appeal for tolerance:

> I'd try to make the class aware that he's a bit different, that he's still a human being, that he's still like them, that he doesn't pose any threat to them. Being gay, it doesn't mean he's going to jump on every classmate. … As an extreme measure, I'd exclude the student from the class and advise going to another school, that is, to a school which would be more accepting. At a school where the majority are, to put it bluntly, non-Slovenians … well, I think they have even more prejudice against it than us … I don't want to discriminate against anybody, but I got the impression they feel endangered more than us … But I would really only exclude him as an extreme measure, because it's already traumatic enough for him to be excluded from the class, let alone being excluded from the school itself. But I think it would be very hard to get the class to accept the student back. It's because there's no raising of awareness about what [homosexuality] is. (Sara, 23, student)

Most participants in the focus groups stressed that they would mainly use conversations and discussions to prevent a student who has come out from being mocked, but not everyone would take coming out as a fact immediately. Some thought it would first be necessary to ensure that the coming out was meant seriously, although others emphasised that it would not be sensible, since anyone who came out to a teacher would surely have thought about it so much that they would know what they were talking about.

> I'd talk to them in some depth, to see if they really meant it, if they know the term, if they know what it's about. Because sometimes people might say it just like that … (Neja, 22, student)

> I think I'd tell him that I respect his decision, that I really esteem him, and then I might ask him how long he's known that or how he actually sees that, how he feels about it, if he has any inclinations …, any dreams, fantasies and so on. I wouldn't intrude into his privacy too much, but just so to see, because children go through various phases and a phase like that … he might only be joking, it might fade away, only be momentary. … If I came across a child who really felt it, I'd say they have my full support. (Maja, 26, student)

Some respondents expressed doubts about their own competence in facing a student's coming out. A gender divide appeared here—although the female students of educational studies generally said they would accept such students and offer them support and help, some male students expressed uneasiness about what to do. Although they would accept them, they would also send them to a school counsellor or a social worker where they would receive more support.

> I'd try to tell him there's nothing wrong with it. … If I were a teacher, I'd tell him to go to the school counsellor if he wants to talk about it more. … He'd get better advice there. (Martin, 27, student)

The students of educational studies thus reported their willingness to try to provide a same-sex-oriented student with an inclusive school environment in various ways. They would react in a similar manner to the coming out of a homosexual teacher. It is interesting that an exploratory study on LGBT teachers in Slovenia (Magić and Janjevak 2011) showed that approximately half the participants (total number of respondents: 123) did not come out in the workplace. What is more, they did not come out precisely because they were afraid that doing so would expose them to their colleagues' chauvinism or that they might even lose their jobs. The respondents are also worried about the reactions of students and their parents. However, the prevailing answer given by closeted LGBT teachers revealed the view that sexual orientation is a personal circumstance which does not need to be discussed at work.

The students of educational studies took a somewhat different view. In principle, they did not oppose the idea of a homosexual teacher coming out at school. They associated an individual's coming out with sincerity, which might gain the respect of students. At the same time, some of them compared coming out—and justified it—with the fact that heterosexual teachers also talk about their privacy at school. Nevertheless, some respondents, following their agreement with homosexual teachers coming out in the workplace, added that they should not be 'too upfront' about it.

> They can say so, but mustn't use it to impose their own opinion, their belief … that others should accept homosexuality or lead them to that. [You have to] present the standpoint objectively. (Neja, 22, student)

> If they say so, there's nothing wrong with that. Perhaps not in the very first lesson when introducing themselves, [but later] during a discussion. Not by saying: 'I'm so-and-so, and I'm a lesbian.' I don't think that's the best way. (Hana, 22, student)

> [They can say so] if it's done in a specific context … Not by coming to every lesson and saying: 'Well, yesterday we made pancakes together …' (Martin, 27, student)

Despite the principled support for teachers not hiding their sexual orientation, respondents said that parents might cause problems for such a coming out. In fact, the whole debate on how to situate homosexuality and same-sex-oriented students and teachers in the school environment kept returning, time and again, to the concern that parents might oppose it.

3.3.   Fearing Parents and Looking For Arguments

> I think parents especially need to be told that your child won't turn gay just like that, just by listening about gays and lesbians. That it's not like someone blowing into you, and you're gay. (Martina, 21, student)

In addition to homosexuality usually not being explicitly mentioned in school curricula (see Komidar and Mandeljc 2009), it seems—drawing on the accounts of the students of educational studies—that the second most important obstacle preserving 'silence on the issue' and consequently the hegemony of heterosexism and homophobia, is parents and their role in the school educational process.

Some students of educational studies thought that parents should be the first to be taught about homosexuality and about why a debate on the matter is important. Others thought that it would be better to introduce the topic without parents' previous knowledge of it or to introduce it into class meetings, which do not need to appear in school curricula. Still others thought they could only resist their parents' protests if the question was systemically solved and if the official curriculum actually encouraged a debate on the subject. In addition to parents, respondents also mentioned the head teacher as the person who could block any debate on the subject during classes. At the same time, they expressed a degree of resignation, saying that teachers have their hands tied and are unable to change parents' standpoints, homosexuality simply remaining taboo.

On the basis of the focus groups' responses, we conclude that most of our interviewees give their parents the legitimate right to interfere with the contents of public school curricula and that the existing curricula do not give many opportunities for discussions about homosexuality and homophobia. However, as far as public schools are concerned, this is not true. Not only does the existing primary school curriculum in Slovenia give opportunities for a debate on homosexuality (for example, human rights, diversity of families, tolerance) but, as Kovač Šebart and Kuhar state (2009: 17), the constitution itself and the human rights value framework with its related obligations stipulate that parents' particular values cannot be the reason enabling them to interfere arbitrarily with the school environment and decide which subjects discussed at school are acceptable or unacceptable. In the same way, Fortin (2011) suggests that all awareness-raising projects, including school debates, should be focused on the issue of homophobia, not homosexuality. He states that debates about homophobia often slide towards etiological debates about homosexuality, questioning the various erotic and sexual details of homosexual activities and suchlike. 'These tendencies,' Funke explains, 'are discriminating, for they treat the individuals in discussion as explanatory objects and consider them as variations or even violations of an alleged norm' (Funke 2011: 225). For this reason, universal human rights should be the centre of any debate. Sexual orientation in Western democracies can no longer be a questioned category, claims Fortin; rather, full citizenship should be taken as the starting point, the right of each person to dignity. We need to enter into a dialogue on the possibilities of co-existence (Fortin, 2011: 35–37). In this framework, also set by the Slovenian constitution, homophobia may be viewed as a form of discrimination and violence which precludes full citizenship.

In point of fact, Fortin's view is not unlike the concept of justice formulated by Nancy Fraser (2002) in her discussion of the status model of citizenship. She maintains that justice can only be achieved through recognition: through the recognition of an unrecognised social group (granting it rights), we allow that group full membership in the community by making it possible for them to cooperate with other members on an equal footing. Regardless of an individual's image of a good life, justice is the only value that is superior to any particular images of a good life. Therefore, the advantage of such a position, which may also be assumed in the educational process, is that it avoids moral judgements and remains in the field of ethics—that is, the question of justice (universal human rights) and injustice (homophobia).

4. Combating Homophobia

Research on homophobic violence in Slovenia (Velikonja and Greif 2001; Švab and Kuhar 2005; Kuhar et al 2008; Kuhar and Magić 2008) and the focus groups with lesbians and gays in our research show how homophobia is a constitutive element of the everyday life of lesbians and gays in Slovenia. The conclusion matches the thesis of Judith Butler (1991) who, rejecting a unified lesbian or gay identity, states that the only thing lesbians and gays have in common is the experience of homophobic violence.

What, then, are the strategies of managing homophobia? On the basis of our focus groups' responses, we can identify five strategies that lesbians and gays use in everyday life: self-censorship, sensitisation, resignation, accommodation and compensation. In different life situations the strategies overlap, that is, individuals apply them simultaneously. In most cases, the choice of a strategy is also related to the level of openness about one's homosexuality. That is, homosexuality in contemporary society is still often understood as deviant, and for this reason many lesbians and gays perceive it as a stigma which is, by its very nature, ambiguous and unclear. As Goffman (1963) claims, its greatest paradox is in its consequences, which may be simultaneously dehumanising and/or inspirational for the stigmatised individual or group.

Stigma, writes Goffman, is the situation of the individual who is excluded from total social acceptance. It means that the stigmatised person has a characteristic which seems highly damaging, that is, it is disreputable, and so that person is viewed as inferior, subhuman. The strategies of facing homophobia can therefore be understood as ways of managing a particular stigma.

Goffman mentions four typical responses that stigmatised persons demonstrate regarding their stigma: (1) correction; (2) compensation (indirect correction); (3) break with reality; and (4) isolation. Correction refers to an individual attempt to correct what they sees as the objective basis of their stigma (for example, undergoing plastic surgery to do away with a physical peculiarity). Compensation (or indirect correction) means a form of indirect correction of one's stigma. The persons involved devote extra effort to the mastery of activities they could not ordinarily do because of their stigma (for example, a blind person learns how to ski). A break with reality actually means reinterpreting one's stigma: the individual employs an unconventional interpretation (in opposition to the stigmatising one) which ascribes the reason for the stigma a different value. Isolation as a way of managing stigma means escaping the reality of everyday life, so that the people in question do not need to face their stigma (Goffman 1963).

Although the strategies of managing stigma that we identified on the basis of our focus groups' responses do not closely match the above-described four typical responses of stigmatised persons identified by Goffman, we can say that self-censorship and accommodation belong to Goffman's first category, compensation to the second, sensitisation to the third, and resignation to the fourth.

Self-censorship

In the analytical sense, self-censorship may be divided into *voluntary* and *mandatory* self-censorship. The main difference is in the subject who imposes self-censorship. As for voluntary self-censorship, the initiative comes from same-sex-oriented individuals (who impose self-censorship on themselves), whereas in the case of mandatory self-censorship the initiative comes from another person (self-censorship is imposed). Although the analytical distinction seems sensible, it is important to stress that voluntary self-censorship can always be traced back to mandatory self-censorship; in cases where it appears as if the individuals involved imposed voluntary self-censorship, censorship is nonetheless imposed on them by society, because it is society which defines those who are to be stigmatised, and individuals only internalise the position.

Our respondents typically brought up voluntary self-censorship in relation to the workplace, understood as a heteronormative space with clearly inscribed definitions of desired masculinity and femininity. Respondents thought that transgression of the matrix (that is, coming out as lesbian or gay) might have a negative impact on the working environment as well as their position at work. They see being in the closet—which actually implies a very strenuous process of keeping up heterosexual appearances—to be a way of avoiding discrimination and homophobia.

Furthermore, the respondents also noticed voluntary self-censorship after having come out to their friends. In particular, they emphasised their fear of any touches or words being understood wrongly after disclosing their sexual orientation, although such friendly touches were entirely taken for granted prior to their coming out.

> As soon as I came out to two girl friends I actually withdrew a bit, just so they wouldn't think I wanted something from them. But they still had exactly the same reactions, and it was even better with further coming outs. Now I don't censor myself so much any more, well, perhaps not at all. (Linda, 20, lesbian)

Mandatory self-censorship as a strategy for facing homophobia generally happens after an individual comes out. It denotes a kind of 'consensual silence' on homosexuality. It looks as if in certain contexts an individual's homosexuality, after coming out, becomes a taboo which is neither discussed nor addressed. This kind of self-censorship essentially means going back into the closet again, for which Kuhar (2007, 2011) uses the term 'the transparent closet'. Power relationships play a very important role in such self-censorship. Accordingly, we observe that, in the family environment, talking about homosexuality after an adolescent has come out is often *regulated* by parents. Parents practically force adolescents to keep silent about homosexuality, which becomes a sort of family secret not to be talked about (Švab and Kuhar 2005). In some cases, silence on homosexuality is preserved long after coming out, which our lesbian and gay respondents experience as a kind of violence they have been forced into through self-censorship.

> I find the fact that they know it at home, but we don't talk about it, psychologically stressful. When, for instance, a pride parade is shown on TV, they discreetly change the channel. For me that is even worse than being openly intolerant. Then you at least know where you are and you can break off relationships with them. But this way … it is known, but it's not talked about. (Čimo, 22, gay)

Sensitisation

Our lesbian and gay respondents emphasised sensitisation, that is, informing the public about homosexuality, as the second important strategy in combating homophobia. The majority—just like the students of educational studies—thought that prejudices against same-sex-oriented people originate in a lack of information and knowledge. The lesbians and gay men in the focus groups stressed that coming out to friends, parents and the more general public is in itself an important way of sensitisation, a strategy for increasing visibility. They reported changes in views on homosexuality among their friends and relatives after they had come out to them, mainly on the basis of the information they had given them.

In addition, respondents stressed the need for institutional sensitisation, which should be a major aim of the educational process. That is, they find that there is not enough debate on homosexuality in schools and therefore, as Matija (26, gay) thinks: 'one fairy tale in ten can really feature two princes'.

Resignation

The third form of facing homophobia is resignation, that is, a withdrawal from situations which respondents perceive as homophobic. They frequently mentioned situations related to the Family Code and homophobic debates both in the media and Parliament. A number of participants reported ceasing to follow events concerning the Family Code, in order to avoid being exposed to homophobic discourse.

Resignation as a strategy for managing homophobia does not necessarily denote the absence of proactive behaviour. Withdrawal from a homophobic situation is certainly proactive behaviour in terms of personal protection and it does represent a strategy of actively managing stigma. We labelled this strategy 'resignation' nonetheless, since individuals 'resign themselves to their fate' of not being able to change the existing situation, so they prefer to withdraw from it.

Accommodation

One of the basic strategies of coping with homophobia employed by homosexuals is accommodation. It signifies various ways of managing individuals' sexual orientations in various life situations. Most of the respondents are out in certain environments but closeted in others, a situation which has a strong determining effect on their behaviour in those particular cases. Some of them drew attention to the public space as one requiring a specific form of behaviour, which means that they accommodate their behaviour so as not to be conspicuous in public or in public spaces. They believe this mimicry to be necessary, since any sign of homosexuality in a heteronormative public space would soon be accompanied by a threat of violence. One respondent thus thought that homosexuality in Slovenia is acceptable as far as it remains somewhere between visibility and invisibility. In other words, homosexuality is acceptable if it is moulded to the heteronormative matrix in a way which neither changes nor threatens it.

> Homosexuality in Slovenia is acceptable if you don't flaunt it too much. If you behave according to the heterosexual pattern, in a heteronormative way, then it's quite okay. Then it's no big deal. But as soon as you get too feminised, too explicitly homosexual, then it's very unacceptable. Then at least a word, if not something else, will fly your way. (Rok, 38, gay)

Compensation

The majority of lesbians and gays in the focus groups thought that, due to their sexual orientation, they needed to be much more successful in all aspects of their lives in order to reach the same goals as heterosexuals. Some of them see their homosexuality as a lack (or they internalise the socially enforced perception of homosexuality as being an inferior sexual orientation), and therefore attempt to be as successful as possible in other areas of their lives, which would presumably make them more socially acceptable.

> We really do take on a big responsibility for this attributed difference. We want to be high achievers. Say, in relation to parents ... I don't know, you pass your exams with distinction, so you're at least clever if you can't be ... (laughter). So they can be proud of you at least in some areas if they can't be in all. I find that an interesting mechanism. ... I think we're stricter with ourselves because of that circumstance. (Nadja, 30, lesbian)

These five ideal types of strategies of managing stigma are part of the everyday practices of managing homophobia. They are linked to the individual's level of being out, to the social context in which they function, and to their own interpretations of how the society around them perceives homosexuality. However, the institutional contexts of dealing with homophobia are also important, primarily antidiscrimination legislation. We therefore asked our respondents about their expectations regarding legislation, especially in terms of its potential prevention of homophobia.

For the most part, respondents referred to the proposal of the new Family Code, in which the rights and obligations of same-sex and opposite-sex partnerships are equated. Their expectations in the area of legislation thus mainly relate to the changes the new Family Code brings. At the same time, the discussion reflected the recent/past legislative changes in the area. Currently, the Registration of a Same-Sex Civil Partnership Act, adopted in 2005 and discriminatory in a number of points, is in force. It is seen by many as a form of symbolic violence inflicted by the state on lesbians and gays, since in the Slovenian legal order the term 'registration' is generally employed for the registration of cars, associations, companies, and so on, but not human beings. Although other European countries regularly use the term 'a registered partnership', in the Slovenian language it is reminiscent of the formal registration of objects. In this context, Slovenian uses the verb 'enter into' (for example, enter into a marriage; Slovenian: *skleniti*), but the proposer of the Act (the centre-right coalition) clearly wished to highlight the symbolic difference in relation to heterosexual marriage also on a linguistic level. The Act is also discriminatory, because it 'legalises' second-class citizenship and, except for the right to inheritance, it mostly imposes obligations on same-sex partners (for example, looking after an ill partner), without the related social, economic and other rights based on the status of next-of-kin as this status is not granted to same-sex couples (Mencin Čeplak and Kuhar 2010).

We can state that participants' expectations concerning the legislation are relatively low. The majority believe that legislation itself cannot have a substantial effect on the social climate and the occurrence of homophobia. However, we can basically distinguish between two types of expectations—pragmatic and symbolic.

Pragmatic expectations primarily refer to the regulation of same-sex partnerships and families. Respondents expect that the state will provide a legislative basis for equal treatment of opposite-sex and same-sex partnerships and families.

Symbolic expectations mostly relate to the consequences which the adoption of the Family Code would have in society. It is thought that adopting the Code would bring about greater acceptance of homosexuals. In addition, the state would send a clear message to the public that discrimination on the basis of sexual orientation is unacceptable. Respondents also expressed their expectations and wishes for stricter sanctions and clearer definitions of hate speech in legislation—particularly when it comes from a position of power. They thought that the discourse used by some Members of Parliament during the debates on the Family Code verged on hate speech, through which the MPs were conveying to the public that such discourse on homosexuality is acceptable.

5. Conclusions

The framework of the discussions held in the focus groups was the binary heterosexuality/homosexuality scheme and its associated heteronormativity. In the focus groups with students of educational studies, the framework set the limits within which homosexuality was to be discussed, as well as the manner in which it was to be discussed. In the focus groups with lesbians and gays, the heteronormative framework was a starting point for the problems which respondents have and which they have to face by means of various strategies.

This research, as expected, showed that breaks and gaps no longer appear in the old places, that is, on the unconditional black-and-white rejection of homosexuality with the simultaneous acceptance of heterosexuality; nowadays, cracks are appearing elsewhere. That is, none of the participating students of educational studies considered homosexuality to be an inappropriate or unnecessary topic for discussion in schools. Quite the opposite: none saw homosexuality in the old framework of mental illness, moral perversion and suchlike. Similarly, all participants recognised homophobia as a prejudice which excludes a certain group of people from social life. Yet, as a rule, they did not question their own positions of power when looking for a solution. They saw the solution to the problem in attempts to include homosexuality in the heteronormative matrix (children need to be shown that lesbians and gays are just like us), but inclusion should not be too forceful, that is, it should not disturb the self-evidence of everyday life (they shouldn't be too 'upfront' when talking about their homosexuality) and should be clearly controlled (homosexuality should be discussed with older children or in the context of other differences).

Lesbians and gays adapt to the described breaks with quite a degree of mimicry, which keeps the heteronormativity of everyday life intact. Individuals can immerse themselves into it only through normalisation, which is nothing but a flexible technique which uses various strategies for managing homophobia. Although it may seem a little trite to emphasise the importance of including the topic of homosexuality in education, our research yet again shows that it is very necessary. And more: mere inclusion does not suffice; it is the way in which the topic is handled that is crucial. Events such as school workshops once a year, or even once every four years, may at first seem as if they were helping to combat discrimination, prejudice and stereotypes, but the effect may be just the opposite. That is, such 'one-offs' of situating the topic in the educational process legitimise its marginality and indirectly reinforce the 'us–them' dichotomy. This was revealed by the answers given by students in the focus groups who advocated 'normalisation' of homosexuality though 'empirical evidence', which would supposedly show that homosexuals are 'so cool', 'okay', 'amusing' and not 'different'—that is, 'normal'. But it is this very 'humanistic position' which is particularly dangerous, as it legitimises difference (or diversity) as something bad and inferior. If schools organise workshops in which children get to know black people, the Chinese, Japanese, the Roma, migrants, disabled people, and so on, they agree to the norm of the normal, embodied by a white, middle-class, heterosexual, physically fit person, and retain its tolerating power relationship with all others. Until, of course, *he* changes *his* mind.

5

Don't Ask, Don't Tell, Don't Bother: Homophobia and the Heteronorm in Hungary

JUDIT TAKÁCS, TAMÁS DOMBOS, GYÖRGY MÉSZÁROS AND
TAMÁS P TÓTH

1. Introduction

'Homophobia is a characteristic feature of the majority identity'—stated a gay interviewee in the early 2000s, when describing reasons why it was not good to be gay in Hungary (Takács 2007). Keeping this in mind, we will use the term homophobia in an interpretational framework, which is more intimately connected to heteronormativity, constituting a major part of a fictional 'truly Hungarian' majority identity, rather than to the concept of homosexuality carrying several denotations and connotations of behaviour, identity, performance and history. In the context of the present study, examining the social functioning of homophobia is interpreted as an awareness-raising tool about heterosexist, heteronormative oppression operating in Hungary and elsewhere— rather than focusing on one's irrational fear of homosexuals, seen as a specific, individual level feature, being largely disconnected from its specific socio-cultural surroundings.

Heteronormative oppression implies that lesbians and gays suffer disadvantage and injustice because of everyday practices resulting from unquestioned norms and assumptions underlying institutional rules (Young 1990). The *heteronorm,* a cultural ideology perpetuating sexual stigma (Plummer 1975; Herek 2004; 2011), can be expressed in systemic violence directed against lesbians and gays, such as the violent attacks in many Eastern European cities witnessed during recent Gay Pride events. The occurrence of these violent attacks can be explained by the fact that in many Eastern European societies, including Hungary, institutionalised social practices encourage, tolerate, and enable the perpetration of violence against lesbian and gay citizens.

Several studies conducted with lesbian, gay, bisexual and transgender (LGBT) respondents point to the problems deriving from their social invisibility: if disadvantages are not made socially recognisable, it is very hard to articulate interests and defend rights. However, as has been emphasised by previous studies (Rivers and Carragher 2003; Švab and Kuhar 2005; Takács 2006), discrimination against LGBT people can remain hidden in a lot of instances because coming out of invisibility is a very critical process for most LGBT people, involving the risk of being ostracised in a heteronormative social environment. Thus when we encounter figures referring to half of Hungarian LGBT respondents experiencing discrimination and prejudice in secondary school, and one third of them suffering disadvantages at their workplace (Takács, Mocsonaki and P Tóth 2008), it must be remembered that most people are afraid to come out as LGBT at school or at work, and that equal treatment practices, recognising sexual and gender diversity among other forms of diversity as enriching features that can positively affect the school environment or the productivity level of work, are still very rare in Hungary.

Although same-sex sexual activity between consenting adults was decriminalised in Hungary in 1961, there have been several manifestations of institutionalised discrimination and 'structural stigma' (Herek 2011) against lesbian and gay citizens, including the different age of consent for same-sex and different-sex partners before 2002, and the present absence of legal institutions such as same-sex marriage or joint adoption by same-sex couples. After the change in the political system of 1989–90 that ended state socialism, social attitudes towards homosexuality became slightly more permissive (Takács 2007). However, in the present European context, Hungary still belongs to those homophobic societies where the acceptance of the freedom of lesbian and gay lifestyles is not at all well developed, an aspect which plays an important role in the functioning of social exclusion mechanisms affecting lesbians and gays. Findings of a recent study (Takács and Szalma 2011), based on large scale European Social Survey data, indicates that among 26 European societies, the greatest level of social acceptance of lesbians and gays was found in Denmark, the Netherlands, France, Sweden and Belgium, while the lowest level of acceptance was found in the Ukraine, Russia, Romania, Croatia, Latvia, Estonia, Slovakia and Hungary. This study also provided empirical evidence that levels of homophobia do not depend only on characteristics of individuals, such as age, gender, education, religion and so on. Certain country level predictors can also be identified: satisfaction with democracy, the introduction of same-sex partnership legislation and the weakening of traditional gender beliefs were shown to have a positive correlation with social acceptance of lesbians and gays in Europe.

According to LGBT respondents, prejudice and discrimination are rooted in ignorance and reinforced by distorted stereotypical representations of what it means to live as an LGBT person (Takács 2006; Takács, Mocsonaki and P Tóth 2008). Consequently, meanings attached to homosexuality can vary to a large extent as has been shown by a recent survey, commissioned by the Hungarian

Equal Treatment Authority, which highlighted major differences between a representative population sample (N=1,000) and an LGBT community sample (N=200) concerning the social categorisation of homosexuality.[1] In the representative sample the highest level of agreement was found with the view that homosexuality is a 'private matter', closely followed by the definition of homosexuality as a 'form of behaviour deviating from social norms and rules'. Defining homosexuality as a 'form of sickness' and the view that 'having a same-sex partner is a basic human right' reflected the same, moderately high, level of agreement, while the definition of homosexuality being a 'sin' had the lowest level of agreement. On the other hand, LGBT respondents expressed the highest level of agreement with the statement that 'having a same-sex partner is a basic human right', followed by a similarly high level of agreement in defining homosexuality as a 'private matter'. Defining homosexuality as a 'form of behaviour deviating from social norms and rules' was received with a medium level of agreement, while definitions of homosexuality as a form of 'sickness' or 'sin' received widespread rejection. The differing categorisation preferences among the LGBT and the representative samples reflect different sets of interpretational frameworks related to homosexuality: while the human rights based approach becomes a very relevant one in the LGBT responses; among non-LGBT respondents the medicalisation approach remains influential, despite the decades old arguments of the World Health Organization and other professional bodies, emphasising that homosexuality is not an illness.

This survey also indicated that about half of the LGBT sample (49%) experienced discrimination—mainly on the ground of sexual orientation (72%), 25% mentioned 'other grounds', 24% referred to their gender, while 17% mentioned their age being the potential cause of discrimination.[2] The most often mentioned forms of discrimination included verbal harassment (63%), followed by humiliation (49%), threats of violence (28%) and public humiliation (24%). Reports of being threatened by violence, harassed by offensive graffiti, being pelted, assaulted and raped were significantly more widespread among LGBT respondents than in the representative sample.

According to Tamás Dombos, who made an overview of over 60 survey-based quantitative studies on homophobia that were conducted in Hungary in the 30 years between 1982 and 2010,[3] homophobia can be interpreted broadly as a phenomenon that includes prejudice, discrimination, violence and other forms

---

[1] See Equal Treatment Authority (2011) *Az egyenlő bánásmóddal kapcsolatos jogtudatosság növekedésének mértéke—fókuszban a nök, a romák, a fogyatékos és az LMBT emberek. Kutatási zárójelentés* (Research report available at www.egyenlobanasmod.hu/tamop/data/MTA_1hullam.pdf).

[2] Respondents could choose more than one option when answering this question.

[3] Homofób társadalom? (Homophobic society?), presentation given at the 'A homofóbia és a transzfóbia elleni küzdelem lehetőségei a mai Magyarországon' (Struggling against homophobia and transphobia in Hungary), 'Citizens in Diversity' dissemination conference organised by IS-HAS, 17 May 2011, Budapest.

of hostile behaviour towards LGBT people, as well as the general notion that homosexuality and bisexuality are inferior to heterosexuality and that gender identities differing from those given at birth are problematic. Homophobia was thus understood not only at the individual, interpersonal level; but is also discussed on the level of deeply held cultural views and institutional norms and practices. Social attitudes towards homosexuality, reflected in the examined surveys, can be categorised into five main models or frames, entailing both the basic understanding of what homosexuality is, and how individuals and social institutions should relate to homosexual and bisexual people. Even though the five frames are representative of certain historic periods, these basic attitudes are also observable at any given time in a cross-section of the population.

The *morality frame* considers homosexuality as an individual choice that can be evaluated in moral terms. According to this frame homosexuality is a sin, because it violates the religious or social laws of a society. Since homosexuality is a sin, it should be punished or at least condemned. The *sickness frame* considers homosexuality as a medical condition usually resulting from a childhood trauma or bad socialisation, something that is beyond the control of the individual. Since the individual does not decide to become homosexual, s/he should not be punished or condemned, but rather helped and cured; people should treat homosexuals with sympathy and pity. The *deviance frame* considers homosexuality as a form of behaviour divergent from widely accepted social norm and rules, which usually implies choice on behalf of the individual, although it does not necessarily imply moral condemnation: it might consist of a value-free, 'cold and factual' attitude towards homosexuality. The *privacy frame* brackets the question of what causes homosexuality and focuses on the fact that the state and society should not intervene in activities that do not cause harm to others, thus homosexuals should do freely whatever they want, as long as it is in private. The public affirmation of homosexuality, however, is problematic as it widens the circle of people affected by it and might cause harm to others, such as impressionable minors. The *human rights frame* starts from the claim that sexual orientation is an integral aspect of personality, usually seen to be the result of a genetic, or other non-alterable biological, non-pathological predisposition (a 'variant of human sexuality'). Since, as with other integral aspects of personality, such as gender, ethnicity, religion and so on homosexuality is also morally arbitrary, the state should protect homosexuals from discrimination and promote their equality.

Between 1996 and 2007 the data shows the slightly growing prominence of the privacy frame and a slight decline in support for the human rights frame. One of the problems with the polling question is the uncertain interpretation of the privacy frame: while it can imply a liberal attitude (this is none of my business, people are free to do whatever they want), it can also imply a refusal to engage with the issue, a support for keeping homosexuality in the closet (they can do whatever they want, as long as I don't have to see them). The options in both types of studies can be further regrouped to two categories: those frames that see homosexuality as some kind of a problem (sin, sickness, deviance) or those that do not (private matter, human right). This regrouping is confirmed by analysing data from a 2010 study of the Hungarian Equal Treatment Authority, in which rather than being given options from which one can be chosen, approval rate of individual items were polled: the factor analysis showed that 67% of variance was explained by these two components.[4]

When focusing on the social embeddedness of homophobia, a functional theory of attitudes can be applied (Herek 1984), identifying three major needs that appear to be met by attitudes towards lesbians and gays. *Experience-based* attitudes derive from past interactions with lesbians and gays, and can be generalised to all lesbians and gays; *defensive* attitudes can help to cope with one's anxieties, especially in the form of externalising inner conflicts; while *symbolic* attitudes, closely related to socialisation experiences, express important values in the process of (publicly) identifying with important reference groups. In this context one can easily see a paradox: on the one hand, because of the perceived hostility of the social environment, lesbians and gays won't come out, while on the other hand, these camouflage-strategies will keep them locked into distant 'mysterious others' categories, and will not provide opportunities for direct everyday interaction between heterosexuals and lesbians and gays. Thus it can be assumed that in present day Hungarian society homophobic attitudes are more likely to have symbolic and defensive functions than be based on actual experiences of interacting with lesbians and gays in everyday life.

This assumption can also be tested in the qualitative empirical findings, gained within the international research project 'Citizens in Diversity: A Four-Nation Study on Homophobia and Fundamental Rights', to be presented in this chapter. The empirical base of the Hungarian part of this research includes 11 focus group interviews which were collected in Budapest, the capital city of Hungary during 2010. Focus group methodology was applied for several reasons, including its focus on socially produced knowledge and performative group dynamics, as well as the opportunity to study sexuality and gender-related issues on the basis of a more egalitarian relationship between researchers and those being researched:

> In a group, if even one person expresses an idea it can prompt a response from the others, and the information that is produced is more likely to be framed by the categories and understandings of the interviewees rather than those of the interviewer. Participants can help each other figure out what the questions mean to them, and the researcher can examine how different participants hear possibly vague or ambiguous questions. This is important in studying sex and gender because these issues are

---

[4] See Equal Treatment Authority (2011) Az egyenlö bánásmóddal kapcsolatos jogtudatosság növekedésének mértéke—fókuszban a nök, a romák, a fogyatékos és az LMBT emberek. Kutatási zárójelentés (Report available at www.egyenlobanasmod.hu/tamop/data/MTA_1hullam.pdf).

'naturalised' to such an extent that it is very difficult to recognise one's own precon-ceived notions, much less challenge others' taken-for-granted assumptions. (Montell 1999:49)

There were four focus group sessions conducted with self-identified heterosexual trainee teachers and students of education (N=20), comprising 16 women and four men. Within these four focus groups there were two sessions, which included only female participants, while the other two sessions also included male participants. The age range of the heterosexual respondents was 20 to 29, and their average age was 23.5. All of them studied in Budapest, but about half of them grew up in a city or a town outside Budapest. Seven focus group interviews were conducted with self-identified non-activist LGBT people (N=33), including eight lesbians, 19 gays and six transsexuals.

Within the LGBT sample no-one identified exclusively as bisexual, which might also imply the rejection of bisexuality as an identity category (as opposed to the understanding of bisexuality as a specific form of behaviour). However, some participants reported on bisexual episodes from their past and present, so we decided to keep the 'B' in the name of the LGBT sample. The LGBT focus group interviews were conducted in specialised sessions: two sessions with only lesbian participants (average age: 32), two sessions with only religious gay men (average age: 28), one session with gay teachers (average age: 36), one session with gay men (average age: 35) and one session with only transsexuals (average age: 40).[5] The age range of the LGBT participants was 19 to 83, all of them living in Budapest. Most of the LGBT participants had completed higher education; five of them had only secondary education.

Heterosexual participants were recruited through the education departments of Hungarian universities, while LGBT participants were recruited through LGBT internet portals and with the help of LGBT NGOs. There were a few participants recruited by a snowball method with the help of those who had already participated in a previous focus group session. The focus group interviews were 1.5 to 2.5 hours long. Following the focus group interviewing procedures, a standard topic guide was applied with open-ended questions around the main themes including the definitions and manifestations of homophobia; inclusion of topics related to homosexuality and homophobia in school activities; fighting homophobia in schools; and resisting homophobia in everyday life. All would-be respondents were provided with an explanation of the study, and willing partici-pants provided written informed consent. All focus group interviews were conducted by two experienced interviewers: one leading the interview, the other observing and providing assistance when necessary. Each respondent chose an assumed name, which was used for their identification in the course of the focus group sessions. The interviews were tape-recorded with the agreement that all

---

[5] The average age would have been only 31 in the trans group without the oldest (83 years old) participant.

audio-material would be destroyed after transcribing. The recorded material was first transcribed verbatim. Transcripts were transformed into a Hungarian code book. The present study is produced by the qualitative analysis of this code book's contents.

2. Contextualising Homophobia as an LGBT Issue

Gay movements have been criticised, especially in North America, for claiming equal rights on the basis of a normalising politics presenting non-heterosexuals as normal, gender conventional, good citizens (Seidman 2002), while, at least since the 1990s, queer activists keep wondering what is happening to the right to be different. A similar argument is presented by Wilchins, when referring to a kind of 'new gay' deal, characterised by 'internalised genderphobia', that is strategic avoidance of non-normative gender issues and norms:

> Gay rights activists have responded to conservatives' attacks by stressing the normality of homosexuals. *We are just like straight people, we just sleep with the same sex.* This strategy has been enormously successful. (Wilchins 2004:17)

Since the extensive overlaps and interrelations between homophobia, transphobia, and genderphobia are hard to deny, homophobia will be contextualised here not as a 'homosexual only' but as a broader issue, which can affect lesbian, gay, bisexual, transgender, queer and (even) straight people.

At the beginning of each focus group session we asked our respondents to tell us who LGBT people are and in which context they encountered this term.[6] This seemed to be an easy exercise for most of them, at least until they tried to decipher the meaning of the 'T'. 'T as in transvestite? Men who dress as women?' asked, for example, Dávid (28 years old), one gay participant. Another gay man thought that transsexuality is a synonym of intersexuality. A female student[7] used a distancing style when referring to LGBT as 'those people' and then added: 'people with ambiguous gender' (Réka, 24 years old). Janka, a 24-year-old female student brought to life a nineteenth-century notion when saying that:

> Homosexuals or lesbians are people who feel different, that is they are men who feel like women or women who feel like men but it's kept deep inside, while transsexuals, I think, will change the outside too.

Apart from the group of transsexuals, there were uncertainties concerning the different meanings of transsexual and transgender, while the trans participants agreed that they would refer to people who wish(ed) to change their official

---

[6] The question was about the meaning of the LGBT acronym.

[7] Student refers to a heterosexual participant, being either a trainee teacher or a student of education.

gender assignment as transsexuals, and those who do not have this wish but do not (want to) fit into the dualistic gender order would be referred to as transgender people.

The lack of clarity around the 'T' in LGBT points to the fact that trans issues are the least socially visible among the socially less visible LGBT issues in Hungary, and thus are often seen as irrelevant as 'there are so few of them'. The ambiguity of trans issues can be rooted in a perception, according to which trans people are some kind of in-betweeners characterised by different degrees of gender transitionality, being an incomprehensible or at least unsettling concept for both the heterosexual and the LGBT respondents. According to the view of Lilla, a 24-years-old female student:

> It's easier for people to accept a person who's attracted to a same-sex partner than a transsexual, well, at least, it's easier for me.

Another female student (Petra, 24 years old) mentioned that even lesbians, at least those she knew, do not want to have anything to do with trans women, who are not 'real women'.[8]

Bisexuality seemed to be a much better-known concept, but the situation of bisexual people was not discussed at all in any of the focus groups, as if they did not exist. In the LGBT groups there was a gay man who admitted that at the age of 18 he was not even aware of the meaning of bisexuality. In the heterosexual groups one participant described bisexuals as 'being excluded by both sides' (Kyra, 24 years old), while others disagreed with her by saying that 'society has the least problem with bisexuals [among LGBT]' (Alma, 20 years old). Previous Hungarian research showed that among gays the definition of bisexuality includes that it is a 'manageable problem' or a 'form of self-deception', a fictional identity strategy 'applied by those who do not dare to come out as gay' (Takács 2004). The silence around bisexuality in our focus groups can also indicate that bisexuality is seen as a 'manageable problem' with not too much social importance, but it can also be interpreted as a sign of rejection of an ambiguous situation.

Heterosexual respondents encountered LGBT topics mainly in the media, especially the tabloid media, but also through friends and family. They also mentioned a few university courses, where they could learn or at least hear about lesbians and gays. LGBT issues were therefore not perceived as being taboo, as one female student pointed out:

> Nowadays you can hear about them ... quite a lot. They're on the news programmes, especially when the Gay Pride march is on, so I think there are no people in Hungary who haven't encountered these people either in person or in a news item. (Janka, 24 years old)

---

[8] Similar arguments were presented, about trans women not being real women, by Janice Raymond in *The Transsexual Empire*, published originally in 1979 (Raymond 2006).

However, this perception might also reflect a somewhat naive projection of personal openness regarding LGBT people to society at large. For example, heterosexual respondents were probably unaware of the very low average number of homosexual friends or acquaintances reported in Hungary.[9]

Besides references to the potentially positive, social visibility-increasing, effect of the media, another female student emphasised the dangers associated with distorted media representations, which can:

> Play a great part in the negative perception of LGBT people. If you watch the Gay Pride on TV, surely they won't be shown in the normal way, even though it would be the goal of the march ... but they will show ... I don't know ... the much more extreme side. (Anna, 25 years old)

However, making a distinction between the favourable 'normal way' and 'the extreme side' of things implies that the rules of norm setting remain the privilege of the speaker-outsider. While the speaker's intention is to point out the distorting effects of the media, the measurement of distortion is a presumably universal code of appropriate behaviour.

Similar distinctions were made by LGBT respondents between normal and extreme behaviour, when the need for Pride marches was contested especially within the group of gay teachers and transsexuals: for some the presence of openly lesbian and gay people on the streets, seen as an act of invading public space with the most public form of coming out, constituted unnecessary extremeness or even provocation, reinforcing the view that homosexuality is a private matter and should be kept that way. In this context, normal behaviour was equated with keeping the expression of sexual preferences mostly hidden, creating a new division between 'extreme activists' and ordinary people, replacing the conventional heterosexual–homosexual divide. This view was reflected in a female student's somewhat paternalistic warning:

> The most useful strategy is to come out in your own little local circles ... and not the militant activist thing ... that can only arouse revulsion. (Nyolc, 23 years old)

Individualised notions of homosexuality, focusing on specific features of individuals to be kept private, which dominated all focus group sessions, seemed to foster the notion that social acceptance of LGBT people is in inverse proportion to their social visibility. In this context social acceptance was interpreted as being tolerated, and equal rights claims were often overshadowed by the convenient application of a 'don't ask, don't tell, don't bother' strategy. These could be seen as rather disappointing results, in view of the fact that most heterosexual participants were young intellectuals with a higher than average level of openness towards LGBT issues, which made them willing to participate in our research—

[9] According to 2009 Eurobarometer data, only 11% of Hungarian respondents reported having homosexual friends or acquaintances, while the EU27 average was 38%; see ec.europa.eu/public_opinion/archives/ebs/ebs_317_en.pdf.

not to mention the LGBT participants, most of whom revealed a certain degree of *externalised heteronormativity* at this point.

However, when respondents were asked whether LGBT people might be at a disadvantage in comparison to others, they presented more nuanced explanations. A female student, for example, explained that:

> Lesbians, gays or transgender people aren't at a disadvantage by definition. They can become disadvantaged, if they suffer discrimination, when society doesn't accept them. (Sári, 23 years old)

Rejecting the essentialising definition of disadvantage implies that the situation of LGBT people should be approached in context-specific ways, by mapping their socio-cultural relations. Students were more likely to think of disadvantage in general terms, manifested, for example, in personal discomfort caused by the conservative, religious mentality of one's family or close community, while at least some LGBT respondents, especially lesbians, interpreted disadvantage in more practical terms, manifested, for example, in the lack of joint adoption rights.

Nevertheless the recognition of disadvantage as being socially constructed was widespread in all focus group sessions: participants listed several elements, potentially contributing to the development of underprivileged situations, which can be different in large cities and in the countryside, among young people and older ones, or in Hungary and outside Hungary. Additionally, the gendered nature of disadvantage was emphasised mainly by the lesbian participants, especially in the case of lesbian women who might easily suffer multiple forms of discrimination in a patriarchal society. At the same time, lesbians were seen as being, at least ostensibly, more easily tolerated, because of the commodification of their bodies.[10] A male student described the power of the heterosexual male gaze:

> A whole industry is built on it … it's perfectly normal if two women are together so you can see this formation more often … and obviously if one woman is beautiful, two women must be even more beautiful. (Cheega, 29 years old)

2.1. Meanings of Homophobia

Several layers and different understandings of homophobia, highlighted by previous research (Roffman 2000; Herek 2004), were also reflected in our findings to be presented here. Homophobia was a familiar concept in the focus groups: all LGBT participants knew the term, and there were only two heterosexual students who had never heard the word. In accordance with criticism about homophobia being a misnomer, which focuses mainly on individual traits,

---

[10] However, according to Tamás Dombos, Hungarian survey findings do not support this view (see Homofób társadalom? above n 3).

and neglecting socio-cultural contexts where hostility towards homosexuality can be deeply embedded (Plummer 1975; 1981; Kitzinger 1987), there was a general agreement that the term can indeed be somewhat misleading, emphasising a specific kind of phobia, the irrational fear of homosexuals, while its central component is not necessarily just fear as it also conveys hostility, rejection, prejudice and readiness to discriminate. A heterosexual female student reported on these interpretational difficulties in the following way:

> In my view, those contra-demonstrators [against the Gay Pride] aren't homophobic. They can't be called homophobic because homophobes would try to avoid homosexuals. They're simply ... well, racist ... perhaps it's not the right word ... but I don't know. So I've some conceptual problems here. Because phobic implies that one is afraid of something. That they try to avoid something as you would avoid plague ... It shouldn't be this! And this is more like aggression. (Piroska, 22 years old)

Respondents registered the difference between homophobic views and discrimination, though it was difficult to define exactly where discrimination starts. For example, according to one gay man:

> Everyone's free to hate certain things, and it's not a problem until this hate is expressed in a formal and public way. (Hajtipajti, 29 years old)

Another gay respondent added:

> It's your right not to like gays or others, but you can't conclude from this that their reason for existence should be questioned. (Gyuri, 32 years old)

The deeply rooted social and cultural embeddedness of homophobia in Hungarian society was illustrated by the anti-faggot jokes and swear words, which were seen as ordinary socialisation experiences from an early age:

> Homophobia is so much culturally embedded in society that even elementary school kids make jokes about it ... they don't know what it's all about exactly ... but through traditional education they can already decode as much that there's a group that's repugnant, obnoxious and repulsive. (Benő, 32 years old)

Anti-gay jokes as elements of a generally homophobic socio-cultural discourse can contribute to the development of 'properly gendered behaviour' prescribed by heteronormative socialisation, not only during childhood but also later at school or in the workplace. These jokes can play an important role in maintaining the illusory assumptions of the heterosexual matrix (Butler 1990), and especially in reinforcing heterosexual masculinity: by pointing to the female-like inferiority of the norm-breaking gay males. Thus some LGBT participants suggested that jokes that make fun of, for example, gays, can be tolerated only if these are told by gays to gays.

In one of the lesbian focus group sessions participants discussed the possible reasons for there not being very many anti-lesbian jokes in the context of patriarchal society:

Alice (33 years old): This is also a sign that lesbians aren't taken seriously in society even at this level, because oh, it [being lesbian] is only a whim, which will pass.

Ivett (29): For men lesbianism is totally unintelligible, I think … it's such an insult for them that they can't [make sense of it].

Conny (24): And here comes into the picture the only so-called joke about lesbians that 'She needs a good screw to stop her being a lesbian', well, how wrong they can be …

Participants vacillated between two main understandings of phobia: expressing fear, which can lead to avoidance as in the case of claustrophobia; or expressing hatred, which can lead to aggression as in the case of xenophobia. Most participants saw homophobia reflecting an intention to intervene in another person's life, mostly on the basis of moral and especially religious arguments, when 'religion can be used as a weapon' (Zoli, 29 years old). On the other hand, silence and reticence were also seen as a means of expressing homophobic rejection. LGBT respondents mentioned that homophobia is value judgmental and closely connected to pathologising views of homosexuality, which define same-sex attraction as sickness, sin or a sign of (moral) inferiority. Heterosexual participants argued that 'what you don't know can become frightful' and referred to ignorance and lack of information as the main causes of homophobia.

Hungary was seen as a generally homophobic country, characterised by different levels of rejection in different socio-economic strata of society. It was also emphasised that similarly to anti-Roma and xenophobic feelings, homophobia can appear in more hidden and coded forms in some segments of the population than in others: among more educated people living in more urbanised environments it is trendier to be tolerant at least at the level of rhetoric. These seem to be realistic perceptions supported by empirical findings (Enyedi, Fábián and Sik 2004; Takács and Szalma 2011).[11] However, since an extreme right-wing party came into the Hungarian Parliament in 2010, directly racist and homophobic forms of public communication started to increase. This was seen, especially by LGBT respondents, as a dangerous tendency:

Alice (33 years old): [The political] system keeps radicalising. It's increasingly tough … I feel increasingly threatened.

Ivett (29): The present mix of right wing politics plus Christianity is the worst possible combination for me, being an atheist lesbian. The change of government swept away women rights and gay rights from the table; this is totally catastrophic, and frightening. The abortion plans [to stiffen abortion regulations] are also frightening … What will happen here? It's really frightening. I started to think about leaving the country.

Respondents also referred to the different degrees of acceptance and rejection of LGBT people by society. According to both LGBT and heterosexual participants,

---

[11] See also Tausz, K (2011) 'Kitöl tartunk jobban: a romáktól vagy az adóhatóságtól? Az ELTE Társadalomtudományi Karának közleménye' Report of the Faculty of Social Sciences of ELTE University, available at www.tatk.elte.hu.

individual lesbians or gay men are easier to accept than a same-sex couple or a larger number of representatives of a social group, for example, at the Pride marches. The functioning of selective acceptance was reported by a gay man in the following way:

> There are these stages: for example, there are those who just don't want to know about it, they say that everyone can do whatever they like but please, I don't want to see any of it. Or they say that you can do it but only at home, others say that they don't mind but they very much hope not to have any gays in their family. These are in fact all homophobic views, representing different degrees of homophobia ... I know certain homophobes who can accept me as a homosexual individual without any problem, but they can't accept that there are more others. (Cassus, 23 years old)

Selective acceptance processes can also reflect gender normalising tendencies inside and outside the LGBT group(s): gender-conventional lesbians and gays seemed to cause less trouble and be easier to integrate not only into society at large but also into a Gay Pride march. For example, a trans man referred to the constant debate as to whether transvestites should be encouraged or allowed to take part in the march in Budapest, especially given the violent attacks against the marchers since 2007. Here the historical role played by transvestites in gay social resistance is countered by their intentionally provoking gender non-conformity:

> Well, a transvestite is a transvestite if he goes out on to the streets as a man dressed like a woman. And yes, it's provoking, and some people think that it's tasteless. But how can one imagine banning transvestites from a Gay Pride March, when they played such a [historical role]? (Beni, 26 years old)

Lesbian participants reported on difficulties butch dykes sometimes have to face because they are seen as 'too masculine', while gay men referred to the masculinity cults generated and maintained in certain gay scenes or subcultures. One gay man brought up the example of gay online dating sites:

> There are these profiles ... really full of passive aggression; you can often read about how disgusting or sickening feminine faggots are, and that they're interested only in straight acting guys. (Benö, 32 years old)

Problematisation of (perceived) gender non-conformity provided a linkage between homophobia and transphobia, though transphobia seemed to be a much less known concept among our heterosexual as well as non-heterosexual respondents than homophobia. To the question of whether or not Hungarian society is transphobic, a lesbian woman replied that 'surely it would be if only they knew what it was'. Participants of the trans focus group manifested the highest level of awareness concerning the functioning of transphobia in Hungary:

> Well, we're bracketed together with gays, anyway ... The majority of society isn't transphobic, but most of them can't really follow what it's exactly. There are some who say that it's just delusion, and the only goal is to make sex between men more acceptable ... they think it's only an alibi for indecent behaviour. (Gyöngyi, 83 years old)

91

They're not afraid of us … it's our existence in society what's frightening … the fact that we exist. (Beni, 26 years old)

Every society of the world is transphobic to a certain extent—but not equally … [what happens at the] Gay Prides can be the measure of its extent. (Barbie, 19 years old)

However, perhaps surprisingly for some, trans participants stated that in their view, in certain respects it is more difficult to live as a lesbian or as a gay than as a transsexual person because lesbians and gays by definition are victims of institutional discrimination as they are denied the right of marriage and joint adoption. In the case of transsexual people institutional discrimination practices are perhaps less salient, legal aspects of gender transition being officially unregulated but following a more or less established legal practice. Still there are two main problem areas where transsexual people might encounter legally prescribed discrimination in Hungary: on the one hand when their rights as patients and their access to state health care might be denied; and on the other, when their rights as married partners and parents may not be respected (Solymár and Takács 2007).

Legal manifestations of homophobia were much more clearly seen by LGBT participants, and especially by lesbians, than by the heterosexual students. A lesbian participant voiced the opinion shared by others:

The present day legal background doesn't provide us with any support if we want to have children. We could have a child [officially] only if we lied through the whole system. (Alice, 33 years old)

Gay participants seemed to be less interested in society at large and the legal norms, which were pictured as distant frameworks, not being relevant (yet or any more) in their everyday life activities. They were more concerned with what they referred to as ordinary manifestations of homophobia, including incidents of verbal and physical aggression, and strategies to avoid these. In fact, one of the most widely used coping strategies seemed to be, especially in the gay teachers' group, not attributing too much importance to the 'problematic situations' they have encountered. One gay teacher explained:

These are mainly just tiny annoying things but I don't think that they would cause big problems in everyday life. If you want to be open [about your gayness] at the workplace … in theory you can't encounter any disadvantage. In practice, on the other hand, things are different. But it doesn't bother me personally, there are certain techniques developed for this and by the time you become middle aged you are well-trained … so if you speak with someone you can size up the situation whether you can speak with that person openly or not … (Ödön, 58 years old)

Gay participants agreed that it is easy to avoid discrimination if one's sexual orientation and related issues are kept secret. However, it was also recognised by them that this self-constrained silencing itself constitutes discriminating disadvantage. Some participants reported on experiences of LGBT people internalising the majority's (hetero)normative perspectives, including ideas that 'perhaps it is better not to come out at all', 'well, other minority groups are also socially excluded', and 'look at other countries where lesbians and gays are in an even worse situation'. These views were accentuated in the religious gay groups, where participants reported on various forms of discrimination they experienced within their religious community, including hostility or even being ostracised, homophobic messages of certain religious doctrines, and prayers said for their cure (that is curing their homosexuality).

Heterosexual students had a more narrow understanding of the legal aspects of homophobia. Most of them concentrated on individuals' rights not to be discriminated against, and did not necessarily equate the lack of legislation concerning same-sex marriage and child-rearing with homophobia. In fact, same-sex family issues seemed to constitute the borderline of the 'normal functioning of society', which should be protected:

Janka (24 years old): This [same-sex marriage] isn't the most important question.

Hold (25): I don't think that this is what needed … and I surely wouldn't advocate childbearing either. Marriage, perhaps … but rather not.

It also turned out that for most of our heterosexual respondents the understanding of having children was limited to adoption related issues, and the possibility that LGBT people can have their own children was missing from their mental map. Thus they haven't considered other options including second parent adoption, having children from previous heterosexual relationships, or artificial insemination either.

3. Building Citizenship through Education

Previous European research findings indicated that young LGBT people face several challenges related to the lack of recognition and full participation opportunities in schools, where heteronormativity seemed to be a precondition for acceptance and appreciation (Takács 2006; 2009). Heteronormative school practices can have serious disempowering effects on young LGBT people: the general practice of silencing LGBT experiences and lifestyles increases their feelings of isolation and invisibility, while potentially contributing to the decrease of their physical and emotional well-being (Quinlivan and Town 1999).

According to a recent survey, half of Hungarian LGBT respondents (N=1,122) suffered from discrimination and prejudice in school: more than 90% of these cases involved bullying by fellow students (94% in elementary and secondary schools and 89% in higher educational settings), while around half of the cases involved mistreatment by teachers (48% in elementary schools, 50% in secondary schools and 57% in higher education), and one-third of respondents reported distorted or totally missing representation of LGBT issues in the school curriculum (Takács, Mocsonaki and P Tóth 2008). Results of a survey carried out by the

Hungarian Equal Treatment Authority, revealed that lesbians and gays in the sample (N=200) tended to be increasingly open about their sexual orientation from elementary school to higher education: the proportion of respondents who did not want or dare to come out among fellow students in elementary school was 39%, it was 32% in secondary school, and 21% at university.[12] At the same time 39% of respondents kept their sexual orientation concealed from their teachers, and 68% reported that discrimination of LGBT people (often or sometimes) happens at school.

It was the general experience of our respondents that while homosexuality and homophobia-related topics are not part of the school curricula, pupils and students frequently discuss these topics at school. Young people were provided with scattered and sometimes distorted information about lesbians, gays or trans people by the media, mainly through television programmes and the internet— but these pieces of information could have been reviewed and structured at school with the help of teachers, some participants thought. The silencing of LGBT issues at school was seen by the LGBT participants as a serious disadvantage, which could threaten one's developing identity and self-esteem. As a gay man explained:

> There was total silence ... in my case it wasn't a real problem ... in fact my life was made quite easy because I heard about gays quite a lot at home, but if that hadn't been the case then I would have felt in school that I got there from God knows where, that there were no gays here before me, and that there are no gays around me, so there must be something very wrong with me. (Gáspár, 43 years old)

Contents of school books were seen as reflecting a white men-centred heteronormative world, for example, they did not include representations of Gypsies or single-parent families, not to mention non-heterosexuals. The only exceptions were certain university classes, where they could encounter LGBT issues, including courses on cultural diversity, social problems (among topics related to deviant youth and drug users), literary theory or American studies.

3.1. When and How to Talk about Homosexuality and Homophobia?

There was a general agreement among our participants that homosexuality and homophobia-related issues should be discussed in schools as these topics are already there—if not officially in the classrooms then informally in the corridors. However, there were very different views about the ways these issues could be or should be presented according to the different interpretational frameworks of homosexuality, which can be identified in present-day Hungarian society as it was described earlier in this chapter. Obviously, presenting homosexuality as a

---

[12] www.egyenlobanasmod.hu/tamop/data/MTA_1hullam.pdf.

moral or medical issue might imply very different personal convictions and beliefs than interpreting non-heterosexual lifestyles as deviant or private matters, not to mention the approach that sees same-sex partner choice as a basic human right. Even though democratic educational principles would require recognising competing conceptions of what can be defined as a good and respectful life (Gutmann 1987), according to our respondents this requirement is rarely put into practice in Hungarian schools.

In theory a basic rule of presenting potentially controversial issues in school is avoiding value-judgements. A female student used the example of drug prevention to illustrate the difficulties one can encounter:

> Drug prevention came to my mind … similarly if we invite someone to give a lecture about homosexuality it implies that we want to know about it more, but possibly not too much … so the borderline between talking one into it or out of it is very thin. (Lili, 22 years old)

Students of education reported that their teacher training programmes hardly provided any guidelines or help to develop skills and competence on how to tackle sensitive issues related to ethnic, religious or sexual minorities in their future teaching practice. Consequently, in accordance with previous findings (Roffman 2000), they did not find it surprising that in many cases teachers could not separate their own moral or religious beliefs from the topics to be taught. It has also emerged from their accounts that their professional training, similarly to most university training programmes in Hungary, had been concentrated mainly on the acquirement of factual knowledge, and when practical or potentially problematic issues were discussed at all, psychological explanations exceeded social scientific approaches. This individualised model of epistemology could have long-lasting consequences in actual teaching practice, too.

Most of the teacher trainee participants agreed that one of the best ways to introduce LGBT issues at school would be to invite guest lecturers who had a certain level of expertise or experience related to these topics, which would provide an external solution to the lack of knowledge and competence as well as the potential personal aversion of the teacher. Inviting someone from outside the school was also perceived as providing some sort of protection against potentially indignant parents, most of whom should also be targeted, at least according to some students, by awareness-raising trainings.

Some of them knew about the 'Getting to Know Gays and Lesbians' educational programme, which was originally introduced for secondary school students and teachers by the Labrisz Lesbian Association in 2000, with the support of the Phare democracy micro-projects programme of the European Union (Borgos 2007). The main goals of this programme included the creation of a safe and unbiased environment in schools for all students, helping students learn to respect each other, increasing teachers' awareness that their students might be lesbian or gay, and providing teachers with guidelines to help their students. In 2003, its scope was expanded to offer a training course on LGBT issues for prospective teachers, psychologists and social workers. Developing a manual for teachers on LGBT issues was also part of this project.

Another frequently mentioned strategy to bring LGBT topics into school was to include them in sex education classes, even though sex education itself is not a very well-developed field in Hungarian public education. The main problem of presenting LGBT issues in the context of sex education derived from the possibility of concentrating too much on sexual aspects at too young an age. Designating the 'right age' for pupils or students to 'get to know (about) lesbians and gays' was another problem, on which no agreement was reached.

The fact that none of the students referred to more institutionalised solutions, such as extending the pedagogical programme of the school to include LGBT issues, or introducing 'safe school environment for all' type of official school policies was probably not a coincidence. These initiatives are not at all wide-spread in the present Hungarian school system, and considering the recent trends in public education their introduction is not very likely in the near future either.

In the LGBT focus groups there was also a certain level of agreement that these topics should be discussed in school. However, LGBT respondents' views reflected a certain level of caution or conservatism concerning its practical realisation. Gay teachers particularly, might be reluctant to discuss the issues: in case talking about homosexuality makes the teacher suspicious that he or she personally might have something to do with it? This cautiousness might be interpreted as part of a self-justifying ego-protection strategy, especially in the case of those LGBT people who cannot or don't want to be out, for example, in their work environment. In our gay teacher focus group, for instance, out of the six members only one is openly gay at his workplace, and he works at a university. For the others who chose the closeted option, it seemed to be harder to introduce the topic of homosexuality at school. One of them pointed to the danger that pupils' curiosity might be aroused this way:

> *Kornél* (58 years old): The other side of the coin is that we know it all too well what happens if there's one such talk or guest lecture organised. Then there's the blasting choir that it's gay propaganda! Of course we reject this view and consider it stupid but if you think more deeply about it, when a teacher comes in and starts talking about gliding, there will be a few children who never heard anything about it before but now they would like to try it. So perhaps it's not so stupid after all [what they say], and we have to take this argument seriously.

> *Ödön* (58): We accept it [our homosexuality] and live with it, and process it completely, but we wouldn't unconditionally wish it for others, if it's avoidable, that they also follow the same path.

A similar debate took place within one of the religious gay men's focus groups when one participant stated that in order to avoid the suspicion of pursuing gay propaganda or being too provocative, LGBT issues should be presented in a neutral way. However, in the course of the discussion neutrality was placed into an unexpected context of presenting gay sex as a potential source of pleasure:

Káleb (29 years old): There should be a neutral way to talk about this.

Researcher: What do you mean by neutral?

Káleb: Just informing them that there is homosexuality and there are gay and lesbian people in a non-value-judgemental way. ... I mean that we shouldn't aim for too much [for example] that it should be included into the National Core Curriculum, and it should be talked about in X number of classes in such and such a way. I just wouldn't like to force thousands of teachers to promote homosexuality in the classroom.

Researcher: In this context references to promoting homosexuality or gay propaganda often occur. You have just mentioned it. What do you mean exactly?

Káleb: I mean that if I am a 15 to 16 year old student I should have a chance to encounter this topic in a neutral way and receive information about it ... I wouldn't say that it's so crucial in someone's personality development as gay but I wouldn't think either that it should be propagated by taking a positive stance ...

Researcher: What would a positive stance be?

Káleb: If a teacher openly celebrates that it's really very much OK to be gay, and would extinguish all homophobes in the class that it's not allowed... I am saying this from the standpoint of someone who is still unsure, who doesn't know anything about it at all.

Becalél (32 years old): This is why I told you my story in such a detailed way to highlight that it was the interest of the pupils that sparked a discussion, they wanted an explanation [in the course of a HIV/AIDS prevention session within a sex education class], they were the ones who wanted to know why gay men get into anal sex practices and what is the physiological reason that makes these acts enjoyable for them ... So where is value judgement in this situation? And where is gay propaganda? They [pupils] were just presented with a piece of neutral information that this can be a source of pleasure. It's a fact, isn't it? So actually the question is how much information you want to keep concealed from them.

Researcher: So how should it be done in your view?

Becalél: In the secondary school ... [because] in the elementary school it would easily become a laughing matter. In the secondary school year students already have some experiences, especially nowadays, and especially if it's about sexuality because as far as I know it's mandatory to cover the topic of sexuality somehow in one way or another. And it shouldn't be a separate class [about homosexuality] but it should be integrated into sex education. And perhaps the extent of the time devoted to this topic shouldn't exactly reflect the 7% proportion of homosexuals in the general population. But it should be integrated somehow ... in a smooth way that we human beings are capable of having a diverse sex life.

Káleb: I agree completely. Actually I had exactly the same thing in mind: in secondary school you have sex education anyway so there should be space to talk about human sexuality, including gayness and transsexuality, and everything that belongs to it ...

This debate can also illustrate that inclusion of homosexuality-related topics in sex education classes was a widespread idea among not only the heterosexual students but also the LGBT respondents although the content and quality of sex education that our participants encountered during their school years seemed to be far from satisfactory. A religious gay man reported on his sex education class experience in the following way:

> In the last year of the [religious] secondary school we had one such class. They thought that at the age of 18 we were not aware of how these things work, but the religious nurse who gave the class didn't really dare to be more explicit than saying that masturbation is no good, and instead we should run two circles (Lapulevél, 25 years old).

A lesbian respondent interpreted sexual education in a broader context, including diversity issues but she also emphasised the role of the educators. Much can depend on whether they are sensitive, open-minded and well prepared:

> This issue should be addressed within sex education … but it should be taught as part of a broader approach that it doesn't matter what the skin colour, the religion, the sexual orientation of people are, they are, we are, all human beings. I remember an interesting case: one of my relatives works as an educational consultant who studied a lot of psychology and pedagogy, and once when I was still in the closet we had a talk. She mentioned that there was a parent who turned to her for advice because the parent thought that perhaps the child might be attracted to same-sex partners. My relative was absolutely outraged about this; she said that there was no such thing as being gay, there are only those who cannot let this phase pass. I asked her: is it like having the flu? It will pass, huh! I was shocked about this narrow-minded approach … and what made it even worse is that she was a specialist in the educational field with a lot of degrees and distinction, not to mention the fact the she was a relative of mine. (Kriszta, 35 years old)

Concerning the right age to introduce these topics to students, most LGBT respondents expressed the opinion that it would be good to start speaking about these issues during the elementary school years and then returning to them from time to time in ways that are appropriate for the specific age groups and circumstances of the students. This can be seen as a novel approach in two respects. On the one hand, according to previous European findings (Takács 2006) a one-off discussion is the dominant model of addressing homosexuality at school, which can reinforce the idea that it is a marginal and controversial issue, a problem in need of a solution. On the other hand, it can also reflect a need felt by our LGBT respondents to break with the monolithically heteronormative presentation of everyday life in school during adolescence. In fact, in one of our lesbian focus groups' participants discussed the idea that children can encounter these issues from a very early age:

> *Szabi* (43 years old): I know about cases when a boy asked the teacher what to do because he thinks he's gay, but he was sent away that there is no need to go anywhere, you will grow out of it, and if you won't, it isn't a problem either.

> *Borbála* (45): I think it's an important point, because in the schools there are school nurses and psychologists, but there isn't anyone there who would help in the secondary school if one thinks that he or she is gay or lesbian … I even had the idea to start a school for only gay pupils and teachers …

Szabi: It's already a topic of discussion among kindergarten kids. In the case of my son, who was brought up by two women, I pretended that he cannot grasp anything from it. [Then he went to kindergarten] and after a few weeks he asked me: you are surely not a faggot, are you? It must have a very pejorative meaning already in the kindergarten. And it's becoming ingrained into children, and especially those who are somehow personally involved, they have to struggle for years to be able to cope with the negative images, indoctrinated into them … they don't even know what it's exactly but it's already clear that it must be something very wrong.

Parental resistance in the context of introducing LGBT topics at school was not discussed in a very detailed way among LGBT respondents. Mainly the gay teacher group members referred to the role parents can play in keeping homosexuality out of school, especially by voting with their feet and taking their child to another school, while the maintenance costs of most Hungarian public schools are covered by normative state contribution, which is determined by the number of students enrolled in a school. In one of the lesbian focus groups, which included one lesbian teacher, participants pointed out that a certain level of parents' awareness-raising might be achieved through the children. Additionally, the importance of including LGBT issues into the official curriculum was emphasised:

Borbála (45 years old): Children can also shape parents' views. Children can learn a certain approach, and then they can influence their parents. And if parents don't want to be shaped then children will leave, when they are 18–20, they will say, thanks a lot, I have had enough now …

Dinnye (21): I think it would lead to a scandal, if children go home and tell their mum that today at school we had a discussion about how nice it can be if two gay people adopt a child, fancy that! And the parent asks immediately, which one [teacher] was it? I will go to see him and tip the table over him.

Borbála: Out of ten how many parents would go into the school to complain? What do you think? Perhaps two. And if it's part of the curricula, parents can't do anything.

3.2. Coming out at School

None of our teacher trainee respondents considered the possibility that LGBT topics could be brought to school by one or some of their students coming out as lesbian or gay. However, when they were asked what they would do in such a situation, after an initial phase of astonishment (this possibility has never occurred to me!), they started to consider it as a realistic option for which they should be prepared, even if it did not seem to be part of their professional training.

Heterosexual students had divided opinions about openly lesbian or gay teachers, where openness always had a sexual connotation. For example, talking about the fact that one has a same-sex partner was interpreted as a somewhat indecent way to disclose intimate matters, while references to one's marital status or having a different-sex partner was not seen as a private matter to be kept secret. This double standard was best illustrated by the view that equated the mention of a teacher's non-heterosexual orientation with reports on a heterosexual teacher's sexual acts:

> It's like I wouldn't talk about how it [sex] went last night, either … if I as a heterosexual would be asked, how was it last night with your husband, teacher? I wouldn't answer because it belongs to my private sphere. (Janka, 22 years old)

> It's not a problem until it doesn't turn out, well, from a professional point of view. It doesn't matter what they do in their private lives, if they're able to leave these aspects outside the school. … And in some cases it can even be seen as an advantage, in the case of encountering a student of the same [gay] type. But it shouldn't be like advertising. (Alma, 23 years old)

Another female student explained that she wouldn't disclose her lesbian orientation because this would put her in a 'queer fish' position, where similar to stigmatising processes (Goffman 1963), one 'peculiar' aspect of her life would overshadow all other aspects of being a teacher. The unwanted distinctiveness of a 'minority person' entails, in her view, that in the eyes of others she becomes the representative of a whole social minority who should be ready face extensive inquiry into her whole life. Nevertheless, she could not decide whether facing never-ending questions about lesbians or hiding one's lesbianism is the more unpleasant experience.

In general, students were not very familiar with the details of the existing equal treatment legislation regarding the rights of lesbian and gay teachers as employees, but they thought it was probably not very easy to fire teachers solely on the ground of their sexual orientation. No-one knew about cases of overt discrimination affecting LGBT teachers, but no-one knew any openly LGBT teachers, either. In this context religious schools were mentioned as exceptions, but even in a religious school there were many other possible excuses for getting rid of those teachers, including LGBT teachers, who are considered unfit to teach there.

LGBT respondents, most of whom faced the difficulties of coming out at school, see these issues from a different angle and point to the feelings of isolation they suffered at school because of the lack of representation of LGBT issues and potential role models. The knowledge that 'you are not alone, that there are many others like you', as one gay teacher stated, was seen to have very important potentially empowering effects for LGBT youth. They also shared negative coping experiences due to the ignorance and hostility of fellow students as well as teachers, often being connected to failing the expectations of behaving according to rigidly separated gender norms.

> I had a short hair cut and I was ridiculed by the others that in fact I must be a man … they threw paper bullets at me, and there were these kind of messages written on the scraps of paper: 'Did they operate you from a man? You must have a hairy chest!' (Adrien, 25 years old)

I can still remember when in the elementary school the form-master ... wanted to teach me how to walk in a proper feminine way in front of the whole class. (Borbála, 45 years old)

LGBT participants did not know any openly LGBT teachers in elementary and secondary schools, although they could report knowing about a few openly lesbian or gay teachers in higher education, where the free choice of classes and the nature of student-teacher interactions can make it easier to 'survive' as a lesbian or gay professor. Coming out as a teacher in Hungarian schools was seen as a dangerous endeavour, by which one can risk losing moral credibility and the trust of students and parents alike. Most LGBT respondents were well aware of the protective environment created for them by the Equal Treatment Act, which was introduced in 2003, but they saw it as providing protection only at a theoretical level. They also knew about the Equal Treatment Authority, where victims of discrimination can turn for redress. One gay teacher reported that studying the homepage of the Equal Treatment Authority provided him with encouragement and hope that he could turn to them should something discriminatory happen to him. However, there was a general agreement that if they want to get rid of someone, they will do it anyway, and it was seen as very unlikely that victims of discrimination would want to return to the scene of their humiliation even in the case of a legal victory.

4. Combating Homophobia

According to a recent survey of the Hungarian Equal Treatment Authority,[13] 49% of the LGBT respondents (N=200) expressed the opinion that during the last 10 years there had been important improvements concerning the social acceptance of LGBT people in Hungary, while 23% saw not just a lack of improvement but also negative developments. The improvements included the introduction of same-sex registered partnership legislation in 2007, the establishment of the Equal Treatment Authority in 2005, and equalising the age of consent in same-sex and different-sex sexual relationships in 2002. Respondents also referred to the functioning of LGBT NGOs and informal communities as well as the annual organisation of the Gay Pride march as important positive features. On the other hand, the list of negative developments included references to the intensifying violence in society, including violent attacks against Gay Pride marches since 2007; the increasing levels of social intolerance, homophobia and xenophobia; lack of political support and the danger of reversal of those rights and legal protection that had been gained. There were also several determining factors identified, potentially contributing to the fight against social discrimination of

---

[13] www.egyenlobanasmod.hu/tamop/data/MTA_1hullam.pdf.

LGBT people, including more publicity and enlightening information on LGBT issues; the coming out of well-known people; increasing social acceptance by media, political, and educational means; rigour in applying the existing legislation, and active involvement of NGOs. Half of the respondents thought that it is primarily society that should change its mentality and behaviour in order to achieve a higher level of social integration of LGBT people, although 9% of the LGBT respondents stated that LGBT people should make more effort themselves to achieve social acceptance.

In our LGBT focus groups there was a mixture of these views, however, concerning practical ways to combat homophobia, the feeling of incapacity and powerlessness seemed to be the dominant one. For example, our religious respondents agreed that in traditional religious communities there is nothing that can be done to combat homophobia, other than leave the community. Others referred to equal treatment legislation as a nice theoretical framework, which can provide some encouragement but not much practical help in preventing discrimination.

4.1. The Discreet Charm of Coming Out

Within the religious gay focus groups, participants emphasised the importance of presenting a personal 'good example' in order to be accepted. Presenting good individual models of 'normal gays' was an important theme in the other gay focus groups, and was seen as a distancing strategy from the 'ass shaking, promiscuous, stereotypical' (Gyuri, aged 32) non-normal gays, who get media attention all too often.

The presentation of good personal examples, however, had to happen in a fixed sequence: first one had to create a general good impression and only then could he admit that he was gay. This rather opportunistic approach, reflecting a majority-oriented minority position, also implies that not everyone deserves acceptance, only those who have first proved themselves to be 'good enough':

> *Orlando* (48 years old): If first they get to know me as a person and like me, and then they hear that I am gay, I will be accepted, but the other way around ... I'm not sure.

> *BP* (33): I agree. First you're just a colleague, just a person, then a cool person, then a friend, and in half a year or two years time it turns out that you are gay, then it's OK. Otherwise if you start with it that you're gay, they will keep a distance and don't want to become your friends.

There were only a few gay men who reported that their coming out was not influenced by the above considerations:

> I don't like this approach that first I should be known and liked by people and then I can tell them that I'm gay ... in my view, if they didn't know that I was gay, they didn't really know me ... because knowing me includes that I'm gay ... and of course, it doesn't start with an announcement like, a minute of silence, please, I want to make an

announcement ... but more like between the lines ... and I'm over it the sooner the better. (Laci, 36 years old)

In this context coming out was interpreted as a form of self-protection from minority stress (Meyer 1995) and unnecessary loss of energy. This approach was based on the realisation that while secrecy can contribute to the maintenance of one's social integrity by helping to avoid stigmatisation, at the same time it can also have serious negative consequences, including stress deriving from information management and leading a double life.

Among lesbian respondents coming out issues were perhaps less emphasised than among gay men, as one of them explained:

This is how women in general are, they don't necessarily want to appear publicly, thus they can function very well even if they have a husband and children, and they can still have a girlfriend at the same time. (Szabi, 45 years old)

4.2. Legal and Political Fronts

Most of our respondents knew and acknowledged the advantages provided by the existing legislative framework, including same-sex registered partnership and equal treatment legislation. One gay man, for example, pointed out that he and his partner combat homophobia by demonstrating with their lifestyle:

We've been living together for many years, we've also registered when it became possible, and this way we were able to erode, at least a bit, the cliché that gays live by themselves for themselves (Becalél, 32 years old).

Lesbian respondents were, however, less satisfied with the existing legal framework, especially those who had or wanted to have children, and interpreted the lack of equality in the field of family law as a violation of children's rights. One of them explained:

We have registered partnership, but who knows for how long? On the other hand, by registering you exclude yourselves from the legal possibilities of raising children. Same-sex partners can't adopt the children of each other either ... one would think that once registered partnership is introduced, it will be coherently followed by providing rights to be able to raise children together ... but no, it won't happen. What can I do? I can sign petitions ... so it will be easier for them to find me when they want to shoot us into the Danube ... and as Hungarian society becomes increasingly impoverished things will get even worse. (Ivett, 29 years old)[14]

---

[14] In 2007, the Gay Pride march, for the first time in 11 years, was violently attacked by extreme right wing supporters, who kept shouting 'Jews into the Danube, faggots to follow!' a reference to shooting Jewish people into the Danube by the Nazis in Budapest during the Second World War. Since 2007 the joint reference to 'dirty faggots, dirty Jews' became a kind of slogan of neo-Nazi anti-gay protestors.

Another lesbian woman added:

> I don't know what can be done officially but I'd like to know, and I'd like to do something about it … increasing visibility at the political level that would be a good solution … but I'm afraid that the present situation is worse than it was a few years ago, and most probably it will get even worse. (Conny, 24 years old).

Many of our respondents agreed that one of the few things that can be done in the present situation is 'not voting for the extreme right' (Alice, aged 33).

5. Conclusion

'Properly' gendered behaviour was shown to be a core issue in an inherently homophobic socio-cultural discourse, prescribed by heteronormative socialisation, while (perceived) gender non-conformity and its social consequences provided a strong link between homophobia, transphobia, and genderphobia. Recognition of the socially constructed nature of gendered disadvantage can make it easy to detect multiple forms of discrimination in a patriarchal society such as present-day Hungary. Similarly, recognising the political interests invested in keeping certain segments of society in disadvantaged position can make it easy to identify intents to intervene in other people's lives, mostly on the basis of moral and/or religious arguments.

In a previous collection of empirical research on everyday life of LGBT people in Eastern Europe it was stated that 'the diverse manifestations of social and cultural homophobia still seems to be a unifying experience for the majority of LGBT people' (Takács and Kuhar 2007:12). Our present findings, especially those connected to the field of education, fit well into this framework. The school environment was pictured as part of a broader men-centred, white, heteronormative social space, which can have serious disempowering effects on young LGBT people. The silencing of LGBT issues at school, perceived as a general experience, was seen by the LGBT participants as contributing to potential disadvantages of LGBT people at a young age by threatening their developing identity and self-esteem. Thus breaking with the uniformly heteronormative presentation of everyday life in school was often mentioned as a desired option.

Accounts of heterosexual students reflected missing competences in their professional training which provides no practical guidelines and an individualised model of epistemology concerning homosexuality and homophobia. Consequently, solutions at the institutional level, such as safe school programmes, were not considered at all. Similarly, the possibility of having a gay student in one's class has never occurred to most students of education, either. They also seemed to apply a double standard, when references to having a same-sex partner were interpreted as a rather indecent way to disclose intimate matters, while references to one's (heterosexual) marital status or having a different-sex partner was not.

Even for the 'most tolerant' students same-sex family issues constituted the border of the 'normal functioning of society' to be protected, thus proving Gregory Herek's view on the intimate connection of sexual stigma with same-sex relationships (2011:414):

> Like sexual orientation, sexual stigma is also about relationships. Whereas enactments of sexual stigma (eg, antigay discrimination, violence) typically target individuals, they are based on those individuals' actual, imagined, or desired relationships with others of their same sex.

LGBT respondents were characterised by a certain level of caution or conservatism, reflecting perhaps a self-justifying ego-protection strategy, when emphasising the importance of presenting LGBT issues at the 'right age' and the 'right way', and referring to the danger that pupils' curiosity might be aroused by talking about homosexuality at school. Sex education seemed to be an appropriate context, favoured by heterosexual and non-heterosexual respondents alike, to present LGBT issues. However, here sex education was understood to cover not only biology of reproduction and/or pleasure but also human diversity issues.

One of the central themes recurring mostly in the gay focus group sessions was the distinction between the 'normal' and the 'extreme' ways to be gay, where normal behaviour was most often equated with hiding expressions of sexual preferences. Consequently, openly gay activists could be seen by definition as acting non-normally, leading to a new division between 'extreme activists' and ordinary people, overshadowing the conventional heterosexual-homosexual divide.

Individualised notions of homosexuality, focusing on specific features of individuals to be kept private, which dominated all focus group sessions, also seemed to foster the notion that social acceptance of LGBT people is in inverse proportion to their social visibility. Thus instead of concentrating on the achievement of full citizenship by claiming equal rights, a more convenient 'don't ask—don't tell—don't bother' strategy was used by many LGBT participants in a context where the legal or structural definitions of homophobia were replaced by an approach focusing on ordinary homophobia manifested mainly in *tiny annoying things* which one can quite easily get used to or avoid. These signs of internalised homophobia (or externalised heteronormativity?) clearly illustrate that at least for a while, gender-conventional lesbians and gays are likely 'to cause less trouble' and be easier to integrate not only into (Hungarian) society at large but also into certain segments of the LGBT population.

6

Homophobia and Ethnic Minority Communities in the United Kingdom

ANDREW KAM-TUCK YIP*

1. Introduction

The UK is widely considered one of the most advanced countries in the EU and the world in terms of legislation on sexual equality. The tumultuous and significant social and cultural change in 1960s witnessed the decriminalisation of male-male sexual acts, with the enactment of the Sexual Offences Act (1967).[1] The following two decades saw a lull in legislative reform in relation to sexual equality, but 1988 marked one of the darkest periods in lesbian and gay history with the enactment of the Local Government Act (1988) with its infamous Section 28 that forbade the 'promotion' of homosexuality in schools, constructing same-sex relationships as 'pretend families' which undermined the sanctity of family and marriage (for example, Weeks 2007).

This section was eventually repealed in 2000 for Scotland and in 2003 for England and Wales. This was widely recognised as one of the incontrovertible manifestations of the commitment to sexual equality of the New Labour government which came into power in 1997. Indeed, 2000s proved to be a stunning decade during which sexual equality legislation of different kinds significantly enhanced various aspects of lesbian and gay life. Following the lifting of the ban of lesbians and gays in the armed forces in 2000, legal reform on sexual equality included the equalisation of the age of consent (2000), the Adoption and Children Act (2002), the Employment Equality (Sexual Orientation) Regulations (2003), the Civil Partnership Act (2004), the Equality Act (Sexual Orientation) Regulations (2007), the Human Fertilisation and Embryology Act (2008), and most recently the Equality Act (2010). This corpus of law firmly establishes

* The author would like to express his deepest gratitude to all respondents who took part in the study. He would also like to acknowledge the significant research and administrative contribution of Dr Alex Toft and Dr Sarah-Jane Page in bringing this project to fruition.
[1] Female-female sexual acts were never criminalised. Its absence speaks volume about the social construction of homosexuality ie the pre-occupation with 'buggery'.

'sexual orientation' as a 'protected characteristic' from discrimination (for a more extensive analysis, see chapter eleven in this volume).

As far as the general population is concerned, research has shown that the UK has become a more tolerant place for sexual difference and diversity. For instance, the annual representative British Social Attitudes Survey has reported an increasing level of tolerance of homosexuality over the past two decades.[2] To summarise, in 1994, 53.8% of the population thought that 'sexual relations between two persons of the same sex' were 'always wrong' or 'almost always wrong'. The percentage dropped to 45.1% in 1998 and 34.1% in 2008. For the same period, the proportion of the sample who thought that they were 'not wrong at all' increased from 22.2% to 29.9%, and then significantly to 42.3%.

In the same series of this Survey, responses to a differently formulated question for different years also demonstrate a similar trajectory. In 1997, 23.4% of the sample 'strongly agreed' or 'agreed' that 'Homosexual relations are always wrong'. The percentage fell to 18.2% in 2006. For the same period, the proportion of the sample who 'strongly disagreed' or 'disagreed' with the statement rose from 38.9% to 51.9%.

The Eurobarometer report series also show that in 2007, 48% of the UK population believed that discrimination on the ground of sexual orientation was widespread. This increased to 50% in 2008, but dropped significantly to 40% by 2009. Furthermore, in 2008, 63% of the UK population also believed that discrimination on the basis of sexual orientation had decreased in the previous five years. In all these cases, percentages for the UK were lower than those of the European average (European Commission 2007; 2008; 2009).

Nonetheless, a more nuanced look continues to tell a cautionary tale: that more progress needs to be made in order to expand the ripple of tolerance and acceptance even more widely. This is because segments of society, structured by, for instance, age, ethnicity, gender, geography, class and religion, often demonstrate differential levels of tolerance of the lesbian and gay population.

The European Union Agency for Fundamental Rights (2009) has reported worrying statistics about the perpetuation of homophobia in British society in different contexts, such as the following:

— A survey of 1,658 lesbian, gay and bisexual persons across Britain shows that 20% of them had experienced bullying from their work colleagues because of their sexual orientation. In addition, those doing manual work were 50% more likely to experience bullying compared to their counterparts in managerial and administrative posts (European Union Agency for Fundamental Rights 2009: 65; for more details, see Hunt and Dick 2008).
— A 2006 survey of 1,100 lesbian, gay and bisexual young people shows that 65% of them had experienced bullying in schools on the ground of their sexual orientation. In addition, 92% of them have experienced verbal abuse,

[2] www.britsocat.com.

including the phrase 'That's so gay', articulated in a pejorative way; and insults such as 'poof', 'dyke' and 'rug-muncher'. Other forms of harassment experienced include: cyber-bullying (41%), physical abuse (41%), death threats (17%) and sexual assault (12%) (European Union Agency for Fundamental Rights 2009: 69; for more details, see Hunt and Jensen 2007).

— Another survey of schools shows that homophobic bullying and harassment continue to persist despite staff awareness. Out of 300 schools studied, 82% of the teachers were aware of verbal homophobia and 26% knew about incidents of physical homophobic bullying. In spite of having general anti-bullying policies in place, only 6% of them explicitly recognised homophobic bullying (European Union Agency for Fundamental Rights 2009: 71).

Against this backdrop, a case study, on which this chapter is based, was undertaken in the UK with the aim to expand and enrich existing research on homophobia, which hitherto focuses primarily on the mainstream 'white' population. Thus, the study turned the spotlight on ethnic minorities, specifically South Asian (the largest group in the UK), African-Caribbean (the second largest), Chinese and African. It aimed to explore how homophobia is constructed and perpetuated within these communities. This was explored through the perspectives of heterosexual women and men, as well as lesbians and gays. Further, the study also examined lesbians' and gays' various experiences of homophobia and their diverse strategies of management and resistance, often emboldened by progressive legal reform. Before the discussion of the empirical themes, however, I shall provide a methodological account to contextualise the case study.

During the fieldwork, which was undertaken between March and December 2010, 25 individual interviews and five focus group interviews were conducted, involving 10 heterosexual women, 10 heterosexual men, 17 gay men and three lesbians (the total sample was 40). All heterosexual respondents were interviewed individually; five lesbian and gay respondents were also interviewed individually, and the remaining 15 were interviewed over five focus groups. The respondents—aged between 19 and 56—were recruited primarily through support groups, personal networks and snowball sampling. Sixteen of them (40%) were students, and 10 (25%) worked in civil service or the voluntary sector. The rest of the sample worked in a host of professions such as social care, medicine and finance, with one being self-employed. Fourteen of them (35%) lived in Greater London, and the rest of the sample came from across England. In terms of ethnicity, 13 respondents were South Asian, and 13 were Chinese. Further, eight respondents were African, and six, African-Caribbean. While all the respondents lived in the UK, and most of them were British, not all of them spoke English with first-language proficiency. This is reflected in some of the narratives presented in this chapter.

The structure of this chapter is informed by the above-mentioned research aims, first exploring the diverse understandings of homophobia, then an analysis of strategies of management and resistance. As this chapter will show, 'homophobia' is a contentious and variously-understood term. Nonetheless, in line with the conception of the research programme within which this study was undertaken, I shall use this term broadly and consistently throughout the chapter. Pseudonyms are used throughout the chapter to protect respondents' identities.

2. Diverse Understandings of Homophobia

The European Union Agency for Fundamental Rights defines homophobia as 'the irrational fear of, and aversion to, homosexuality and to lesbians, gays and bisexuals stemming from prejudice' (2009: 8). In this definition, the term 'phobia' underscores notions such as 'fear' and 'aversion', which signify a psychological and individualised dimension. Nonetheless, at the academic level, 'homophobia' is a contentious term and scholars do not speak with one voice in this respect (for a detailed discussion of this concept, see for example, Adam 1998; Bryant and Vidal-Ortiz 2008; Herek 2004; Murray 2009).

In one of his many publications in this area, Herek (2004) proposes a more layered understanding of this phenomenon, focusing on the term 'hostility'. Herek's formulation is important because it encourages us to understand hostility towards lesbians and gays at three inter-connected levels: (1) cultural/ ideological (that is, hierarchical power relations between heterosexuality and homosexuality, resulting in the hegemonisation and normalisation of the former, and the stigmatisation and subordination of the latter); (2) institutional/ structural (that is, antipathy, indirect or deliberate silencing and marginalisation of homosexuality, leading to lesbian and gay interests and needs not being incorporated into policies and practices); and (3) individual (that is, negative, discriminatory and prejudicial attitude and/or behaviour on, for instance, a moral basis). He labels the hostility on these three levels as, respectively, 'sexual stigma', 'heterosexism', and 'sexual prejudice' (Herek 2004: 14). Whatever the definitions and foci of 'homophobia', it is important to conceive it as not only an individual's emotional, intellectual and behavioural reactions, but also attitudes and practices pertaining more broadly to group, community, and culture (O'Donohue and Caselles 1993). This multi-layered conceptualisation frames the case study, and themes this chapter explores.

2.1. 'Homophobia'—Heterosexual Respondents' Perspectives

Among heterosexual respondents, there was a distinct dislike—or at least discomfort—about the term. This feeling was based on the assertion that 'homophobia' denotes a psychological pathology. It implies that a homophobic individual possesses an irrational fear that undermines her or his reasoning faculty. Many heterosexual respondents argued that, on the contrary, their objection to—or concern about—certain aspects of homosexuality was based on reasoned and sound evaluation and judgment, informed by a host of ethical, moral and practical principles. Thus, these respondents lamented the tendency of some lesbians and gays to label all questioning heterosexuals as 'homophobic'. They felt strongly that this potentially militant and rigid attitude was counter-productive, because it did not offer any space for dialogue. In fact, it unintention-ally led to silencing and polarisation which, paradoxically, were outcomes that lesbians and gays fought hard to eradicate (Manalansan 2009). Jamimah, a 20-year-old heterosexual woman of South Asian origin, expressed this view strongly:

> I wouldn't want people to call other people homophobic. [*Interviewer*: Would you be offended?] Yeah. Even if I don't agree with it [homosexuality], I would still be. I'm not homophobic; it's just that I don't agree with it. I don't hate them. It's like saying everyone hates them; like people getting scared … It's not like I hate gay people but I don't agree with what they do.

Of course, not all heterosexual respondents shared Jamimah's view. Nonetheless, those who were committed to sexual equality did acknowledge that—despite their own positive attitudes toward lesbians and gays—inaccurate and prejudicial perceptions and attitudes were pervasive amongst their ethnic communities. Such inaccurate perceptions could be organised into four broad categories: (1) homosexuality is an illness or abnormality, signifying an individual's inability to function fully in society; (2) homosexuality is against nature, because lesbians and gays cannot procreate in the traditional sense; (3) lesbians and gays have confused gender and sexual identities, thus not behaving as 'proper' women or men; and (4) sexual equality legislation would promote sexual immorality, by making lesbian and gay 'lifestyle' more visible and represented in public spaces.

These pervasive and entrenched perceptions constitute a powerful ideological structure that legitimises and perpetuates the exclusivity and moral rightness of heterosexuality. They also construct a pathologising and moralistic framework within which lesbians and gays must manage and negotiate their everyday life. From the perspective of these heterosexual respondents who were committed to sexual equality, their ethnic communities constituted an overwhelmingly and predominantly heteronormative space. This implies that one's belonging to such a space was contingent upon being heterosexual, or at least being publicly perceived as being heterosexual. Therefore, an open lesbian and gay identity could undermine this tacit and fragile belonging, or worse, lead to the expulsion from such a space. In this context, lesbians and gays became, in some ways, 'occupants of a strange land', constantly carrying with them the awareness of the condition imposed by the heteronormative structure, and the costs of not complying with it. These are issues that I shall develop later, from the perspectives of lesbian and gay respondents.

2.2. 'Homophobia'—Lesbian and Gay Respondents' Perspectives

To many lesbian and gay respondents, 'homophobia' generates a host of meanings, constructed and reinforced by their own experiences. These meanings include: fear, hate, ignorance, misunderstanding, discrimination and gender-role stereotypes pertaining to homosexuality. The following exchange in a focus group, among some gay men from African communities, illustrates some of these perceptions:

> *Xola* (aged 24): [Homophobia is] hatred. A lot of hatred for me personally, and not being accepted.
>
> *Abiodun* (25): It's very negative. It's hatred.
>
> *Interviewer:* And what's the hatred towards?
>
> *Xola:* Us; individually as human beings, and also for who we are as people. That doesn't help us to function mentally properly in a nice way. We are given signals that we are not functioning properly. And then they take it to the next level where it will not be comfortable to talk about it.
>
> *Erasto* (aged 26): And the religion as well.
>
> *Interviewer:* Religion? … So people are homophobic because of their religion?
>
> *Erasto:* Yes. I've come across that. Even with my own brother, he doesn't even want to see my face. He won't even listen to me, my own brother. I can't even see my nephews and nieces because of it. If he sees me in the street he would make sure we would not see each other face to face.

In the same vein, Liweng, a 28-year-old gay man of Chinese origin, elaborated on homophobia being a form of fear:

> Homophobia: it's being scared of people who are gay, [that] they are with the same, not opposite. It's about being scared of gays and not wanting to be around people who are gay … Can be nasty and fights and hurting people about being gay and what they do in their life. Being a homophobic [person] is not accepting people at all who are gay because they are gay: the lifestyle, what they do together, who they are … [even] things you don't think about [such as] how you look and what you say, walking, friends, dressing and walking through the towns. It's not good for people and it shouldn't happen. But it does because they don't understand what it is to be a gay and what our life is, the style of our life and what we do together, and me and my partner too … It's misunderstanding, yes, and it's other things too. Misunderstanding, it's the start, and then it goes to things like shouting at people and being not nice to people, causing hurt to people because they don't like them. It is everything about being gay … you know, being different and being something else. They are scared of it I think, like the word phobia. They are scared of us being gay, and it's different to them. Perhaps we will make them gay or something. Like if they see us walking down the road and around the town, it will rub on them and make them like me or something and it will make them gay too. They think it will spread onto them and make them gay too. They are scared of that because they want to do what is the 'right' thing for their family and the parents. They

112

don't want no shame or problems with being gay so they want to keep away from it ...
They are against ... everything about being gay.

The typical narratives above clearly demonstrate the underlying properties of 'homophobia'. It is predicated on the ignorance, misunderstanding and fear of—even the hatred towards—the difference that lesbians and gays embody and represent. This difference is more than just difference. It is also constructed as a threat to the norm, in other words, heterosexuality. This difference represents a corrupted—and most of all—corrupting force, which must therefore be contained (within the private sphere), if not eradicated altogether. This problematic difference then becomes something threatening that has to be policed, monitored and managed, in order to minimise its contagious potential, particularly on the young. I shall return to these themes later.

To many lesbian and gay respondents, the perception of homosexuality as a threat to heteronormative sexual and gender orders was often fuelled by religion (for example, conservative religious teachings; see Herek, Gillis and Cogan 2009; Negy and Eisenman 2005), cultural norms and practices (such as emphasis on marriage and childbearing), as well as the media (for example, portrayal of gender and 'lifestyle' stereotypes with gay men being effeminate and promiscuous; see Brown and Groscup 2009; Goodman and Moradi 2008; Schope and Eliason 2003). This could lead to the avoidance of lesbians and gays, which compounds ignorance and prejudice.

Significantly, we can see the discrepancy in the understandings of homophobia between most heterosexual respondents (represented by Jamimah) who rejected the psychological and medicalised conception, and many lesbian and gay respondents who tended to evoke precisely such a conception. This raises the important question of terminology—and its affective implications—in dialogue and education about sexual difference and diversity. Therefore, in some contexts at least, it may prove to be more productive ultimately to frame unequal treatments of lesbians and gays as 'discrimination', 'hostility' 'prejudice' or 'negativity' (or a combination of these), which is more recognisable in the everyday lexicon, rather than 'homophobia', which is far more emotive; and to some, condemning.

3. Differential Levels of Tolerance

While some heterosexual respondents unequivocally and fully accepted lesbians and gays on account of their commitment to sexual equality and human rights, many of them took a more tentative and hesitant approach. They demonstrated differential levels of tolerance of homosexuality, contingent upon the specific manifestation and context, including the type of homosexuality (lesbianism or male homosexuality). Although the analysis here is based on the narratives of heterosexual respondents, lesbian and gay respondents also articulated their experience of these differential levels of tolerance in their everyday life. Indeed, this experience constantly reminded them of being 'tolerated but not fully accepted'.

These differential levels of tolerance could be broadly organised into four. The highest level of tolerance of homosexuality was evident in the fact that no heterosexual respondent argued that homosexuality should be re-criminalised. However, there was a minority view that lesbians and gays should be—and could be—'reformed' through counselling and/or spiritual intervention. This medically but more often religiously-informed perspective reflects the belief in the possibility and the desirability of 'straightening' lesbians and gays; that they, who have sexually and morally strayed, could be 'cured' and brought back to the fold of 'normality', namely heterosexuality. Underpinning this perspective are two related ideologies. First, homosexuality is a consequence of nurture; in other words, it is an outcome of specific experiences in primary and/or secondary socialisation (for example, sexual abuse in childhood, peer influence). Secondly, even if a homosexual sexual orientation is innate, the 'expression' of it (engaging in same-sex sexual acts) is morally unacceptable. This orientation/expression dichotomy offers lesbians and gays two choices: abstinence or heterosexual marriage (for a more extensive discussion of this see Balkin, Schlosser and Levitt 2009; Erzen 2006; Gerber 2008).

At the second level, all heterosexual respondents, whatever their own views on homosexuality, thought that lesbians and gays—as individuals—should not be discriminated against because of their sexual orientation, for instance, in the areas of education, employment, and provision of goods and services. Further, they also argued that lesbians and gays should be protected against hate crime and hate speech, thus indirectly indicating their support for some sexual equality legislation. However, there were exceptions in the case of employment. Some respondents argued that certain professions were not suitable for lesbians and gays, for instance, religious leadership or priesthood (because of religious censure of homosexuality) and teaching (because of teachers' position of power in relation to children and young people). Xian, a 22-year-old heterosexual woman of Chinese origin, expressed this view:

> I think it [whether it is desirable for a lesbian or gay teacher to be employed] depends upon what the content of the teacher's job is. I think if they could affect the children a lot ... If his teaching content [is not] too related to his homosexuality, then it's OK. If the teacher's job relates to heterosexuality or homosexuality, but if it's a very close relationship, I would prefer that [the teacher is not gay] ... If you're in a primary school a teacher is like ... you have to play with the children, you have to teach several subjects. And to play with the children all the time, that means affect the children a lot.

Xian's opinion represents a minority view compared to the general population, since three quarters of the UK population are reportedly now comfortable with having their child taught by a lesbian or gay teacher (Danish Institute for Human

Rights 2009). Nonetheless, it does highlight the complication that could ensue when the emotive issue of 'child protection' or 'child welfare' is evoked, a point that I shall elaborate later.

Some heterosexual respondents also emphasised the importance for a lesbian or gay not to 'flaunt' her/his sexuality in public spaces, particularly the work place (for example, not to display her/his partner's photo). This shows the public/ private divide often implicitly but systematically imposed on lesbians and gay people, to be 'respectable' in public spaces structured by heterosexist norms, as a condition to be tolerated. This 'privatisation' of lesbian and gay sexuality under-pins the continued and entrenched argument that their sexuality is a private issue, thus of no consequence to the public arena. As scholars of intimate/sexual citizenship have repeatedly reminded us, this private/public dichotomy forms an impediment to the recognition of lesbian and gay interests and needs to be taken seriously in public spaces, and being incorporated into policy, political and public consciousness (for example, Oleksy 2009; Richardson 2000; Smith 2010).

While some respondents made no distinction between lesbianism and male homosexuality, others viewed them differently, with the former generally less negatively perceived, because it was considered less transgressive of the dominant gender and sexual orders. Linda, a 35-year-old heterosexual woman of Chinese origin, explained:

To be honest, I feel I can accept lesbian relationships more than gay. Yeah ... I don't know, because as a woman I feel it's very normal for women to touch and feel and we like to hold hands and just feel close. But for men I kind of feel strange to see two men holding hands, I have to say. Although I may not show it, I still feel interesting because it's two men walking in the street. But two girls holding hands together is very normal because I do that myself ... For girls it's very normal. I don't know about here but in our culture it's very OK for close friends to hold hands ... not really hold hands but to cross arms walking together ... But for men, men tend not to do it. They only tend to do it with their girlfriends or wife. When you see two men holding hands it seems odd. I always see holding hands as not really a man thing. It's not like a macho thing to do. Yeah, it's quite feminine.

Linda's attitude towards lesbianism and male homosexuality—which is directly informed by a rigid dualistic construction of gender and gender relations—has been well-documented in scholarly literature (for example, Kimmel 2000; Rah-man and Jackson 2010).

On the third level—which, as with the fourth level, focuses on the relational— the tolerance of homosexuality becomes more complicated and contentious. Some heterosexual respondents supported the Civil Partnership Act (2004) because of their commitment to sexual equality and human rights for lesbians and gays. Often underpinning this commitment was a 'love discourse', which broadly recognised that, far from being pathological and promiscuous (especially in the case of gay men), lesbians and gays were capable of forming long-standing, loving and committed relationships; and such qualities ought to be legally and socially affirmed and promoted, despite the variant sexual type of the relationship. Andrew, a 26-year-old heterosexual man of Chinese origin, expressed this view:

> I think it [Civil Partnership Act (2004)] is probably a step in the right direction ... Yeah ... it's good I think; like in terms of stability. And I suppose it sends a message that this thing is for real and that the relationship is committed. Yeah, people have a problem with relationships if they are not serious, don't they? I do anyway. I think if people are serious then they need to act serious ... [I]t makes it real in a way.

In contrast with Andrew's stance, some heterosexual respondents demonstrated a qualified tolerance of this development. This applies particularly to those who considered 'marriage' a social institution and cultural practice exclusive to heterosexual couples. Thus, while they supported the legalisation of same-sex partnerships, they would object to such legalisation evoking 'marriage'. I would contend that this has much to do with the entrenched cultural and ideological link between marriage, children and family, widely considered the cornerstone of society. Thus, the legalisation of same-sex relationships was tolerable (for its domestication and privatisation of same-sex intimacy), but calling it 'marriage' would put it on an equal legal—and more significantly, moral—footing with an exclusively heterosexual institution, thus devaluing an institution that was perceived as the foundation of society. In other words, legalisation of same-sex relationships is one thing, but labelling it as 'marriage' would be too close for comfort; too close to the moral foundation of society. The narratives below illustrate this attitude:

> A contract like that [civil partnership] would be OK ... That would keep them together. It is not a marriage though ... [I]t is not a real relationship and it's not a Christian thing, no it's not [a] religious thing and I don't think it should be. Not a Christian thing, no. That would not be right. (George, a 32-year-old heterosexual man of African-Caribbean origin)

> No, I don't think they should have the right to get married ... because I wouldn't see that as getting married because it's two males or two females. I wouldn't say that the marriage law [that includes same-sex couples] should be there. And I don't think they should have the right to have children ... But everything else, yeah, they should probably [be treated equally] ... You know, these laws [on legalisation of same-sex partnerships, adoption, parenting], if they all came into place then quite a lot of people would become homosexuals; so there would be quite a lot of problems in society because of the children thing and parents ... same-sex parents. Yeah, we [would be], well, indirectly encouraging people to be homosexuals. (Jamimah, a 20-year-old heterosexual woman of South Asian origin)

The concerns encapsulated in the narratives above were illustrated even more evidently in the contentious issue of same-sex parenting and family, which is the last of the four differential levels of tolerance. Underlining this concern was the perceived well-being of the child, underscored by the 'two daddies' or 'two mummies' discourse that renders same-sex family a problematic space for the development of a psychologically and socially well-adjusted child, who was free from, for instance, confusion about gender roles and ridicule in the school playground owing to her/his family set-up. This is clearly illustrated in Jamimah's view. In the narrative below, she considered a heterosexual single-parent family preferable to a same-sex family with both parents:

> If a child had two women [as] mothers, it would be a bit weird saying, my mum; Which mum? If he was a boy he might be a bit more confused if he had two female parents and if there was a female [child] with two male [parents] then I think that would be a hard situation … [I]f she saw both of her parents doing things that men do she might look at it a bit differently than other people; she might not know what is expected of her. Like if she went to school and the wider society, she might think, 'What shall I do?', because her parents are a bit different … Even if it was a boy because his parents would be a bit … people say homosexual [men] are a bit feminine. He might not know what is expected. If he went to school and teachers were like, boys do football and girls do netball, he might wonder why and feel a bit excluded … But I'm not saying they have to have a dad and mum but it is best to. You might have a mother and the dad has died or something but then it would still be OK. I think that one [single-parent family] would be better. The child would know that there has to be a dad and you can't have two female mums.

Some heterosexual respondents also expressed concerns that a child in a same-sex family might grow up to be lesbian or gay as a result of 'over-exposure' to homosexuality. As I have already argued, this concern is underpinned by the perception of homosexuality as a corrupted and corrupting force or existence that would contaminate the 'purity' of the defenceless child. Some respondents went as far as evoking the human rights discourse to justify this; in this case, not the human rights of the parents, but that of the child: the right to be free from such psychological and social influences and complications. The view of Weng-chao, a 19-year-old heterosexual man of Chinese origin, which according to him also reflected a dominant community view, is representative of this argument:

> The child who is subjected to this social background [same-sex family] may adopt their views and may become homosexuals themselves. I can see why they [the community] are worried about [it]. If that carries on a large scale, it does mess up the family system and the breadwinner, care-giver kind of thing. I do think that a child needs a strong masculine role model and a gentle female feminine role model. It gets confusing for the child if they grow up in the environment and everyone else has a mummy and daddy and he has two mummies or two daddies. It's not really about the homosexual couples in a way. It's more about what is going to affect the child. I don't think that homosexuals shouldn't be allowed a child of their own, but in a way I can see why it could affect the child in a negative way … If he grows up in that environment he could be subjected to all sorts of disadvantages. Maybe in the school he gets bullied because of his parents being different. Maybe he feels left out. So I'm seeing the disadvantage purely on the child rather than the parents. The parents wanting a child, I don't see a problem with that. But a child growing up in that environment may affect him is a negative way in the future.

Jamimah's and Wengchao's views are consistent with findings reported in existing research. Focusing on the UK, the Danish Institute for Human Rights (2009: 6) reports that:

> Despite increased governmental attention toward LGB parenting rights, according to Stonewall there is only limited acknowledgement that same-sex couples are capable of constituting a family and that LGBT parents are raising children across the UK. It is assumed that gay parents have a negative impact on the upbringing of children and do not constitute a 'real' family. Stonewall also notes that the level of acceptance of LGBT persons drops significantly when discussing LGBT family rights such as having children.

While some heterosexual respondents argued that it was better for a child to be raised by a heterosexual single parent, or even in an orphanage, rather than same-sex parents, other respondents offered a contrasting view, asserting that it was a loving and supportive family environment that was paramount for the well-being of the child, rather than the family type. This narrative below is articulated by Samuel, a 32-year-old heterosexual man of African-Caribbean origin:

> At the moment there are a lot of children in the care system and in homes. They haven't got role models and they are exposed to crime; probably underage sex too. And some children will get into trouble. If some people of the same sex who really love the child and have the interests of the child at heart, as long as the child has freedom of choice; and they are going to give them a stable relationship and put love in their life, I think that is certainly better than putting them in a home where there's no boundary. The needs of the child need to be put into account. From that perspective the child will be better off with someone of the same sex if they are monitored.

In summary, we can see that heterosexual respondents had different understandings of sexual equality and rights. Therefore, the dualistic and essentialising 'pro-gay' or 'anti-gay' formulation of their attitudes would be too simplistic, incapable of capturing the nuances of their perceptions and attitudes. Of course, this also complicates the operationalisation of the term 'homophobia' or 'homophobic'. For example, which of the above-cited heterosexual respondents demonstrates homophobia? Which of them is homophobic? These are not straightforward questions to answer.

The point about children is also related to the contentious issue about progressive sex and relationship education taught in schools. While no heterosexual respondent argued that such education should be removed from the school curriculum, opinions about whether homosexuality should be included in the curriculum were divided to say the least. Some respondents felt strongly that homosexuality should be addressed in school because it reflected the diversity of sexuality and relationships in contemporary society, thus promoting inclusivity and tolerance. Further, it also offered a safe space for students to discuss such matters, regardless of sexual orientation, thus contributing to their sexual and emotional development.

Nonetheless, some respondents articulated strong objection to such a move. Often they were not even entirely comfortable with sex and relationship education per se, at least for pre-university students, even when it focused on heterosexuality exclusively. Below is a typical argument:

> I personally, if I have a child in school, I of course don't want him or her to be affected by it [the discussion of homosexuality]. If he's a bit shaken and if he's a really a male and has some doubt about his inner self, I hope that he can lead a normal life and could be in a normal way. And at that stage he's affected by the teachers saying homosexuality is very normal, I obviously don't like it as a parent … I don't have a child but when I do I would stand on the side that I hope my children are not affected by that … I don't like it because the teacher has a great effect on the children. Children have no solid judgement on what the teacher says. (Xian, a 22-year-old heterosexual woman of Chinese origin)

Indeed, the issue of sex and relationship education involving children and young people within the school context is itself a hot potato. Its contentiousness is significantly amplified when homosexuality is added to the mix. This is an issue with significant policy and practice implications. On the one hand, positive and accepting attitudes towards social diversity (including sexual diversity) are most effectively inculcated from a young age, particularly within the context of the school, where different perspectives could be rationally discussed and debated. However, it is precisely the nature of this context and its participants that generates emotive opposition in some quarters to such an educational endeavour. This is where the fault line lies. Implicated in the vortex of intense emotions are not only the issue of sexual diversity and lesbian and gay rights, but also the citizen rights of children and young people in relation to parenting rights and responsibilities. No doubt this controversy will persist for some time to come (e.g. Shipley forthcoming; Rasmussen 2010).

3.1. Contributing Factors Informing Differential Levels of Tolerance

There were diverse factors that informed the heterosexual respondents' varied understandings of sexual equality and rights in general, and their differential levels of tolerance towards homosexuality in particular. For those who thought that lesbians and gays should be treated equally as heterosexuals in all aspects of life, their commitment to the discourse of equality and human rights was explicit. The vast majority who demonstrated differential levels of tolerance of homosexuality attributed their attitude to social and cultural upbringing, having internalised parental and community values that did not affirm lesbian and gay sexuality. They also argued that the schooling system did not contribute to an inclusive understanding of sexual difference and diversity. These processes and practices collectively concretised and perpetuated the heteronormative framework that informed construct their perceptions and behaviour.

Another significant factor was the dominant perception of 'homosexuality as a western/white disease', which has been well-documented in research on ethnic minorities' attitudes in this respect, particularly among those of minority religious faiths (Siraj 2009; Yip 2004; Yip with Khalid 2010). In a nutshell, this racialisation of sexuality constructs homosexuality as a preserve of the white majority, a function of its perceived secularity, cultural degeneracy, sexual permissiveness and excessive individualism. From this racialised perspective, to be homosexual is to be white. Put differently, homosexuality equates with whiteness; thus, being lesbian or gay is being white. Sociologically, this is an example par excellence of identity construction and contestation that marks out the 'Other' ('them'—the dangerous) as contaminated and contaminating, while one's own group ('us'—the pure) as the anti-thesis; the repository of everything that the 'Other' is not. Therefore, a non-white person who assumes a lesbian or gay identity is perceived to have abandoned her/his 'pure' cultural and religious heritage, and embraced and embodied the 'Other'. It signifies not only sexual, but also cultural, religious and moral degeneration.

From this perspective, legal reform that extends equal rights to lesbians and gays is socially and politically mistaken, as well as morally dangerous—at least in some contexts—because it undermines the moral foundation of the society. Andrew, a 26-year-old heterosexual man of Chinese origin, explained this from his parents' point of view:

> Chinese people don't talk about things like that [sexuality], I would because I've been here all of my life and it doesn't mean anything like that to me, but my parents never talked about sex or anything. I learned everything I know from bits at school, films … Yeah … no, no, my parents wouldn't even mention opposite sex people having sex, not even to think about homosexual people … They would say that Chinese people can't be homosexual … Yes, they would say Chinese people can't be homosexual, it's something that is here and is part of Britain and England and the British culture, I'm sure of it. When I ask them about things on TV or we talk about things on TV they scowl and say, 'It wouldn't be like back home, people cheating on each other and doing things that they shouldn't, it's part of being here'… In a way I can see what they are saying, that it's a British thing because of the way that our culture is. It's free and we can do lots of things, all sorts of things.

Religion—more accurately conservative religious teachings that only legitimise heterosexuality—could also form a powerful justification for the censure of homosexuality (Gerhards 2010; Rosik 2007). For instance, Peter, a 37-year-old heterosexual man of African origin, who admitted that he did not know any lesbians or gay men, articulated the typical 'against nature' argument, supported by religious beliefs:

> I have heard about homosexuality back home but it's a closely guarded secret. It's not something that people discuss. Traditionally it's maybe a taboo subject and you don't claim to be a homosexual or if someone is believed to be in that act anyway in the society, they would probably be an outcast and not accepted by the society. [*Interviewer:* Why?] I think basically it's like traditional beliefs of Christianity background. When it

comes to sexual relationships it always states that it's a man and a woman so I think people just believe that it's the opposite sex when it comes to sexual relationships. Yes, that is something taught throughout your life ... [I]t is different in the UK. In [home country] it's rare and a closely guarded secret if it happens within the community. It's not publicised and it's not something that is recognised socially so it's very different here, it's accepted here and it's publicised and it's regarded as a normal thing rather than a taboo as we regard it in [home country]. It's a taboo to do homosexual acts anyway ... Well from my personal point of view the [home country's] approach is right because of what we believe and our religion. From my point of view even here in the UK I think if you draw a graph you can say this is the norm, this is the standard. So if the standard is heterosexuality then somebody who is homosexual then that is not the standard, it's not within the standard parameters of life or something like that. So I don't think it should be public, it should not be easily regarded as a common thing ... It's not the norm, a [homo]sexual relationship. If you look naturally, and sexual relationships even in the animal kingdom, in maybe the plant kingdom you will find that there is male and female to reproduce. For human beings there is male and female to reproduce and if it comes to sexual relationships, the design is that they were meant to meet and reproduce.

The sentiments that Peter expressed are well-documented in literature on some heterosexuals' negative feelings towards homosexuality (for example, Siraj 2009). Of course, conceiving homosexuality as 'not normal' or 'against nature' does not necessarily mean that a heterosexual individual would act in a discriminatory fashion towards lesbians and gays in all contexts. It is important to acknowledge this affective-behavioural difference. Yeefang, a 22-year-old heterosexual man of Chinese origin, for instance, articulated this point, on the basis that each individual had the right to lead a happy life:

Now, it [homosexuality] is nothing different [from] heterosexuality. As long as people are happy, that's fine. Something I'm concerned about is not about homosexuality, it concerns the attitude towards them, towards the rest of society. As long as the people don't disturb the rest of the people or disturb them, that's fine.

Interestingly, religious faith could have a positive effect on some heterosexual respondents' perception of homosexuality, which underlined their acceptance of it, as Anand, a 25-year-old heterosexual man of South Asian origin, explained:

I am a Hindu and was brought up Hindu and to be honest there is in Hinduism, we don't have our commandments as such, but we do have something similar in terms of how we should behave as people and treat others as people, and I think a lot of it is based on really just accepting people for who they are and really loving people for whatever they are. There isn't in Hinduism that says bad things or prohibits homosexuality or doesn't give any stories or parables about being punished or being wrong ... [T]here is nothing written at all about homosexuality ... There isn't anything said about homosexuality being bad. I think that is probably another influence on my beliefs, there isn't anything written in black and white, or things said in religious circles and temples about it being wrong.

Anand's narrative is important because it reminds us of the inaccuracy of popular discourse that often habitually and uncritically constructs religion as intrinsically homophobic, by conflating official teachings articulated by religious authority structures and individual religious believers. While there is no denying that religious spaces generally lag behind secular spaces in endorsing sexual equality legislation and demonstrating lesbian and gay-friendly attitude and practices, there are inter and intra-religious similarities and differences—in terms of theology, tradition and practice—that must be taken into account. The continued ideological propensity to cast religion and homosexuality as oppositional opposites, occupying each end of an unbridgeable gulf, would not contribute to the development of a more nuanced and productive understanding of their intricate and multi-dimensional relationship (for example, Yip forthcoming; Yip, Keenan and Page 2011).

4. Experiencing Homophobia

So far this chapter has focused primarily on heterosexual respondents, offering a nuanced exploration of their varied views on, and attitudes towards, homosexuality and sexual equality. This—and the next—section focuses exclusively on lesbian and gay respondents, specifically on their experience of homophobia (or at least sexual prejudice), and their management of, and resistance to it in the everyday context.

Given the legal advancement within the UK context with regard to sexual equality, it is sometimes mistakenly thought that the UK is a lesbian and gay haven, characterised by the bright lights of London, Manchester or Brighton. This research, which has taken a more layered look at lived reality by turning the spotlight on ethnic minorities, has generated findings that are consistent with the three challenges that many lesbians and gays face within the EU context, as the European Union Agency for Fundamental Rights (2010) recently highlighted: living in silence and invisibility, suffering violent attack, and receiving unequal treatment.

Indeed, lesbian and gay respondents had had varied experiences which they perceived as a manifestation of homophobia. These experiences include: verbal abuse (by far the most commonly reported), physical assault, threat, gossip and joke, rejection by family/friends/relatives, heterosexism in mainstream culture, and the silence about homosexuality within their ethnic communities. The last manifestation—community or cultural silence—is particularly profound, because it signifies the lack of dialogue—or worse, the absence of awareness that such a dialogue is indeed needed—about sexual diversity and equality within such communities. Therefore, while overt opposition to homosexuality is no doubt worrying, silence about it also produces similar effects—the denial of lesbian and gay existence and experiences. This is highly consistent with the 'homosexuality is a western/white disease' discourse I have already discussed: the attitude that there is no lesbian or gay man in their community, so there is no need to discuss such an issue within that context. This silence reflects the 'deafening loudness' of heteronormativity: the cultural ideology and norms, as well as institutional and individual practices that implicitly and systematically legitimise and hegemonise heterosexuality (Hockey, Meah and Robinson 2007).

There is no doubt that some lesbian and gay respondents experienced in their daily lives the weight of cultural sanction of homosexuality. The cultural silence on homosexuality which heightened the implicit pressure of 'compulsory hetero-sexuality' led some of them to conceal their sexual identity out of fear, and 'pass' as heterosexuals, which are typical management strategies of a stigmatised identity that Goffman (1963) has famously expounded. These strategies also illustrate the responses to the condition of belonging to a fiercely heteronorma-tive space that I have already discussed. To belong, one has to toe the line and indirectly collude in the perpetuation of the heteronormative character of the space, thus exacerbating the silence and invisibility it engenders.

Some respondents also avoided spaces that were overtly heterosexist where playing the heterosexual game would prove to be too stressful. Some had also suffered mental health problems as a result of this. The focus group exchange below, among gays from African communities, brings such realities to the fore:

Erasto (aged 26): I used to live in [place's name] so there is a really big [his ethnic] community there … When they noticed me on the street, and if they asked me, I tell them, 'Yes, I am [gay]'. I think like five or six times they have attacked me, beat me up, put me in a hospital. They have smashed my house; they came to where I live.

Interviewer: And you still carried on telling them that you were gay?

Erasto: Yes.

Interviewer: So that's important to you?

Erasto: Yes. I have been punched once, it was a big punch but this man asked me, 'Are you gay?', and I said, 'Yes'. Some of them, they have spit on me, when I go shopping. When they see me they say, 'This is the man'. 'Are you gay?' I say 'Yes', and they spit on me. I call the police, I always call the police, but when I call the police they run away.

Interviewer: Apart from religion, what do you think the [ethnic] community has against being gay? Why would they physically attack you?

Erasto: Because they are ashamed.

Ayodele (aged 31): It's an issue of pride and I also think 'cleanness' as well.

Erasto: Feel ashamed. When you say you are [ethnic community/nationality] and gay you think the nation would be ashamed.

Abiodun (aged 25): It's pride and you are not only bringing shame to your direct family but also your clan.

Interviewer: Someone mentioned cleanliness, what did you mean by that?

Ayodele: You guys can correct me if I am wrong but I think the [ethnic] community see being gay as something unclean, sort of smears the [ethnic community's] reputation. They like to think of themselves as good people and homosexuality as seen as deeply terrible so it tars the image that [ethnic community] hold.

Erasto: They don't believe that someone has been born gay or homosexual, they don't believe it. They tell stories of gays and gay women being abused when they were young, things like that. But they don't believe people have been born that way.

Abiodun: They definitely think it's a choice [to be lesbian and gay].

The focus group exchange above clearly illustrates the various factors that underpin homophobia that many heterosexual respondents reported, either as their personal views or those of their ethnic communities. These factors often operate inextricably on the cultural, ideological, institutional and individual levels. These multiple levels constitute a normative web within which individual and social actions are suspended.

Similarly, another focus group interview with gays of South Asian and African-Caribbean origin also brought up accounts about negative experiences of homophobia, but they also acknowledged the power of the law on sexual equality:

Avikar (aged 34): I haven't actually experienced it [homophobia]. Apart from when I came out to my parents. Generally, especially when it comes to society in general, like services, the NHS or whatever, I don't know. It's never been an issue really.

Falit (34): I think you have to be a strong character not to experience homophobia in its ugliest form. When we were at school we were trying to find ourselves, and know who we were. It was very much more vulnerable and open to that kind of distrust and that kind of hatred I suppose. But now we are older, I don't think anyone would dare say anything detrimental about me being gay at work or anywhere that I go. We are just too strong characters. You would just tell them to fuck off, wouldn't you?

Johnny (37): I think as well, they wouldn't dare say at work because you have got the law behind you.

Falit: Yeah, we are more empowered now. But if you take that away, we are still quite strong characters within ourselves to not to attract that kind of attention.

Johnny: In [town's name] when I first came out, I had been chased, been called names, been strangled. I've had literally someone jump on my back and try to strangle me all because I am gay ... One place I worked I misplaced the keys and this woman was getting upset about it and she turned around and said, 'Well it's because you are a puff'. And actually her words were, 'You've lost the keys because you are a fucking puff'. And I just turned round to her and said, 'My sexuality has nothing to do with this, leave it alone'.

Falit: Who said that?

Johnny: Some old cow I worked with, she's dead now.

There is a positive dimension to the exchange above, in that the respondents recognised the empowering potential of sexual equality law, and their having experienced such empowerment. This signifies the close relationship between the law and civil society. As I have argued, within the UK at least, progressive legal reform has played a significant role in the shift of social attitude towards homosexuality. The law has emboldened some lesbians and gays to be more open about their sexual orientation and live their sexuality more visibly, knowing that there is legal recourse if need be. It has also generated more space for debate and dialogue. In turn, increased social visibility, representation and political clout have served to accelerate progressive legal reform. This point is elaborated further in the section below.

5. Managing and Resisting Homophobia

Many lesbian and gay respondents, being aware of the lack of tolerance of homosexuality within their ethnic communities and beyond, chose to conceal their sexuality. This is a direct outcome of being sensitive to the negativity surrounding their sexuality, embedded in everyday interactions and the socio-cultural terrain across which they navigate. Minghua, a 31-year-old gay man of Chinese origin, explained:

> I've to be so careful you know. You will never know what people think, what they would do. Some friends know I am gay. But to other people I just, you know, sort of lie or gloss over the issue. I guess I don't feel, you know, secure and safe. My parents live nearby and I have many extended family people … So it's like, keeping your head down, be quiet kind of thing.

Minghua's view and action encapsulate the heterosexist currents that silence and make invisible lesbian and gay presence in everyday life. Lesbians and gay men like him have to develop the routine of performing the heterosexual role and incorporate that into their everyday presentation of the self. This performance, as in any other performance, has its own script, vocabulary, rules of engagement and bodily rituals that need to be competently executed to ensure its authenticity and believability.

On the other hand, lesbian and gay respondents who were confident about their sexual identity and rights devised a host of strategies to resist the manifestations of homophobia within their ethnic communities and society at large. Undoubtedly, they felt empowered by progressive legal reform.

One of the strategies such respondents employed was to be open about their sexuality, despite the risk. This openness served various purposes. First, it fundamentally challenged the entrenched perception that lesbians and gays did not exist in their communities. The imposed absence was therefore broken. Secondly, it could provoke controversy and discussion, thus challenging the deafening 'cultural silence' I have already discussed. The habitual silence therefore found a voice, however tentative. Finally, increased visibility offered a message of hope to those who were not open about their sexuality, demonstrating the possibility of integrating their sexual and ethnic identities. This often became a starting point for the construction of support networks, some of which developed into political activism; as Amanda, a 49-year-old lesbian of African-Caribbean origin, explained:

> Well I think research like this which is sort of implicitly saying we are here, we are queer, get used to it, is helpful. But people are just going to have to get used to it … If you said to anyone [that] in the state of Virginia [USA], it was not until 1967 the Supreme Court ruled that a black woman could marry a white man … I think that's when it was and how it went … but they wouldn't believe it, [but] it was in living memory that things were so difficult. I just think that a lot of this is, it's not a moral ground; it's just grounds of bigotry and a misguided sense of superiority. [So] the more this is challenged, it can only do good. And I think that people being out, even though there are risks to being out, and going about their business. I think the fact that me and my partner are seen just to be going about our business and looking after our parents and having our own family, it does have an effect because lesbians and gays don't become the 'Other'; they are just another person down the road who is just living a normal life and trying to deal with the challenges the same as you and me. Yeah. So being out helps, even though it carries risks.

In the view of some respondents, while the support from the lesbian and gay community was no doubt important, lesbian and gay-friendly segments of ethnic minority communities could also offer support. Aijaz, a 50-year-old lesbian of South Asian origin, explained:

> I think my experience, my relationship, has been very positive for me. Being part of an LGBT community has been positive. I think there's a lot of courage and resilience and positivity and humour in lesbian, gay, bisexual and trans communities. Obviously some people are badly hurt by their experiences. A lot of people have got through that to express something very positive, which is something about life in society in general. Likewise within BME [Black minority ethnic] communities, there's been a lot of resilience that has seen people through sometimes difficult times and perhaps has widened society's horizons. There are a lot of positive things and maybe learning about the value of diversity; learning that there isn't only one acceptable way to be human; learning to think about ethical values rather than simply accepting what one is told can be very important and positive. That has been positive for me.

Whatever their strategies, the vast majority of lesbian and gay respondents felt empowered by the various legal reform on sexual equality, believing that legal progress was crucial to bringing about social progress in this respect, though there was still more work to be done. The focus group exchange below, among respondents from South Asian communities, illustrates this:

> *Falak* (aged 36; gay): I think one of the good signs is that I notice a lot of schools have it in their school policy under their bullying policy. They make it quite clear any homophobia-related bullying will also not be tolerated and I think that is a good sign. But I worry that you know, there are still [homophobia] … The word 'gay' is used to refer to anything that is just not cool, and teachers aren't picking up on this.

Aninash (aged 41; lesbian): It's more of a recent thing these days.

Falak: But I'm guessing that maybe teachers are just turning a blind eye to that. If someone started saying that's so black, that just wouldn't work. So maybe there's an issue about the practice of this, how it's monitored [that] is lacking.

The exchange above focuses on schooling and education, an area, as I have discussed, that remains highly emotive and contentious, particularly because it involves children and young people (for example, Guasp 2009; Hunt and Jensen 2007). On the other hand, the exchange below, among South Asian and African-Caribbean gay men, focuses on the legalisation of same-sex partnerships:

Avikar (aged 34): I think it's good that they have got them [various pieces of sexual equality legislation] there. We've come a long way to actually get them passed and recognising same-sex relationships, for example. I think it makes it a lot easier for gay people to direct their life the way they want it. If they want to have kids, they want to get married and have some sort of legal status, of being in a relationship, then that is fine. But I still think, I just don't understand why two men or two women can't get married.

Johnny (aged 37): I've heard they are actually challenging it. They have had four gay couples go and apply for marriage and four straight couples apply for a civil partnership. And each time they have all been turned away due to the law. They are going to write and take legal action saying that it's discrimination.[3]

Avikar: Of course it is. You have the European Court of Human Rights, you know, what rights have I got if I ever wanted to get married to another man? It is still, I would have to have a civil partnership. That is still putting gay people in a separate group isn't it, as second class citizens, because marriage is still at the top and then you have civil partnerships. [But] in Sweden you can get marriages for all.

Johnny: I think it's a good idea in that it gives a legal protection to people.

Falit (aged 34): It's an empowerment, which is good.

That the respondents above drew strength and courage from sexual equality legislation is indisputably evident. However, whether an individual lesbian or gay man is able to exercise her/his rights covered by such legislation is contingent upon her/his personal circumstances. For instance, James, a 28-year-old gay man of Chinese origin, who was not open about his sexuality to his family, would not be able to capitalise on the Civil Partnership Act (2004)—as least for the moment. He explained:

Well, I'm not sure personally what I think about this [Civil Partnership Act] because it will never happen to me. I don't even know about living with someone, perhaps my partner. I do know [that] I [won't] be able to do that because of family pressures; and what would I say if they wanted to come round? They would want to help me move in.

---

[3] The respondent was referring to the on-going *Equal Love Campaign*, organised by *Outrage!*, the LGBT human rights organisation. More information can be found at www.equallove.org.uk.

Why am I moving in with a man, they would probably ask me. I wouldn't blame them for asking. He could be a roommate or something. But that might go on for a long time. I would like it to go on for a long time I think. We get on very well and I want to be with him a lot. So I would think about it. In terms of partnerships, I think it [the legislation] is good. Yes, it's good. But I don't think I can use it myself; it won't be useful to me.

James' narrative raises an important point. Although progressive legal reform in principle benefits all lesbians and gays, the resources needed to operationalise and live out such progress are inequitably distributed. Heterosexist cultural norms and practices, among other factors, structure this distribution (for example, Szymanski and Gupta 2009). In James' case, his concern about contradicting established cultural norms and practices militate against the empowering potential of the legislation. This illustrates the importance of empowering individuals in the negotiation and management of cultural norms in everyday context.

6. Concluding Remarks

This chapter has explored, from the point of view of heterosexuals as well as lesbians and gays from ethnic minority communities, the diverse understandings of homophobia and the various factors that construct the differential levels of tolerance of homosexuality. Across the ethnic communities studied, there were respondents who were highly supportive of sexual equality and the human rights of lesbians and gays. However, these respondents also acknowledged that their own attitudes were generally out of sync with the predominantly heteronormative view of sexuality that their communities upheld and perpetuated, which were also shared by some heterosexual respondents.

Furthermore, the study has also presented the voices of lesbians and gays in terms of their experiences of homophobia, and their strategies of management and resistance. In this respect, progressive legal reform has unleashed empowering potential; however, individuals are differentially enabled in this process, depending on their personal circumstances.

I shall conclude this chapter by highlighting three points. First, the research findings have shown that heterosexual respondents did not all understand the meanings of the words 'homosexuality' and 'homophobia'. Thus, it is difficult to ask questions such as, 'How many of the 20 heterosexual respondents are homophobic'? The answer depends on what 'homophobia' or 'homophobic' means to them. Furthermore, it depends on whether it is female or male homosexuality. More importantly, it also depends on the specific aspect of homosexuality to which we refer. As I have argued, this lays on all of us the responsibility of resisting loose and lazy usage of such terms.

The second point is that, in order to tackle homophobia, we cannot focus solely on changing attitudes of individuals. That is no doubt important, but institutional practices and cultural systems such as the media, the work place and schools also need to become more aware of the existence of lesbians and gays, and more committed to making their lives and experiences visible, without the fear of rejection and exclusion (Fone 2000). Culturally, lesbians and gays need to be de-sexualised and humanised, in the sense that, as a culture we need to develop the habit of seeing lesbians and gays as a social group, a human group—with all its talents and flaws—and not only as a sexual group. Thus, the lesbian and gay identity ought to be embraced as a social and a human identity, not just a sexual identity; because the sexual is but a part of the whole human.

Third, broadly speaking, the law cannot legislate against homophobia. What it can do is to legislate against discriminatory behaviour or acts, committed by individuals, groups or institutions on the basis of sexual orientation. Therefore, a heterosexual individual could hold intense anti-lesbian and gay feelings ('covert homophobia'), but as long as she/he does not behave in a discriminatory way towards a lesbian or gay ('overt homophobia'), she/he has not fallen foul of the law. In other words, 'covert homophobia' is 'legal'—or more accurately, it falls outside of the remit of the law. Nonetheless, as a liberal democratic society, we do have the responsibility to promote a better understanding of sexual diversity and difference, as part of the kaleidoscope of human existence. Thus, 'covert homo-phobia' is a social issue that needs to be addressed and resources of various kinds need to be made available for such education. The challenge in this respect is that educational efforts need a lot of resources and the outcome often takes time to materialise. Changing entrenched social attitudes, particularly in relation to sexuality and gender, is a time-consuming and energy-sapping endeavour.

This also requires the lesbian and gay community to be patient and actively engaged in dialogue with the heterosexual community, but also amongst them-selves. The responsibility rests on the heterosexual as well as the lesbian and gay communities. Overly enthusiastic efforts in this respect by the lesbian and gay community are likely to be misconstrued as disingenuous and militant ideologi-cal and political strategy that prove to support, rather than counter, anti-lesbian and gay rhetoric and activity. In this respect, I think it beneficial to heed the advice offered by Murray:

> I want to draw attention to the plurality of locations and the density of debate within and between borders … in order to illustrate the discursiveness through which homo-sexuality and homophobia continue to be debated, rethought, and created anew … . No nation, no culture, no group, no individual is traditionally, essentially, permanently, *naturally* homophobic. Homo hatred arises out of historical confluences of diverse political, economic, and cultural dynamics; it does not sit uniformly, timelessly, or completely within any cultural, sociopolitical, or economic formation. (2009: 189–90; emphasis in original)

In his analysis of legislation and policy on, as well as social attitudes towards, homosexuality in 27 European countries, Gerhards (2010) concludes that improved education and improved socio-economic conditions would lead to more tolerance of homosexuality, with the emergence of post-materialist values that emphasise self-expression and self-actualisation. On the other hand, Rye and Meaney (2009) argue that increased contact and awareness would contribute to the reduction of misunderstanding and hostility towards lesbians and gays (see also Brown and Groscup 2009). As I have argued above, such efforts must focus not only on individuals, but also institutions and cultural systems and spaces, by challenging—to evoke Herek's (2004) work again—the sexual stigma, heterosexism and sexual prejudice that are often invisible, implicit and quiet, yet stubbornly embedded and powerfully structured the everyday interactional web.

There is no doubt that legal reform at national and EU levels play a crucial role in combating discrimination against lesbians and gays. At the social and cultural level, the process is likely to be more time-consuming and convoluted. Persistence and commitment from all parties, including the heterosexual majority, would be required to achieve the noble goal of unity in diversity. Thus:

> Since diversity enriches the Union, the EU and its Member State must provide a safe environment where differences are respected and the most vulnerable protected. Measures to tackle discrimination, racism, anti-semitism, xenophobia and homophobia must be vigorously pursued (Council of the European Union 2009: 14).

PART II

RECOGNISING AND COMBATING HOMOPHOBIA IN AND WITH THE LAW

7

Introduction to the Legal Case Studies

ALESSANDRO GASPARINI AND ROBERT WINTEMUTE

The aim of this second part of the book is to ask whether there is any evidence of homophobia 'in law' (in the drafting, interpretation and application of legal rules by public institutions and authorities in each of the four countries), and whether homophobia can be fought 'with law' (by considering four particular areas in which the law might be used in each country). In conducting this research, the authors have adopted a 'legal process' approach, which means searching for interactions between all the component parts of a legal system, not only legislation, academic commentary and judicial rulings, but also hidden factors supporting the existing rules within each country's legal system. The resulting analysis considers the legal system as part of a society. It therefore focuses both on the process leading to the adoption of existing legislation, and on the substantive reasons given to justify that legislation.

To make the results of the research comparable, the legal analysis has been conducted using a shared approach. The first important issue was to define the sources of law to be analysed. All the authors agreed on a broad interpretation of the words 'law' and 'legal', taking into account not only statutory law and case law, but also so-called 'soft law', administrative practices, the discussion of bills within parliamentary committees, and all decisions of public authorities, even if they are not legally binding.

Secondly, the legal team agreed to confine its research to four areas, which were chosen because they are related to the protection of fundamental rights, and because of the potential need in these areas for EU harmonising measures: (1) 'hate crimes' and 'hate speech'; (2) education at all levels; (3) free movement, immigration and asylum; and (4) cross-border reproductive services.

The first and second areas are related to EU competence because, in the case of racial discrimination, EU institutions have already taken action in relation to 'hate speech' and 'hate crimes',[1] as well as discrimination and harassment in

---

[1] Council Framework Decision 2008/913/JHA of 28 November 2008 on combating certain forms and expressions of racism and xenophobia by means of criminal law, OJ L328/55 (6 December 2008).

education.[2] The first area has been chosen because homophobia in society is often expressed through 'hate speech', which can incite 'hate crimes' (crimes of violence motivated by prejudice or hostility towards lesbian, gay and bisexual persons). The relationship between laws against 'hate crimes', 'hate speech' and other 'discrimination' can be explained as follows. Homophobia can be expressed through violence (fists), expression (words), or discriminatory acts (decisions). Anti-discrimination legislation (such as national laws implementing Council Directive 2000/78/EC) focuses mainly on discriminatory acts or decisions that deny opportunities, for example, access to employment or vocational training. Criminal legislation often supplements anti-discrimination legislation through special provisions on crimes of violence motivated by homophobia. The legislation may employ either or both of two methods: (1) it may create new, special offences with higher maximum penalties; or (2) it may make the prejudice or hostility of the convicted person an aggravating factor in determining the appropriate sentence under an existing, general offence. This kind of crime is known in the USA as a 'hate crime', which is a convenient shorthand in English. Laws against 'hate crimes' are intended to provide extra condemnation of crimes that target minorities and make the victims afraid to be visible or to mix with members of the majority.

Criminal legislation also supplements anti-discrimination legislation by prohibiting expression that incites hatred, discrimination or violence against individuals because of their sexual orientation. This kind of expression is known in the USA as 'hate speech', which is also a convenient shorthand in English. Laws against 'hate speech', which are permitted by the European Court of Human Rights (ECtHR) under Article 17 or 10(2) of the European Convention on Human Rights (ECHR),[3] but not by the First Amendment to the United States Constitution,[4] are partly preventive in nature. They are intended to discourage expression that could cause persons hearing or reading it to engage in acts of discrimination or violence against members of a minority.

The second area has been chosen because homophobic attitudes are often developed in schools, and bullying of students perceived to be lesbian or gay is not challenged by teachers. Children are not born homophobic. Hostility towards lesbian and gay individuals must be learned, at home from parents and siblings, at school from teachers and classmates, and from the media. Laws banning homophobic hate speech seek to prevent harmful messages spread by the media.[5] Respect for family life will generally prevent the law from interfering with the

---

[2] Council Directive 2000/43/EC of 29 June 2000 implementing the principle of equal treatment between persons irrespective of racial or ethnic origin OJ L180/22 (19 July 2000), Art 3(1)(g).

[3] See, eg *Le Pen v France* (20 April 2010).

[4] See *RAV v City of St Paul*, 505 US 377 (1992).

[5] The media outlet is not itself criminally liable for hate speech, if its intention is not to spread hate, but rather to educate the public about the existence of the phenomenon. See *Jersild v Denmark* (ECtHR, 23 September 1994).

messages children receive from their parents and siblings, but schools are an important venue in which teachers have the opportunity to either encourage or discourage homophobic attitudes on the part of their students, which could later be expressed as homophobic hate crimes, hate speech or discriminatory acts when their students become adults.

The third and fourth areas reflect the fact that homophobia (in the broad sense of rejecting equal opportunities for lesbian and gay people) causes the introduction or maintenance of directly or indirectly discriminatory rules and practices in national law, some of which fall within the competences of the EU. Two examples have been chosen: free movement of lesbian and gay persons (immigration of same-sex partners of EU citizens, and asylum claims by lesbian and gay individuals from outside the EU), and cross-border reproductive services (children are born as a result of medical services provided in one Member State and then live under the legislation of another Member State).

The link between homophobia and the third and fourth areas can be explained as follows. In England and Wales, section 28 of the Local Government Act 1988 (to be discussed in chapter eleven) was, until its complete repeal in 2003, an example of homophobia in legislation, which effectively stated that same-sex couples are 'pretended families'. The failure of national immigration laws to recognise same-sex couples as families can create obstacles to the free movement of EU citizens and their partners. Likewise, national immigration laws that fail to take seriously claims of lesbian and gay asylum-seekers from outside the EU may force these individuals to return to their home countries, where they risk suffering homophobic persecution.

Similarly, in countries that allow unmarried individuals to adopt children, legislation or policies that exclude lesbian and gay individuals from this opportunity can now be described as homophobic. In *EB v France* (2008), the ECtHR held (by 14 votes to three on the principle) that this form of exclusion is discrimination which violates Article 14 of the ECHR combined with Article 8. The principle was best stated by the President of the ECtHR, Judge Costa, in his dissenting opinion (he dissented on the application of the principle to the facts of the case):

> [T]he message sent by our Court to the States Parties is clear: a person seeking to adopt cannot be prevented from doing so merely on the ground of his or her homosexuality … our Court … considers that a person can no more be refused authorisation to adopt on grounds of their homosexuality than have their parental responsibility withdrawn on those grounds … I agree.[6]

---

[6] *EB v France* (ECtHR, 22 January 2008).

The ECtHR's reasoning should also apply, a fortiori, to countries that allow unmarried heterosexual women to request donor insemination.[7] The homophobia of excluding lesbian women from this opportunity, in countries where it exists, is even clearer. It amounts to a government saying to lesbian women that it is better for children not to be born at all, and never to live, than to be born to lesbian mothers. Unlike in the case of adoption, in which there is sometimes a possibility that a child could be placed with a 'traditional family' (a married, different-sex couple), children born to lesbian women after donor insemination will either be born to these women, or not at all. Because Articles 56 and 57 of the Treaty on the Functioning of the EU protect freedom to provide and receive services (including reproductive and other medical services) in other Member States,[8] the legal problems faced by children of lesbian and gay parents (born after their parents received reproductive services in another Member State) are a matter that should be of concern to EU institutions.

It should also be borne in mind that reproductive services are used mainly by different-sex couples with joint fertility problems (one member of the couple cannot produce fertile eggs or sperm). The service often involves, not 'treatment' of the infertility (which is impossible), but the substitution of donor eggs or sperm for the missing eggs or sperm. Thus, when a lesbian woman with a female partner seeks access to donor insemination, she is seeking: (1) access to a technique that, in most countries, is already authorised for different-sex couples; and (2) the same respect for her choice of partner that different-sex couples receive. A heterosexual woman with a male partner, whom she loves but who is sterile, is not asked to replace him with a fertile man (to solve their joint fertility problem). Similarly, a lesbian woman with a female partner, whom she loves, should not be asked to replace her with a fertile man (to solve their joint fertility problem, that is, two women cannot conceive a child without donor sperm).

In the four legal case studies that follow (read together with the four sociological case studies in Part I), it should be clear to the reader that in countries where the legal system decided to take action (by 'recognising and fighting homophobia'), the social situation is not always dramatically better than in countries where no laws have been passed, in which the status quo amounts to 'ignoring and condoning homophobia'.

As in Part I, the results of the case studies will be reported in the following order: Italy, Slovenia, Hungary and the UK. This should enable the reader to appreciate that Italy lacks specific legislation with regard to the four areas, that

---

[7] There is not yet any case law on this question, but a Chamber has ruled that Austrian legislation prohibiting particular techniques of assisted reproduction violates the ECHR. See *SH & Others v Austria* (ECtHR, 1 April 2010; reversed by Grand Chamber on 3 November 2011).

[8] See, eg Case C-157/99, *Geraets-Smits and Peerbooms*, [2001] ECR I-5473, para 53: 'It is settled case-law that medical activities fall within the scope of Article 60 [now 57] of the Treaty'.

Slovenia and Hungary are in an intermediate position, and that the UK has the most complete set of rules dealing with the four areas. The four countries will be compared across the four areas in chapter twelve.

8

Homophobia in the Italian Legal System: File not Found

ALESSANDRO GASPARINI, CATHY LA TORRE, SILVIA GORINI AND MONICA RUSSO*

1. Introduction

A peculiar aspect of the Italian legal system is its resistance to confronting homophobia in every aspect of social life. Apart from the explicit prohibition of discrimination in the field of labour law (required to implement Council Directive 2000/78/EC), and the list of forms of persecution justifying international protection, no reference to sexual orientation can be found in Italian statutory law (Bilotta 2005), and the word 'homophobia' hardly ever appears in court judgments or administrative documents. To understand the reasons for this we need to widen the field of analysis to parliamentary debate; to focus on the legal reasoning of judges who have to decide on cases not covered by specific legislation; and to consider examples from Italian society (calls for law reform from judges and non-governmental organisations).

Although Italian criminal law contains specific provisions to punish conduct based on racial, ethnic, national or religious hatred, conduct motivated by homophobia is not covered. A recent bill aimed at combating homophobia failed on the basis of generic references to freedom of expression, freedom of religious teaching, the danger of legitimising every kind of sexual deviation, and the need to avoid unjustified special protection for homosexuals.[1]

---

* Sections 1, 3 and 4 to this chapter were written by Alessandro Gasparini. Cathy La Torre wrote section 2, Silvia Gorini section 5 and Monica Russo section 6.

[1] On 18 May 2011, the Justice Committee of the Italian Parliament refused its preliminary approval of the bill introducing an aggravating circumstance based on discrimination on the grounds of sexual orientation. The discussion moved to the General Assembly of the Parliament where, on 26 July 2011, the majority rejected the law by approving the same prejudicial question that was presented in October 2009 (see section 2.2). It should be noted that the Minister for Equal Opportunities, after having supported the law, abstained from voting.

Similarly, in legislation concerning schools and universities, prevention of homophobia has not been a priority. Only in recent years has the Ministry for Equal Opportunities stressed the importance of promoting educational programs aimed at increasing awareness of all kinds of discrimination and intolerance including those based on sexual orientation. Indeed, the educational system lacks disciplinary sanctions against homophobic bullying and appropriate sex education in school curricula (about which political parties cannot agree). Conservative Catholic culture is the main obstacle to modern secular education and to any law which may be viewed as a threat to the traditional concept of the family.

Italian laws on free movement and family reunification, formally implementing EU directives, exclude homosexual couples because of the absolute denial of any kind of recognition of same-sex partnership. The Italian Parliament and the Italian Government refuse to accept legal recognition of a lasting relationship between two people of the same sex, even though in 2010 the Constitutional Court stated the possibility (or necessity?) for legislators to regulate these situations (explicitly excluding marriage). The resistance to accepting homosexuality as a 'normal' state for an individual is even clearer in the refugee decisions of the Italian Court of Cassation, which reject the existence of a criminal law for those who 'act in a homosexual manner' as a sufficient reason for asking for international protection.

Lastly, legislators have expressed their resistance towards homosexuals in the law concerning medically-assisted procreation, which explicitly excludes same-sex couples. Italian law generally restricts joint parenthood to the union of man and a woman and, apart from a few exceptions, does not permit adoption by a single person.

2. Hate Crime and Hate Speech

2.1. Legislation against Hate Speech

Article 3 of the 1947 Italian Constitution states that 'all citizens have equal social dignity and are equal before the law, without distinction of sex, race, language, religion, political opinion, personal and social condition'.[2] Because sexual orientation is included under 'personal and social condition', the principle of non-discrimination is fully recognised within the Italian legal system.

Italian legal protection against discrimination is most comprehensive with regard to discrimination on racial and ethnic grounds (Legislative Decree 286/1998, Act 300/1970, Legislative Decrees 215/2003 and 216/2003). The first law

---

[2] Translation by the Interpreters—Translator Office of the Chamber of Deputies, available at www.camera.it/Camera/view/doc_viewer_full?url=http%3A//en.camera.it/4%3Fscheda_informazioni%3D23&back_to=http%3A//www.camera.it/38%3Fconoscerelacamera%3D28.

against discriminatory demonstrations (of a racial nature) was Act 645/1952, which gave effect to the Constitution's ban (in Transitory Disposition XII) on reorganising the Fascist Party, including a ban on racist propaganda. Later, Act 654/1975 implemented the 1966 International Convention on the Elimination of all forms of Racial Discrimination.

Act 654/1975 (Article 31(a) and (b)), as amended by Article 13 of Act 85/2006, punishes

> with detention of up to a year and six months or a fine of up to 6,000 EUR anyone who spreads propaganda founded on notions of superiority or racial and/or ethnic hatred, or instigates others to commit or commits acts of discrimination on racial, ethnic, national or religious grounds, with imprisonment for between six months and four years anyone who, in any way, incites others to commit or commits acts of violence or acts of incitement to violence on racial, ethnic, national or religious grounds.

Case law affirms that the law indicates an offence motivated by specific intent, characterised by the awareness and intent to damage the human dignity of a person from a different racial, ethnic or religious background.[3] Such distinction acquired further relevance because the 2006 amendment replaced, in relation to 'acts of discrimination', the word *incitement* with the word *instigation*. This means that the prosecution must prove not only the possibility of the discriminatory speech to cause others to commit discriminatory acts; they must also provide specific evidence that a discriminatory act was committed because of the discriminatory speech.

To date, Italy has not extended the 'hate speech' content of Act 654/1975 ('spread[ing] propaganda founded on … hatred', 'instigating others to commit … acts of discrimination', 'incit[ing] others to commit … acts of violence') to sexual orientation or gender identity. However, since the XV legislature (April 2006-February 2008), a number of bills have been proposed, all aiming to extend Act 654/1975 to sexual orientation and gender identity.[4] In 2007, the Prodi Government attempted to introduce this measure in an amendment to a decree in matters of public order.[5] However, the decree was not converted into a law. Later, Parliament decided to follow normal procedure and proposed a unified text in January 2008.[6] Not even this was approved, due to the crisis in the Prodi Government which led to the early dissolution of Parliament.

In the XVI legislature (from April 2008), the Committee for Justice began to examine two bills (AC 1658 and AC 1882), which sought to add sexual orientation and gender identity to Act 654/1975. During the Committee's debate, it

---

[3] See Court of Cassation, III Criminal Section judgment of 28 February 2002 No 7421; Court of Verona, judgment of 2 December 2004.

[4] The first attempt can be found in Bill No 2169, presented on 25 January 2007. See www.legxv.camera.it/_dati/lavori/stampati/pdf/15PDL0036970.pdf.

[5] Law Decree of 1 November 2007, No 181.

[6] House of Deputies, Bill 1249-ter, available at leg15.camera.it/dati/lavori/stampati/pdf/15PDL0036970.pdf.

immediately became clear that it would be difficult to agree a text. Instead, a decision was made to work on a text (AC 1658–1882-A) which did not amend Act 654/1975, but introduced a new aggravating circumstance (sexual orientation) into Article 61 of the Penal Code, in relation to offences committed with criminal intent against an individual's life and safety.[7]

The major LGBT associations rejected the new bill as insufficient to prevent an escalation in violence against LGBT people. The choice not to extend to sexual orientation the crime of instigating discrimination and inciting hatred would, for example, make it impossible to punish extremely serious cases, such as those which occurred in Rome in 2009, when neo-fascists plastered walls with posters exhorting readers to put gays in the arena of the Colosseum with lions. Opposition to extending the crime of instigation was based on the concern that it would limit freedom of opinion, guaranteed by Article 21 of the Constitution. In this regard, it is necessary to note that the issue of the relationship between crimes relating to opinions—which include racist propaganda—and freedom of thought has been widely debated both among scholars and in case law (see Amato and Barbera 1997: 277; Pace 1992: 414; Pace and Manetti 2006). Criticism alone, even if it is severe, cannot be a crime unless there is a danger that it might objectively incite public disorder or disobedience.[8]

The case law of the supreme courts offers an interpretation of Act 654/75 which is also compatible with Article 21 of the Constitution. In a 1993 judgment, the Court of Cassation (I Criminal Section, 29 October 1993, RV 196583) stated that the law which punishes acts of propaganda relating to claims of racial superiority

> is not directed towards the limitation of thought aimed at exalting or undermining various races ... The aim is to prevent ideologies containing the seed of subjugation from leading to aberrant discrimination and the ensuing danger of hatred, violence and persecution.

A widely-known case involved the leaders of an Italian political party (Lega Nord), who had promoted a campaign to collect signatures to remove a nomadic community of Sinti gypsies from within city limits. In this case, the judges stated that 'thought in itself can be expressed as long as it does not harm or endanger other constitutionally guaranteed rights, such as human dignity, racial or cultural identity, sexual orientation, religious beliefs or reputation'.[9] According to these judgments, it seems reasonable to state that punishment for those actions contained in Act 654/75 does not infringe Article 21 of the Constitution.[10] Because the bills under discussion sought merely to extend the existing ban on

[7] See www.camera.it/126?pdl=1658&tab=5&leg=16.
[8] See report to the Justice Commission by Diletta Tega available at www.forumcostituzionale.it/site/images/stories/pdf/documenti_forum/paper/0095_tega.pdf.
[9] Court of Verona, judgment of 2 December 2004.
[10] See also Court of Cassation, I Criminal Section judgment of 28 February 2001 No 341.

racist 'hate speech' to LGBT persons, the concerns expressed by some members of the Committee for Justice seem to have had no basis in constitutional law.[11]

2.2. Legislation against Hate Crime

Despite the opposition of the major LGBT associations, the Committee decided to bring to Parliament a unified text which only included the aggravating circumstance of crimes committed on the grounds of sexual orientation and sexual discrimination (a term that was intended to exclude gender identity). Notwithstanding the bill's less ambitious aim, it was rejected by the Assembly, following approval of a prejudicial question presented by the UDC group (centre party) on 13 October 2009 (see European Union Agency for Fundamental Rights 2010). The prejudicial question claimed that the bill would violate Article 3 of the Constitution (under the assumption that those who are subjected to violence, allegedly on the grounds of sexual orientation, would benefit from a privileged form of protection versus those who are simply subjected to violence) and Article 25 of the Constitution, due to the vague meaning of the term 'sexual orientation'.

According to the supporters of the prejudicial question, in violation of Article 3 of the Constitution, the bill introduced differential treatment on the grounds of an unreasonable element, assuming that sexual orientation would cover any orientation towards any kind of sexual activity, including incest, paedophilia, zoophilia, sadism, necrophilia and so on. However, this assumption seems to be completely unjustified, as the term 'sexual orientation' does not refer to any specific kind of sexual behaviour, but rather to a personal characteristic of people who feel an affectionate, romantic and/or sexual attraction towards people of the same sex (see Dynes 1990; Sell 1997), or the opposite sex, or both. The Italian legal system already punishes the above types of sexual behaviour through penal measures, because they are considered to be damaging to the victim, whether the behaviour is different-sex or same-sex. At the same time, Italian law explicitly protects sexual orientation, through the legislation implementing Directive 2000/78.

2.3. The New Perspective of Criminal Courts: LGBT Organisations as Injured Parties

The first judgment to make explicit reference to sexual orientation dates back to 1994, when the Court of Cassation sentenced a teacher for verbal abuse of a

---

[11] The Commission asked for the opinions of two legal experts, Professor Diletta Tega and Profesoor Mario Ronco. Professor Tega was in favour of extending the existing legislation on hate speech to cases of homophobia, rather than creating a specific aggravating circumstance; however, Professor Ronco disagreed, because of the possible violation of fundamental constitutional rights, such as freedom of expression, religion and education. For a critical analysis of Ronco's arguments, see section 6.

student, whom he had addressed with epithets such as 'stupid', 'imbecile' and 'gay'. In this case, the adjective 'gay' was considered an offence, due to its offensive content and the intentions of the teacher.[12] But it was not until 2009, that a homophobic motive started to take on legal relevance in the criminal process. For the first time, the Court of Rome (18 November 2009) openly recognised a homophobic motive in relation to the attempted murder of a young homosexual man, who had been stabbed outside a dance venue called 'Gay Village'. By virtue of this recognition, the court authorised the NGO Arcigay to participate in the trial as plaintiff jointly with the victim. Following this precedent, the Court of Pordenone (10 December 2009) identified a despicable homophobic motive in an attack against a disabled young man on the grounds of his homosexuality. There were similar outcomes in the case of a young gay man who had suffered defamation (Court of Bagheria, 14 October 2010), and in the Court of Rimini (25 January 2011), which permitted Arcigay to participate in a trial against an individual who had sexually abused a young man because he was homosexual. This admission of an LGBT organisation as an injured party in a criminal trial shows that Italian judges are beginning to recognise crimes committed from a motive of homophobia and, applying Article 91 of the Criminal Procedure Code, bypassed the strict limitations created by the lack of legislation on anti-LGBT 'hate crimes'. The efficacy of this solution will depend on the final judgments in these cases. In any case, it is unacceptable that full responsibility for protecting gay and lesbian rights should be placed on a private non-profit organisation when it is the state which should grant these rights through clear legislation.

3. Education at all Levels

3.1. Confronting Homophobia in Italian Schools

Homophobic bullying and related acts of discrimination against pupils who are, or are presumed to be, gay or lesbian are quite common in Italian schools, but official data is only available for the last few years. Since 2008 Arcigay has been monitoring the situation of homophobic bullying in schools at all levels, and drawing attention to the problem by sending the results of its reports to public institutions, in particular to the Presidency of the Chamber of Deputies of the Italian Parliament.[13] It appears that the most frequent episodes consist of verbal abuse which often degenerates into acts of violence.

---

[12]   Court of Cassation, V Criminal Section, judgment of 28 October 1994.

[13]   See in particular the research and observations of Arcigay: Project 'Schoolmates', 2007, supported by the European Commission and Daphne (Lelleri 2007), and the more recent 'Interventi di prevenzione contro il bullismo a sfondo omofobico', 2010, co-financed by the Ministry of Labour and Social Policies (Prati 2010). The Minister for Equal Opportunities

A survey of Italian laws concerning education shows that, to date, no national policies, programmes or specific actions to combat homophobic bullying in schools, have been developed. Furthermore, no resources have been provided to support professionals, parents, carers and pupils in developing anti-bullying policies. In spite of news items about students who have committed suicide because of bullying and discrimination due to perceived lesbian or gay sexual orientation (or, in many cases, their gender non-conformity), neither public opinion nor government have seemed to consider bullying as an important nationwide problem requiring serious measures. The significance of existing legislation will be examined in the light of its efficacy in recognising and combating homophobia, with particular attention to the question of sexual education in schools, which could play an important role in preventing episodes of discrimination and violence based on sexual orientation.

3.2. Homophobic Bullying: Useless Tools of Legislation

The general law concerning the organisation of schools at all levels in Italy is Legislative Decree 287/1994 (School Consolidation Act). It gathers together all the rules covering the education system, both public and private, and provides general principles for the regulation of every single kind of school, from elementary to secondary school. Article 397 deals with the School Inspectorate. Traditionally, the duty of school inspectors has been to monitor and in some cases punish any behaviour by students or teachers which is against the law. In the last 20 years, school inspectors have also taken on the duty of promoting good practice and preventing conflict.

A regulation of the Ministry of Education, University and Research (MIUR) contained in Decree of the President of the Republic 260 of 21 December 2007, expanded the role of school inspectors to include the phenomena of bullying and deviant behaviour. The same principle was confirmed by Article 3 of the MIUR Decree of 27 February 2008, which states that inspections must also address the problem of bullying in schools.[14] In theory, the inspectors must investigate, sanction, and prevent bullying in schools and report all known episodes of bullying to the MIUR. In practice, however, effective means of implementing these regulations are still missing. Above all, the inspectors must be competent to deal with the matter, yet there is no requirement that they have adequate knowledge to deal with problems related to discrimination and bullying based on sexual orientation and gender ientity.

---

announced that a survey is to be conducted during 2011 to better identify the phenomenon of homophobia in schools.

[14]   Available at www.edscuola.it/archivio/norme/decreti/dm27208.pdf.

In an explanatory note dated 31 July 2008,[15] the MIUR stated that it considered it a priority to combat increasing episodes of bullying in schools, and asked all schools to amend their own internal regulations by introducing proper sanctions (not only punitive, such as expulsion or detention) and to cooperate with families in order to better educate students in 'respect for others'.

Even this formal act does not explicitly mention the issue of homophobic bullying. Moreover, based on the absence of competence and in the name of school autonomy, the Ministry avoided creating an effective mechanism to deal with bullying.

The Italian Parliament has hardly dealt with the problem of bullying at all and has paid even less attention to the specific question of homophobic bullying. On 19 July 2007, in the preceding legislature (2006–2008, when the left-wing party was in power), in the VII Committee (Culture, Science and Education) of the House of Deputies, Deputy Alba Sasso presented a resolution about the need to promote cultural and educational projects in schools, aimed at combating bullying and homophobia. This Parliamentary Resolution No 7/00251,[16] referred to episodes which had occurred in the previous school year: in particular, the case of a 16-year-old student in Turin, who committed suicide because he had been a victim of constant homophobic bullying by his schoolmates[17]. This resolution had very little influence on the policy of the government, which faced a crisis the following year and resigned its mandate.

The second time the Italian Parliament discussed the problem of homophobia was with a question (No 4–04378) to the Ministry of Equal Opportunities on 9 March 2010. On that occasion, referring to new episodes of homophobia in Rome, Pisa, Pavia and Mestre (where, in particular, a 13-year-old boy was a victim of bullying by his schoolmates, who filmed him and published the video on a well-known social network), the Minister was again asked what kinds of initiatives the Government planned to address the escalating situation.

The Minister recalled the 8 October 2009 meeting with LGBT associations at the Ministry of Equal Opportunities, when the public campaign against homophobia was announced. It consisted of a television 'spot' against homophobia released on 9 November 2009 on all national television channels and a series of leaflets distributed in schools. There are no official data regarding the success of this campaign. The Minister also referred to an agreement with the Ministry of Education (signed on 3 July 2009) concerning 'Anti-Violence Week' (12–18 October 2009), the first of its kind within the Italian Government. This initiative produced public debates in the assemblies of secondary schools and institutions facing the problem of various kinds of bullying including homophobia. Under the agreement, parents should play a more active role in the activity promoted by

[15] Available at www.edscuola.it/archivio/norme/decreti/statuto3.html.
[16] Available at www.branchedati.camera.it/sindacatoispettivo_15/showXhtml.asp?high Light=0&idAtto=14642&stile=6.
[17] Available at www.arcigay.it/matteo,-martire-del-pregiudizio.

the Ministry of Education. The intention is to enhance awareness of the problem of discrimination among students of all schools, by promoting dialogue between teachers, students, psychologists and the police about discrimination based on race, religion or gender. The agreement also provides information about the need to respect the law and prevent any kind of violence including that based on discrimination, which is to be included in school curricula.

In addition to the meeting with LGBT associations and introducing 'Anti-Violence Week', the Minister noted the role played by UNAR (Office for the Elimination of Racial Discrimination), an institution directed by the Ministry for Equal Opportunities which also covers discrimination based on sexual orientation and gender identity. This office was created by Legislative Decree 215 of 9 July 2003, to implement Directive 2000/43/EC, and is regulated by the Decree of the President of the Council of Ministries of 11 December 2003. The Minister also drew attention to its 4 August 2008 agreement with the Italian Institute of Statistics (ISTAT) to develop a survey on discrimination based on gender, sexual orientation, gender identity and ethnic origin (results expected in 2011), and to agreements with local administrations, especially at the regional level, concerning the creation of anti-discriminatory centres with the aim of combating, among other things, homophobia (see also Trappolin and Motterle, chapter three in this volume).

It is too early to analyse the impact of these initiatives. The critical point is that the various agreements are too general and are not binding. Educational authorities remain free to decide when and how to deal with such a problem and, in the social context of Italian society, good intentions may have ineffectual results. A more active role has been played by local provincial or municipal administrations which, in cooperation with private LGBT associations, have promoted and financed activities with teachers to better identify strategies to combat homophobic bullying and to find ways to deal with the bullies and their victims.[18]

Despite the numerous cases of bullying in state schools and investigations carried out by LGBT associations,[19] there is very little case law related to homophobic bullying. One case may be given as an example,[20] because of its peculiarity and significance. In a secondary school, a student was bullying one of his schoolmates (an 11-year-old boy), preventing him from going into the boys' toilet and taunting him with expressions like: 'You can't get in, you are a gay, a wimp'. His teacher, realising what was happening (partly because some students told her), decided to give the bully special detention. She ordered him to write

---

[18] See, eg, the European NISO project, coordinated by the Province of Rome and started in April 2011. The project aims to promote a wider knowledge and understanding of fundamental rights among young people specifically in terms of the right to non-discrimination on the grounds of sexual orientation. The project will engage young people in an active research process based on active learning methods and promote a deeper understanding of LGBT people's rights as fundamental human rights.

[19] See above n 15.

[20] Court of Palermo, judgment of 27 June 2007.

out 'Sono un deficiente' ('I am stupid') one hundred times, to mark the seriousness of his behaviour and make an example of him for the other students. The student's parents responded by reporting the facts to the police and accusing the teacher of excessive punishment (Art 571, Penal Code). The court found the teacher not guilty: what she had done was the only effective way of punishing the student. This case highlights the need for national policies and programmes to provide teachers with the guidelines and support they need in order to protect their students from this kind of harassment and to teach respect for diversity.

Apart from primary and secondary schools, the particular situation of Italian universities must be examined. They legally enjoy an autonomy broader than that of schools, and have their own internal governance structure, covering all aspects of the administration of university life. Italian law only stipulates general principles concerning the methods of selecting professors, researchers and other employees, who are all public servants.

The recently issued 'University Act'[21] clearly requires universities to adopt an ethical code (Art 2(4)). Some universities had already adopted this kind of code, see for example, the University of Bologna's 2006 code,[22] Article 1 of which rejects every form of discrimination, including discrimination based on sexual orientation. No disciplinary proceedings can be initiated on the basis of this code, but the Rector (the head of the university) can admonish the person who infringed the regulation, either orally or in writing. The Academic Senate of the State University of Milan decided to take similar action after a homophobic episode.[23] The original idea behind this code was that it would form part of the employment contracts of those who work for the University, so that it could be legally enforced. In March 2010, an employee of the University verbally abused a 19-year-old student while he was putting up a poster advertising a discussion about a film with a gay theme. The employee praised violence against homosexuals, shouting at the student: 'Don't you dare put up another one or I'll kill you! You're the dregs of mankind, there's no place for you here!'[24] In addition to the new code, it is worth noting that the State University of Milan was the first

---

[21] The Italian Parliament has recently approved a new law concerning universities, the Parliamentary Act 40 2010, which has not changed the situation. In particular, the Act delegates to the government the power regulate Italian universities. The text of the Act is available at http://www.normattiva.it/uri-res/N2Ls?urn:nir:stato:legge:2010;240.

[22] Available at http://www.unibo.it/NR/rdonlyres/F77752F4–9741–4D2C-9378–707F227 1172C/65325/Codiceeticoversionefinaleedefinitivaago2006.pdf.

[23] See a reference to this code at www.universita.it/statale-milano-codice-etico-omofobia/.

[24] The facts have been reported by local newspapers. See,eg, www.milano.repubblica.it/ cronaca/2010/03/12/news/milano_omofobia_all_universita_statale_e_il_caso_finisce_al_ senato_accademico-2642066/.

university in Italy to start a course (from 20 January 2011) entitled 'Homosexuality: a world within the world', an optional course for students of law, philosophy, sociology and history.[25]

3.3. Sex Education in Schools

Convention underlies every society and there is no doubt that a culture of respect for others must be one of the first things taught in schools. In order to encourage respect for different sexual orientations, it is crucial for schools to provide proper sex education. In the early 1970s, a political and academic debate opened on the topic of sex education in all state schools. Especially important was the position of the Catholic Church, which plays an influential role in the political arena.[26] According to Catholic doctrine, the main teacher of sex education should be the family followed by the Church, and finally, in a complementary way, state institutions including schools.[27] This point of view was shared by some MPs, who considered it dangerous to legally authorise schools to educate children about sexuality, because it would conflict with the roles of the family and the Church. The parliamentary debate that began in 1975 has yet to end.

The first bill concerning sex education in state schools was presented on 13 March 1975 (Perico 1972; Bini 1975; Lener 1977; Galli 1979). It was followed by Bill 471 (Ferrari, 31 July 1979).[28] Bill 1315 (Anselmi, 23 January 1980),[29] and Bill 3711 (Greggi, 25 October 1982).[30] None of them was passed.

A new bill was presented during the XI Legislature (1992–94) on 10 November 1992.[31] The same text was presented during the XII Legislature (1994–96), as Bill 2389 (7 April 1995), during the XIII Legislature (1996–2001), as Bill 218 (9 May 1996), and during the XIV Legislature (2001–06), as Bill 354 (30 May 2001, Information and Sex Education in Schools).[32] The new bill seeks a balance

---

[25] All information is available on the website of the association of gay and lesbian students of the State University of Milan: www.gaystatalemilano.it/proj/lab_1011.php.

[26] The strict links between the Church and the Italian State have historical origins that cannot be explained here, but education is one of those matters (together with the family) that the Italian State left under the influence of the Church. For a recent comment on this issue see Prosdocimi 2006 and Locati 2009.

[27] See the Encyclical *Divinis Illius Magistri* by Pope Pio IX, dated 1931, quoted in the report to the Bill No 3711, 3.

[28] Available at legislature.camera.it/_dati/leg08/lavori/stampati/pdf/04710001.pdf. In the following legislature this bill was again proposed: see Bill 98 of 12 July 1983.

[29] Available at legislature.camera.it/_dati/leg08/lavori/stampati/pdf/04710001.pdf. See also Pieraccioni (1981) and Quarenghi (1983).

[30] Available at legislature.camera.it/_dati/leg08/lavori/stampati/pdf/37110001.pdf.

[31] Three different bills were unified: Bill 179 of 23 April 1992, presented by Deputy Artioli of the Socialist Party, Bill 954, presented by Deputy Poggiolini of the Republican Party, and Bill 1593 presented by Vendola and Mita of the Communist Party.

[32] The Bill is available on the website of the Italian Parliament at http://legxiv.camera.it/_dati/leg14/lavori/stampati/pdf/14PDL0000900.pdf.

between different political points of view, stipulating that state schools at every level, in cooperation with families, must make their contribution to inform and educate students in a culture of responsible sexuality (Art 1). This education, according to this bill, is not part of the school curriculum, but must be taught with the cooperation of teachers of various subjects (that is, it should be interdisciplinary; Art 2). The aim of sex education must be decided by the Ministry of Education with specific decrees, to be updated regularly (Art 3). At the same time, the teachers involved in these programmes must attend special courses (Art 4). In addition, schools, together with parents and (in the case of secondary schools) students, must plan special programmes for extracurricular activities, to be carried out with external experts. Lastly, the new bill provides for specific examinations on sex education in university courses for teachers.

The new bill was added to a more general bill on reform of the education system on 18 February 2003.[33] In the end, the political majority decided to delegate the content of school teaching programmes to the Government by Act 53/2003, which does not refer specifically to sex education. Article 2(1)(b) refers to the spiritual and moral education, also inspired by the principles of the Italian Constitution, but it is difficult to interpret this provision as including awareness of different sexual orientations. In the meantime, many private specialist associations offered courses for children although only a few schools were prepared to devote extracurricular hours to sex education. What is currently offered to students in Italian state schools is merely sex information (not education) offered by biology teachers. The topic of responsible sexual behaviour remains the monopoly of teachers of religion.

Although Parliament has failed to act, the Court of Cassation has stated a clear constitutional principle regarding sex education in schools. In a recent judgment, the court ruled that, under Articles 33 (freedom of teaching) and 34 (compulsory education) of the Italian Constitution, schools have the power to select programmes and educational methods, although these may be at odds with the values held by students' families.[34] Indeed, teachers should educate students in a way which may partially or totally contradict their families' cultural and political opinions, not only with reference to sex education, but also history, philosophy, science and citizenship education. The public interest in public education prevails over the right or duty of parents to educate their children. Parents may invoke a so-called 'legitimate interest', a weaker form of right that the court must balance against a superior general interest. Despite the court's judgment, it is

[33] First by another bill presented to the competent committee of the House of Deputies (No C 3387), available at legxiv.camera.it/_dati/leg14/lavori/bollet/frsmcdin.asp?percboll=/_dati/leg14/lavori/bollet/200211/1126/html/07/&pagpro=60n4&all=off&commis=07. See also Bill No S 1306-B (available at www.senato.it/leg/14/BGT/Schede/Ddliter/19153.htm) during the debate by the competent committee of the Senate.
[34] Court of Cassation, judgment of 5 February 2008 No 2656.

common to hear political statements that entirely ignore the constitutional protection of state schools.[35]

4. Free Movement, Immigration and Asylum

4.1. Homophobia and Immigration Laws in Italy

Limiting the fundamental right of free movement and family reunification enjoyed by all EU citizens, directly or indirectly on the basis of their sexual orientation, may be viewed as a form of homophobia.[36] Although no legal rule explicitly limits the rights to freedom of movement, family reunification, or asylum on the basis of sexual orientation (an explicit rule would be a clear and direct violation of the Italian Constitution, Art 3, principle of equality), in many situations, the exercise of these rights is precluded or made more difficult for homosexuals.

In Italian immigration and asylum law, an important role is played by European Union law, especially the Free Movement Directive 2004/38/EC, the Family Reunification Directive 2003/86/EC, and the Qualification Directive 2004/83/EC.[37]

On the one hand, implementation of these three directives obliged Italian legislators to amend very restrictive national rules. On the other hand, it has created a complex area of law, which varies between EU and non-EU citizens.

The general statute on immigration is Legislative Decree 286/1998 (Consolidation Act on Immigration, CAI),[38] which is now applicable to all non-EU citizens, and was twice amended to implement EU Directives. With regard to asylum,

---

[35] See Declaration of the President of the Italian Government: 'We will never let schools inculcate values different from those taught by families' (available at www.corriere.it/politica/11_febbraio_26/premier-pericolo-comunista_dc34f1e4–41a4–11e0-b406–2da238c0fa 39.shtml).

[36] In this sense, see comparative legal analysis by the European Union Agency for Fundamental Rights (2010) on homophobia, transphobia and discrimination on grounds of sexual orientation and gender identity.

[37] In its December 2008 report to the European Parliament and the Council on the application of Directive 2004/38/EC (Free Movement Directive), the Commission took the view that, while the interpretation given to 'family member' by the Member States during transposition of Article 2(2) was satisfactory, the transposition was 'less satisfactory' with regard to the rights of other family members under Art 3(2) of the directive. The European Parliament, citing the Fundamental Rights Agency report in its Resolution of 2 April 2009 on the application of Directive 2004/38/EC, expressed its concern about the 'restrictive interpretation by Member States of the notion of 'family member' (Art 2), of 'any other family member' and of 'partner' (Article 3), particularly in relation to same-sex partners, and their right to free movement under Directive 2004/38/EC' (Preamble, para S).

[38] Available at www.camera.it/parlam/leggi/deleghe/98286dl.htm.

Article 19(1)[39] stipulates a general principle of non-expulsion for members of certain social groups who are victims of persecution in their country of origin, even though they do not have refugee status.[40] This principle grants the minimum protection offered by Article 3 of the European Convention on Human Rights (ECHR), and prevents the state from expelling an immigrant who resides legally or illegally in Italy, even if the state claims that the immigrant is a threat to public order or national security.

Article 19(1) applies whether or not the individual has applied for refugee status or other subsidiary protection, if the judge establishes that there is a risk of persecution as a consequence of expulsion. If Article 19(1) applies, no crime is committed if a foreign national stays in Italy, notwithstanding a police order.

This protection clause is also acknowledged in Article 14 of Legislative Decree 251/2007, implementing Directive 2004/83/EC. This legislative act is very important, because it refers to sexual orientation as a possible reason for persecution that could justify an asylum claim. The Legislative Decree refers to sexual orientation in Article 8 (Reasons for persecution), Article 3 (Assessment of facts and circumstances) and Article 7 (Acts of persecution), which give new interpretations to the CAI, especially to Article 19(1), as will be explained later.

In order to complete the legal framework, it is also necessary to recall Legislative Decree 25/2008, implementing Directive 2005/85/CE, and later amended by Legislative Decree 159/2008 and Act 94/2009. The Legislative Decree 25/2008 regulates the procedure to obtain recognition of refugee status, whereas Legislative Decree 251/2007 covers the substance of the right to claim refugee status.

Also worthy of mention is Legislative Decree 5/2007, implementing Directive 2003/86/EC, which amends the provisions of the CAI concerning family reunification, with regard to non-EU citizens legally resident in an EU Member State, especially Article 29, and adds a new Article 29b on family reunification of refugees. The Legislative Decree restricts the right to obtain residence permits to the spouse, children and parents of the non-EU citizen.

As regards immigration of homosexuals as individuals and couples within the EU, the relevant statute is Legislative Decree 30/2007, which implemented Directive 2004/38/EC, and was later amended by Legislative Decree 32/2008. The 2007 Decree created a new set of regulations for EU citizens. From a brief reading of the parliamentary debates,[41] it is clear that the main concern of the Italian

---

[39] Legislative Decree 286/1998, Art 19: 'The expulsion of a foreign national who may be a victim of persecution because of race, gender, language, citizenship, religion, political opinions, or personal or social condition, or may risk being sent to another state where protection against persecution will not be afforded to that person, cannot be ordered'.

[40] Art 19(1), ibid, mentions gender and personal or social conditions, but not sexual orientation or gender identity.

[41] The whole discussion is available at legxv.camera.it/_dati/leg15/lavori/nfas/schededibattito/asp/NuovaScheda_xhtml.asp?sFile=IdDibNL2_3184.xml&ns=2&sFonte=B&Depu=&ancora=undefined.

Parliament was to avoid legitimating in the Decree what Italian family law does not recognise: a family outside the traditional concept of the union between a man and a woman who are legally married. Legislative Decrees 5/2007 and 30/2007 offer clear examples of a possible form of discrimination based on sexual orientation, because a key role is played by the legal concept of family or cohabitation and the evidence necessary to prove it.

The EU Directives and the Italian Decrees contain a definition of 'family member' referring to spouses, to registered partners (depending on the host state's treatment of registered partners) and de facto partners, which comes into conflict with Italian family law, which does not recognise same-sex marriage, any other form of same-sex registered partnership, or even same-sex de facto couples (Bilotta 2008; Bonini Baraldi 2010).

According to case law, a marriage (even when celebrated outside Italy) is recognised by the Italian State only if the partners are of different gender.[42] This approach was recently confirmed by the Italian Constitutional Court[43] which was asked to decide on the constitutionality of the articles of the Civil Code which appear to prohibit same-sex marriage. The constitutional judges refused to extend the general right to marry to homosexual couples, declaring that this decision was to be made by legislators and not by the courts.[44] Even the right to compensation for the death of a same-sex partner has no clear recognition in Italian case law, with the exception of two recent interim procedural decisions taken in a pending first instance case.[45]

---

[42] See, in particular, the Court of Latina, decree of 10 June 2005 No 3 (comments by Schlesinger 2005; Bonini Baraldi 2005; Cavana 2005; Orlandi 2005; Dosi 2005; Danovi 2006. See also Mosconi and Campiglio 2006: 62). On the judgment in the same case rendered by Court of Appeal of Rome, decree of 13 July 2006 (Sesta 2007), and an old case of the Court of Rome, 28 June 1980, comments by Galletto (1982).

[43] The latest decision of the Constitutional Court on this matter is order No 4/2011, issued on 5 January 2011, which rejected the review of constitutionality of Arts 93, 96, 98, 107, 108, 143, 143-bis, 156-bis and 231 of the Italian Civil Code, which refer to marriage as the union between a man and a woman. In this decision, the Court confirmed its precedents. See, in particular, judgment 138/2010, followed by order 276/2010. In the same sense, see also orders 16/2009, 34/2009, 42/2009. In its decision, the Constitutional Court stated that, according to existing laws, in particular Art 29 of the Constitution, that article must be interpreted in the light of existing law and it is not possible for the judiciary to create a new concept of family, which only legislators may do. On the interpretation of this judgment, Italian scholars disagree. See eg, D'Angelo, Spinelli, Silvis, Calzaretti, Melani, Pezzini, Pugiotto, Dal Canto, all available at www.giurcost.org/decisioni/index.html.

[44] It should be stressed that, in the above-mentioned decision 138/2010, the Constitutional Court, in affirming the competence of Parliament to regulate same-sex couples, recalled Art 2 of the Italian Constitution, which refers to the fundamental rights of human beings.

[45] See Order of the Court of Milan, 17 November 2009, according to which the same-sex partner may be part of the trial as a person who suffered from the commission of a crime. In the same sense, see Criminal Court of Rome, 2007.

4.2.   Free Movement and Family Reunification within the EU: Formal Implementation of EU Directives Conceals Discriminatory Regulations

In the above-mentioned legal framework, the regulations governing family reunification are different, not only for two EU citizens forming a couple, but also for an EU citizen and a non-EU citizen lawfully residing in another Member State, and an EU citizen and a non-EU citizen residing outside the EU. These differences derive from the different regulations that apply. In the first situation (two EU citizens), Legislative Decree 30/2007 applies. In the second situation (EU citizen and non-EU citizen legally residing in EU), Legislative Decree 5/2007 applies. The third situation (EU citizen and non-EU citizen residing outside the EU) would be governed by the general provisions of the CAI.

Let us examine an example of each situation. In the first situation, an Italian man asks his Spanish male partner (who is not a worker, a student, or self-employed or self-sufficient, and therefore does not have an independent right of residence) to join him in Italy. Because both are EU citizens, Legislative Decree 30/2007 applies. According to Article 2(1) of the Decree, a family member is the spouse, the registered partner (if the host state recognises that status), a child under the age of 21 or dependent, or a dependent parent. Article 2(1) does not explicitly exclude married or registered same-sex couples from the right of residence, but Italian courts may not interpret Article 2(1) in a way that contradicts the Civil Code, which clearly states that the only marriage that is valid in Italy is opposite-sex marriage.

As for registered partners, the Decree reproduces the wording of the EU Directive, even though this provision cannot be applied in Italy, which has no registered partnerships, even for opposite-sex couples. The only legally recognised family is that based on marriage. For same-sex couples, it is necessary to make reference to Article 3 of Legislative Decree 30/2007, which refers to unregistered, cohabiting partners. A same-sex couple, although legally married according to the law of another EU Member State (such as Spain), is treated by Italian law as an unmarried couple: their marriage is considered void (and in some cases totally non-existent)[46] as contrary to public order.

Article 3(2)(b) raises two questions. First, while Article 3(2)(b) of the Directive refers to 'the partner with whom the Union citizen has a stable relationship, duly attested', Article 3 of the Decree reads: 'the partner with whom the Union citizen has a stable relationship, duly attested by the State of the Union citizen'. The additional requirement, which is arguably contrary to the Directive, could exclude an EU citizen whose stable relationship is attested by a Member State other than their own, including an Italian citizen returning to Italy after living in

---

[46] For opinions expressed by Italian Courts on the recognition of a same-sex marriage, see nn 44 and 45.

another Member State. It should be noted that at the time of writing, the Law Decree no 89 of 23 June 2011 had changed the expression 'duly attested by the State of the Union citizen' with 'officially attested' (art 1(1) a): this amendment should have avoided the discriminatory effect towards same-sex couples whose relationship is not attested by the State. Unfortunately, in the conversion of the decree into Act 129 of 2 August 2011, this amendment has been removed. Secondly, Article 3(2) does not confer an absolute right as does Article 3(1), but rather imposes an undefined obligation to 'facilitate' entry and residence. Because Italian law does not identify the criteria to be applied when exercising discretion with regard to such applications, same-sex couples requesting residence receive inconsistent decisions from the public administration or the local courts. Should the partners demonstrate that they have a stable relationship by supplying letters, photographs or statements of witnesses? Are they required to produce legal certificates? Would these legal documents be recognised and accepted by the Italian administration and courts? Would the evidence of several years of cohabitation and the sharing of family responsibilities, such as bringing up a child, be sufficient?

4.3. Family Reunification with Non-EU Family Members: Reference to National Law excludes Same-sex Couples

The above-mentioned Legislative Decree 5/2007 (implementing Directive 2003/86/EC) modified Article 29 of the CAI, which provides that the Italian State shall authorise the entry and residence of the sponsor's spouse and the under-age children of the sponsor and her/his spouse. Italy chose not to exercise the option, under Article 4(3) of the Directive, to authorise the entry and residence of the

> unmarried partner, being a third-country national, with whom the sponsor is in a duly attested stable long-term relationship, or of a third-country national who is bound to the sponsor by a registered partnership.

This clear choice, confirmed by a recent judgment of the Court of Cassation,[47] did not take into account Article 5 of Directive 2003/86/EC: 'Member States should give effect to the provisions of this Directive without discrimination on the basis of … sexual orientation'.

The case of Roberto Taddeucci and Douglas McCall soon demonstrated the discriminatory effects of the Italian legislator's choice.[48] Mr Taddeucci, an Italian national, obtained from New Zealand recognition of de facto partner status with his partner, Mr McCall, who is a citizen of New Zealand. The administration denied Mr McCall a residence permit in Italy on the basis of a family tie with

---

[47] Court of Cassation, judgment of 17 March 2009 No 6441 (hearing on 30 September 2008). For a complete analysis of this important judgment which represents a precedent on this topic, see Acierno 2009: 458.

[48] Court of Appeal of Florence, judgment of 12 May 2006.

Mr Taddeucci. The Court of First Instance ruled that the permit should be granted, but the Ministry for Internal Affairs appealed. According to the Court of Appeal of Florence, Italian law requires Mr McCall to be a family member of Mr Taddeucci to qualify for a residence permit. Although New Zealand recognised the couple's status as cohabitants, New Zealand is not an EU Member State. As long as there is no Italian law recognising de facto unions for the purpose of immigration, family re-unification will not be available to same-sex couples. The decision of the Court of Appeal to reverse the trial court's decision was affirmed by the Court of Cassation (decision 6441, 17 March 2009). *Taddeucci & McCall v Italy* (Application No 51362/09) is, at the time of writing, pending before the European Court of Human Rights (ECtHR).

4.4. Asylum and Subsidiary Protection: Omissions of the Italian Legislature in Implementing Directive 2004/83/EC

As mentioned above, Legislative Decree 251/2007 (implementing Directive 2004/83/EC) is the main Italian law on the procedure for granting refugee status (which is also mentioned in the Constitution, Article 10(3)). Article 10(1)(d) of the Directive reads as follows:

> depending on the circumstances in the country of origin, a particular social group might include a group based on a common characteristic of sexual orientation. Sexual orientation cannot be understood to include acts considered to be criminal in accordance with national law of the Member States. Gender related aspects might be considered, without by themselves alone creating a presumption for the applicability of this Article.

However, Article 8(1)(d) of the Directive reads as follows:

> Depending on the circumstances in the country of origin, a particular social group might include a group based on a common characteristic of sexual orientation. Sexual orientation cannot be understood to include acts considered to be criminal in accordance with Italian law.

The reference to 'gender related aspects' was omitted to restrict interpretation of the expression 'sexual orientation'.

Under Articles 3 and 8 of the Decree, the individual claiming international protection must provide documentary or other evidence. But if none is available, the applicant's statements are sufficient, if they are found to be coherent, plausible and consistent with specific and general information relevant to the applicant's case. The application is more credible if it was made at the earliest possible time, unless the applicant can demonstrate a good reason for not having done so. In addition, Article 8 explains what may be considered acts of persecution, such as acts which are sufficiently serious by their nature or repetition as to constitute a severe violation of basic human rights, including: acts of physical or mental violence (including acts of sexual violence); legal, administrative, police and/or judicial measures which are in themselves discriminatory or which are implemented in a discriminatory manner; and prosecution or punishment which is disproportionate or discriminatory.

Despite the breadth of the Decree, the Court of Cassation has applied it in a very restrictive way. For example, the case of F (16417/2007),[49] involved a gay male citizen of Senegal where homosexuality is punished with imprisonment for between one and five years. In its decision, the Court of Cassation stated that homosexuality is a human condition worthy of protection and expression of personality pursuant to Article 2 of the Constitution. Persecution is a cruel form of minority oppression conducted in a way that is contrary to human rights. In order to grant asylum, evidence of the persecution of homosexual people in the applicant's country is required, and the homosexuality of the person who requests protection must be strictly proven. In stating these principles, the court quashed the first instance decision and sent the case to a second judge to determine whether in Senegal being homosexual is itself a crime (which can be prosecuted), or whether only homosexual practices are punished. Secondly, the second judge would have to verify that F's homosexuality has been proven, an oral interrogation being sufficient.

In 2008, the second judge (a Justice of the Peace in Turin), applying the Court of Cassation's principles, rejected the asylum petition, because Senegal's criminal law punishes immoral acts of homosexuals but not homosexuality as a condition in itself. The judge added that persecution in Senegal can easily be avoided by concealing one's sexual orientation.

The same approach was followed by the Court of Cassation in case 2907/2008,[50] in which S, a homosexual immigrant from Morocco, was expelled by a police order. The Court of Cassation remanded the case to the territorial court to ascertain whether Morocco punishes not only external manifestations of homosexuality (sexual behaviour), but also homosexuality as a personal condition (sexual orientation).[51] The judge must find a balance between public security and individual protection, partly because refugee status based on the risk of persecution is a special exemption.

In a more recent case,[52] the Court of Cassation followed its judgments 16417/2007 and 2907/2008. A Tunisian man claiming to be homosexual gave as evidence the testimony of a French national that he was a victim of persecution while in Tunis, because he had been found in an apartment having sex with

[49]   Court of Cassation, judgment of 25 July 2007 No 16417.

[50]   The Morocco case: *Public Prosecutor v S*, Decision of Court of Cassation, first criminal section, judgment 2907 dated 18 January 2008. The difference between this case and the Senegal case is the kind of liability. In the first case, the man was charged with having infringed the criminal law by staying illegally in Italy. In the second, the object of the case was the legitimacy of the police order of expulsion.

[51]   For an analysis of the legal reasoning used by the Court of Cassation on sexual orientation and behaviour in granting humanitarian protection, see section 6.2.

[52]   Court of Cassation, judgment of 28 October 2009 No 41368.

another man. But the court rejected the Tunisian man's appeal against expulsion, because there was not enough evidence to prove that homosexuals are persecuted in Tunisia simply because of their inclination, rather than because they practise their different sexuality.

These decisions of the Court of Cassation perfectly match the point of view constantly expressed by the Catholic Church.[53] The Vatican makes a clear distinction between sexual orientation (which can be understood as referring to feelings and thoughts), and sexual behaviour. Only criminalisation of the former (feelings and thoughts) is illegitimate because it violates human rights. Instead, it is possible to forbid some types of sexual behaviour (such as paedophilia and incest), as the state has the duty to regulate social behaviour. Similarly, when the Court of Cassation declares that LGBT status is worthy of international protection, it implicitly states that it is legitimate to punish a homosexual person simply because that person decides to express her/his sexuality in a sexual relationship. This reasoning conflicts with the ruling of the European Court of Human Rights in *Dudgeon v United Kingdom* that private same-sex sexual activity is protected by Article 8 of the ECHR.[54]

Some first instance courts have taken a completely different approach. For example, the Justice of Peace of Genoa held on 10 July 2010 that DO, an Ecuadorian gay citizen, could not be expelled because of the risk of violence and discrimination in his country, even though the crime of 'homosexualism' was struck out by the Constitutional Court of Ecuador in 1997. The judge recognised his right to international protection because public authorities in Ecuador tolerate violence against homosexual people. In particular, she quoted Article 10 of the Italian Constitution:

> The foreigner who is denied in his own country the real exercise of democratic liberties guaranteed by the Italian Constitution has the right of asylum in the territory of the Republic, in accordance with the conditions established by law.

A case decided in May 2011 by the Commission of Caserta may give the Court of Cassation an opportunity to reconsider its case law. In 2008, Joshua, a 28-year-old Nigerian gay man and a member of a Christian community, escaped from Nigeria where he might have been tortured and sentenced to death, after his male friend's Muslim family had discovered their sexual relationship and reported it to the police. In February 2008, the *Nigeria Observer* published his picture and details of the warrant for his arrest, in which the police promised a reward for handing him over to the authorities. If he is forced to return to Nigeria, Joshua could be imprisoned for 14 years and subjected to 100 lashes. He

---

[53] See 'Vatican addresses UN debate on sexual orientation', statements of the Permanent Representative of the Holy See to the United Nations in Geneva at the 16th Session of the Human Rights Council available at www.radiovaticana.org/EN1/Articolo.asp?c=471925.

[54] *Dudgeon v United Kingdom*, App No 7525/76, Council of Europe: European Court of Human Rights, 22 October 1981, available at: http://www.unhcr.org/refworld/docid/47fdfaf7d.html.

would also risk, according to the principles of sharia law, being killed by the fundamentalist tribe to which his friend's family belonged.

5. Cross-border Reproductive Services

5.1. Legislation and Parliamentary Debates

Act 40/2004 (19 February 2004) was the first law passed by the Italian Parliament to regulate Assisted Reproductive Technologies (ART). Before that time, almost any form of ART was available, at least in a private clinic, if a patient requested it and a doctor was willing to provide it. Even Act 40/2004 does not respond to all the social questions relating to the complex world of parenthood. At a first reading, the law appears to be a list of prohibitions, only allowing ART in a very small number of cases. Instead of balancing the desire for parenthood with the possibilities opened up by new technologies, the law expresses a very conservative viewpoint on reproduction, and some of its articles appear to violate rights recognised by the Italian Constitution.

Act 40/2004's regulation of ART is made up of so many prohibitions, and such detailed bureaucratic procedures, that it greatly restricts access to ART and prevents many categories of people from becoming parents. It forbids the donation of both sperm and ova, and also heterologous insemination (use of any sperm other than the sperm of the woman's male partner). In other words, single women and homosexual couples are not allowed to use ART. Only heterosexual couples are allowed to use ART but even they are required to use their own reproductive material.

Article 4 states that recourse to ART is allowed only when the impossibility of removing the causes which do not allow procreation have been medically ascertained (even if the causes cannot be explained), or in a case of medically certified sterility or infertility. Article 5 states that subjects allowed to use ART must be adult couples, of different gender, married or living together, both of an age of potential fertility and alive at the time of recourse to ART. Article 12(6) prohibits surrogate maternity and provides for prison sentences of up to two years and fines of €600,000 to €1,000,000 for anyone who practices or promotes it. This means that no-one, neither an individual nor a couple, can turn to a woman who is willing to 'lend' her own uterus and, if deemed to be useful, her reproductive material, for the period of the pregnancy. Act 40/2004 also prohibits couples who are fertile but have genetic disorders from using diagnostic tech-niques to ascertain the health of an embryo.

After approval of law 40/2004, discontent about its restrictions produced a social and political movement opposed to its limitations and four referendums for its partial repeal were proposed in December 2004. Briefly, the four referen-dum questions were: (1) to cancel the reference to the rights of embryos; (2) to cancel the prohibition of heterologous insemination; (3) to cancel the ban on producing more than three embryos at the same time; and (4) to cancel the prohibition of scientific research on embryos. Many movements and groups (women's movements, movements for the development of scientific research, and in general all LGBT movements) actively intervened in the debate supporting the pro-referendum campaign, often clashing with the so-called 'pro-life' movement, and Catholic morality and ethics. Because of the large-scale campaign for abstention made by the Catholic organisations, the position of the highest ecclesiastical hierarchies, and the lack of concern on the part of much of the population, the referendum on 12–13 June 2005 did not reach its quorum, leaving the situation unchanged.

5.2.   Prohibitions and Legislative Vacuums: Consequences and Effects

The first effect of Italian restrictions on the use of ART was greatly to increase so-called 'procreative tourism' to states where these techniques are easily accessible. 'Procreative tourism' is a real phenomenon involving lesbian and gay people in Italy, who escape to countries which, compared with Italy, are considered procreative paradises (Falletti 2007). For example, on 23 December 2002 Greece passed a law allowing the use of heterologous insemination, insemination of single women, *post mortem* insemination, and surrogate maternity. For heterosexual women with no male partner and lesbian women living alone or with a female partner, the problem is slightly simpler than for gay men. Indeed, a fertile woman can become pregnant by resorting to a donor (anonymous or not) in a European country that allows the use of heterologous ART by women without male partners, and then manage the pregnancy and childbirth in Italy. In such cases, there are no legal prohibitions to recognising that the woman who gives birth to a child is that child's biological mother, even if a woman has another woman's fertilised ovum implanted in her own uterus (Schuster 2011). However, Italian law does not permit the woman's female partner to adopt the child and become its second legal parent.

For gay men, either single or living as a couple, the situation is more difficult, because a man cannot have a child without a woman's aid. One option in these cases is surrogate maternity. It generally involves two women: the donor, who gives ova, and the carrier, who accepts the fertilised ova, continues the pregnancy and gives birth to a child. This child is the natural child of the man who provided the sperm, who therefore becomes its legal guardian. The carrier renounces all rights to the child before its birth, or immediately after, and in the future will not be considered in any way the legal parent of the child (Schuster 2011). Of great importance is the contribution of each person involved, the genetic mother, the carrier mother of an embryo which is not hers, and the man who fertilised the first woman's ovum. This type of situation requires clear agreements identifying the rights and choices of all those involved.

It is important to stress that surrogate maternity is strictly forbidden in Italy and in many European countries, or is permitted with considerable restrictions. At the time of writing, for gay men, surrogate maternity is practical only in some states of the USA (especially California) and a few other countries such as India and Ukraine. Article 12(6) of Act 40/2004 states:

> Any person who, in any form, creates, organises or advertises the marketing of gametes, embryos or subrogation of maternity shall be punished ....

However, Article 3 of the Italian Penal Code states that the conduct which constitutes a crime must take place in Italy. Therefore, if the practice is performed abroad, in countries where it is lawful, it should not be a crime under Italian law.

5.3. Case Law

The only case law on parenthood and homosexuality deals with separation of spouses and custody of their children, in which the condition of homosexuality of one of the two parents is declared and is often the reason for the separation (Oberto 2010). As required by *Mouta v Portugal* (1999), Italian courts have recently developed a positive attitude towards the condition of homosexuality of one of the spouses. They have ruled that cohabitation of an ex-spouse with a partner of the same sex is not sufficient reason to derogate from the strong presumption of joint custody for both parents of the child(ren).[55]

On 28 June 2006, the Court of Naples, in a case of separation of spouses, affirmed the suitability of the homosexual parent to have custody of the minor, affirming that

> the attitude of more or less veiled hostility towards homosexuality on these matters is the result of mere pseudo-cultural stereotypes, expressions of moralism and not shared ethical principles, without, however, a legal basis ... Indeed, homosexuality is a personal condition, and not a disease; likewise, homosexual relations are not, in themselves, risk factors or reasons for a negative juridical evaluation when compared with heterosexual relations. Parents' homosexuality is considered—for this matter—not differently from political, cultural and religious preferences, which are irrelevant for the purposes of custody. This is even truer with reference to high socio-cultural contexts, like that of one of the parties, where ancient prejudices towards homosexuality should be over-looked.

Similarly, on 15 July 2008, the Court of Bologna concluded that the homosexuality of one of the parents did not justify an exceptional grant of exclusive custody to the other parent. The parent's homosexuality was not a reason to

---

[55] See Art 155 *et seq* of the Italian Civil Code, after the reform on joint custody (Law 54 2006).

derogate from the rule of joint custody, since homosexuality does not affect a parent's capacity to raise their children.

In Italy, these decisions constitute an important acknowledgement of the suitability of gay people to undertake parental roles, and further the desire of some for parenthood. However, the cases concerned family ties which were already in place. ART raises the question of whether there exists in Italy a right to procreation, or a right to be a parent. On this topic, there are important judgments of the Court of Rome which, in dealing with surrogacy (before Law 40/2004 was passed) acknowledge that surrogacy agreements involve interests that deserve legal protection. The court interpreted the couple's aspiration to parenthood as the expression of a 'genuine right to procreate', based on the broader right, guaranteed and protected by the Italian constitution, to the manifestation and development of one's personality.[56] In this case, the Court of Rome, in opposition to the decisions of other courts (for example, Monza[57]), considered ART as a way to satisfy the desire to be a parent and the right to procreate. This was why they considered surrogacy lawful.

After Act 40/2004 was passed, surrogacy agreements, on which previously courts had expressed their opinions by invoking the right to procreation, became unlawful. This has not prevented Italian courts from addressing the important issues of the right to procreate, protection of the status of women, and the right to health of those involved, in cases requiring a constitutionally valid interpretation of Act 40/2004.[58] In particular, the civil courts of Florence and Catania[59] have raised the issue of the constitutional validity of the prohibition of heterologous insemination in Act 40/2004, Article 4(3), under Articles 2, 3, 31, 32 and 117 of the Constitution. They did so because of the ECtHR's Chamber judgment in *SH & Others v Austria* (1 April 2010; reversed by Grand Chamber hearing on 3 November 2011). In finding a violation of Article 14 combined with Article 8 ECHR, the Chamber held that, when it is a matter of an important aspect of an individual's private life, the regulatory power of the state had to be limited. Considering that the desire to have a child was a particularly important aspect, the prohibition of heterologous ART did not represent a proportionate solution.

Inspired by the ECtHR, Italian courts have raised the question of the constitutional legitimacy of the absolute prohibition of heterologous ART, which affects a fundamental right, the right to procreation, and discriminates against sterile or infertile couples according to the gravity of their pathological condition. The future decision of the Constitutional Court could represent an important opening in the field of ART in Italy, even though it would not affect the restriction of

[56] Court of Rome, 17 February 2000 and 27 March 2000.
[57] Court of Monza, 27 October 1989.
[58] Verdict No 151/09 of the Constitutional Court which rephrased Art 14 of Law 40, removing the duty to implant no more than three embryos, their simultaneous implantation, and the prohibition of cryoconservation of other embryos produced.
[59] Court of Florence, 13 September 2010, and Court of Catania, 21 October 2010.

ART to heterosexual couples. It could constitute an important affirmation of the right to procreation and a signal of hope that, in the near future, single and gay people might also be granted access to ART.

6. Law, Politics and Homophobia

6.1. Stereotypes, Prejudice and Stigma: The Challenge of States

There is a flourishing sociological and anthropological literature on stereotypes, prejudice and stigma in society, which are important causes of discrimination (see Fredman 2002). Scholars have emphasised how these phenomena can be analysed as ideological assumptions about the social classification of groups and the perpetuation of differentiated access to power and resources (Boni 2008: 23). The simplified interpretation of society as a collection of social groups (internally homogeneous and externally different from all other groups) implicitly denies heterogeneity, subjectivity and agency to social actors. 'Differences' between social groups thus become the main parameter used to activate including/excluding mechanisms. On the basis of factors such as race, gender, religion and sexual orientation people are catalogued, interpreted, accused, defended or reduced. The presumed 'value system' of a social group is attributed to all of its 'members', and 'difference' becomes the ideological ratio for discrimination.

From a sociological or anthropological perspective, although discrimination mechanisms operating in society have been well identified and described, it is not always easy to talk openly about 'discrimination' within legal systems. Both politicians and lawyers are influenced by the society they grew up in and live in. They may therefore incorporate (sometimes critically) stereotypes, prejudices, and even social stigma towards certain groups. Their most difficult and important challenge is how to avoid these factors (little direct knowledge, or fear of or prejudice against, the group) influencing their judgement and their work. Apart from the potentially prejudiced thinking of these individual actors, the difficulty, legally speaking, is to determine when a state is in breach of its constitutional and international duties of non-discrimination, equal treatment and respect for human dignity. Although it is clear that discrimination mechanisms operate at the social level, it is sometimes harder to conceptualise discrimination by the law. Yet the collective decisions of members of a legislature to pass new discriminatory laws, to refuse to repeal existing ones, or to refuse to prohibit discrimination by public and private actors, can hardly be described as anything other than 'discrimination by the law'.

This book seeks to examine how states react to social claims by LGBT citizens by means of a cross-comparative method. Through four case studies, the juridical analysis has tried to show, on the one hand, the various 'legal boundaries' an EU Member State can call into question when rejecting specific claims to rights and, on the other hand, the solutions other EU Member States may adopt in accepting and regulating those same claims. This analysis shows how legal frameworks can, in the presence of political will, move beyond their own boundaries and how change, challenges and demands arise which require continuous remodeling of our juridical structures. We do not argue here that legal boundaries are only used instrumentally as an excuse to reject new demands for rights, but that politics has the power to determine the agenda for legal change. This may happen for many reasons (primarily electoral advantage), but what we examine below is whether politicians and law professionals, when explaining their rejection of certain claims, can be influenced by, and use in their decisions, the same prejudices that the law (at a higher and 'ideological' level) is presumed to combat in the name of equality. This means critically analysing the surviving contradictions of modern states, which are deemed to be based on strong democratic and egalitarian legal frameworks (in which discrimination is prohibited) while still having serious difficulty in guaranteeing equality for all 'citizens' (in a broad sense), regardless of their being part of some so-called 'minority group'. The following analysis focuses on the Italian case.

6.2.   'Being Homosexual' and 'Acting in a Homosexual Manner': Judicial Reasoning about Sexual Behaviour

Article19 of Legislative Decree 289/98 forbids the expulsion of foreign citizens from Italy to a state where they may be persecuted for, among other things, their sexual orientation. Three interesting judgments of the Court of Cassation trace the limits to this protection. The three judgments, dealing with citizens of Senegal, Morocco and Tunisia, claiming to be gay and seeking refugee status in Italy, were discussed in section 4.4.

How is it possible, from a juridical point of view, to explain such a differentia-tion, that is the separation of homosexuality from sexual behaviour? Can sexual identity and behaviour be considered as two separate spheres with only the former deserving legal protection? What kind of humanitarian protection is the system actually offering to foreigners, if they can be repatriated to the country which 'merely' persecutes their behaviour? The message from the Court of Cassation seems to be: 'Act like a heterosexual and you won't be persecuted'. This interpretation is based on the common prejudice that homosexuality may be considered as something which people may legitimately be asked to hide, a 'practice' which should be carried out in private because it is socially embarrass-ing. No humanitarian protection is therefore granted when persecution in that country is the consequence of actions revealing, as the court affirms, 'diverse sexuality' or even 'indecent behaviour in public'. Is this interpretation based, not on strong judicial reasoning, but on a common prejudice influenced by the 'naturalisation' of heterosexuality and the hierarchisation of sexuality? As shown in the following paragraphs, this 'naturalistic' interpretation of heterosexuality is not confined to decisions of the Court of Cassation.

6.3. The Italian Constitution: The Concept of Family as 'Natural Society' and Heterosexuality as a Social Model

It is perhaps superfluous to stress that discrimination based on sexual orientation, at least against lesbian, gay and bisexual individuals (and in some cases also against same-sex couples), is forbidden in Italy and all EU Member States. Despite this, the Italian political system on one hand and the judiciary on the other, still have difficulty—for different reasons—in handling many demands made by LGBT people. How do politicians and lawyers explain barriers to the evolution of LGBT rights? What kind of political, legal or social discourse is used to forbid advances on these grounds? Is political and legal discourse influenced by stereotypes and stigma towards this group?

As seen in section 4, the concept of family in Italian law, important for freedom of movement and family reunification, is that of a heterosexual married couple, in conformity with a narrow interpretation of Article 29 of the Italian Constitution, which excludes homosexual or heterosexual unmarried couples.[60] Article 29 subsection I(1), states: 'The Republic recognises the rights of the family as a natural society founded on marriage.' The debate on what the adjective 'natural' actually means is vast and we cannot analyse it in detail here. Briefly, we emphasise that, during the debate on Article 29 within the 'Constituent Assembly' (the body charged with drafting the Constitution between June 1946 and January 1948), the Christian Democrat Party struggled for and gained the insertion of this formula defining the family as a 'natural society', affirming an original right which pre-existed the state, and also limiting recognition of the family to the model regulated by the state (marriage). No explicit reference to heterosexual couples was inserted in the text, but the widespread interpretation of this article (by scholars, judges and politicians) was that it applied only to different-sex couples.

Although the Constituent Assembly certainly had in mind, at that time, the heterosexual family, the tendency by many politicians (and some scholars) to stand by that interpretation of the norm has frozen the evolution of LGBT rights. The continued reference to the original desire of the 'founding fathers' to regulate only married couples leads to controversial results.

First, it allows 'naturalisation' of the concept of heterosexuality, which acquires a superior status because it is seen as 'natural behaviour', as the 'natural' social model to which all other forms of sexuality must be compared, and the mechanism of reproduction of the social (and biological) order. Therefore, even though homosexuality is accepted in the private sphere, it becomes unacceptable

---

[60] On the legal concept of family in Italian law, see section 4.1.

when it publicly claims to be equivalent to heterosexuality (Borrillo 2009: 11). Homophobia may thus be considered, at least in part, as the fear that this identity may be publicly acknowledged.

Secondly, the reference to a static concept of 'family' does not allow the necessary continuous reinterpretation of the concept of 'culture' on which it is based. The concept of culture which underlies the interpretation of Article 29 is evidently essentialist: culture is considered as a static set of values, incapable of change over time. In this view, the idea of family of the Constitutent Assembly in 1946 was the same as that of the Italian legal framework of that period. In these circumstances, Italian society does evolve, but its legal foundations remain inert and unaccepting of social change. This strict interpretation of Article 29 of the Constitution traces a kind of undefeatable anthropological and cultural model of the heterosexual family. We can see some examples of this attitude in the following case.

In its decision of 10 June 2005 regarding a request for recognition and transcription in the public registry of a same-sex marriage contracted in the Netherlands, the Court of Latina explained:

> The Constituent Assembly, when recognising 'the rights of the family as a natural society' wished to refer to the traditional relationship of marriage between persons of different sex, according to an interpretation founded, even before that in law, on the sentiment, culture and history of our national community', and, 'given the evolution of Italian society, same-sex marriage conflicts with the history, tradition and culture of the Italian community, as acknowledged by the law ... which no evolutive interpretation, even sympathetic towards a shared social feeling, could overcome.[61]

This narrow interpretation of Italian 'culture' evidently tends to leave the difference unchanged and prevents legal change through the recognition of new rights and new social realities. Anthropologically speaking, the court saw the Italian social system as unvaried in a diachronic sense. The concepts and meanings used by the Constituent Assembly have remained unchanged as far as the social meaning of the family is considered. 'Culture' is described as a static 'heritage', rooted in the moral value of heterosexuality as a 'natural' issue, simply recognised by the law.

In addition to this, we must emphasise that, even when judges do not share this kind of interpretation of society, the possibilities of recognising new forms of partnerships in the Italian legal system are quite limited in the absence of new legislation. Refusal to transcribe the relationships of same-sex couples (registered outside Italy) in the Italian system has been upheld by other courts: examples are the Court of Appeal of Rome (13 July 2006), the Court of Appeal of Florence (27 May 2008), the Court of Venice (4 February 2009), and the Court of Turin (18 May 2009).

---

[61] See above n 42.

Judges are asking for modifications to be made to the Italian legal framework, but see themselves as powerless to make them. In all these cases, they base their reasoning on two essential legal arguments: (a) because there is no binding legislation at European level on same-sex marriage, every state is free to regulate the matter, and no automatic translation of new family systems from other national systems can be authorised; and (b) only legislators, and not judges considering the evolution of habits and changes in society, can define the status of same-sex couples. Thus no tortuous interpretation of the law is necessary to force the recognition of new social realities.[62]

It seems obvious that a political step is required to give judges the instruments they need to respond to social claims. But we should ask ourselves: is the idea of 'family' described above shared among politicians? What causes the reluctance to give Article 29 a broader interpretation? What do politicians think about LGBT claims? In the following sections, we shall see that the silence of the law in many cases reflects the discomfort, difficulty or unwillingness of the political class to adapt the Italian legal framework to social changes.

6.4. The Ghosts of Politicians: Parliamentary Debates on Homosexuality and Homophobia

The first parliamentary debate on homosexuality took place during the discussion of Law Decree 122/1993, outlining emergency measures against 'racial, ethnic and religious discrimination'. On this occasion, a proposal to extend all provisions against racism to crimes committed on the grounds of sexual orientation was submitted, which would have put homophobia and racism on an equal footing. This proposal was not included in the final text of Law 205/1993 (the so-called Mancino Law), which was limited to racism. Only 10 years later, to comply with its EU obligation to implement Council Directive 2000/78/EC, Italy had to adopt its first law (Legislative Decree 216/2003) against discrimination based on sexual orientation. During the Prodi Government in 2007, a bill on same-sex unions was discussed, but the collapse of the government ended the debate.

In Section 2.2 the legal arguments used by politicians to postpone the draft bill on 'hate crimes' have been described. Here, we analyse the 'social' arguments which politicians involved in the debate used to justify their unwillingness to approve the bill and ask whether stigma and prejudice do operate and produce definite effects even in political debate.

---

[62] The decisions of the Constitutional Court described in section 4.1 are particularly interesting. The Court stressed how, according to existing laws, in particular Art 29 of the Constitution, it is not possible for the judiciary to create a new concept of family, because this power lies only in the hands of legislators.

Luca Rodolfo Paolini, a member of the Northern League Party, criticised several parts of the proposal. First, in his opinion, the phenomenon of homophobia in Italy did not reach the 'dramatic' dimensions described by Arcigay. By belittling the phenomenon of homophobia and downgrading it to simple episodes of 'taunting', he characterised the bill as punishing behaviour which, although contemptible, does not deserve to be treated as a crime. Secondly, he argued that extending hate crime legislation to sexual orientation would be an unacceptable restriction of freedom of expression, for example, his own party's ability to oppose joint adoption by same-sex couples.

Roberto Rao, an MP for the Christian Democratic Union, added a 'biological' explanation for his opposition to the proposal. Although homophobia must be socially stigmatised, ascribing gender differences to Article 3 of the Constitution (on equality) would lead to misinterpretation of the Constitution. Sexual differences, in Rao's opinion, are biological, and differentiate men and women:

> Admitting that sexual difference is due to cultural influence or orientation, as a subjective interpretation of sexual desire, which could change during people's lives, would clear the way for an intolerable degenerative spiral of all principles and fundamentals of our society and culture ... Embracing the ideology of gender means contesting the more widely related concept of the family as a union founded on marriage and the general natural interpretation of affection and sexuality.[63]

Anti-discrimination measures should cover only 'sex' discrimination, because the concept of gender, in his opinion, 'may refer to transexuality, intersexuality and transgender status, which could eventually be addressed by an ad hoc provision'. Sexual orientation should be replaced by 'homosexuality', as the former 'may entail all sexual tendencies including incest, paedophilia, zoophilia, sadism, masochism and other sexual choices'. Besides his biological discourse, Rao emphasised how the legislative proposal could create intolerance towards those people who, according to their ethical or religious beliefs, defend 'the importance of nature before the law', and 'heterosexuality as an indispensable condition of anthropological identity and sociality'. Finally, he explained that, as it was impossible to identify clearly the motive for a crime, the victim of violence based on sexual orientation would be granted a privileged position when compared with any other kind of victim, violating the principle of equality stated in Article 3 of the Constitution.

In his report to the Justice Committee, Mario Ronco (a professor of criminal law at the University of Padova) criticised the proposal for other reasons. In his view, including sexual orientation among discriminatory factors would lead to the dangerous situation of excessively increasing the number of types of behaviour believed to be discriminatory. In his view, discrimination is a broad concept,

---

[63] http://www.camera.it/453?bollet=_dati/leg16/lavori/bollet/200909/0915/html/02#INT18n1.

and labelling discrimination on the basis of sexual orientation as a hate crime would unacceptably increase the role of criminal law.

As an example of what he defines as an 'aberrant consequence', Professor Ronco described the case of a mother who tried to persuade her daughter not to marry a bisexual man because it would damage the stability of their family, or the case of a father who would not let his son rent an apartment (owned by his father) if he were to live in it with a same-sex partner. In his opinion, these examples demonstrated how constitutional rights would be narrowed by such a provision, which would violate Article 21 (freedom of expression) and Article 30 (right of parents to educate their children) of the Constitution. Even freedom of association and freedom of religion would be violated if this proposal were to become law, putting at risk those religious doctrines and educational systems which defend the supremacy of heterosexuality under natural law. In addition, Professor Ronco stressed that including 'gender identity' as a discriminatory factor would make it impossible to criticise those kinds of sexual behaviour labelled as paraphilia (including sadism or masochism). Besides the risk of restricting important constitutional rights, he emphasised the risk that hate crimes could subvert criminal law as law based on objective facts. Hate, in his view, is 'a passion naturally embodied in human psychology' which acquires importance only once it leads to a criminal offence.

According to Professor Ronco's argument, prohibiting hate crime is extremely dangerous for the freedom of citizens, because hate crimes are essentially founded on private and often unconscious motives. Criminal law would undergo a disproportionate process of ethicisation. Discrimination based on racial, ethnic, or religious factors regulated by the Mancino Law, was an exception within the system of criminal law, which finds an explanation in historical reasons and on the level of violence often attained by these acts. Conversely, extending the provisions of the Mancino Law to discrimination on the grounds of sexual (or even gender) orientation would constitute a clear signal of unacceptable trespassing from 'criminal law based on facts' to 'criminal law based on intimate attitudes'. Lastly, in his opinion, the real aim of the proposal was to promote values centred on the denial of morphological sexual differences.

The ideas expressed by these MPs and by Professor Ronco reveal the fear and prejudice towards homosexuality which is still harboured in political and social discourse. Sexual differences are described as mere biological facts, differentiating men and women. Accepting homosexuality as a sexual orientation, on the same level as heterosexuality, represents a great danger for the 'values' of 'mainstream heterosexual Italian society'. The discourse is too often focused on offensive or irrelevant comparisons between homosexuality and incest, paedophilia, zoophilia, sadism or masochism. The opening of the legal system to LGBT protection and rights would therefore represent not only a 'cultural' threat but also a religious threat: what would happen, asked Professor Ronco, to all those people who 'legitimately' defend the supremacy of heterosexuality under natural law? Do we want expression of religious belief to be restricted in the name of homosexual rights? The question seems to be: do we really want to challenge our cultural foundations by recognising homosexuality as equal to heterosexuality?

Describing heterosexuality as a social value, a cultural pattern and a religious belief is often a useful way to postpone legal reforms relating to LGBT civil rights and discrimination on the grounds of sexual orientation. The unwillingness or inability to find a political solution permitting legal reforms does not help either judges or society. This kind of political discourse and the silence of the law are blocking the evolution of the Italian legal system and political and social debate. The courts alone cannot respond to social claims, and cannot take Parliament's place in filling legal gaps. And society, for its part, cannot regulate itself: it needs a clear legal framework and the definition of new rights.

9

Traits of Homophobia in Slovenian Law: From Ignorance towards Recognition?

NEŽA KOGOVŠEK ŠALAMON

1. Hate Crime and Hate Speech

In general, Slovenian law cannot be described as directly homophobic. There are no provisions that prohibit homosexual behaviour in a way that would be different from heterosexual sexual behaviour of the same kind. For example, sexual intercourse with a person under the age of 15 is prohibited, regardless of whether it is homosexual or heterosexual. In other words, the minimum age of consent is the same for homosexuals as heterosexuals.

Before going into details, it should be stressed that the term 'homophobia' (in Slovenian *homofobija*) does not occur at all in the criminal legislation and is not defined in the Slovenian Language Dictionary.[1] If the law addresses the issue of homophobic violence, it uses more general terms, such as unequal treatment on the grounds of sexual orientation. For that matter, provisions concerning hate crimes and hate speech in the Slovenian legal system must be analysed in the wider context of both anti-discrimination and criminal law.

1.1. Legislation against Hate Crime and Hate Speech: Incitement to Hatred, Violence and Intolerance based on Sexual Orientation

The main source of criminal law provisions related to the prohibition of hate crime is the Criminal Code,[2] which defines the crime of the violation of equality (Article 131) and the crime of incitement to hatred, violence and intolerance (Article 297). The latter provision in fact criminalises both hate speech and some forms of hate crime. Article 297 (incitement to hatred, violence and intolerance) states that one who publicly encourages or incites ethnic, racial, religious or other

---

[1] Available at bos.zrc-sazu.si/sskj.html.
[2] Kazenski zakonik (KZ-1), Uradni list RS, št 55/2008.

hatred or intolerance, or incites another type of intolerance based on physical or intellectual impairment or *sexual orientation*, is liable to imprisonment for a maximum of two years (section 1). The fact that sexual orientation is included as a motive in Article 297 of the Criminal Code is the result of recent developments. That is, the definition of this crime was revised in 2008, as the same provision in the 1994 Criminal Code[3] did not cover sexual orientation-related motives; it covered only motives based on race, ethnicity and religion. The definition of the then Article 300 stated that

> whoever provokes or spreads ethnic, racial or religious hatred or spreads ideas of superiority of one race over another, or provides any kind of assistance at racial activities, or denies, minimises the meaning of, approves of or advocates genocide, shall be punished with imprisonment of up to two years.

With the addition of the concept of *sexual orientation* (in Slovenian *spolna usmerjenost*) to the law, a problem might arise regarding the meaning of this concept. The Slovenian Language Dictionary does not define the term; it only defines 'homosexuality' with the words 'sexual inclination towards persons of the same sex'. Accordingly, it is not surprising that, particularly in parliamentary debates by opponents of equal rights for same-sex couples, sexual orientation is often mentioned together with various types of sexual deviation, such as paedophilia or incest.[4]

The insufficient protection of the 1994 Criminal Code which prohibited only hate speech concerning race, ethnicity and religion has also been mentioned in parliamentary debates. For example, a member of the National Assembly, Ms Majda Širca, highlighted the fact that the existing article prohibiting hate speech is outdated, as it does not offer protection to groups defined on other personal grounds, including sexual orientation. She proposed a provision which would include an open-ended list of grounds that would offer protection from hate speech based on any personal grounds. In the debate, Ms Širca invoked the position taken by legal theory in the field of criminal law which was of the opinion that the law should be amended in this respect.[5] Although the first proposal for the new Criminal Code did not foresee any change to the previous Article 300, after this parliamentary debate the need for revision was considered and the provision was finally changed, with a view to offering protection to groups defined not by an open-ended list of grounds, but specifically by listed personal circumstances, which included sexual orientation. The reason for not retaining an open-ended list of grounds and for specifying instead the grounds on which hate speech is prohibited, is that an open-ended list of grounds would

---

[3] Kazenski zakonik (KZ), Uradni list RS no 63/1994, as amended.

[4] See, eg, the discussion of France Cukjati, member of the Slovenian Democratic Party, 19th Regular session (part 5) of 31 March 2011.

[5] Majda Širca, member of the ZARES parliamentary group, 38th Regular Session of the National Assembly of 8 November 2007.

be too general and flexible (and could lead to the limitations of freedom of speech known under the previous communist regime). The Criminal Code must contain clear provisions in accordance with the principle *nullum crimen sine lege,* which requires that an individual should be able to understand which type of speech is prohibited, in order for a certain act to be considered a crime.[6] This position is inconsistent with Article 131 (see below section 1.2) on the crime of violation of equality, which does contain an open-ended list of grounds.

If an act of incitement to hatred, violence and intolerance is committed through a publication in the media, the media editor may also be punished for the crime, except in cases where the act is committed in a live broadcast and could not have been prevented (Article 297, section 3, Criminal Code). If the act is committed in a way which constitutes an aggravated type of this offence, that is, by coercion, maltreatment, endangering of security, desecration of national, ethnic or religious symbols, damage to the movable property of another, or desecration of monuments or memorial stones or graves, punishment for the perpetrator is imprisonment for up to three years (Article 297, section 4, Criminal Code). In addition, if the act is committed by an official, with abuse of official position or of power, the sanction is imprisonment for up to five years (Article 297, section 5, Criminal Code).

The main provision of Article 297 of the Criminal Code, stated in section 1, shows that one of the key elements required for the action to be considered a crime of incitement to hatred, violence or intolerance is that it was done in a way which made the incitement public. This excludes all acts of hate crimes or hate speech carried out away from the public eye; these can be prosecuted in accordance with other more general provisions of the Criminal Code (see below). The potential problem that may arise due to limiting the prohibition of hate crime and hate speech to public acts has also been highlighted in parliamentary debates by Members of Parliament,[7] as well as by the Legislative-Legal Service of the National Assembly (*Zakonodajno-pravna služba Državnega zbora*), a professional body within the National Assembly which examines the legal coherence of adopted laws. The representative of the Legislative-Legal Service even pointed out that limiting protection to public hate speech would be inconsistent with the Constitution which, in Article 63, prohibits any kind of incitement to inequality or intolerance, regardless of whether or not it is carried out in public. However, in spite of these objections, the fact that the incitement must be public in order to be criminal remained in the wording of the provision of Article 297 of the Criminal Code.

All other acts motivated by hate which are not covered by Article 297 of the Criminal Code are dealt with by the criminal justice system within the context of

---

[6] *Cf* Dimitrij Kovačič, MP for the Slovenian Democratic Party, 38th Regular Session of the National Assembly of 8 November 2007.

[7] Majda Širca, member of the ZARES parliamentary group, 38th Regular Session of the National Assembly of 8 November 2007.

other crimes, for example, murder (Article 116, 2008 Criminal Code); threat to safety (Article 135, 2008 Criminal Code); violent conduct (Article 296, 2008 Criminal Code); light, severe or particularly severe bodily injury (Articles 122, 123 and 124, respectively, 2008 Criminal Code) and so on. The motive of hate or homophobia may be taken into account as an aggravating element in any of the sub-definitions of criminal acts (for example murder motivated by violation of equality) or in sentencing (see below). Parliamentary debates have highlighted the fact that the hate element should have been taken into account more often in relation to these general acts, but also that specific crimes should be added to cover general acts which are committed with discriminatory motives.[8] Nonetheless, proposals have not been taken up by the parliamentary majority, the counter-argument being that these definitions of crime also protect from discriminatory motives and that specifying new hate crimes differentiated from ordinary crimes only by motive is unnecessary.[9]

In relation to hate speech in the media, the relevant provision is contained in Article 8 of the Media Act,[10] which states that it is forbidden to incite violence or war on grounds of ethnicity, race, religion, sexual orientation or other inequality or to provoke ethnic, racial, religious, sex or other hatred and intolerance through the media. To some extent, protection from hate speech which is targeted at a specific individual is—at least theoretically—also provided for in the Act Implementing the Principle of Equal Treatment,[11] which in Article 5 prohibits harassment on any personal grounds (which includes sexual orientation) as one of the forms of discrimination. If harassment is carried out in the form of oral or written statements, it is difficult to distinguish it from hate speech. There is, however, a problem of enforcement of the provision on harassment, as the Act Implementing the Principle of Equal Treatment does not specifically identify which inspectorates competent to issue binding decisions can enforce the Act (for more details on enforcement of this Act see below sections 1.4 and 2.1). The answer to this question is clear only in the field of employment, as the prohibition of harassment is also included in Article 6(a) of the Employment Relationship Act,[12] for which the designated enforcement body is the Employment Inspectorate. Accordingly, the problem arises if harassment takes place in areas which are not covered by any of the inspectorates, or if the inspectorates which cover a specific area do not consider themselves competent to enforce the provisions of the Act Implementing the Principle of Equal Treatment (as their

[8] Božo Strle, representative of the Legislative-Legal Service of the National Assembly of the Republic of Slovenia, 38th Regular Session of the National Assembly of 8 November 2007.
[9] Robert Marolt, Representative of the Ministry of Justice, 38th Regular Session of the National Assembly of 8 November 2007.
[10] Zakon o medijih–uradno prečiščeno besedilo (official consolidated text), Uradni list RS no 110/2006.
[11] Zakon o uresničevanju načela enakega obravnavanja–Uradno prečiščeno besedilo (official consolidated text), Uradni list RS no 93/2007.
[12] Zakon o delovnih razmerjih, Uradni list RS no 42/2002 and 103/2007.

competence in the matter is not specifically stipulated by this law). To examine complaints on discrimination and harassment, a special equality body has been established, as required by the Racial Equality Directive. In Slovenia, this body is called the Advocate of the Principle of Equality which, however, lacks any significant powers (see section 1.4 below).

1.2 Legislation against Hate Crime: Homophobia as a Violation of Equality

There is another crime related to the prohibition of discrimination included in the Criminal Code: the crime of violation of equality, defined in Article 131. It is important to set out the relationship between this crime, on the one hand, and the crime of incitement to hatred, violence and intolerance, on the other. The crime of violation of equality provides that (Article 131, section 1):

[W]hoever prevents or restricts another person's enjoyment of any human right or fundamental freedom recognised by the international community or laid down by the Constitution or legislation, or grants another person a special privilege or advantage on the grounds of ethnicity, race, color, religion, ethnic origin, gender, language, political or other belief, *sexual orientation*, social status, birth, education, social position or any other circumstance, shall be punished through a fine or sentenced to imprisonment for a maximum of one year. (emphasis added)

The same punishment is imposed for cases where an individual or an organisation is persecuted for advocacy of equality of people (Article 131, section 2). If these two crimes are committed by an official person by abuse of office or abuse of official authority, the punishment imposed is imprisonment for up to three years (Article 131, section 3). Sanctions for the crime may include both imprisonment as the main sanction and a fine as an additional sanction. Fines are calculated according to the daily earnings of the defendant and his family obligations, and may range from 30 to 360 times daily earnings, depending on the gravity of the offence (Article 47, Criminal Code). In cases of hate crime or hate speech, the provisions of Article 131 may be used only when the abuse amounts to a deprivation or restriction of a certain human right or fundamental freedom. The wording of the definition of this crime shows that violation of equality covers *acts* (both commissions and omissions) but not *speech*, and includes a condition that, by such acts the enjoyment of certain human rights or fundamental freedom is prevented or restricted. Therefore, the act of incitement to hatred, violence and intolerance covers hate *speech* which would otherwise not be subject to criminal prosecution.

The Criminal Code also includes some other definitions of serious crimes such as torture and murder, committed on certain personal grounds, which may include sexual orientation. That is, the provision of Article 116 of the 2008 Criminal Code specifically defines the criminal act of murder committed due to violation of equality and prescribes a sentence of imprisonment of at least 15 years. With regard to torture, Article 265 of the Criminal Code states that one who intentionally causes severe pain or suffering for a reason based on violation of equality, may be imprisoned for between one and 10 years. If such severe pain or suffering is caused by a person in an official capacity, the sanction is imprisonment for three to 12 years. Both these crimes were only added to the Criminal Code in 2008.

If a case of homophobic crime cannot be subsumed under any of the acts that include a homophobic and discriminatory motive as one of the elements of that crime, and the case is treated as an 'ordinary' one (for example, an assault or an act of violence), the homophobic or discriminatory motive may be taken into account by the court in determining the sentence. This is provided for by Article 49, section 2 of the 2008 Criminal Code which states that, at the time the sentence is set (the sentence is subject to legal minimum or maximum limits), the court must take into account all mitigating or aggravating circumstances of the case, in particular, the level of the perpetrator's criminal responsibility; the *motives* for which that person committed the crime; the level of threat to or violation of the value protected by the law; the circumstances in which the crime was committed; the previous record of the perpetrator; the perpetrator's personal and economic situation; behaviour after the commission of the crime; and any other circumstances relating to the perpetrator's personality. This means that, in the case of homophobic crimes, the court may take into account the words used by the perpetrator to express homophobia, if that crime for any reason cannot be prosecuted according to the law covering crimes related to discrimination.

The law covering minor offences committed for discriminatory or homopho-bic motives is the Protection of Public Order Act.[13] According to this Act, certain minor offences (violent and provoking behaviour; indecent behaviour; damaging an official inscription, sign or decision; writing on or defiling buildings, or destroying state symbols), if they are committed with *discriminatory motives*, are considered to be aggravated forms of minor offences for which a higher fine is prescribed. For example, for a minor offence of violent behaviour, a fine of 60,000 to 120,000 tolars (the current value would be from €250 to €502) could be imposed, whereas if this minor offence is committed with the purpose of inciting ethnic, racial, gender, religious or political intolerance or intolerance based on *sexual orientation*, the perpetrator may be punished with a fine of at least 200,000 tolars (currently €837). This provision is used when the motive of hate is clearly expressed and can be proven.

In Slovenian law there is no definition of gender identity-based violence. There are the above-mentioned references to violence based on sexual orientation but there is no reference to transgendered persons. It is even questionable whether violence perpetrated for motives related to gender identity would be treated as hate violence at all, or whether they would be treated as an aggravated form of

---

[13] Zakon o varstvu javnega reda in miru, Uradni list RS no 70/2006.

the general provisions relating to violence. The personal grounds of being a transgender person may, however, be taken into account in Article 131 of the Criminal Code (violation of equality) which includes an open-ended list of protected grounds, as well as in Article 20 of the Protection of Public Order Act, which only uses a general reference to discriminatory motives, and there is no reason not to cover the issue of gender identity.

1.3. The 'Black Hoods' Case

So far only one criminal case concerning hate crimes on the grounds of sexual orientation has been decided by the criminal courts in Slovenia. The facts of the case are as follows. On 25 June 2009, a group of men dressed in black hoods, caps and masks, carrying torches, stones and pieces of asphalt, came to the Open Café in Ljubljana, which is known to be gay-friendly. At the moment of the attack, the café was hosting a literature evening during the Pride Parade week. While attacking the café, the men screamed offensive slogans, calling gay people *pedri* (faggots). During the attack, a man standing outside the café received several injuries. One of the windows of the café was broken and one of the torches was thrown inside. Three of about eight perpetrators were identified and prosecuted for the crime of incitement to hatred, violence and intolerance, as well as for the crimes of 'violent conduct' and 'causing general danger for the public'. Other perpetrators remain unidentified.

The district criminal court in Ljubljana found the three defendants guilty as accomplices to a crime of public incitement of hatred, violence or intolerance, in accordance with Article 297, paragraphs I and IV of the Criminal Code, in connection with Article 20 of the Criminal Code (defining complicity). Each defendant was sentenced to imprisonment for 18 months (upon appeal the higher court lowered the sentences to seven months for two defendants and to five months for the third defender). In addition to the statements of many witnesses, confirmation that the three masked defendants were on the scene holding the torches was obtained from DNA forensic tests and phone-call transcripts, proving that at the critical time the defendants had been communi-cating with each other. In house searches of the defendants' homes the police discovered literature of national-socialist ideology. The court did not accept the defendants' plea that they were only expressing their opinion about public expression of one's sexual orientation. It found that both the attack and the equipment used during it had been organised and prepared in advance, and accompanied by hate speech, and that the day before the attack some members of the attacking group had gone to check the café to see how many people were there and if any of them were armed. However, the court did not find the defendants guilty of the crime of 'violent conduct' under Article 296 of the Criminal Code, arguing that the elements of this crime were already subsumed in the crime of public incitement of hatred, violence and intolerance. The defendants were also found not guilty of the crime of 'causing of general danger' as it was not possible to establish precisely which one of the defendants threw the torch into the café (as it might have been one of the men who has not been identified). As the man who was hurt in the incident was by coincidence a gay-rights activist who paid particular attention to the motives of the crime, the case has always been treated as a 'hate crime case'.

The outcome of the case, and one that is important for legal theory, was that the court decided that public incitement to hatred, violence or intolerance already includes violent conduct, which means that a person cannot be prosecuted for both crimes at the same time. Consequently, the crime of public incitement to hatred, violence and intolerance not only covers hate *speech* (as had been believed until then) but also hate *crime*. The Higher Court confirmed the judgment in its entirety, but it lowered the sentence to seven months imprisonment for two defendants and five months for the third one.[14]

The fact that this is the only hate crime case concerning sexual orientation deliberated by courts in Slovenia and that there are no other convictions in this area of law, does not reflect the actual situation, as often: (a) hate crimes are not dealt with as such but as crimes defined in other more general terms without mention of the motives; (b) not all gays and lesbians disclose their sexual orientation when reporting a crime; and (c) the people who are victims of such crimes very rarely report the events to the police. The report 'Tell On' (*Povej naprej*) from 2010 in which the responses of 140 people were collected and analysed, states that 92% of the respondents who had experienced hate crime or hate speech due to their sexual orientation, did not report the crime to the police (Magić, Kuhar and Kogovšek 2008). The 8% who did report it were persons who had disclosed their sexual orientation to family, friends and others. Being 'out' is therefore very important in deciding whether or not to report a crime. The respondents stated that fear was one of the main reasons for not reporting the crime, in that their case would not be dealt with appropriately by the criminal justice system; they would be mocked by the police; and, following their report to the police, they would be even more exposed to abuse. It seems that this impression is unfounded, as 60% of those who had reported a crime stated that the attitude of the police towards them was neutral, while 40% stated that the attitude of the police towards them was supportive. Other respondents' statements on the question as to why they did not make a report at the time show that the victims believed that the violence they had undergone was not that bad (34%); they would not achieve anything by reporting the crime (27%); they were afraid they would be exposed to even more violence (9%); they had not considered the option of reporting (6%); they did not trust the police (6%); they were afraid that by reporting the crime they would have to disclose their sexual orientation to the police (3%); and they feared the police would not believe them

---

[14] Judgment of the Higher Court Ljubljana no II KP 5357/2010 of 15 June 2011.

(3%). Also, quite often the victims did not link the violence that they had undergone with their sexual orientation and assumed that they were just random victims. Other earlier research carried out in 2005, in which 443 people participated, also revealed that hate violence is highly prevalent in the lesbian and gay community. The research showed that 53% of respondents were subject to violence motivated by their sexual orientation. Similar data had been obtained by an even earlier survey of 2001 (Danish Institute for Human Rights 2009).

One of the reasons for the low number of cases concerning homophobic crimes is the fact that the new Criminal Code, which prohibits sexual orientation-related hate speech and hate crimes, only came into force on 1 November 2008. Only hate speech and hate crimes which took place after that date could be prosecuted. However, there are other more systemic barriers to the prosecution of homophobic hate speech and hate crimes. The problem of insufficient activity on the part of the Prosecutor's Office on hate crime reports was initially made public by the Human Rights Ombudsman of Slovenia who, reporting for the year 2008, took the position that the activities of the Prosecutor's Office in this area 'cannot be positively assessed',[15] meaning that much more could have been done The reaction of the prosecution to this statement that 'prevention is better than repression', disappointed the Ombudsman, who insisted that 'a serious and fast reaction of the prosecution on instances of public incitement to hatred, violence and intolerance and their sanctioning is the best prevention'.

Homophobic hate speech is not the only type of speech that is difficult to prosecute, as the situation does not differ greatly in relation to racist speech. Even though racist hate crimes and racist hate speech had already been prohibited in 1994 by the first Criminal Code adopted in Slovenia since its independence (within the crime of incitement to hatred, violence and intolerance, defined in Article 300 of the 1994 Criminal Code, now contained in Article 297 of the 2008 Criminal Code), only a small number of cases have been handled by the courts so far.[16] The fact that racist hate speech and hate crimes have been prohibited for about 14 years longer than homophobic hate speech and hate crimes has not had much effect in this respect.

1.4. The Advocate of the Principle of Equality and the Human Rights Ombudsman: A Soft Approach to Tackling Homophobia

With the enforcement of the Act Implementing the Principle of Equal Treatment, a special body called *Zagovornik načela enakosti* (Advocate of the Principle of

---

[15] Republic of Slovenia, Human Rights Ombudsman, *14th Regular Annual Report of the Human Rights Ombudsman of the Republic of Slovenia for the Year 2008* (available at www.varuh-rs.si/fileadmin/user_upload/pdf/lp/Varuh_-_LP_2008_-_ANG.pdf).

[16] See, eg, Judgment of County Court in Ilirska Bistrica no K 50/99 of 31 December 2001, or Judgment of County Court in Lendava of 27 December 2005.

Equality) was introduced within the *Urad Vlade RS za enake možnosti* (Government Office for Equal Opportunities) on 1 January 2005. The Advocate of the Principle of Equality, a one-person institution established as an equality body in Slovenia, is competent to examine complaints filed by victims of discrimination or harassment and to issue non-binding opinions with recommendations. This body clearly has only limited powers and for this reason it cannot be defined as an enforcement body. If its recommendations are not respected by the violators, the Advocate may refer the case to the competent inspectorate. As already briefly mentioned, the problem arises when there is no competent inspectorate for the area in which harassment took place, or if the inspectorate which is otherwise competent for a certain area (for example, the market or school inspectorate) does not consider itself competent for issues of discrimination, as its competence is not specifically designated in the Act Implementing the Principle of Equal Treatment.

The Advocate is competent to examine complaints of alleged discrimination on the grounds of gender, ethnicity, race or ethnic origin, religion or belief, disability, age, *sexual orientation*, or other personal circumstance, in both the public and private spheres. Very few cases concerning sexual orientation are sent to the Advocate which makes this ground one of the least reported. The second task that the Advocate carries out is the provision of advice and support to victims of discrimination. The main mandate of the Advocate is prevention and raising awareness on issues which constitute discrimination and harassment, while repressive and prosecutorial powers remain with the police and the prosecutor's office. This means that, in instances of hate speech or harassment in bars and cafés, on the street, or in any other public or private place outside the work environment, even if the Advocate decides that there was discrimination and issues a non-binding opinion with recommendations, no further enforcement action is available to victims if the recommendations are not respected.

Another non-judicial mechanism available for victims of hate speech is the Human Rights Ombudsman, an independent public body which is positioned outside all three main branches of power. In accordance with Article 159 of the Constitution of the Republic of Slovenia, the Human Rights Ombudsman is competent only for the public sector. This means that, in the case of hate speech or hate crime, it cannot bring any procedures against private individuals as alleged perpetrators of hate crimes or hate speech, but it can monitor procedures taking place before state bodies or local government bodies. If, for instance, the police or a prosecutor's office do not react to or deal with complaints of hate crime or hate speech, or if their procedures are not sufficiently effective, the Human Rights Ombudsman may alert those authorities to the fact. It does not, however, have the competence to interfere with pending court procedures, due to the principles of division of powers and independence of the judiciary. As defined in the Human Rights Ombudsman Act, the Ombudsman may issue an opinion on whether or not a violation of rights has occurred but these opinions are not legally binding. The Human Rights Ombudsman's annual reports do not contain any specific information on homophobic speech or homophobic crimes in Slovenia, but only highlight the lack of legal protection in cases of hate speech and hate crimes prior to the 2008 Criminal Code.

1.5. Code for Regulation of Hate Speech in Slovenian Web Portals

As a response to internet media forums, which form the main public arena for hate speech, a 'Code for regulation of hate speech in Slovenian web portals' has been signed by six media companies and is still open for signature by other internet forums.[17] The code was prepared by the Center for Safer Internet and its anti-hate speech internet point is called The Web Eye (*Spletno oko*) and is located at the University for Social Studies (*Fakulteta za družbene vede*).[18] The code addresses problems with hate speech on the internet (some internet forums enable internet users to post comments anonymously, without any previous registration that would enable the user to be identified in cases of hate speech which constitute a crime of incitement to hatred, violence and intolerance) and problems with investigations of those crimes encountered by the police and the prosecutor's office. The code binds its signatories to introduce a system of moderation in their forums, in accordance with the guidelines prepared by a working group comprised of the representatives of the signatories of the code, and the system of registration of internet users who wish to post comments on the specific forum. The code also obliges its signatories to include both a warning to their forums that hate speech may constitute a crime of incitement to hatred, violence and intolerance under Article 297 of the Criminal Code, as well as to provide a button next to each comment which other users may press to report comments which, in their opinion, amount to a crime. Pressing this button leads a user to a standardised form for reporting internet hate speech to The Web Eye as a centralised point, which then helps to clarify which cases amount to hate speech and which do not, and reports those which do to the police.

---

[17] Kodeks za regulacijo sovražnega govora na slovenskih spletnih portalih, signed on 14 December 2010 by media compagnies Dnevnik, Delo, Večer, Siol, Žurnal24 and RTV Slovenia.
[18] For more information about Web Eye (*Spletno oko*) see www.spletno-oko.si/en.

2. Education at all Levels

2.1. Prohibition of Homophobic Treatment in Schools: The Problems of Generality and Unenforceability

As in the area of hate crimes and hate speech, the legal sources in the field of education do not contain any references to homophobia. There are provisions prohibiting sexual orientation discrimination in schools but their wording is very general: Article 2 of the Act Implementing the Principle of Equal Treatment includes prohibition of direct and indirect discrimination as well as harassment based on any personal circumstance (including sexual orientation) in all fields of social life, including that of education. This means that, in principle, in cases of discrimination in the field of education, the alleged perpetrator would be punished for a misdemeanour by a competent inspectorate which, in the case of education would be the School Inspectorate, operating within the Ministry of Education and Sports. But this might not necessarily be the case. According to Article 2 of the School Inspection Act,[19] the School Inspectorate is competent to monitor the respect of laws and other Acts regulating the organisation and activities of up-bringing and education carried out by pre-school institutions, elementary schools, music schools, lower and middle vocational schools, middle technical and professional schools, high schools, higher professional schools, schools for students with special needs, organisations for adult education, and private entities carrying out public educational programs.

The problem with this provision is that it limits the competence of the School Inspectorate to monitor compliance with legislation concerning the *organisation and activities of schools*, but not other laws which cover education, such as the Act Implementing the Principle of Equal Treatment which prohibits discrimination in the area of education. This may give rise to the above-mentioned problem of the School Inspectorate declaring itself incompetent for issues of discrimination, despite a referral by the Advocate of the Principle of Equality (a general provision allows the Advocate to forward the case to a competent inspectorate if duly produced recommendations are not respected). Such declarations have been made by the inspectorates competent in the areas of housing and trade.

Protection from discrimination, including homophobic acts at all levels of education, is guaranteed not only to students and pupils but also to teachers. However, teachers who are also employees of the educational institution enjoy a much stronger legal position, as they can also invoke the legislation governing employment relations, in which the definition of labour inspectorate competences is significantly clearer. As opposed to the 'missing link' between the

---

[19] Zakon o šolski inšpekciji–uradno prečiščeno besedilo (official consolidated text), Uradni list RS no 114/2005.

definition of competences of the School Inspectorate and anti-discrimination provisions, the link between the labour inspectorate and anti-discrimination provisions is clear, as the latter are also explicitly included in the Employment Relationship Act.

The fact that sexual orientation has been included in the protected grounds in the education system shows that the legal protection set up in Slovenia exceeds the personal and material scope of the EU anti-discrimination directives, which require that the field of education should be protected from discrimination only in relation to racial and ethnic origin (as required by the Racial Equality Directive) or that protection from discrimination based on sexual orientation should be guaranteed only in the fields of employment and vocational training (as required by the Employment Equality Directive). The reasons for including the prohibition of discrimination based on sexual orientation in the law are not made clear in parliamentary debates. In fact, Members of Parliament in the legislative process did not discuss issues of homophobia in schools when passing this law. It seems that inclusion of all areas (in terms of material scope) and all grounds (in terms of personal scope) was a matter of practical importance, in which different levels of protection for different discriminated groups were avoided. Another possible explanation is that in the Constitution discrimination is also generally prohibited, without limiting legal protection to certain areas of life.

The legislation of the Republic of Slovenia applying to the field of education comprises the Elementary School Act, Gymnasium Act, Vocational Education Act, Higher Education Act, Post-secondary Vocational Education Act, and Graduation Examination Act. None of these Acts includes any additional provisions on the prohibition of discrimination. Equal treatment of students in Slovenian schools is in fact protected at the level of implementing Acts—for example, by Article 2 of the Rules on the Code of Conduct in Secondary Schools,[20] which states that a student has the right to equal treatment irrespective of sex, race, ethnicity, religion, or social status of the family or other personal circumstances, as well as to a safe, healthy and supportive working environment. Many schools also have their own codes of conduct. However, in spite of provisions that are available for legal protection, students rarely rely on them in cases of discriminatory behaviour based on sexual orientation (Maljevac and Magić 2009). The lack of more specific protection within the education laws indicates that the Act Implementing the Principle of Equal Treatment must be used in such cases as an 'umbrella' Act.

Some of the listed laws do include positive obligations on the part of educational institutions to pursue goals related to equal treatment and prohibition of discrimination. For example, Article 2 of the Elementary School Act states that one of the goals of elementary education is to learn mutual tolerance, respect for

[20] Pravilnik o šolskem redu v srednjih šolah, Uradni list RS št 43/2007.

differences, cooperation with others, and respect for human rights and fundamental freedoms, in order to develop pupils' capacity to live in a democratic
society. Similar provisions can be found in each of the laws, for example, Article 2
of the Gymnasium Act, Vocational Education Act and Post-secondary Education
Act include in their goals the development of consciousness of the rights and
duties of a human being and a citizen (except for the Higher Education Act which
contains no provisions of this kind at all). An important provision is also that of
Article 7, section 1 of the Act Implementing the Principle of Equal Treatment,
which states that the National Assembly, the Government, the ministries and all
other state bodies and bodies of local government, have within their powers, the
duty to create conditions for equal treatment irrespective of any personal
grounds, by raising awareness and monitoring the situation in this sphere, as well
as by legislative and political measures. Although public schools are not specifically mentioned in this provision, they are public institutions which must abide
by the same rules.

The inspectorates and courts in Slovenia have not yet decided on cases of
discrimination based on sexual orientation in the field of education. However,
this does not mean that such cases do not occur. Research on harassment and
violence relating to sexual orientation in schools shows that such events occur
very often, and also points to the fact that teachers do not react to acts of
discrimination and harassment among peers. The main reason why cases do not
reach the courts is that the victims do not resort to legal remedies (Maljevac and
Magić 2009).

2.2. Integration of the Concepts of Homosexuality and Homophobia in School Curricula

'Soft' law is an important source of law in the field of education which, apart
from general organisational and institutional framework issues, cannot be governed by binding legislation. One source that may be considered soft law, which is
worth examining, is the so-called learning plan (*učni načrt*)[21] for elementary
schools. This lists topics that pupils should cover in the course of the educational
process and that should be reflected in school textbooks. In the learning plan,
only one reference is made to the term 'sexual orientation', in relation to the
curriculum for fifth grade (attended by 10 year-olds), in which students are
expected to learn about diversity, including different types of sexual orientation.
However, there is a problem in achieving this principle, as school textbooks do
not always mention sexual orientation or same-sex families (Danish Institute for
Human Rights 2009: 7).

---

[21] Annual learning plans for schools are prepared by the national Education Institute of the
Republic of Slovenia and are accessible at www.zrss.si/default.asp?link=predmet&tip=3&pID=
63&rID=731.

Ksenija Komidar and Saša Mandeljc, who analysed the learning plan from the wider perspective of inclusiveness of the issue of sexual orientation, found that the plan includes topics such as learning about different types of families and forms of social communities and developing a tolerant attitude towards them; learning about different kinds of people in terms of their gender, age, religion, sexual orientation and ethnicity; and challenging certain stereotypes such as HIV/AIDS being a disease of homosexual people. Their analysis showed that homosexuality and homophobia are not explicitly included among topics in the students' learning plan. They stressed that the aim of including certain topics in the learning plan is to prevent teachers from avoiding discussion about them in the classroom. Their review of textbooks also showed that homosexuality and homophobia are not included, as is required by the learning plan. Nor is homosexuality explicitly mentioned in any of the school textbooks, which raises the question of whether the learning plan (as an example of soft law in the educational system) is adequately followed. Some teachers compensate for the lack of information in textbooks by taking advantage of any incidents in the class (for example, name calling) as an opportunity to talk about the issues of homosexuality. However, practices in addressing this issue differ from teacher to teacher (Komidar and Mandeljc 2009).

The missing references to education concerning issues of homosexuality in school curricula are compensated for by some schools, which offer optional courses on human rights, taught by non-governmental organisations (NGOs), for example, Amnesty International Slovenia, Association Legebitra and so on. These NGOs have recently come under attack, with accusations that they promote homosexuality in schools. The attacks were made both in the media and within parliamentary debates,[22] as well as in the form of criminal reports filed directly against them.[23] No information is available on whether or not the police have initiated any investigative actions as a result of these reports.

2.3. 'Proud of my Sex/Proud of my Pole' School Campaign

Specialised bodies competent in the area of anti-discrimination and human rights have not yet had the chance to examine many cases related to homophobia. However, there was one interesting case considered in 2010 by the Advocate of the Principle of Equality. The Advocate examined a complaint concerning the campaign of the Ministry of Education and Sports entitled *Ponosen sem na (s)pol* (Proud of my sex, or proud of my pole—the title uses a pun which is a play on the fact that one's sex is at the same time another person's opposite sex, and that two persons create two different poles and complement each other). The aim of

---

[22] See eg, the parliamentary debate at the 29th Regular Session of the National Assembly of 17 March 2011.
[23] The information is based on the author's personal discussions with representatives of these NGOs.

the campaign was, according to the Ministry, to encourage young people to think about safe sex, which they could confirm by signing a declaration stating that they are proud of their (biological) sex.

The Advocate of the Principle of Equality found that the campaign calls upon students to take a public position about some of the most private spheres of their lives, connected with their personal and psychological integrity, personal rights and human dignity. From the campaign materials, it was not clear what guarantees existed to protect students' personal data and their right not to declare these facts publicly. Although the campaign's main aim was, according to the Ministry, to raise awareness of the importance of safe sex, it was not accompanied by any educational activities; so its effect in promoting safe sex is highly questionable. The Advocate found that the complementary materials of the campaign were based on the assumption that humanity consists of two sexes which jointly maintain civilisation, which requires students to be 'proud' of a classic heterosexual orientation.

The Advocate of the Principle of Equality issued a (non-binding) opinion, stating that the campaign was an example of direct discrimination based on 'sex identity', as well as of indirect discrimination on the ground of sexual orientation, as it disregards students with past, current and/or future experience of homosexual, bisexual or transsexual orientation and/or change of their 'sex identity'. The Advocate called upon the Ministry to discontinue the campaign and to prevent its continuation in schools, to include sex education in school curricula, and to prepare the content of curricula in cooperation with experts from all related professional areas, in such a way that the curricula will include content on social gender and the phenomena of different 'sex identities', without any discrimination on the grounds of sexual orientation, as well as information on all social views on various sexual practices. In order to address the damaging effects of the campaign, the Advocate recommended that the Ministry carry out activities to enhance awareness on the part of students of the importance of tolerance and equal treatment of sexual minorities. The Advocate asked the Ministry to report to the Advocate within 60 days on measures taken with a view to implementing these recommendations.[24]

The case is interesting from various perspectives. It shows how institutionalised heteronormativity at the highest level, such as the Ministry of Education, can interfere with the educational process and spread ideas which may lead or contribute to homophobia in society. It also shows that, instead of thinking about the ways in which homophobia in society could be reduced by reforming school curricula, the institutions are actually helping to maintain the current situation, which is predominantly marked by silence, as is evident from the Slovenian sociological case study in chapter four of this volume. Finally, it remains to be

[24] Opinion of the Advocate of the Principle of Equality no 0921–22/2010–7 of 6 September 2010.

seen whether or not the Ministry of Education will follow the recommendations of the Advocate and, if it does not, what the outcome will be, due to the limited powers assigned to the Advocate.

3. Free Movement, Immigration and Asylum

As in other fields of law, the term 'homophobia' cannot be found in Slovenian legislation concerning asylum and immigration. However, this legislation can have both negative and positive effects on issues related to homosexuality, such as family reunification, the rights of same-sex partners deriving from their partnership, and the rights of children living in families of same-sex partners.

The relevant legislation in the field of free movement, immigration and asylum in relation to sexual orientation comprises the Aliens Act,[25] regulating the entry and residence of foreigners in Slovenia (both EU citizens and third-country nationals) and the International Protection Act,[26] regulating the status of asylum-seekers and beneficiaries of international protection and the procedures for acquiring international protection in Slovenia. Two main questions arise in this area: (1) whether or not homosexual married, registered or cohabiting partners are recognised as family members who can claim family reunification rights under Slovenian legislation; and (2) whether persecution due to sexual orientation is a reason for which refugee status can be granted. In relation to these questions, whether or not there is evidence of institutional homophobia in these fields of law can also be examined. This section is organised in three parts: (1) family reunification and free movement of same-sex partners of EU citizens; (2) family reunification of third-country nationals and refugees; and (3) asylum and international protection.

3.1. Family Reunification and Free Movement of Same-Sex Partners of EU Citizens

With regard to family reunification rights, the Aliens Act and the International Protection Act are neutral with respect to sexual orientation. However, in their practical application, same-sex partners are treated less favourably. That is, EU citizens (and Slovenian nationals) have the right to family reunification with the following family members who are not Slovenian nationals:

---

[25] Zakon o tujcih—uradni prečiščeno besedilo, Uradni list RS no 64/2009. On 27 June 2011 a new Aliens Act was published (Zakon o tujcih (ZTuj-2), Uradni list RS, št 50/11), recognising the right to family reunification to registered partners as well. The Act entered into force on 27 July 2011, and will be used from 27 October 2011 onwards.

[26] Zakon o mednarodni zaščiti, Uradni list RS no 111/2007 as amended.

(1) sponsor's spouse;[27]
(2) sponsor's unmarried children under the age of 21;
(3) spouse's unmarried children under the age of 21;
(4) sponsor's or spouse's unmarried children over the age of 21 and sponsor's or spouse's parents, whom the sponsor or spouse is obliged to provide for under the law of the sponsor's or spouse's country of nationality; and
(5) parents of the sponsor until the latter reaches 21 years of age.

However, there is a provision in the Aliens Act which may be used for borderline cases such as those involving unmarried same-sex couples and their children. That is, a competent body may exceptionally recognise family reunification rights to other relatives of the sponsor if special circumstances indicate the need for family reunification in Slovenia (Article 93(k) of the Aliens Act), which is a provision which may be used by sponsors who are Slovenian nationals or EU citizens and who are claiming family reunification rights.

The question is whether there are any specific reasons for non-inclusion of registered partners among family members defined by the Aliens Act. The provision of Article 2(2)(b) of the Directive 2004/38/EC, which governs free movement rights of EU citizens, states that the definition of family members should include

> the partner with whom the Union citizen has contracted a registered partnership, on the basis of the legislation of a Member State, if the legislation of the host Member State treats registered partnerships as equivalent to marriage and in accordance with the conditions laid down in the relevant legislation of the host Member State.

Does Slovenia treat registered partnership as being equivalent to marriage? Taking into account only legislation that is currently in force, the answer is no as the rights of spouses frequently exceed the rights of registered partners. However, the adoption of the Family Code will change the answer to this question if it comes into force. The Family Code adopted in 2011 recognises equal rights to same-sex partners compared with opposite-sex partners, except for the right to marry, the right to joint adoption, and the right to automatic recognition of parental rights for the biological parent's registered partner. This means that, through this law, same-sex partnership would be brought much closer to marriage. The Family Code, however, has not yet entered into force, because conservative groups filed a demand for a referendum, which can only be prevented by the Constitutional Court if it finds that the referendum would lead to 'unconstitutional consequences'. In spite of this obstacle, the mere process of adopting the Family Code has had positive effects, especially the introduction of the new Aliens Act.[28] This Act, which was adopted in 2011 (it will come into force

---

[27] With the 2011 Aliens Act, comes into use on 27 October 2011, registered partners were included among close family members who can claim family reunification rights.
[28] Zakon o tujcih (ZTuj-2), Uradni list RS no 50/2011.

from 28 October 2011), defines registered and cohabiting partners as family members who will have access to family reunification rights. This means that, from October 2011 onwards, these rights will also be recognised for same-sex registered partners. In the case of cohabiting same-sex partners, these rights will be recognised only after (and if) the Family Code enters into force, because it is the Family Code that legally recognises cohabiting same-sex partners.

When the relevant provisions of both the 1999 and 2011 Aliens Acts were adopted in the parliament, there was no debate among the Members of Parliament on whether or not registered partners and cohabiting partners (in the case of the Aliens Act) should be entitled to family reunification rights. That is, this option was not even included in the drafts prepared by the government, and consequently was not debated as a possible option.

Nonetheless, by excluding registered and cohabiting same-sex partners from family reunification rights, the existing 1999 Aliens Act interferes with Article 8 of the European Convention on the Protection of Human Rights and Fundamental Freedoms (guaranteeing the right for respect of private and family life) in connection with Article 14 of this Convention (prohibiting discrimination on the grounds of sexual orientation). For such interference not to constitute a violation of the Convention, very weighty reasons would need to be presented by the state parties to the Convention, to justify unequal treatment of EU citizens, migrants and refugees by these two laws. It may be concluded that, with respect to the recognition of family reunification rights to same-sex partners and some of the children living in the families of same-sex partners, Slovenian law does reflect homophobia and the heteronormativity prevalent in the society.

As regards same-sex partners of Slovenian nationals who are EU citizens and their free movement rights deriving from their EU citizenship, it is evident from the stated provisions of the currently valid Aliens Act that, unless they are married, they cannot invoke their family reunification rights, but only their independent free movement rights deriving from their individual EU citizenships, regardless of who their same-sex registered or cohabiting partner is. However, the situation would be different if a Slovenian national or an EU national married in a country which also allows same-sex couples to marry. In such a case, the Republic of Slovenia would be obliged to recognise family reunification rights to such spouses as to opposite-sex spouses, due to the general prohibition of discrimination defined in Article 14 of the Constitution. That is, in both cases the applicants for family reunification rights would be spouses, regardless of their gender or sexual orientation.

With its adoption the 2011 Aliens Act partly remedied this void. While the sex of the partners is irrelevant for registered partners (according to the principle of non-discrimination both homosexual and heterosexual partners would have to be recognised as close family members according to these new norms), it remains relevant for cohabiting partners, who are defined by the legislation in the field of family relations. The latter, as explained below, currently only recognises hetero-sexual partners as being able to form a cohabiting partnership.

3.2. Family Reunification of Third-Country Nationals and Refugees

The situation is not very different as regards the family reunification rights of sponsors who are third-country nationals or who have international protection (refugee status or subsidiary protection) in Slovenia. Article 16(b) of the International Protection Act which defines the family members of the person who was granted international protection, includes:

(1) a spouse of the person or extramarital partner in a permanent relationship as defined in accordance with the Aliens Act and Marriage and Family Relations Act;[29]
(2) children of the couple defined under (1) if they are unmarried and unprovided for, regardless of whether they were born in or out of wedlock or if they were adopted;
(3) minor unmarried children of the person who was granted international protection if that person has custody of the children and regularly provides for them;
(4) minor unmarried children of the spouse or extramarital partner of the person who has been granted international protection, if the partner has custody of the children and regularly provides for them;
(5) adult unmarried children of the person who has been granted international protection (or of their spouse or extramarital partner) who, due to physical or mental condition, are not capable of providing for themselves and taking care of their rights and interests; and
(6) parents of unaccompanied minors.

From the group of family members which includes spouses and extramarital partners, all registered couples, including same-sex couples, are excluded. This means that, if a person is granted international protection in Slovenia and has a registered same-sex partner from a third country, that person cannot invoke the right to reunification with the partner, meaning that that partner does not have the right to move to Slovenia and be granted international protection under Article 17 of the International Protection Act. In addition, if same-sex partners are not married or registered, but have lived in the country of origin in an extramarital (civil, cohabiting) partnership and one of them is granted international protection in Slovenia, the other partner cannot claim family reunification

---

[29] Zakon o zakonski zvezi in družinskih razmerjih—Uradno prečiščeno besedilo, Uradni list RS no 69/2004. With the 2011 Aliens Act which is not yet in use, registered partners were added to close family members who can invoke family reunification rights (see Art 47).

rights. Article 12 of the above-mentioned Marriage and Family Relations Act states that a long-lasting relationship between a man and a woman who are not married has the same legal standing as marriage. Thus an extramarital relationship which is considered to be equal to marriage is recognised only for opposite-sex partners and excludes same-sex partners. In other words, due to the stated definition of extramarital partnership, two same-sex partners living together in a 'long-lasting life community' could not claim either the status of an extramarital relationship or equal rights as opposite-sex partners in the same situation could. This further means that, in the case of cohabiting same-sex partners, one of whom would be granted international protection in Slovenia, the other would not be able to claim family reunification rights according to Article 17 of the International Protection Act.

This leads to the fact that the children of a registered or cohabiting same-sex partner of the person who was granted international protection are also not recognised as family members, unless they are adopted by the refugee (second-parent adoption), in which case they are in an equal position to that refugee's biological children. The question is whether or not a same-sex partner's child, over whom the refugee has parental rights automatically at birth as the parent's registered partner, is considered to be a family member, as that person is not the biological or adoptive parent of the child. The law does not regulate this situation, and it is presumed that application for family reunification for such a child would probably be rejected.

A similar question arises concerning family members of unaccompanied minors which, under point 6 above, are limited to the unaccompanied minor's parents. According to Slovenian legislation, a person is considered to be the parent of a child only if that person is the child's biological or adoptive parent, but not if that person is a same-sex or opposite-sex partner of the parent or a same-sex parent who has obtained parental rights automatically at the moment of birth of the child as for same-sex registered couples. Nevertheless, in order for child's rights to be protected, such a parent should also be considered the child's official parent, with equal rights to those of the biological or adoptive parents.

Another question which remains unaddressed by the International Protection Act is how the competent bodies would treat same-sex spouses, that is same-sex partners married in a country which also allows marriage between same-sex partners (for example, South Africa). According to the general prohibition of discrimination defined in Article 14 of the Constitution, which includes protection from any kind of discrimination, including discrimination on the grounds of sexual orientation[30] and gender, the competent bodies would be obliged to treat

---

[30] Despite the fact that sexual orientation is not explicitly included in the list of protected grounds in Art 14 of the Constitution of the Republic of Slovenia which guarantees equality, the constitution covers an open-ended list of grounds, as it ends with the clause 'or any other personal circumstance'. That this general clause includes sexual orientation was explicitly confirmed by the Constitutional Court. The case concerned equal treatment of registered

same-sex spouses equally to opposite-sex spouses, regardless of the fact that in Slovenia marriage for same-sex partners is not accessible—that is, these two partners would not be demanding the right to marry, but the right to family reunification which is recognised for all spouses. In other words, the law does not state that family reunification rights will only be recognised for those spouses who are considered as such in accordance with the Marriage and Family Relations Act (this condition is specifically set out only for unmarried cohabiting partners who are considered as such under this law).

A similar situation concerns family reunification rights under the Aliens Act, which defines the family members of a sponsor who is a third-country national. The term 'sponsor' is used by the Family Reunification Directive 2003/86/EC, which defines it as (Article 2(c)):

> a third-country national residing lawfully in a Member State and applying or whose family members apply for family reunification to be joined with him/her.

Sponsors who are third-country nationals have the right to reunification with their family members if they (the sponsors) reside in Slovenia on the basis of a residence permit.

Persons who are considered to be family members in this case are (under Article 36 (3) of the Aliens Act):

(1) a spouse;[31]
(2) minor unmarried children of the sponsor;
(3) minor unmarried children of the spouse;
(4) parents of a third-country national who is a minor; or
(5) adult unmarried children or parents of the sponsor or spouse for whom the sponsor or the spouse are obliged to provide under the law of the country whose nationals they are.

As in the case of family reunification rights recognised for persons with international protection, registered or cohabiting same-sex partners of the sponsors are not automatically included among family members whose right to family reunification is recognised, even though this possibility is provided for by the optional provision of Article 4.3 of the Family Reunification Directive. Consequently, the right to family reunification with the sponsor is also not recognised for minor unmarried children of the sponsor's same-sex partner, unless such children are adopted by the sponsor (second-parent adoption). It is questionable whether the right to family reunification would be successfully claimed by the registered same-sex partner's minor unmarried children over whom the sponsor obtained

---

same-sex partners with married couples in inheritance issues. See Judgment of the Constitutional Court of the Republic of Slovenia no. U-I-425/06 of 2 July 2009.

[31] Note that with 2010 Aliens Act, which is not yet in use, registered and cohabiting partners have been added to close family members of the sponsor who can invoke family reunification rights. The law will be used from 28 October 2011 onwards.

parental rights automatically by birth (that is, assumption of parenthood), since that situation is not regulated in Slovenian law. By the same analogy, automatic granting of parental rights at the child's birth would be legally equal to adoption or other forms of assumption of parenthood, such as the case in which the mother's spouse is automatically considered to be a child's father if the child is born in wedlock or within a period of 300 days after the termination of marriage (Article 86, Marriage and Family Relations Act).

As in the case of family reunification rights of EU citizens, the competent body may exceptionally consider other relatives of the sponsor to be family members, provided that specific circumstances speak in favour of family reunification in Slovenia (Article 36(4), Aliens Act). This is a general clause which takes into account different cultural backgrounds of large families exceeding three linear generations. There is no reason why it could not also have been invoked by families of same-sex partners, in order to pursue their equal rights regardless of sexual orientation and gender of the partners. So far, there have not been any cases adjudicated by the courts in Slovenia on this matter.

This shows that the only difference which exists in the law concerning the nationality status of sponsors (whether they are third-country nationals, EU citizens or Slovenian nationals) is the age of unmarried children who may be granted family reunification status, while there are no other differences concerning the same-sex partners of the sponsors. A comparison of family reunification rights of sponsors with those of persons with international protection shows that the scope of family members who are recognised is more extensive in the field of international protection, as in that field family reunification rights are also recognised for cohabiting partners. However, this does not have any effect on same-sex partners and their family members, as their extramarital partnership is not recognised under Slovenian law.

As in the case of EU citizens, the 2011 Aliens Act (which will be in force from 28 October 2011), introduces changes in relation to family members of third-country nationals as well. Under this law, the right to family reunification will also be recognised for registered and cohabiting partners. From October 2011 registered same-sex partners will no longer be legally insecure. However, for cohabiting same-sex partners to obtain access to family reunification rights, the entry into force of the Family Code is required, because it is this law that recognises cohabitation of same-sex partners.

3.3. Asylum and International Protection

In the field of asylum, the International Protection Act follows the 1951 Convention Relating to the Status of Refugees and its 1967 Protocol, by providing that refugee status is granted to a person who, owing to a well-founded fear of being persecuted for reasons of race, religion, nationality, membership of a particular social group, or political opinion, is outside the country of his nationality and is unable, or owing to such fear is unwilling, to avail himself of the protection of that country; or who, not having a nationality and being outside the country of his former habitual residence as a result of such events, is unable or, owing to such fear, is unwilling to return to it (Article 2, section 2, International Protection Act).

The relevant ground of persecution that gays and lesbians may invoke is membership of a particular social group, if they have been subjected to persecution due to their sexual orientation. Article 27, section 6 of the International Protection Act recognises homosexuality as a possible element which may constitute membership of the particular social group (in this case, a sexual minority) as a form of persecution in respect of which international protection can be granted. For that matter, Slovenian asylum legislation could be regarded as anti-homophobic, but it should be emphasised that the inclusion of the reference to sexual orientation was the result of a 'top-down' approach, as it took place during the transposition of Article 10(1)(d) of the Council Directive 2004/83/EC of 29 April 2004 on minimum standards for the qualification and status of third-country nationals or stateless persons as refugees or as persons who otherwise need international protection and the content of the protection granted (known as the Qualification Directive).

So far, there have been five asylum-seekers who have claimed refugee status in Slovenia due to persecution based on their sexual orientation—two from Kosovo, and one each from Iran, Bosnia and Herzegovina, and Croatia. For the purposes of this analysis, it was only possible to obtain information on three of the cases: those related to asylum-seekers from Kosovo, Bosnia and Herzegovina, and Iran. In the first case, the two asylum-seekers, who are a male-male couple from Kosovo, claimed they had been persecuted due to their homosexuality. Persecution took place in the form of harassment by various people in Kosovo, and one of the asylum-seekers claimed he was raped by three men while his partner was forced to watch. They did not report this to the police as they did not believe any report would be taken seriously. The first instance body competent to determine refugee status, the Sector for International Protection of the Ministry of the Interior, refused their application,[32] explaining that their statements did not match and were incoherent and therefore not credible (the statements to which this conclusion related were about the weather conditions at the time of the rape, the men's whereabouts after it, and the reasons for not reporting it to the police). In the procedure for international protection, the competent body did not seek to establish whether or not the two asylum-seekers met the conditions for international protection, that is, whether the acts they had been subjected to amounted to persecution in the sense of Article 26 of the International Protection Act (which defines the nature of the acts which constitute persecution). Nor did any

---

[32] See Decision of the Ministry of the Interior no 2142–425/2006/7 (1352–12) of 29 January 2007.

competent body elaborate on whether or not the asylum-seekers were members of a particular social group defined by homosexuality, or whether Country of Origin Information for Kosovo confirms their statements of persecution (an objective element of asylum procedure). In other words, according to Article 22 of the International Protection Act, the competent body does not even refer to the Country of Origin Information if the general credibility of an asylum-seeker and their claims is not established. Following the negative decision at the first instance, the couple sought judicial review by filing a lawsuit in the Administrative Court, in accordance with Article 74, section 1 of the International Protection Act. They claimed that, if the first instance body was of the opinion that their statements were contradictory, they should have been given the chance to clarify them, which was not the case. The Administrative Court found in their favour, due to a violation of the rules of administrative procedure, and returned the case to the Ministry of the Interior as the first instance body.[33] The Ministry filed an appeal against the Administrative Court decision to the Supreme Court. The Supreme Court confirmed the judgment of the Administrative Court, which meant that the Ministry of the Interior was obliged to conduct the asylum procedure again.[34] However, the asylum-seekers had left the Asylum Home and had not returned within three days which, in accordance with Article 50, section 2 of the International Protection Act, meant that their asylum application was deemed to be withdrawn; consequently their procedure was terminated.[35] The Netherlands, which was the country to which they had gone, returned them to Slovenia according to the Dublin II Regulation procedure, and they filed a new application for international protection in Slovenia, which at the time of writing was still pending.[36]

In the second case concerning Bosnia and Herzegovina, the asylum-seeker claimed that he had been subject to persecution because of his homosexuality. He had been rejected by his family and beaten. However, this case too, has not yet been examined on its merits. The Sector for International Protection of the Ministry of the Interior established that the asylum-seeker had left his country many times and had lived in Slovenia before, on a work permit issued for seasonal work. Accordingly, the Ministry took the position that the asylum-seeker could have applied for asylum many times previously. Since he had not done so, he did not meet the provision of Article 55 of the International Protection Act,

---

[33] See Judgment of the Administrative Court no U 435/2007–7 of 25 March 2008.

[34] See Judgment of the Supreme Court of the Republic of Slovenia no I Up 165/2008 of 14 May 2008.

[35] See Conclusion of the Asylum Section of the Ministry of the Interior no 2142—425/ 2006/24 (1352–12) of 3 June 2008.

[36] According to a Fundamental Rights Agency report which mentions the same case, the two people were (allegedly) told by the staff member of the Slovenian asylum authorities that homosexuality can be cured by therapy (Danish Institute for Human Rights 2009: 10).

which requires that an asylum application be submitted as soon as possible. The Ministry rejected the application as manifestly unfounded.[37]

In the third case, the asylum application was lodged by an asylum-seeker from Iran, who claimed persecution due to his sexual orientation and mentioned fear of the death penalty, to which he would be exposed in Iran if he were caught engaging in homosexual activity. His application was rejected by the Ministry of the Interior on the grounds that his claims presented in the asylum application differed from the statements he had made at the oral interview conducted within this procedure. For example, the competent body concluded that the timing of various events was described differently when the application was lodged, compared with the description provided at the interview. When the applicant was confronted with the inconsistencies, he was not able to provide any explanation for them. Another reason for rejecting the application was that, according to the Ministry, some of his statements were not credible. For example, he claimed that the wife of his partner knew about their relationship, but only reported it to the police two years after she gained that knowledge. The Ministry decided not to consider this statement as credible, since homosexuality is a serious crime in Iran and it was not clear to the Ministry why the partner's wife would wait two years. In this case, the asylum application was considered in the accelerated procedure and rejected as manifestly unfounded, as in the case of the Kosovo applicants. When the applicant sought judicial review before the Administrative Court, the latter confirmed its first instance decision. The applicant finally appealed to the Supreme Court of the Republic of Slovenia, which found in his favour.

The Supreme Court judged that the Ministry had not clarified whether or not there was a threat of the death penalty in Iran, foreseen in accordance with Iranian criminal law if the applicant was caught engaging in homosexual activity as a non-political act. In addition, according to the Supreme Court, the Ministry would have to clarify whether the death penalty for such a crime is foreseen only for persons with homosexual orientation or also for persons who do not have such orientation but are apprehended while engaging in homosexual activity. The Supreme Court stated that examination of these facts is necessary, since if the threat of the death penalty truly existed in such cases, the application would have to be heard in a regular (not accelerated) procedure, which requires a full examination of all elements of the definition of a refugee. Specifically, the Supreme Court instructed the Ministry to examine the nature of Iranian criminal law in respect of such crimes, whether the Iranian courts issue judgments after carrying out a full criminal procedure in such cases, and if death penalties are decreed on the basis of such judgments.[38] In spite of appealing successfully to the

---

[37] See Decision of the Ministry of the Interior no 2142–1/2010/6 (1232–04) of 12 July 2010.
[38] Judgment of the Supreme Court of the Republic of Slovenia no I Up 1435/2005 of 15 December 2005.

Supreme Court, the applicant was not granted refugee status by the administrative body. For the purposes of this chapter, however, the reasons for the refusal could not be ascertained.

These three cases are, of course, not sufficient to establish any trends in relation to applicants claiming persecution due to sexual orientation. However, they are consistent with the general administrative practice of the Ministry of the Interior in the field of international protection, which rejects a large majority of asylum applications, most of them manifestly unfounded, due to the alleged lack of credibility of the asylum-seekers' statements.[39]

4. Cross-border Reproductive Services

4.1. Donor Insemination and the Legal Position of Children

In Slovenia, donor insemination is regulated by the Infertility Treatment and Procedures of Biomedically-Assisted Procreation Act. This Act takes the approach that donor insemination is one of the procedures for treatment of infertility, which means that establishment of infertility is one of the conditions of eligibility for these procedures which are paid for by the medical insurance scheme. The beneficiaries of infertility treatment procedures are defined in Article 5 (section 2) of this Act which states that eligible persons are

> a man and a woman who live in marriage or in extramarital partnership, who, in the light of medical science, cannot expect to achieve conception by means of sexual intercourse and cannot be assisted with other types of infertility treatment.

Another exceptional option for using donor insemination is allowed in cases where this would prevent the transmission of a severe genetic disease to the child (Article 5, section 3). This means that donor insemination in Slovenia is not available for single women or women with female partners, regardless of their nationality.

In 2001, the government proposed that artificial insemination services also become available for single women. On 19 April 2001, amendments to the Act were adopted, although 34 members of the parliament filed an initiative for a legislative referendum, which is a possibility provided for in the Constitution. The referendum results of 17 June 2001 prevented the amendments to the law

---

[39] In 2008, about 85% of asylum applications on which a decision was issued were rejected. See Republic of Slovenia, Ministry of the Interior, Directorate for Migration and Integration, *EMN Annual Policy Report 2009* (available at www.emn.intrasoft-intl.com/Downloads/download.do;jsessionid. . . ? fileID=1038).

from entering into force,[40] with a vote of 72.36% against the amendments. Consequently, assisted reproduction services only remain available to married and unmarried male-female couples.

For artificial insemination, the cells which are used are generally those of a man and a woman who are married or who live in extramarital partnership (Article 8, section 1). Exceptionally, donor semen or donor ova may be used if, according to medical science, there is no possibility that insemination with cells from a man and woman who are married or who live in an extramarital partnership would be successful, or if other procedures have been unsuccessful (Article 8, section 2). In any case, artificial insemination with donor semen and donor ova used at the same time is not permitted.

Since some EU Member States do allow access to donor insemination for single women or female-female partners, which is available to citizens of other EU Member States, the question arises as regards what rights the inseminated woman's female partner might have after her return to Slovenia and the child's birth.[41]

In Slovenian law, such a situation is not explicitly foreseen. The only legally available option is adoption, provided for in Articles 134 to 153 of the Marriage and Family Relations Act. In relation to adoption, there are three possible situations: (a) when a single person adopts a child; (b) when the partner of the parent adopts a child (second-parent adoption); and (c) when two partners adopt a child (joint adoption). The 1976 Marriage and Family Relations Act clearly defines only single adoption and joint adoption, whereas second-parent adoption is defined indirectly. That is, Article 138 of the Act states that married partners can only jointly adopt a child, except in the case when one of the spouses adopts a child of the other spouse. Article 135 also states that no-one may be adopted by more than one person, except in the case of a joint adoption by spouses. However, the law does not explicitly regulate a situation in which one person who is not a spouse, but a registered or cohabiting partner of the parent, wishes to adopt the partner's child. Legal theorists took the position that the lack of clear rules does not prevent the parent's partner from adopting the partner's child (second-parent adoption) since this is still in accordance with the principle that no-one may be adopted by more than one person except in the case of joint adoption by spouses. This position was also supported by the Supreme Court.[42]

This means that second-parent adoption is also available for female-female partners, one of whom would give birth to a child with the assistance of donor

---

[40] See Nataša Velikonja, *Zgodovina aktivizma za legalizacijo gejevskih in lezbičnih partnerskih zvez v Sloveniji*, available at www.ljudmila.org/lesbo/raziskave/ZgodovinaAktivizma.pdf.

[41] The same questions are raised by *Gas and Dubois v France*, a case pending before the European Court of Human Rights. See Robert Wintemute, 'Written Comments of FIDH, ICJ, ILGA-EUROPE, BAAF & NELFA to the European Court of Human Rights' in *Gas & Dubois v France*, 11 December 2009.

[42] See Conclusion of the Supreme Court of the Republic of Slovenia no II Ips 462/2009–9 of 28 January 2010, point 15. See also Novak 2007.

insemination performed in another EU Member State. In such a case, the adoptive parent would obtain all parental rights equally with the parent who gave birth to the child. If the second parent does not wish to adopt the child, that person would have no parental rights in relation to the partner's child, as only the rights of the mother who gave birth to the child would be recognised immediately after birth. It is questionable whether this is in accordance with the principle that the best interests of the child should be followed in all laws and procedures concerning children.

In July 2011 the first such second-parent adoption was carried out in practice. One of the partners in a lesbian couple filed for adoption of her partner's biological child. Her application was first rejected by the centre for social work, but on appeal it was approved by the Ministry of Labour, Family and Social Affairs. The Ministry justified its decision, stating that the second-parent adoption is still in accordance with the principle that no-one may be adopted by more than one person, except if the adopting parents are two spouses. The Ministry also stated that the law does not contain any limitations with regard to the marital status, sex or sexual orientation of the adoptive parent. It concluded that limiting second-parent adoption to male-female couples only would violate the principle of non-discrimination.[43] The decision is considered to be a landmark case, showing that the existing legislation adopted 35 years ago already allows for second-parent adoption, and that this procedure will remain accessible for same-sex partners even if the Family Code, which contains specific provisions allowing second-parent adoption, does not enter into force.

4.2. Surrogacy and the Legal Position of Children

In Slovenia, obtaining parental rights through surrogacy is not permitted by law. By definition, surrogacy implies the need for assisted reproduction services, such as artificial insemination of donor ova or the ova of the surrogate mother (in the latter case, the surrogate mother is also the genetic mother of the child). For this reason, the provisions prohibiting surrogate motherhood are contained in the Infertility Treatment and Procedures of Biomedically-Assisted Procreation Act. Article 7 of this Act states that a woman who intends to give the baby to a third person after birth (with or without financial compensation) is not entitled to assisted reproduction services. If this provision is not respected, the person who provides such services is punished for a misdemeanour in accordance with the law, or may be found guilty of a crime specified in Article 121 of the 2008 Criminal Code. The punishment for such a crime is imprisonment for between six months and five years.

---

[43] Ministry of Labour, Family and Social Affairs, decision no 12030–7/2011/4 of 14 July 2011.

As in the case of donor insemination, the question arises as to the nature of the parental rights in Slovenia of couples who become parents to a child by surrogacy which takes place abroad, especially in another EU Member State where surrogacy is legal. If only one person from the same-sex couple obtained parental rights in relation to the child, the procedure is the same as in the above-mentioned cases of female-female partners who received assisted reproduction services in the form of donor insemination abroad. In such a case, the same-sex partner of the couple who did not obtain parental rights would have to undertake the second-parent adoption procedure.

However, if both same-sex partners legally become parents in the Member State where the child was born through surrogacy, a different procedure applies. First of all, if surrogacy is performed abroad, it is not considered to be a crime in Slovenia. Secondly, in such a case, both partners probably became legal parents because of a formal judicial decision by the competent court in the country where the child was born. This decision is usually necessary, as otherwise the woman who gave birth to the child would legally become a mother, which is not the intended result of surrogacy. In such cases, second-parent adoption is not an appropriate procedure as both partners are already recognised as parents of the child in another EU Member State, so that the aim of any further procedure would be to obtain recognition of their existing parental rights in Slovenia. In such cases, the procedure for recognition of foreign judicial decisions must be carried out in accordance with the Private International Law and Procedure Act.[44]

According to Article 94, section 1 of this Act, a foreign judicial decision is treated equally with a decision issued by a court of the Republic of Slovenia, and has the same legal effect as a domestic decision, only if it is recognised by a court of the Republic of Slovenia. One of the more important elements which must be considered in such procedures is that a foreign judicial decision is not recognised if the effect of its recognition would be contrary to the public order of the Republic of Slovenia. In this aspect, public order should not be understood as all the norms and provisions of the currently valid legislation in Slovenia, but only as a basic principle of law (Kramberger Škerl 2008). In other words, in such cases the courts in Slovenia are not allowed to examine whether or not the same type of decision would be possible under Slovenian law, but can only evaluate the effects of the recognised decision and their relation to public order. In this particular case, this means that the court would have to take into account, for example, the rights of the child and evaluate whether it is in the best interests of the child to have its parents recognised in the country of its birth but not in Slovenia. At the time of writing there have been no cases in which a child was born through surrogacy in another EU Member State to a same-sex couple who are Slovenian nationals. However, there has been such a case in which the child

---

[44] Zakon o mednarodnem zasebnem pravu in postopku, Uradni list RS no 56/1999.

was born in the USA. In this case, the parental rights of the same-sex (male-male) couple were recognised, through the procedure for recognition of foreign judicial decisions.[45]

This shows that, even though assisted reproduction in Slovenia is not in principle available to same-sex couples, there are ways of recognising parental rights deriving from cross-border reproductive services provided within the framework of EU Member States or other countries. In general, reproductive services in Slovenia are deemed to be widely available, as several assisted reproduction attempts have been paid for by medical insurance, which may be considered, at least implicitly, as a recognition of the right to be a parent. However, this right is only recognised for male-female partners, and not for individuals or same-sex couples. The current state of the law reflects the position in the legislation (which is discriminatory in relation to the family status and sexual orientation of those eligible for assisted reproduction). It still remains to be seen what the development of the right to be a parent will be, if and when the courts start to decide cases in this area.

5. Concluding Remarks

To conclude, a basic legal framework in relation to incidents of hate crime and hate speech, as well as protection of discrimination, is now in place. There are no provisions in the law which would in any way prohibit expressions of homosexuality. Although no legal provision explicitly prohibits homophobia in general, there are several provisions in place which protect an individual from specific forms of homophobic act or speech. Therefore, we can by no means conclude that Slovenian law is openly homophobic. However, a close examination shows that there are several gaps in the legislation, with regard both to enforcement procedures and substantive rights, which contribute to the persistence of homophobia in society. Accordingly, there is much room for improvement with a view to building a comprehensive system which would effectively contribute towards fighting homophobia. For the most part, the law is a reflection of developments in Slovenian society, which is especially true of sexual orientation and homophobia. So far, Slovenian law-makers have not been able to take steps which would fully reflect that change of social attitudes towards homosexuality. Certain positive traits of the law, such as relatively wide anti-discrimination protection and inclusion of specific crimes in the criminal legislation, should not be taken as evidence that the legal system as a whole is free of homophobia. As with Slovenian society in general, the law in this field is marked by silence (perhaps even ignorance). In other words, it is not so much marked by specific provisions

---

[45] See Decision of the District Court (*Okrožno sodišče*) of the Republic of Slovenia no I R 226/2010 of 26 April 2010.

as it is by the lack of other provisions: it is what is not written in the law but what should be that characterises the level of homophobia, both in the law and in society.

10

Fighting Homophobia in Hungarian Law: Slowly Evolving Standards

ESZTER POLGÁRI*

1. Hate Crime and Hate Speech

1.1. Legislation against Hate Speech

In order to try to stop the spread of racist and homophobic intolerance, the Hungarian Parliament has attempted to enact more effective and tailored hate speech legislation several times. All of the proposed bills were vetoed by the then President of the Republic and later quashed by the Constitutional Court. The court has not been willing to lower the constitutional standard of protection afforded to freedom of expression. Although all attempts aimed at broadening the criminal prohibition of hate speech beyond 'incitement to hatred' have failed, the issue has been kept on the agenda and legislators seem to be conscious of the problem. Apart from criminal law protection against hate speech, personality rights protection under the Civil Code and the harassment provisions of the Act on Equal Treatment offer limited possibilities of combating homophobic speech, as the emerging case law shows.

The most severe forms of hate speech are currently sanctioned by criminal law, providing very limited protection against homophobic speech. The current version of the Criminal Code[1] defines incitement to hatred as follows:

Article 269—Incitement against a community

A person who incites to hatred before the general public against:

---

* Shortly after this chapter was finished, the new Basic Law of Hungary was adopted, changing among other things the rules of the Constitutional Court, limitation of rights and access to constitutional review. As the Law will come into force on 1 January 2012, this chapter reflects the rules in force at the time of writing.
[1] Act No IV of 1978 on the Criminal Code (hereinafter Criminal Code).

203

a) the Hungarian nation,
b) any national, ethnic, racial group, or any group of the society, shall be punishable for such an offence with imprisonment of up to three years.

The reference to 'any group of the society' has been part of Article 269 since the transition when the socialist crime of 'Insult against the Community' was amended.[2] Initially, Article 269 prohibited incitement against—among others—the Hungarian nation or any nationality, the constitutional order of the Hungarian People's Republic, and any people, religion or race. In addition, it provided limited protection for groups: the protected grounds were race, religion or socialist conviction. The text enacted in 1989 established that:

(1) Anyone who, before a large public audience, incites hatred against:
  a) the Hungarian nation, any other nationality
  b) people, religion or race, or any group of society shall be punishable for a felony offence with imprisonment of up to three years.
(2) Anyone in the same circumstances who uses an offensive or denigrating expression or commits similar acts against the groups defined in the first paragraph shall be punishable for an offence with imprisonment for up to one year, corrective training or a fine.

The above text of Article 269 was challenged before the Constitutional Court (*ex post facto* review). In 1992, the Constitutional Court declared that the second paragraph of Article 269 was unconstitutional: the court emphasised that freedom of expression (Article 61 of the Constitution[3]) had only external limitations and that, as long as the expression remained within those limitations, it deserved protection, regardless of the veracity or value of the speech itself. While the restriction on freedom of expression and press under Article 269(1) was justified by the historically-proven harmful effect of incitement to hatred, the protection of fundamental constitutional values and the fulfilment of international obligations, Article 269(2) singled out expressions on the basis of their content. In case of the behaviour defined in paragraph (1), the impact and consequences for the individual and for society were so grave that other forms of accountability were inadequate to deal with those publicly inciting to hatred. In the case of paragraph (2), other legal means than criminal law offered adequate remedy.[4] Following the Constitutional Court's milestone decision in 1992, Article 269(1) remained in force unaltered.

---

[2] Act No XXV of 1989.
[3] Article 61(1) of the Constitution of Hungary (in force at the time of writing): 'In the Republic of Hungary, every person shall have the right to freedom of expression and to freedom of speech, and furthermore to the right to receive and impart information of public interest.'
[4] Constitutional Court Decision No 30/1992 (26 May) Most of the decisions of the Constitutional Court mentioned are available in English on the court's website at www.mkab.hu/index.php?id=home_en.

In 1996, Parliament amended Article 269 of the Criminal Code.[5] The new version prescribed the following:

[A] person who incites to hatred before the general public against:

a)   the Hungarian nation,
b)   any national, ethnic, racial or religious group, or any group of the society, or commits another act suitable for the arousal of hatred shall be punishable for such an offence with imprisonment for up to three years.

The new wording of the Criminal Code thus eliminated the reference from point a) to 'any other nationality' and criminalised a further act ('another act suitable for the arousal of hatred'). This provision was also challenged before the Constitutional Court, which declared that penalising any kind of act which was capable of inciting hatred among the general public violated the constitutional principle of rule of law and legal certainty, as the provision in question (Article 269, as defined in 1996) was not clearly phrased and was not sufficiently specific. Thus, the restriction on freedom of expression was unnecessary and disproportionate.[6] The court kept the remaining parts of Article 269 in force.

The next attempt of the Parliament to amend Article 269 of the Criminal Code came in 2003. The legislator's proposed text tried to follow the Constitutional Court's expectations and enact a provision aimed at criminalising the milder forms of hate speech (that is, those which do not reach the level of incitement to hatred):

(1)   Any person who before the general public inflames to hatred or calls for violent acts against any nation, any other national, ethnic, racial or religious group, or any other group of the society commits an offence punishable with imprisonment of up to three years.
(2)   Any person who before the general public insults dignity by
       a)   disparaging or humiliating others on the basis of national, ethnic, racial or religious identity, or
       b)   stating that on the basis of belonging to a national, ethnic, racial or religious group, any person or group of persons are inferior or superior, commits an offence punishable with imprisonment of up to two years.[7]

The President of the Republic, before signing it, sent the Bill passed by the Parliament to the Constitutional Court for preliminary review. In his petition, the President claimed that the wording 'inflame to hatred' ran the risk of lowering the threshold of protection provided for freedom of expression. He also criticised the phrase 'calls for violent action' as it did not imply the need for actual violation of individual rights. In addition, in his opinion, Article 269(2) was unconstitutional, since it only protected the public peace in an abstract and

---

[5] Act No XVII of 1996.
[6] Constitutional Court Decision No 12/1999 (21 May).
[7] Bill no T/5179 (2003).

general way—a limitation which was unacceptable under Article 61 of the Constitution, which guarantees freedom of expression. The Constitutional Court, although accepting many of the President's comments, emphasised that the legislator's intent was to depart from the constitutionally acceptable 'incitement to hatred' and to criminalise instead 'inflaming to hatred' and 'calling for violent acts' in Article 269(1)—thus also including less dangerous conduct in the same criminal offence. None of these types of conduct—as the court's reasoning went—reached the constitutionally required minimum level of punishability, and for this reason unnecessarily restricted freedom of expression. As regards the modified Article 269(2), the Constitutional Court found that, when trying to protect human dignity and public peace against hate speech, the legislator failed to choose the least restrictive means. The court reiterated its earlier stand on abusive speech: according to the above-mentioned 1992 decision, criminal sanctions may be applied only in defence of other constitutional rights and only when unavoidably necessary. The proposed version of Article 269 was thus found in violation of the Constitution and the previous wording of the Criminal Code remained in force.[8]

In 2008, the Parliament changed the approach: instead of trying to include further acts in Article 269 (incitement to hatred), a new provision was proposed. The new statutory definition of hate speech in Article 181/A of the Criminal Code would have criminalised 'disparagement':

(1) Any person who in relation to the Hungarian nation, any national, ethnic, racial religious group, or any group of society before the general public uses or circulates expressions which are capable of denigrating a member of a given group or violating human dignity, commits a misdemeanour punishable with imprisonment of up to two years.

(2) Under paragraph (1) any person is punishable who before the general public uses gestures—especially those which are reminiscent of a totalitarian regime or ideology—which are capable of denigrating the Hungarian nation or any group of society, in particular national, ethnic, racial or religious groups, or of violating these groups' human dignity.

(3) Any person who in connection with a political party or political activity of civil organisation in relation to a public appearance
a) uses or circulates expression capable of denigrating the members of that particular group, or of violating their human dignity,
b) acts as described in paragraph (2) shall not be punishable.[9]

The President of the Republic, again, requested a preliminary review from the Constitutional Court; he considered the new criminal provision to be in violation of Article 61 of the Constitution. In its decision delivered in 2008, the Constitutional Court recalled that freedom of expression was guaranteed, regardless of the veracity or content of the expression, hence the legislator could only use the

---

[8] Constitutional Court Decision 18/2004 (25 May).
[9] Bill No T/2785 (2008).

means of criminal law in extreme cases, that is, when the expression was capable of instigating intense emotions in the majority of people, when the speech endangered fundamental rights which enjoyed a prominent place among constitutional values, and when the expression constituted a clear and present danger of breaching the public peace. In the case of the newly-enacted criminal provisions, the victims of the crime were neither physical persons nor clearly defined members of a group. It was an intangible offence which did not require the actual violation of individual rights or even any threat to them. A person could be convicted even if no-one's personality rights had been violated. It would have been sufficient if the expression or the gesture in an abstract sense were capable of violating human dignity. The aim of the amendment was clearly to punish hate speech, even when the injured party could not be identified and disparagement was based on belonging to one of the protected groups. In the Constitutional Court's opinion, it was legitimate to protect people who refused to become a 'captive audience' forced to listen to hate speech. The problem with the proposal was that it would have punished all forms of hate speech, including cases in which the issue of a captive audience did not arise.[10]

In conclusion, despite all the recent efforts of Parliament, no new hate speech legislation has been passed, because of the increased protection afforded by the Constitutional Court to freedom of expression.[11]

In addition to criminal law protection against 'incitement to hatred', victims of homophobic speech—especially in cases of milder forms of expressions targeted at a particular person—may seek a remedy in civil law. The Civil Code offers such remedies within the framework of protecting personality rights under the following conditions:

Article 76
Any breach of the principle of equal treatment; violation of the freedom of conscience; unlawful deprivation of personal freedom; injury to body or health; contempt for or insult to the honour, integrity, or human dignity of private persons shall be deemed as violations of personality rights.

Article 84
(1) A person whose personality rights have been violated shall have the following options under civil law, depending on the circumstances of the case:
   a) that person may demand a court declaration of the occurrence of the infringement;
   b) demand to have the infringement discontinued and the perpetrator restrained from further infringement;

---

[10] Constitutional Court Decision No 95/2008 (3 July).

[11] There is, however, some inconsistency in the jurisprudence of the Constitutional Court and the standards of the President resorting to preliminary review. In 2010—by Act No XXXVI of 2010—Parliament criminalised denial of the Holocaust: Article 269/C of the Criminal Code protects the 'dignity of a Holocaust survivor' by prohibiting denial of the fact that the Holocaust happened. The law came into force without any constitutional objection.

c)   demand that the perpetrator make restitution in a statement or by some other suitable means and, if necessary, that the perpetrator, at his own expense, make an appropriate public disclosure for restitution;

d)   demand the termination of the injurious situation and the restoration of the previous state by and at the expense of the perpetrator and, furthermore, to have the effects of the infringement nullified or deprived of their injurious nature;

e)   file charges for punitive damages in accordance with liability regulations under civil law.

(2)   If the amount of punitive damages that can be imposed is insufficient to mitigate the gravity of the actionable conduct, the court shall also be entitled to penalise the perpetrator by ordering that person to pay a fine to be used for public purposes.

(3)   The above provisions shall also apply if the infringement occurred through the publication of an illegal advertisement.

Article 85

(1)   ... personality rights may only be enforced personally. A person with limited legal capacity may take action in person in protecting personality rights.[12]

The protection of personality rights is not specifically aimed at providing legal remedies against homophobic speech although, through the reference to the principle of equal treatment and human dignity, it does supply a sufficient legal basis for such civil law claims. One of the main deficiencies of the civil law regulation is that it only provides protection if the speech is targeted directly at identifiable individual(s), which makes the regulation difficult to use against general homophobic expressions, no matter how harmful they may be.

In 2007, the Parliament tried to remedy this problem—the need for a victim in a strict sense—and added a subsection to Article 76 of the Civil Code:

Article 76/A

(1)   The violation of personality rights shall be established in particular in the case of public and gravely insulting conduct which targets racial identity, belonging to a national or ethnic minority, religious or other conviction, sexual orientation, sexual identity or any other essential attribute of one's personality and which refers to a group of people having such an attribute that is in a minority within society.

(2)   The injuring party cannot refer in defence of his contested conduct that it has been not directly and identifiably aimed at a party or parties enforcing a claim on the basis of paragraph (1).

(3)   The claims under Article 84(1) may also be enforced on the motion of any social organisation or public interest foundation established for the protection of human rights. These organisations can only bring a claim under Article 84(1) point e) [punitive damages] in the interest of the insulted community and for the benefit of one of the public interest foundations.

---

[12]   Act no. IV of 1959 of the Civil Code of Hungary.

(4)   The claims specified in paragraphs (1)-(3) may be enforced by initiating a legal action within 90 days after the alleged violation of rights have occurred.[13]

The Bill was a remarkable step for the LGBT community, as it would have explicitly provided personality rights protection against homophobic speech or conduct within the framework of the Civil Code. The President of the Republic—again in defence of freedom of expression—refused to sign it and requested a preliminary review from the Constitutional Court. In his petition, the President claimed that the proposed legislation imposed a disproportionate restriction on freedom of expression. The President questioned the existence of personality rights of groups. In his interpretation, the amendment rested on the assumption that the insult aimed at the community resulted in violation of the subjective rights of community members. He was concerned about the fact that the new provision failed to take into consideration the intensity of the relationship between the group and its members, as well as the size and the definition of the community considered as forming a group. Furthermore, the President argued that the minority position of a particular group within society does not justify offering it a privileged status.

In its decision, delivered in 2008, the Constitutional Court shared the President's reservations and declared the proposed amendment unconstitutional. The court emphasised that only natural persons have human dignity and thus that only they—in their status as individuals—are entitled to legal protection. The court also found the definition of groups problematic: considering the great number of personal traits that are suitable for determining personality and forming a group, the legal regulation fails to reduce the restriction on freedom of expression to the minimum. The right to bring actions by civil organisations was impossible to interpret within the current legal framework, as they would have applied individual legal remedies.[14]

In November 2008, the then governing party submitted to Parliament a new proposal on civil law remedies against hate speech: a bill providing the necessary legal means for protection against certain activities which might seriously harm a person's dignity.[15] The proposal was passed by Parliament, but the President of the Republic sent the bill to the Constitutional Court for preliminary constitutional review. The Constitutional Court has not yet delivered its decision.

The newly proposed Act would provide protection against degrading or threatening behaviour targeted at members of a group. Protected groups are identified on the basis of belonging to a national or ethnic minority, religious conviction or sexual orientation. The available remedies would be the same as for a violation of personality rights. The Act would provide protection against degrading or threatening behaviour targeted at members of a group. Considering

---

[13]   Bill No T/3719.
[14]   Constitutional Court Decision No 96/2008 (3 July).
[15]   Bill No T/6219.

the recent constitutional changes, it is very uncertain whether the Constitutional Court will deliver a decision on the case at all, and even if it does, whether it will change its earlier position on the protection of freedom of expression.

Lastly, after all the failures of the hate speech amendments, individual Members of Parliament submitted a proposal which aimed at removing the constitutional barrier.[16] It would have amended Article 61 of the Constitution guaranteeing freedom of expression by introducing a limitation clause, thus excluding the possibility of relying on the text of the Constitution in defence of speech harming the dignity of communities. The proposal did not receive the support of the Government, nor the necessary two-thirds majority in Parliament. The amendment was widely criticised by civil society organisations for disproportionately restricting freedom of expression.[17]

In addition to the remedies provided by the Civil and Criminal Codes, the definition of harassment in the Act on equal treatment and promotion of equal opportunities (ET Act)[18] in Article 10 is also worthy of mention:

> (1) Harassment is a conduct of sexual or other nature violating human dignity related to the person's characteristics as defined in Article 8, with the purpose or effect of creating an intimidating, hostile, degrading, humiliating or offensive environment around that person.

The harassment powers of the Equal Treatment Authority (ET Auth)[19] allow it to provide a legal remedy in cases where the protection of personality rights cannot be pursued, and an *actio popularis* claim might be initiated on the grounds of this provision, with the possibility of the ET Auth imposing a public interest fine. For the ET Act, the prohibition of harassment aims at combating behaviour and actions violating the human dignity of a person. Acts violating Article 84 of the Civil Code, cited above, may be very different, ranging from mocking an individual on the basis of their actual or assumed sexual orientation, through anti-gay/lesbian jokes, to actual physical violence. The ET Auth, or the court adjudicating on the basis the ET Act, must primarily consider the affected person's subjective perception of the situation and reach an objective decision on the basis of that perception. The rules on evidence as specified in the ET Auth's rules of procedure are also applicable in cases of alleged harassment: petitioners must prove that they have suffered a disadvantage (due to a violation of their dignity or the fact that, in their opinion, a hostile, degrading or offensive environment was created around them). Respondents must prove that they were not obliged to respect the principle of equal treatment (that is, the provisions of

---

[16] Bill No T/9584.

[17] On the position of the Hungarian Civil Liberties Union see www.mixonline.hu/Cikk.aspx?id=30393.

[18] Act No CXXV of 2003 on Equal Treatment and Promotion of Equal Opportunities (hereafter ET Act).

[19] For detailed information on the Equal Treatment Authority, see www.egyenlobanasmod.hu/index.php?lang=en.

the ET Act) in the particular case or that they had acted in accordance with the law. During the procedure, naturally, respondents may defend the content of any allegedly harmful expression (Kárpáti et al 2006).

1.2. Legislation against Hate Crime

Since 2008, LGBT communities fall within the scope of Article 174/B of the Criminal Code, which criminalises violence against a member of a community. In addition to national, ethnic, racial and religious groups, a general reference to 'any other group of society' was included, which, according to the interpretation of the Ministry of Justice, also includes sexual minorities. This position also seems to be supported, at least in some cases, by police practice; there have already been some investigations initiated against offenders for homophobic hate crimes under this provision.

Until the 2008 amendment, LGBT people were left without any criminal law protection against crimes motivated by homophobic hate. In 1996, a new provision was added to the Criminal Code, which provided additional protection to certain groups, but none of them covered LGBT people.[20] The pre-2009 Article 174/B (the 2008 amendment came into force on 1 February 2009), prohibited violence against a member of a national, ethnic, racial or religious group with the following wording:

Article 174/B

(1) The person who assaults another person because that person belongs or is believed to belong to a national, ethnic, racial or religious group, or coerces that person by violence or threats into doing or not doing or into enduring something, commits an offence and shall be punishable with imprisonment for up to five years.

(2) The punishment shall be imprisonment from two years to eight years, if the act of crime is committed:
    a) by force of arms,
    b) in an armed manner,
    c) causing a considerable injury of interest,
    d) by torture of the injured party,
    e) in groups,
    f) by criminal conspiracy.

As this provision created a *sui generis* crime, with more rigorous sanctions for violent acts motivated by racial or religious hatred, until the 2008 amendment, homophobic hate crimes were only prosecuted as 'ordinary' offences such as disorderly conduct or causing bodily harm.

In response to the violent attacks during and after the 2007 LGBT Pride events, in 2008 Parliament amended the above-mentioned Article 174/B of the Criminal

---

[20] Act No XVII of 1996.

Code by adding to national, ethnic, racial and religious groups a reference to 'any other group of society'. This provision, which has been in force since 1 February 2009, prohibits the following conduct:

Article 174/B

(1) The person who assaults another person because that person belongs or is believed to belong to a national, ethnic, racial or religious group, or any other group of society, … commits an offence and shall be punishable with imprisonment of up to five years.
(2) [same as before amendment].[21]

The legislator's intent—according to the explanatory report attached to the Act—was to provide more efficient and deterrent sanctions against those violating basic rights, including freedom of assembly. The drafters realised that groups other than those already protected were subject to discriminatory acts or violent attacks. However, despite the efforts of LGBT organisations, the amendment fails to specify which groups are protected. The explanatory report claims that the groups falling within the scope of protection, because of their very diversity, cannot be named. What is decisive when establishing the offence is whether the person or persons were subject to violence or any other act prohibited by Article 174/B on the basis of belonging to one clearly identifiable community.

The Háttér Support Society for LGBT People requested clarification from the Ministry of Justice on the interpretation of 'any other group of society', as in the parliamentary debate two proposals had directly or indirectly (by referring to the ET Act) suggested the inclusion of an explicit reference to sexual minorities. The Government did not support any of these proposals. However, an official statement signed by Ms Katalin Gönczöl, State Secretary for Criminal Policy at the Ministry of Justice, confirmed that the legislator's intent was to cover sexual minorities (sexual orientation and sexual or gender identity) as protected groups. In the same statement, the Ministry also informed the Háttér Support Society for LGBT people that it was planning training in cooperation with the Advocate General and the National Judicial Council, to ensure uniform interpretation of the amendment.[22]

Although considerable resources have been devoted to developing a national crime prevention strategy, the programme completely ignores the LGBT community as a potential victim group. The website devoted to the social and police components of the strategy makes no mention of the needs of the victims of homophobic hate crimes.[23] Currently, there is no reliable database providing guidance for researchers as to the numbers of registered homophobic hate crimes and the outcomes of prosecutions. There have been attempts to collect data on

[21] Act No LXXIX of 2008.
[22] The statement is on file with the author.
[23] See www.bunmegelozes.hu/.

hate crimes, but all of them approach the problem from either the perpetrator's or the victim's point of view, or include only certain crimes, thus often providing naturally distorted data.

The *modus operandi* in force until 12 March 2009 was applicable to cases in which, on the basis of well-founded suspicion, an investigation was ordered. The register did not include all cases: only intentional crimes were considered, and only a few groups were included. The questionnaire to be filled out by the police only required information on sexual orientation in the case of victims.[24] In 2001, the police started to collect data on the sexual orientation of the alleged perpetrators of homicides. The Order on the rules of crime analysis prescribes that a form with 256 questions must be filled out in all cases of murder. It must be done on a case-by-case basis and the police can choose the answers to each question from an exhaustive list. A question on sexual orientation is included among those concerning the personality and the personal circumstances of the defendant.[25] Lastly, in 2003, Robotzsaru-2000 (Robocop-2000) replaced the previous method and created a unified system for collecting data. However, there is no publicly accessible information about the types of data which are collected.

1.3. Case law related to Events surrounding Pride Marches

Since 2007, there has been heavy opposition to LGBT Pride marches in Budapest. In that year, the police were unprepared. Violent counter-demonstrators and peaceful marchers were allowed to march side by side without significant police protection or separation, which put the marchers' safety at direct risk. In 2008, police cordons were erected along the route of the march, although counter-demonstrators were free to throw eggs, potatoes and even heavier and more dangerous objects (cans, stones and so on) at Pride participants, without effective interference from the police. As a result of these events—especially street fights between police and counter-demonstrators—several people were arrested, many of them for throwing eggs. Earlier in 2008, while he was giving a speech (at an event other than Pride), the Mayor of Budapest also had eggs thrown at him. A public debate began about the criminal nature of such acts: both the courts and the prosecution were of the opinion that throwing eggs without causing physical harm constituted a form of symbolic expression and thus enjoyed constitutional

---

[24] Order No 22/2000 (XII. 29) on interim rules of the Modus Operandi register.
[25] Order of the National Police Headquarter No 13/2001 (10 February) on rules of crime analysis.

protection (Julesz 2008).[26] However, the report of the Parliamentary Commissioner for Civil Rights[27] published after the march emphasised that throwing eggs and other objects at peaceful marchers cannot be considered as an act protected by the right to freedom of expression.[28]

The attackers arrested during or after the 2008 Pride March were all charged with hooliganism. The Pest Central District Court acquitted one of them: the defendant had allegedly only been carrying one egg, and threw it at the marchers believing that his action was not illegal. The court reasoned that, due to prevailing public opinion and the differing opinion on the legal nature of the act, he could reasonably have believed that his act (throwing the egg) was not punishable as a crime.[29] The other defendant was eventually convicted for breach of the peace: unlike the first offender, he resisted the police and tried to hide his face while throwing eggs at the marchers. He was fined less than €200.[30]

The judgments were widely criticised by both politicians and NGOs. The Parliamentary Commissioner for Civil Rights requested clarification from the Supreme Court on the legal status of throwing eggs. In a statement dated 29 September 2008, the Supreme Court stated that, when a person throws objects at another person—even if those objects are not capable of causing physical harm, the thrower commits a crime. The act is considered as defamation (through actions rather than words) or, in more serious cases, hooliganism.[31] The Prosecutor General also confirmed this interpretation, emphasising that defamation is punishable only as private motion; no investigation can be started *ex officio*.[32]

Those demonstrators who clashed violently with the police were treated more severely by the authorities: those who were part of the group which attacked the police were given suspended prison sentences and were also forbidden from attending any kind of public gathering where more than 50 people were present.[33]

---

[26] The author of the study maintains that the law usually treated such incidents as acts falling under the prohibition of libel/defamation and causing bodily harm. Prior to the Pride events, the conflict of free speech and human dignity was not even an issue in such criminal cases.

[27] For further information on the legal status, tasks and competences of the Ombudsman, see www.obh.hu/allam/eng/index.htm.

[28] ÁJOB Projektfüzetek—Gyülekezési jogi project, 2009/1—Freedom of assembly project.

[29] Case No 11.Sze.11.280/2008/2. All court cases mentioned in this study are available at www.birosag.hu/engine.aspx?page=anonim.

[30] Case No 11.Sze.11.282/2008/2.

[31] See Opinion no 71, Criminal Law Section, file no 2008.El.II.E.3/10 (available at www.l-b.hu).

[32] A summary of the press release published by the speaker for the Attorney General is available at www.jogiforum.hu/hirek/18311#axzz1KWvmE8nS.

[33] Information on the court proceedings are available at www.napiaszonline.hu/aktualis/melegfelvonulas__masfel_ev_felfuggesztett_5585.

A few days before the 2009 Pride March, some extreme right-wing figures published online articles which explicitly called for violence against the participants.[34] The Pride organisers complained to the police, claiming that that there was proof of preparation of violent crime against a member of a community. One of the accused has been charged, and the case is pending. On his first appearance in court in March 2011, he was found guilty, but was only sentenced to probation for two years.[35]

Although the Pride marches in 2009 and 2010 went relatively smoothly, due to extreme police protection and the choice of less central, relatively isolated locations, several participants were attacked on leaving the events. This common problem is one which, from the very beginning, the police failed to treat as a hate crime prohibited by Article 174/B of the Criminal Code. It is important to note that violence against a member of a community is a crime which can be prosecuted *ex officio*, and is unlike the less serious offence of causing bodily harm, for which the victim must submit a private motion to have the police start an investigation. The different categorisation of the acts necessarily means different punishments: while violence against a member of a community is punishable with imprisonment, merely causing bodily harm—especially in the case of first offenders—is sanctioned by a fine, which has a significantly weaker deterrent effect. This is why NGOs, headed by the Hungarian Civil Liberties Union, asked law-enforcement authorities to treat such cases with due care and to consider indicators which would support a more serious classification for the offence.[36] In addition, specific training on hate crimes (based on international standards and comparative studies) was offered to the police by the Háttér Support Society for LGBT people.

Pride events not only attract violence, but also provide a venue and an alleged reason for engaging in homophobic speech. The National Radio and Television Commission[37] (NRTC) has received several submissions from LGBT organisations complaining about the one-sided, false and partial portrayal of LGBT communities by television channels. These complaints were usually submitted against TV programmes broadcast shortly before the Pride marches. In July 2001, the public television's popular weekly news programme showed a report about the differing views concerning homosexuality and the Pride March. It portrayed the LGBT community as sick, dangerous and harmful to young people. In addition to misleading and out-dated statements, the editors gave television time to religious views claiming that, according to the Bible, homosexuality is a sin. The NRTC, accepting the decision of the Complaints Committee, found that the national television had violated the principle of diversity and balance,

---

[34] Available at www.kuruc.info/r/6/45812/.
[35] The judgment was still not available at the time of writing.
[36] The press release of the Hungarian Civil Liberties Union is on file with the author.
[37] Replaced by the Media Council. (Act CLXXXV of 2010 on Media Services and Mass Media). Further information is available at www.mediatanacs.hu/english.php.

and failed to provide a true picture of the LGBT community. The way the programme was edited and cut could reasonably have contributed to the growth of social intolerance towards the LGBT community. The NRTC requested the broadcasting of a statement containing the reasons for its decision in the public television editors' next programme.[38]

Two years later, again in relation to the Pride March events, Hírtévé—a right-wing affiliated news channel—organised a talk show in which the participants openly incited hatred against the LGBT community. The Háttér Support Society for LGBT People submitted a complaint to the NRTC. In the meantime, the television channel provided an equal amount of time for representatives of the LGBT community to rebut the stereotypical and hateful statements made in the impugned programme. In return, Háttér withdrew its complaint.[39]

In 2009, LGBT organisations won a huge victory against Echo TV which, in a programme covering the LGBT Equality (Pride?) March entitled 'Nonsense', allowed a guest speaker to make unequivocally homophobic statements which were capable of fuelling the already existing intolerance. The NRTC suspended the broadcasting privileges of Echo TV for 90 minutes.[40]

Although most of the cases submitted to the NRTC have been successful, homophobia remains widespread in broadcasting.

1.4. Alternative Protection against Hate Speech: the Equal Treatment Authority and the Prohibition of Harassment

As stated above, in principle and in practice, the provision on harassment in the ET Act[41] can provide protection against hate speech directed against LGBT people. Since its foundation in 2005, the ET Auth has had several occasions to rule in cases where complainants alleged violation of the prohibition of harassment. In 2006, the petitioner, a mother, claimed violation of the ET Act because the head of her child's school had asked a question about her daughter's sexual orientation ('Are you [and your friend] lesbians or what?') in front of the entire class. In the mother's view, this could create a hostile environment for her daughter. The petition was eventually rejected by the ET Auth since—according to its reasoning—the head of the school had never intended to violate the human dignity of the child, and in the proceedings she apologised several times for her question, while admitting that it could have given rise to misunderstandings. The decision emphasised:

---

[38] NRTC Decision No 1472/2001 (26 October).
[39] Information about the case is available at www.hatter.hu/programjaink/jogsegelyszolgalat/jelentosebb-ugyeink/hir-tv-teriteken-2003.
[40] NRTC Decision no 2500/2009 (16 December).
[41] Act No CXXV of 2003 on equal treatment and promotion of equal opportunities.

Harassment always presupposes the intention of the respondent to create a hostile environment. It is rarely one single act, most of the time it is composed of a series of actions which result in creating a degrading environment around the targeted person.[42]

In 2009, the ET Auth again rejected a complaint submitted by a lesbian couple living in a shelter for the homeless. The couple alleged that the remarks made by the employees of the shelter questioned their sexual orientation, and that the employees failed to protect them from other residents. The shelter was able to justify its actions: it could provide documentary evidence that the complainants had disturbed others several times with their behaviour, and many complaints had been submitted against them. Moreover, another lesbian couple who were former residents of the shelter supported the position adopted by the authorities, stating that they had not experienced any kind of hostile attitude during their stay.[43]

In 2010, in an important decision, the ET Auth found an employer to be in violation of the principle of equal treatment as defined by the ET Act, because the petitioner's colleagues and superior had created a hostile environment around her on the basis of her sexual orientation. As part of the procedure, witnesses were questioned and confirmed that one of the employers regularly mocked the petitioner and told jokes about her sexual orientation. On this employer's initiative, the victim's sexual orientation became the subject of various workplace discussions. During the hearing, the employer admitted that although his remarks had been made 'in good faith', he might have offended the employee, but he had not intended to harass her within the meaning of the ET Act's definition. The company where both people worked tried to defend itself by emphasising that it could not assume responsibility for remarks made by its employees, but the ET Auth rejected this argument. The reasoning behind this decision stressed the fact that violating the prohibition of harassment does not presuppose intentional acts; actions or behaviour which potentially have the effect of creating a degrading environment could also be illegal. In practice, expressions or jokes not intended to humiliate the person towards whom they were directed but which, in the subjective perception of the victim, were degrading, fall under the prohibition of harassment. The company was fined approximately €800.[44] This decision by the ET Auth contradicts the above-mentioned Decision No 611/2006, because it lowers the threshold for establishing harassment, especially by making it possible to violate the prohibition of harassment with non-intentional acts. Creating a hostile environment need no longer be intended, as long as it is the result (based on the victim's subjective perception) of the perpetrator's conduct. It is to be hoped that this interpretation will be maintained for future guidance.

[42] Equal Treatment Authority Decision No 611/2006.
[43] Equal Treatment Authority Decision No 499/2009.
[44] Equal Treatment Authority Decision No 49/2010.

2. Education at all Levels

2.1. Sex Education in Public Schools: Fostering Tolerance among Students

In addition to providing specific knowledge in various disciplines, states are unquestionably under the obligation to provide—through education—socially important information of a more general kind. Sex education has been widely disputed over the past few decades, and has been discussed by the various organs of the Council of Europe.[45] It appears to be commonly accepted that sex education must be part of school curricula, although it may not amount to indoctrination or the advocacy of specific kinds of sexual activities.[46] The legislation in Hungary—on the face of it—provides a sufficient basis for creating an LGBT-friendly school environment: according to the various laws, school curricula must foster tolerance and respect for human dignity. However, actual practice at times falls below these prescribed standards.

The basic legislation in the field is the Hungarian Act on public education.[47] It contains general rules on state-run kindergarten and school education and teaching, as well as on related services and the control of activities carried out by these institutions. It defines the basic rights and obligations of students and teachers together with the responsibilities of educational institutions. Among its basic principles, the Act requires, among other things, that the institutions falling within the scope of the regulation be responsible for the physical, intellectual, emotional and moral development of children and students. Article 10(2) specifically provides:

> The personality, human dignity and rights of a child/student shall be respected, and protection shall be provided for them against physical and mental violence. Children and students may not be subject to corporal punishment, torture or cruel and humiliating retribution or treatment.

Students may freely express their opinions as long as no-one's human dignity is violated, and this puts the responsibility on schools to protect a child's dignity against harmful acts or speech by fellow students.

The ET Act also contains rules which are important in the field of education. It provides a comprehensive protection against discrimination, including in the area of education. With regard to all areas within its material scope, the ET Act explicitly prohibits direct and indirect discrimination on the basis of 'sexual

---

[45] There have been cases on sex education, both before the European Court of Human Rights, and the European Committee of Social Rights (which supervises the implementation of the European Social Charter).

[46] See *Kjeldsen, Busk Madsen and Pedersen v Denmark* 5095/71; 5920/72; 5926/72 (7 December 1976), A23, para 54.

[47] Act No LXXIX of 1993 on public education.

orientation' and 'gender identity'. In addition, the ET Act makes harassment, unlawful segregation, and retaliation or victimisation, illegal. Its material scope covers education at all levels and, apart from the general prohibitions, detailed rules apply to education. According to Article 27(1):

The principle of equal treatment extends to any care, education and training

a)   carried out in accordance with requirements approved or ordered by the State, or
b)   whose organisation is supported by the State
    ba)   by direct normative budgetary subsidy, or
    bb)   indirectly, especially by releasing or clearing taxes or by tax credit.

The ET Act also names a few areas where the principle of equal treatment is to be applied, although the list is not exhaustive. These are: defining and setting requirements for education; evaluation of performance; providing and using services related to education; access to benefits; providing accommodation and dormitories; issuing certificates, qualifications and diplomas; providing access to vocational guidance and counselling; and termination of relationships related to participation in education.

School curricula are regulated by government decree. Although the Government Decree on the National Basic Curriculum[48] (NBC) does not explicitly mention homosexuality or the rights and lives of LGBT people, there are certain values and goals therein which are broad enough to cover these areas. The Annex of the Decree contains the specific rules of the framework curricula (detailed below), within which schools are free to design their own curricula. Among the common values of teaching, the document states:

[t]he spirit of the NBC is defined by the Constitution of the Hungarian Republic and Hungarian laws, in particular the Act on public education, national and international norms on human rights, the rights of the child, the rights of national and ethnic minorities and the equality of the sexes.[49]

The NBC envisages a school where the values of democracy, humanity and respect for the individual are appropriately represented. It aims to create a school environment which promotes equal opportunities and tolerance.

The NBC also defines the basic competences schools must develop in students. One of these is 'Social and Citizens' Competence', including knowledge of citizens' basic rights as defined by the EU Charter of Fundamental Rights and other international documents. The Decree makes reference, in particular, to making students aware of diversity and cultural identities in Europe.

'Physical and moral health' is also listed among the key competences. The school—according to the Decree—is an inevitable source of information on

---

[48]   Government Decree No 243/2003. (XII 17) on the National Basic Curriculum (hereinafter NBC).
[49]   NBC, Section II—Common values of school teaching and education.

sexual culture and sexual behaviour, and it is the task of teachers to prepare children and adolescents for a healthy family life.[50]

Although the NBC only provides guidance for preparing the curricula of schools, its values and goals have the potential to permit incorporation of LGBT-related topics into teaching. The exact content of the curricula varies from school to school; for example, some institutions allow LGBT NGOs to give presentations to children, so as to incorporate the issue of non-heterosexuality into their education.

For primary and secondary schools, the NBC is supplemented by a Ministry of Education decree concerning framework curricula.[51] In its annex, the decree provides the basic guidelines that primary and secondary schools (including vocational training schools) must follow when designing their own teaching plans. The guidelines follow the basic values and goals articulated in the NBC, and propose ways in which the issue of differences in general, and homosexuality in particular, could be addressed.

The Decree first mentions homosexuality in 11th grade (students aged 16–17) biology teaching. The module on 'Regulation and Reproduction', within the general topic of 'Hormone Systems and Reproduction', devotes a section to sexuality and family planning. The Decree prescribes a general framework regarding matters which should be covered during these classes: in addition to ethical considerations surrounding family planning (especially abortion), homo-sexuality and infertility (possible causes, in vitro fertilisation, and so on) are to be taught. The sessions covering this topic must also cover 'decisions and choices in the light of Christian values'. Secondly, also for the 11th grade, the Decree— without mentioning a connection with any specific subject—sets up certain themes, all divided into modules. The general topics are: basic knowledge about life, humans and the environment. In order to help schools draw up a matching learning plan, the decree specifies the problem, learning activities, and already existing and acquirable knowledge. A separate module covers the sexuality of adults and 15.5 hours are to be spent on this. The aim of the module is to establish health-conscious behaviour and the need for and interest in valuable human relationships. The module also explicitly sets out, as one of its aims, to prepare students to live according to their chosen sexual identities. One of the problems which must be explored in schools is the changing social perception of homosexuality and the level of tolerance of sexual differences. Related activities are: individually gathering information (for example, from the media) about LGBT communities, and in-class discussions about society's attitudes towards differences in this field. Teachers are to provide students with new information and knowledge about sexuality, different sexual orientations, and different gender identities.

---

[50] NBC, Section III—Common goals of school teaching and education.
[51] Decree No 17/2004 of the Ministry of Education on issuing and validating framework curricula.

Lastly, in providing basic competence in the natural sciences, the Decree proposes that schools should include in their teaching plans for 10th grade students (aged 14–15) four sessions about (human) reproduction. In these classes, the primary and secondary sexual differences between men and women are to be described, together with the concept of heterosexuality and homosexuality. The legislator envisages discussions and demonstrations about the male and female body, guided debates about gender identity, the equality of the sexes, and tolerance of non-heterosexuality. Students should be able to realise that 'homosexuality is not merely a matter of choice (but is also determined genetically) and that an important role is played by the family in the development of personality'.

While legislation provides fairly detailed rules on how to design school curricula, actual life in schools is very much under-regulated. The current Hungarian legislation provides only partial protection against bullying: in principle, the above prohibition of harassment in the ET Act is capable of offering remedies for the victims of school violence based on their actual or perceived sexual orientation. However, the legislation is not accompanied by a consistent policy or programme that would raise awareness among students and their teachers, and which would be suitable for eliminating homophobic violence from schools.

In addition, despite the relatively progressive legislation, LGBT topics in schools are still rarely covered, and the 'issue' of non-heterosexuality is still the subject of frequent debates in Parliament. In 1996, the Ministry of Education, as part of the 'All Different, All Equal' campaign, sent out posters to schools, which aimed at fostering tolerance among students: one of the pictures showed a gay couple. The conservative opposition parties vehemently attacked the Ministry in Parliament, claiming that the campaign promoted homosexuality, which is 'harmful for society', especially since the country's population is decreasing each year. Most of the opposing MPs referred to homosexuality as an illness for which no tolerance was needed. Even the moderate opposition voices denounced the poster as 'bad'.[52]

As mentioned above, there has been a civil initiative aimed at lowering the barriers around the topic of sexuality, especially around the lives of LGBT people. It seeks to promote tolerance by offering talks for schools about LGBT topics. On 19 December 2000, one of the representatives of the extreme right-wing party made a speech denouncing the education programme of Labrisz, a Hungarian lesbian NGO. He claimed that Labrisz tried to 'recruit' new members and compared their talks in schools to sex tourism. He stressed that sexuality was a private matter and that the Ministry of Education had no role in promoting any of its forms. The Secretary of State representing the Ministry, who was a member of the then governing conservative party, emphasised that discussions on sexuality could be conducted by trained professionals and was clearly regulated by the

---

[52] See Parliamentary Records from 13 February 1996. Available at www.parlament.hu.

law on public education, although NGOs could not be forbidden from taking initiative and sending letters directly to all schools. The MP initially posing the question felt relieved, although he reiterated that homosexuality was a deviant behaviour. In his reply, the Secretary of State implicitly accepted that homosexuality was deviant. The programme, despite initial difficulties, still runs relatively successfully.[53]

The examples discussed above clearly indicate that there is still strong resistance towards anything which does not fit into the majority's heteronormative world view. The law and practice in the field of education still seem to be far apart, and it is probably practice that requires more change in the future than the law.

2.2. The Limitations of Equal Treatment: Excluding a Gay Student from a Theology Faculty

The most famous case in the field of education concerned the expulsion of an openly gay student from theological studies. The man attended the Faculty of Theology of the Károli Gáspár University, which is run by the Hungarian Reformed Church. The Faculty primarily educates theologians, ministers and teachers of religious education. On 10 October 2003, the Faculty Council adopted a statement on the religious and moral approach towards homosexuality, claiming that the University could not, according to the Bible, support same-sex relationships, same-sex marriage, adoption by same-sex couples, or the training of teachers of religious education and ministers who were sexually active lesbians or gay men. On the same day, an openly gay student was expelled from the university, because his sexual orientation made him unsuitable for the career of a minister. The decision to expel the student was appealed. The Metropolitan Court quashed the Faculty Council's decision: the scope of the Act on Higher Education also extends to universities maintained by churches. According to the Act, a student may be expelled from a university as a result of a disciplinary proceeding. The internal rules of the University made no mention of gay students being unsuitable for training, and the decision of the Faculty Council did not meet the formal requirements of the Act on Public Administration in force at that time. In the end, the student in question continued his studies at another university.[54]

In a parallel proceeding, the Háttér Support Society for LGBT People (as plaintiff) submitted an *actio popularis* complaint (based on the ET Act) on 10 February 2004, alleging breach of the right to equal treatment in Article 76 of the Civil Code. The basis of the submission was the statement adopted in October 2003 and made public in January 2004: Háttér argued that, in practice, the

[53] See Parliamentary Records from 19 December 2000.
[54] For the chronology of the case see www.otkenyer.hu/ref-ugy.php.

Faculty Council's position made participation in the education offered dependent upon a person's sexual orientation. By denouncing same-sex relationships and lifestyles, the university in question excluded non-heterosexuals from the education of ministers and theology teachers, and thus made heterosexuality a precondition for admission to the Faculty of Theology. The statement thus violated the right to equal treatment of LGBT people as a social group (Kárpáti 2005).

The first instance court summarily dismissed the petition submitted in defence of openly gay students.[55] The Court of Appeals also decided in favour of the university. In its more detailed judgment, the Court of Appeals emphasised that, in the case of religion-based education, the educational institute was entitled to express its religious views and principles, to take a stand matching its moral convictions and religious dogma, and make decisions about eligibility to be trained as a minister in line with its beliefs. Before starting their university studies, candidates for the titles of minister and teachers of religion take a voluntary oath, stating that they comply with the teachings of the church and also the regulations of the Faculty Council. In the view of the Court of Appeals, because the Faculty Council's statement was based on the religious principles advocated by the Reformed Church, the university in question had not arbitrarily discriminated, and had not exceeded the limits of its constitutionally guaranteed freedom of expression and religion.[56]

Háttér, in response to the negative judgment, submitted a motion for review by the Supreme Court. Although the Supreme Court rejected the petition, the judgment clarified important questions relating to the application of the ET Act. First of all, the court stressed that a religious entity may be exempt from the principle of equal treatment when exercising religious functions, but this does not mean that all church-related activities fall into this category. On the contrary, the ET Act covers church-run universities. Secondly, Háttér, as an organisation interested in representing the LGBT community, had the right under the ET Act to initiate *actio popularis* proceedings in defence of the principle of equal treatment. Lastly, the Supreme Court considered whether the university was obliged to respect the principle of equal treatment in this particular case. The court found that the university could provide a rational explanation for its position regarding openly gay students training to be ministers or teachers of religion, because they must comply with the moral teachings of the church. In this situation, the ET Act explicitly provides an exemption. Although the claim was rejected, the Supreme Court made several important findings, which paved the way for *actio popularis* actions under the ET Act.[57]

---

[55] Metropolitan Court, Case No 19.P.21788/2004/10.
[56] Budapest Court of Appeals, Case No 2.Pf.21318/2004/4.
[57] Supreme Court, Case No Pfv.IV.20687/2005/5.

3. Free Movement, Immigration and Asylum

3.1. Immigration of Same-sex Partners

With the coming into force of the Act on registered partnership (RPA),[58] the situation of registered same-sex partners wishing to immigrate to Hungary improved significantly. However, the improvement is only partial in the case of *de facto* (unregistered or cohabiting) same-sex partners, and in the case of asylum-seekers fearing persecution in their home countries.

Article 3(1) of the RPA states that (unless the RPA otherwise provides or explicitly excludes the application of it), the rules covering marriage are also to be applied to registered partnerships. Where the law mentions spouses, registered partners are also to be included, and the rules covering widow(er)s and divorced persons are to be applied to the surviving registered partner or former registered partner, respectively. As none of the immigration-related rights are mentioned by the RPA as exceptions, registered partners are to be treated on an equal footing with spouses in the field of immigration. In addition, the explanatory report to the RPA specifically refers to the equal rights of registered partners in immigration proceedings.

The Háttér Support Society for LGBT People requested clarification from the Immigration Authority as to the interpretation of Article 3(1) of the RPA in immigration procedures. In a statement dated 7 December 2010, the Immigration Authority reiterated the principle that, in deciding on the entry, temporary stay and residence of registered partners, the same rules shall apply in the case of spouses. However, the Authority emphasised that, in its interpretation, this only applies to partners who entered into a registered partnership in Hungary. This interpretation is clearly *contra legem*, against the legislative intent,[59] and contrary to Article 2(2)(b) of Directive 2004/38/EC, which grants 'family member' status to 'the partner with whom the Union citizen has contracted a registered partnership, on the basis of the legislation of a Member State'. The Directive refers to the legislation of 'a Member State', not 'the host Member State'.

---

[58] Act No XXIX of 2009 on registered partnership (hereinafter RPA).
[59] Correspondence on file with the author.

3.2. Freedom of Movement of EU Citizens and Nationals of EEA States

The Act on the entry and residence of persons with the right of free movement and residence[60] (Act No I of 2007) covers nationals of any Member State of the European Union, and countries which are parties to the Agreement on the European Economic Area, Article 3(1) of the RPA also applies here: registered partners are in the same position as spouses. Article 2 defines 'family members' for the purposes of Act No I of 2007: it includes among others: (a) the spouse of an EEA national; (b) the spouse of a Hungarian citizen; (c) the descendants of an EEA national or a Hungarian citizen and those of the spouse of an EEA national or a Hungarian citizen who are under the age of 21 and are dependents; and (d) unless otherwise prescribed by the Act, dependent relatives in the ascending line of an EEA national or a Hungarian citizen and of the spouse of an EEA national or a Hungarian citizen. By virtue of the RPA, the spouse in this case also means the registered partner.

However, because de facto different-sex and same-sex partners are not mentioned in the Act, their situation differs from that of married different-sex partners and registered same-sex partners. However, Article 2(bh) makes it possible for the competent authority to authorise any other person as a family member, so that there is also the possibility of recognising a de facto partner. This Article could be used to discharge Hungary's (undefined) obligation to 'facilitate' the entry and residence of the partner in 'a durable relationship', under Article 3(2)(b) of Directive 2004/38/EC.

3.3. Third-Country Nationals

The rules applicable to third-country nationals are contained in the Act on the entry and stay of third-country nationals (Act No II of 2007). Article 3(1) of the RPA is also applicable in their case, and requires that registered partners be treated like spouses. Act No II of 2007 defines family members as: (a) the spouse of a third-country national; (b) the minor children (including adopted and foster children) of a third-country national and their spouse (common child); (c) the minor children (including adopted and foster children) of a third-country national if the third-country national has parental authority and the children are dependent on them (child of the third-party national); and (d) the minor children (including adopted and foster children) of the spouse of a third-country national if the spouse has parental authority and the children are dependent on them (child of the spouse). It is clear that spouse in this case also means

[60] Act No I of 2007 on the entry and residence of persons with the right of free movement and residence. The English text of all immigration laws is available at www.bmbah.hu/jogszabalyok.php.

registered partner. However, the de facto partner's situation in the immigration procedure is not defined. Neither the law nor practice provide any guidance on how de facto partners who wish to join their partners in Hungary to enter into a registered partnership under Hungarian law, are to be treated. Furthermore, for the purposes of the Act, registered partnerships—in principle, regardless of the place of registry—are to be treated as equal to marriage. The Immigration Authority has not yet clarified how a foreign registered partnership that provides substantially fewer rights than a Hungarian one will be treated. If there are major differences, the Authority may decide to treat the foreign one differently from a Hungarian one.

In a lengthy procedure, the Supreme Court, in its capacity as a review court, eventually confirmed that, in the case of cohabiting same-sex partners, the partner is also to be taken into consideration in determining the foreigner's place of abode and residence. In one case, the petitioner, a Romanian national who had been living in Hungary since 1998, had studied and then worked legally in the country. Since 2002, he had lived in his partner's apartment. In order to receive a permanent residence permit, the couple entered into an agreement signed in front of a notary, stating that the petitioner freely used his partner's apartment and that, in case of need, the partner also provided financial support. During the proceedings, they were able to provide evidence that they lived in a partnership based on emotional and financial cooperation. As the first instance forum, the Immigration Authority rejected the request: neither the applicant's place of abode nor his maintenance was sufficiently secure. On appeal, the Metropolitan Court rejected this reasoning and stressed that, although the petitioner could not be considered a family member under the Civil Code, a de facto partnership could be established also by same-sex partners, and partners were to be considered as members of the family. When the law refers to long-term partners, same-sex couples could not be excluded.[61] The Immigration Office requested a review by the Supreme Court, which upheld the lower court's decision, adding that, if the agreement of the partners regarding financial support was not legally forbidden, it should be considered in the immigration proceedings.[62] Although the Supreme Court's decisions are not treated as legally binding precedents, the judgment nevertheless indicates a clear turning point in the interpretation of the law.

3.4. Asylum

Act No LXXX of 2007 regulates asylum proceedings. Among family members, the Act also lists the foreigner's spouse. As in the case of EU citizens, EEA nationals,

[61] Case No 20.K.31.868/2005/4. The reasoning was in line with the Constitutional Court Decision No 14/1995 (III.13) which found that the exclusion of de facto same-sex partners from benefits provided by the Civil Code was in violation of the Constitution.
[62] Case No Kfv. II. 39. 032/2005/5.

and third-country nationals, by virtue of RPA Article 3(1), registered partners are also included when spouses are mentioned. Article 2 of Act No LXXX of 2007 defines family members as: (a) spouse; (b) children (including adopted and foster children); and (c) parent(s), if the person seeking recognition is a minor. The Act makes no reference to de facto partners, and the Immigration Authority has no discretionary power under the Act to recognise such persons on account of their living in a de facto relationship with their partner. In such cases, both partners must seek recognition individually. Sexual minorities are also recognised—in principle—implicitly in the definition of a safe third country:

Article 2:

i)   safe third country: in the context of the applicant the country where the applicant stayed or travelled through prior to his/her arrival in the territory of the Republic of Hungary and had the opportunity to submit an application for recognition as a refugee or for subsidiary protection, provided that the refugee authority ascertained that in the given country

ia)   the applicant's life and liberty are not jeopardised for racial or religious reasons or on account of his/her ethnicity, membership of a social group or political conviction and the applicant is not exposed to the risk of serious harm;

ib)   the principle of non-refoulement is observed in accordance with the Geneva Convention;

ic)   the rule of international law, according to which the applicant may not be expelled to the territory of a country where s/he would be exposed to death penalty, torture, cruel, inhuman or degrading treatment or punishment, is recognised and applied, and

id)   there is protection available in accordance with the Geneva Convention.

Article 64(2) further clarifies the situation of LGBT people in asylum proceedings: depending on the circumstances in the country of origin, a particular social group may include a group based on a common characteristic of sexual orientation and gender-related aspects. For the purposes of this provision (which implements Article 10(1)(d) of Directive 2004/83/EC), 'sexual orientation does not include acts related to the defendant's sexual orientation, which qualify as crimes under the rules of Hungarian law. In Hungarian criminal law, there are no specific crimes in which the defendant's sexual orientation must be considered.

It is difficult to describe the situation of LGBT asylum-seekers. The decisions of the Hungarian Immigration Authority cannot be researched without special permission allowing access to the files. Thus, the case law introduced below cannot provide a conclusive evaluation of the current jurisprudence in the field, since only those cases which are appealed by the asylum-seeker reach the court. However, the low number of appeals indicates that the Immigration Authority's decisions are rarely disputed.

In Hungary, the Metropolitan Court has exclusive jurisdiction in immigration cases in which petitioners may file an appeal against the Immigration Authority's negative decision. From case law (available since 2008), it is notable that only two judges preside over most trials involving the question of granting asylum or a related status to a third-country national. As of January 2011, there were six judgments available in the publicly accessible judicial database;[63] in none of them did the court rule in favour of the petitioner, which means that the court consistently upheld the decision of the Immigration Authority. In some cases—as shown below—the court correctly established the inconsistency of the evidence of the asylum-seeker, and noted the fact that their sexual orientation was only one of many reasons invoked in support of their application. In other cases, however, the court seemed to overlook some important factors relating to the merits of the case. In line with Hungarian data protection regulations, all information which may connect a particular person with a particular case has been omitted. This means, in practice, that one may find only accidental references to the country of origin. This makes critical evaluation of the decisions almost impossible.

There are several similarities in the judgments which may be attributed to the fact that only two judges deal with most asylum cases. The first remarkable point in common is that the judgments consistently use gender identity and sexual orientation as synonyms. In a 2009 judgment, the Metropolitan Court used the following wording: 'the petitioner ... based his request for asylum status on the fact that considering his gender identity he is homosexual'.[64] The court also required in each case that the petitioners show that they were subject to actual persecution—either by the state authorities or by other social groups. If the persecution was by other social groups, the court always asked the petitioners to prove that the state was unable to protect them. If the applicants failed to seek a state remedy against their attackers, the Hungarian court did not find that they had a well-founded fear of persecution. It is noteworthy that, in the case of a gay couple who suffered regular beatings in the streets at night by persons objecting to their relationship, the court did not find it sufficient that they had reported the violence to the police. According to its reasoning, the petitioners could not prove that they were the ones who had been attacked and had reported the crime to the state authorities. The Hungarian court seems to put an extra burden on asylum-seekers: it is not enough for them to tell their story consistently and to substantiate their persecution; the judges want to see copies of written reports submitted to the police in their home countries. In addition, in one case in which the applicants were from Mongolia, the court ruled out the possibility of being persecuted simply on the basis that the country—presumably Mongolia—does not criminalise same-sex relationships and at the same time prohibits discrimination. As a final argument for rejecting their claim, the court proposed that the applicants could have sought help from non-governmental organisations dealing with LGBT rights in their home country.[65]

[63] www.birosag.hu/engine.aspx?page=anonim.
[64] Case No 21.K.32936/2009/7.
[65] Case No 21.K.34681/2008/2.

Another argument appearing repeatedly in judgments is that, if the petitioners live a closeted life and keep their affection hidden from the public, they could avoid the feared persecution. In 2009, the court stressed that the attacks had always taken place in the evening or at night, when the petitioner had attracted the attention of homophobes by publicly showing his affection for his partner.[66]

There are naturally instances in which the story told by the petitioner is inconsistent, or in which grounds are fabricated to support the petition. In one case, the applicant mentioned his sexual orientation only five months after the first interview held in the asylum procedure.[67] However, the fact that asylum-seekers do not reveal their sexual orientation as lesbian or gay in the first hearing does not automatically mean—contrary to the position of the court—that it is heterosexual. In the case of a lesbian applicant, her lawyer stressed that her lack of information about Hungary, the situation of LGBT people, and the applicable legislation could have justified her caution. The asylum-seeker, a lesbian woman from a country at war, had been granted the status of a person recognised as being able/allowed to stay, and her sexual orientation and the fear of being persecuted on these grounds came up in the periodical review procedure. However, the court established that the principle of non-refoulement was applicable, and withdrew her recognised status. Her current status is unknown. The reasoning of this judgment has several flaws, which shows stereotypical thinking on the part of judges. First of all, it was inconceivable for the judge that a woman could realise that she is lesbian during her marriage to a man. The court used the petitioner's statement as proof of an inconsistent personal story and commented as follows: 'the fact that she married a man questions her lesbianism, as it is obvious if she had been lesbian she would not have entered into marriage'.[68]

The court practice in the case of asylum-seekers claiming that they are being persecuted on the basis of their sexual orientation is rather underdeveloped and reflects the stereotypes present in the wider society. Unfortunately, the lack of references to the country of origin in the decisions makes it impossible to evaluate the court's assessment of the risk of persecution in the home country. It seems that, in cases reaching the court level, it is extremely difficult to prove that the petitioner meets the requirements of the Geneva Convention, because they are persecuted on the basis of their sexual orientation. Even in cases where asylum-seekers have provided substantial evidence and a coherent personal history, the court has failed to grant refugee status.

---

[66] Case No 21.K.32987/2009/5.
[67] Case No 21.K.32936/2009/7.
[68] Case No 17.K.33.929/2008/10.

4. Cross-border Reproductive Services

4.1. Assisted Reproduction for Single Women

Since 2006, the law covering health makes it possible for single women (regardless of sexual orientation) to participate in assisted reproduction.[69] The current legislation on assisted reproduction according to the Act on health is the following:

Article 167

(1) Reproduction procedures may be performed on married couples or on two persons of opposing genders living together as common-law spouses if, for reasons of health existing among either party (infertility), it is highly probable that a healthy child cannot be produced through natural means. Among common-law spouses, the procedures only may be conducted if neither of the partners is married to another person.

...

(4) In the case of a single woman reproduction procedures may be performed if by way of her age or medical condition (infertility) it is highly probable that she cannot produce a child through natural means.[70]

Although the Act mentions married couples, by virtue of an exception in Article 3(4) of the RPA, Article 167(1) of the Act on health does not apply to registered partners. The RPA lists among the few differences between married couples and registered partners participation in assisted reproduction, in addition to joint adoption of children, and the right to take the partner's name. Article 165 of the Act on Health defines single women as 'a woman of age who at the time of starting the procedure is neither married to nor cohabiting with a partner'. This means that lesbians cohabiting with their partners or living in registered partnerships are not allowed to participate in assisted reproduction. Single women are allowed to participate (regardless of sexual orientation) if they are infertile or, due to age, likely to become infertile soon. The reference in Article 167(1) to 'two persons of opposing genders living together as common-law spouses' is arguably contrary to the principle of *Karner v Austria* [2003].[71]

The 2005 Act on health brought significant changes in access to reproductive services. The original 1997 version of the Act on health allowed only married and different-sex cohabiting couples to participate in assisted reproduction. In discussions with the Minister for Equal Opportunities, LGBT organisations proposed extending artificial insemination to lesbian couples as early as 2003. Following a 2005 parliamentary decision requiring the government to draw up an action plan

---

[69] Amended by Act No CLXXXI of 2005. The modified text came into force on 1 January 2006.
[70] Act No CLIV of 1997.
[71] *Karner v Austria* 40016/98 (24 July 2003), Reports of Judgments and Decisions 2003-IX.

on the problem of infertility,[72] the government proposed to amend the Act on health in order to extend the categories of women who were allowed to donate ova. Following proposals from the Hungarian Civil Liberties Union, socialist and liberal MPs submitted amendments to the bill to extend assisted reproduction to single women and to liberalise surrogacy.[73] The surrogacy proposal did not gather enough support to be put to the vote, and a competing amendment about assisted reproduction for single women with slightly different wording (and limiting assisted reproduction to Hungarian citizens), was also submitted: it gathered more support in the committees and was adopted by Parliament. In the final reading, the government proposed to remove the citizenship limitation, arguing that the autonomy to make health-related decisions is part of human dignity and thus cannot be limited by citizenship. The amendment was adopted, opening up the possibility of artificial insemination for foreign single women.[74] Assisted reproduction for women living in lesbian partnerships has not been put on the agenda at all and, although the liberals strongly argued that anyone who wants to have children should have the possibility of doing so and that no group of people should be excluded, this does not seem to include lesbian women. A conservative MP criticised the proposal to extend assisted reproduction to single women by arguing that it would lead to unforeseen consequences, even child-bearing by same-sex couples.

4.2. Practice

The topic of extending assisted reproduction services for LGBT people has rarely been discussed. In relation to the RPA and its explicit exclusion of same-sex couples from joint adoption, some liberal members of Parliament raised equality concerns. These were always rebutted on the basis that consensual decision-making requires compromises: the institution will be introduced, but only with reservations on rights.[75]

Similarly, there is no court practice in Hungary regarding cross-border reproductive services. On the basis of interviews, the following can be established: the law allows the possibility of reproductive procedures for single women, and lesbian couples use these avenues more often—by circumventing the law, often with the help of their gynaecologist. A collection of interviews published in 2010 confirmed this trend: lesbian couples admit that, instead of registering their

[72] Decision of the Parliament No 62/2005 (VI.28).
[73] On the position of the Hungarian Civil Liberties Union see www.tasz.hu/betegjog/13.
[74] All related parliamentary documents, including committee positions, proposed amendments, etc are available at www.parlament.hu/internet/plsql/ogy_irom.irom_adat?p_ckl=37&p_izon=18093.
[75] See eg, the Parliamentarty debate of the Constitutional, Judicial and Standing Orders Committee on 9 September 2009. Available at www.parlament.hu/biz38/bizjkv38/AIB/0909091.htm.

partnership, they undergo artificial insemination as single women and arrange custody in private contracts (naming a guardian in case of the death of the partner) (Sándor 2010).

In addition, since the rules are more liberal and the success rates are higher than in neighbouring countries, Hungary serves as a receiving country in this regard. However, some of the interviewed lesbian couples were of the opinion that—out of fear of illegality—they would rather raise the necessary funds and have artificial insemination procedures carried out outside the country. Since surrogacy is illegal in Hungary, gay couples have no other choice than to pay for such services outside Hungary, for example in the United States.[76]

Children born by donor insemination in another EU Member State, third country or Hungary may not be adopted by the same-sex partner of the mother because step-parent adoption is not legally available. There had been proposals allowing for second-parent adoption for cohabiting partners, but due to the change of government the previous draft of the new Civil Code was withdrawn. As at September 2011 the new version has been made public.

---

[76] Interview correspondence on file with the author.

11

Homophobia and United Kingdom Law: Only a Few Gaps Left to Close?

ROBERT WINTEMUTE

1. Hate Crimes and Hate Speech

1.1. Criminal Legislation against Hate Crimes

Legislation against homophobic hate crimes in 'the United Kingdom of Great Britain and Northern Ireland'[1] consists of the Criminal Justice Act 2003 (England and Wales), the Offences (Aggravation by Prejudice) (Scotland) Act 2009, and the Criminal Justice (No 2) (Northern Ireland) Order 2004. The 2003 Act for England and Wales followed legislation on hate crimes against racial or ethnic minorities in 1998,[2] and against religious minorities in 2001 (especially hate crimes against Muslims triggered by the 11 September attacks).[3] It took five years to extend the 1998 legislation on racist hate crimes to homophobic hate crimes, despite the bombing of the Admiral Duncan gay pub, Soho, London on 30 April 1999, which killed three people and injured over 60.[4]

Under section 146 of the Criminal Justice Act 2003 (in force from 4 April 2005), courts are obliged to treat as an aggravating factor, in considering the seriousness of an offence prior to selecting the appropriate sentence, the fact:

(2) . . .

(a)   that, at the time of committing the offence, or immediately before or after doing so, the offender demonstrated towards the victim of the offence hostility based on

---

[1]   This is the official name of the country, which consists of four parts: England, Wales, Scotland and Northern Ireland. For additional legal information about the UK, including some legal history, see Wintemute (1994; 2005) and the thematic study of the European Union Fundamental Rights Agency available at www.fra.europa.eu/fraWebsite/attachments/LGBT-2010_thematic-study_UK.pdf.

[2]   Crime and Disorder Act 1998, ss 28–32.

[3]   Anti-Terrorism, Crime and Security Act 2001, s 39 (amending ss 28–32 of the 1998 Act).

[4]   See *The Independent* (London) (1 May 1999), 1.

(i)   the sexual orientation (or presumed sexual orientation) of the victim, or ...
(b)   that the offence is motivated (wholly or partly)
(i)   by hostility towards persons who are of a particular sexual orientation.

If the offence was committed in any of these circumstances, the judge must state in open court that this is the case, and must increase the sentence.[5] While the 2003 Act provides for increased sentences for aggravating circumstances related to race, religion, disability or sexual orientation,[6] hate crimes based on race or religion receive a second form of condemnation. This is because the Crime and Disorder Act 1998 also creates special offences with higher maximum penalties. These offences are known as 'racially or religiously aggravated' assault, criminal damage and public order offences.[7] It is not clear why the UK Government decided to introduce a hierarchy of grounds of discrimination into 'hate crimes' legislation, rather than adopt a consistent approach with regard to all grounds. One advantage of the 'racially or religiously aggravated' offences is that they appear as separate categories in national crime statistics.[8]

The Scottish legislation is very similar to the 2003 Act, except that it substitutes 'malice and ill-will' for hostility, and applies both to sexual orientation and 'transgender identity'.[9] The Northern Ireland legislation is also very similar, except that it refers to 'hostility towards ... members of a sexual orientation group', which means 'a group of persons defined by reference to sexual orientation'.[10]

A 'hate crime' is usually proved through evidence that the attacker used offensive words to describe the victim's actual or presumed sexual orientation, at the time of the crime, or immediately before or after the crime. However, the words need not be offensive, and any reference to the victim's actual or presumed sexual orientation could be sufficient proof of motivation. For example, in a recent attack which London police are treating as homophobic, the attackers first asked the victim 'Are you gay?', before stabbing him in the chest and leg.[11]

There do not appear to be any appellate court decisions in which the homophobic hate crime legislation has been interpreted. However, media reports indicate that sentences are being increased by trial courts. Two of the most prominent cases were the killings of Jody Dobrowski in 2005, and Ian Baynham in 2009. Mr Dobrowski was punched and kicked to death by Scott Walker and Thomas Pickford in a South London park (Clapham Common). Because his face was so badly injured that his family could not identify him, his fingerprints had

---

[5]   Section 146(3).
[6]   Sections 145–46.
[7]   Sections 28–32.
[8]   See rds.homeoffice.gov.uk/rds/pdfs10/recorded-crime-2002–2010.xls.
[9]   2009 Acts of the Scottish Parliament 8, s 2.
[10]   Statutory Instrument 2004 No 1991 (NI 15), Art 2.
[11]   See www.pinknews.co.uk/2011/02/17/four-men-arrested-over-camden-gay-stabbing (attack on 14 February 2011).

to be used.[12] 'The killers could be heard by witnesses screaming anti-gay insults as they beat the barman to death.'[13] The two accused pleaded guilty to murder and were sentenced to life imprisonment. The 2003 Act was applied when the trial judge ordered that they must serve a minimum of 28 years in prison.[14]

Mr Baynham was attacked near Trafalgar Square (the centre of London) by Ruby Thomas and Joel Alexander, fell, struck his head, and died 18 days later from a brain injury. The two attackers were convicted of manslaughter (unintentional killing) and sentenced to six years in prison. The sentence of Ms Thomas was increased by one year because she had shouted 'fucking faggots' at Mr Baynham and his friend, just before the attack.[15]

How prevalent are homophobic hate crimes in the UK? One indication can be seen from the Crown Prosecution Service's statistics on prosecutions for homophobic incidents in England and Wales (some of which might involve 'hate speech' or harassment rather than violence).[16] These have increased from 822 in 2006–07 to 1,152 in 2009–10, a net increase of 40% in three years. This compares with an increase from 11,713 in 2006–07 to 12,131 in 2009–10 for prosecutions involving racial or religious prejudice, a net increase of 3.6% in three years.[17] The 1,152 prosecutions in 2009–10 probably understate the seriousness of the problem, because it is likely that many homophobic crimes are not reported to the police. Research commissioned by the non-governmental organisation Stonewall found in 2008 that 20% of lesbian and gay individuals had experienced a homophobic hate crime or incident in the last three years, that in 16.7% of cases the incident involved a physical assault, and that experiencing a physical assault was twice as likely for lesbian and gay individuals from ethnic minorities (8%) than for all lesbian and gay individuals (4%), but that in 75% of cases the victim did not report the crime or incident to the police.[18]

It is also difficult to estimate the chilling effect that fear of hate crimes has on public expression of affection by lesbian women and gay men.[19] Although, in theory, greater visibility of same-sex couples should reduce social prejudice and

---

[12] See www. bbc.co.uk/news/1/hi/5087286.stm.

[13] See www.timesonline.co.uk/tol/news/uk/crime/article717120.ece.

[14] See www.cps.gov.uk/publications/prosecution/htc_toolkit.html.

[15] See www.guardian.co.uk/uk/2011/jan/26/ruby-thomas-sentenced-fatal-homophobic-attack.

[16] See also www.copfs.gov.uk/Publications/2011/05/Hate-Crime-Scotland-2010–11 ('448 charges ... with an aggravation of sexual orientation' in Scotland in 2010–11).

[17] See www.cps.gov.uk/data/hate_crime/hate_crime_key_findings/CPS_hate_crime_prosecution_by_hate_crime_type_2006_2010.csv.

[18] See 'Homophobic hate crime: The Gay British Crime Survey 2008', available at www.stonewall.org.uk/documents/homophobic_hate_crime__final_report.pdf; 'Homophobic hate crimes and hate incidents 2009' (www.stonewall.org.uk/documents/sexual_orientation_hate_crimes_paper.pdf); 'Blow the whistle on Gay Hate' (www.stonewall.org.uk/documents/stonewall_gay_hate.pdf), a guide intended to encourage reporting.

[19] See eg, www.bbc.co.uk/news/uk-england-london-13103647 (two men ejected from pub for kissing).

hate crimes, fear of hate crimes creates a vicious circle, reducing the visibility of same-sex couples and helping to maintain social prejudice.[20] The smaller number of prosecutions for homophobic hate crimes, compared with racist or religious hate crimes, is probably the result of the combination of lesbian and gay individuals' lower visibility and lower numbers, compared with members of non-white ethnic minorities, who made up 7.9% of the UK's population in 2001.[21]

In conclusion, there can be no doubt that, in the UK, government and civil society actors are taking homophobic hate crimes seriously. The Crown Prosecution Service has a webpage with several publications on the prosecution of homophobic hate crimes.[22] In London, the non-governmental organisation Galop specialises in 'challenging homophobic and transphobic hate crime', and has published a detailed study of the problem.[23] At least two police forces, Grampian (Scotland) and North Wales, display rainbow flag stickers in stations to encourage gay people to report homophobic crime.[24]

1.2. Criminal Legislation against Hate Speech

The UK's legislation against homophobic hate speech consists of Part IIIA of the Public Order Act 1986 (England and Wales), as amended in 2008, and Part III of the Public Order (Northern Ireland) Order 1987, as amended in 2004. There is still no legislation in Scotland. The UK's first prohibition of racist hate speech appeared in section 6 of the Race Relations Act 1965, which came into force on 8 December 1965, just before the United Nations General Assembly's resolution of 21 December 1965, adopting and opening for signature the Convention on the Elimination of all forms of Racial Discrimination (CERD). Article 4 of CERD obliges States Parties to:

> [D]eclare an offence punishable by law all dissemination of ideas based on racial superiority or hatred, incitement to racial discrimination, as well as all ... incitement to ... acts [of violence] against any race or group of persons of another colour or ethnic origin.

A similar obligation appears in Article 20(2) of the 1966 International Covenant on Civil and Political Rights (ICCPR):

[20] See www.bbc.co.uk/news/uk-11831556.
[21] See www.ons.gov.uk/.../ethnicity/...ethnicity...ethnicity.../focus-on—ethnicity-and-identity-summary-report.pdf.
[22] See www.cps.gov.uk/publications/prosecution/homophobia.html.
[23] See Galop, 'Filling in the blanks: LGBT hate crime in London', available at www.galop.org.uk/wp-content/uploads/2009/05/filling-in-the-blanks-low-res.pdf.
[24] See http://www.pinknews.co.uk/2011/10/14/north-wales-police-to-display-rainbow-flag-in-stations.

Any advocacy of national, racial or religious hatred that constitutes incitement to discrimination, hostility or violence shall be prohibited by law.

Since 1965, the UK has taken a consistently strict approach to banning racist hate speech. The main prohibition is found in section 18 of the Public Order Act 1986 (which applies to England, Wales and Scotland):[25]

(1)   A person who uses threatening, abusive or insulting words or behaviour ... is guilty of an offence if
    (a)   he intends thereby to stir up racial hatred [hatred against a group of persons defined by reference to colour, race, nationality (including citizenship) or ethnic or national origins], or
    (b)   having regard to all the circumstances racial hatred is likely to be stirred up thereby [unless] ...
(5)   ... [he] was not aware that [his words or behaviour] might be threatening, abusive or insulting.

The prohibition incorporates the broad concept of 'race' used in UK anti-discrimination legislation,[26] which has been interpreted as protecting the Jewish[27] and Sikh[28] minorities (who are simultaneously ethnic minorities and religious minorities), but not the Roman Catholic and Muslim minorities (who are non-ethnic religious minorities). In Northern Ireland, there was no need to stretch 'race' to cover ethnic-religious minorities, because Article 8 of the 1987 Order has always included 'religious belief' in the definition of 'hatred'.

After the attacks of 11 September 2001, the UK Government sought to protect Muslim individuals against the increased hostility they faced (from non-Muslim individuals who blamed all Muslim individuals for the attacks), by adding religion to the legislation on racist hate crimes and hate speech in England and Wales. The hate crimes amendment succeeded in 2001,[29] but the hate speech amendment was blocked by the upper (legislative) House of Lords in 2001 and 2005 as an unjustified interference with freedom of expression. Opponents of the amendment sought, in particular, to preserve the right of comedians such as Rowan Atkinson to make fun of religions and religious officials. When the amendment was finally passed in 2006,[30] the prohibition of incitement to religious hatred was considerably weaker than the prohibition of incitement to racial hatred. The main prohibition was inserted into the Public Order Act 1986 as section 29B:

(1) A person who uses threatening words or behaviour ... is guilty of an offence if he intends thereby to stir up religious hatred.

---

[25]   See s 42(2) of the 1986 Act.
[26]   Equality Act 2010, s 9(1).
[27]   *R (on the application of E) Governing Body of JFS*, [2009] UKSC 15.
[28]   *Mandla v Dowell Lee* [1983] 1 All England Reports 1062.
[29]   Above, n 3.
[30]   Racial and Religious Hatred Act 2006. Section 3(4) makes it clear that the Act applies only to England and Wales and not to Scotland.

It is not enough for the words or behaviour to be 'abusive or insulting', as in the case of racist hate speech, they must be 'threatening'. Moreover, the accused must have intended to stir up religious hatred. Unlike in the case of racist hate speech, it is not enough that the words or behaviour were likely to stir up religious hatred, and that the accused was aware that they might be threatening.

Not only is the main prohibition weaker, the 2006 amendment includes a 'protection of freedom of expression' exception which, if interpreted broadly, could deprive the prohibition of most of its symbolic and practical value. Section 29J states that:

> Nothing in ... Part [IIIA of the Public Order Act 1986] shall be read or given effect in a way which prohibits or restricts discussion, criticism or expressions of antipathy, dislike, ridicule, insult or abuse of particular religions or the beliefs or practices of their adherents ... or proselytising or urging adherents of a different religion ... to cease practicing their religion

The exception appears to make a very fine distinction between, for example, expressing dislike, ridicule, insult or abuse of Islam or the beliefs or practices of Muslims (which is permitted), and expressing dislike, ridicule, insult or abuse of Muslims as individual human beings (which is prohibited). It would seem that religious hate speech is permitted in England and Wales, as long as the speaker chooses their words carefully, and focuses on particular religious beliefs or practices rather than on the adherents of the religion. There is no equivalent to Section 29J in Northern Ireland.

In 2008, when the UK Parliament decided to extend (in England and Wales, but not Scotland) the prohibitions of incitement to racial and religious hatred to hatred on grounds of sexual orientation,[31] it had to choose between the stronger 'race model' and the weaker 'religion model'. Given that it was unlikely that lesbian and gay individuals would receive better protection than non-ethnic religious minorities, it is not surprising that the weaker 'religion model' was chosen. As a result, the main prohibition of incitement to religious hatred (section 29B(1)) was amended by adding at the end 'or hatred on grounds of sexual orientation', defined in section 29AB as 'hatred against a group of persons defined by reference to sexual orientation (whether towards persons of the same sex, the opposite sex or both)'. This means, as in the case of religious hate speech, that the words or behaviour must be 'threatening', not merely 'abusive or insulting', and that the accused must have intended to stir up hatred on grounds of sexual orientation. The 2008 amendments also include a 'protection of freedom of expression' exception, section 29JA, modelled on the section 29J exception for religion:

---

[31] Criminal Justice and Immigration Act 2008, s 74 and Sch 16, amending Public Order Act 1986.

In this Part [IIIA], for the avoidance of doubt, the discussion or criticism of sexual conduct or practices or the urging of persons to refrain from or modify such conduct or practices shall not be taken of itself to be threatening or intended to stir up hatred.

As in the case of section 29J, the section 29JA exception appears to make a very fine distinction between criticising the sexual conduct or practices of lesbian and gay individuals or same-sex couples (which is permitted), and criticising lesbian women and gay men as individual human beings (which is prohibited). Like section 29J, section 29JA guts the prohibition of homophobic hate speech of most of its symbolic and practical value. It would seem that homophobic hate speech is permitted in England and Wales, as long as the speaker chooses their words carefully, and expresses their hostility towards same-sex sexual activity and couple relationships, rather than towards lesbian and gay individuals. There is no equivalent to section 29JA in Northern Ireland, where 'sexual orientation' was added to the definition of 'hatred' in 2004,[32] and where racist, religious and homophobic hate speech are treated in the same way, that is Great Britain's 'race model' applies to all three. Indeed, the Northern Ireland prohibition provides slightly stronger protection against all three forms of hate speech, because it covers not only 'stirring up hatred' but also 'arousing fear',[33] with both 'hatred' and 'fear' defined as including a hatred against, or fear of

a group of persons defined by reference to religious belief, sexual orientation, disability, colour, race, nationality (including citizenship) or ethnic or national origins.[34]

In Scotland, as at 1 September 2011, it is surprising to note that hate speech targeting Muslims, Roman Catholics, lesbian women, or gay men is legal, because the Scottish Parliament (to which the UK Parliament has devolved, since 1998, power to legislate over criminal law for Scotland) has yet to create new offences of incitement to hatred based on religion or sexual orientation. The Scottish Government's 'Offensive Behaviour at Football and Threatening Communications (Scotland) Bill', introduced on 16 June 2011, would create a new offence of communicating threatening material with intent to stir up religious hatred, as well as a more specific offence, applying only to regulated football matches, of

expressing hatred of, or stirring up hatred against, a group of persons based on their membership (or presumed membership) of … a religious group … [or] a group defined by … sexual orientation … [or] transgender identity.[35]

---

[32] Criminal Justice (No 2) (Northern Ireland) Order 2004, SI 2004 No 1991 (NI 15), Art 3, adding 'sexual orientation, disability' to the definition of 'hatred' in the Public Order (Northern Ireland) Order 1987, Art 8.

[33] 1987 Order, Art 9.

[34] 1987 Order, Art 8 (as amended in 2004).

[35] See www.scottish.parliament.uk/s4/bills/01-offbehfoot/b1s4-introd.pdf.

The non-governmental organisation Equality Network has argued that the more general offence of 'communicating threatening material' should be extended to cover disability, race, sexual orientation, and transgender identity, as well as religion.[36]

In conclusion, the UK has legislation prohibiting hate speech, but it suffers from major inconsistencies. The highest standard of protection is found in Northern Ireland (the location of a long-standing ethnic-religious conflict), where racist, religious and homophobic hate speech are treated in the same way. In England and Wales, there is a clear hierarchy between racist hate speech, which enjoys a much higher level of protection, and religious and homophobic hate speech, which is permitted as long as the speaker chooses their words carefully. In Scotland, the same hierarchy exists, but the gap is greater because there are no statutory offences applying to religion or sexual orientation. The European Court of Human Rights (ECtHR) permits prohibitions of hate speech, but does not yet require them.[37] The UK has decided, for England, Wales and Scotland, that the harm caused by racist hate speech justifies the interference with freedom of expression. It is hard to understand why the freedom of expression argument has been given much greater weight (through the section 29J and section 29JA exceptions in England and Wales, and the absence of any statutory offences in Scotland) in the case of religious and homophobic hate speech.

A recent example of expression that might constitute illegal hate speech in some European countries is a newspaper column using the phrases: 'a Government-backed drive to promote the gay agenda'; 'the ruthless campaign by the gay rights lobby to destroy the very concept of normal sexual behaviour'; 'the latest religious believers to fall foul of the gay[-led] inquisition'; 'It seems that just about everything in Britain is now run according to the gay agenda'; and 'the seemingly all-powerful gay rights lobby carries all before it'.[38] Certainly, the phrase 'all-powerful Jewish lobby' would risk a prosecution in some European countries.

The 2008 amendments banning homophobic hate speech in England and Wales came into force on 23 March 2010. The first prosecution using the new offence (as opposed to more general public order offences) was announced on 28 January 2011, when two men were charged with distributing a leaflet outside a mosque, and with pushing it through the letterboxes of some homes. The leaflet was entitled 'The Death Penalty?' and said that lesbian and gay individuals should be executed.[39]

---

[36] See www.equality-network.org/Equality/website.nsf/webpages/A81952051718638080257 8BD00528621.

[37] See *Aksu v Turkey* (ECtHR, 27 July 2010; Grand Chamber hearing on 13 April 2011).

[38] Melanie Phillips, 'Yes, gays have often been the victims of prejudice. But they now risk becoming the new McCarthyites', *The Daily Mail* (London), at www.dailymail.co.uk/debate/article-1349951/Gayness-mandatory-schools-Gay-victims-prejudice-new-McCarthyites.html.

[39] See www.pinknews.co.uk/2011/01/28/men-charged-with-anti-gay-hatred-over-execution-leaflets.

2. Education at all Levels

In the early 1980s, attempts by some local governments and some state schools to promote 'positive images' of lesbian and gay individuals triggered a powerful political backlash: the enactment of section 28 of the Local Government Act 1988 for England, Wales and Scotland (but not Northern Ireland):[40]

A local authority shall not

(a)   intentionally promote homosexuality ... [or];

(b)   promote the teaching in any maintained [state-funded] school of the acceptability of homosexuality as a pretended family relationship.

This statutory language was extremely offensive to lesbian and gay individuals in the UK. It can be compared with equivalent language in relation to religion or race: 'the acceptability of Hinduism, Islam or Judaism as pretended religions', or 'the acceptability of persons of Asian, African or Caribbean origin as pretended human beings'.

The rationale behind section 28 (and unequal ages of consent to sexual activity in the criminal law) was that being lesbian or gay is a 'contagious affliction'. To stop it from 'spreading', lesbian and gay adults should have no contact with children, whether as teachers or parents, and children should not hear anything about them that is not clearly negative and disapproving. This social fear of lesbian and gay individuals has gradually been replaced by respect, and in particular by a broad social understanding that a child's sexual orientation is determined at birth, or in the early years of childhood, meaning that there is no possibility of a teacher's changing a child's sexual orientation through so-called 'promotion'.

Section 28 was repealed for Scotland in 2000, and for England and Wales in 2003.[41] Although it must have had a chilling effect on the discussion of same-sex sexual activity and couple relationships in schools, and on efforts by teachers to address bullying of lesbian and gay students, it did not give rise to a single reported judicial decision. Its rationale was repudiated by UK legislation, the Sexual Offences (Amendment) Act 2000 (equalising the age of consent) and the Civil Partnership Act 2004 (allowing same-sex couples to register their relation-ships and acquire almost all of the rights and duties of married different-sex couples). Its rationale has also been rejected by the ECtHR, in its 2003 judgment holding that unequal ages of consent violate Articles 14 and 8 of the European

---

[40]   The Act inserted a new section 2A into the Local Government Act 1986.

[41]   See Ethical Standards in Public Life etc (Scotland) Act 2000, s 34; Local Government Act 2003, s 127(2) and Sch 8, Pt 1 (England and Wales; in force from 18 November 2003).

Convention on Human Rights (ECHR),[42] and in its 2010 judgment holding that cohabiting same-sex couples enjoy 'family life' under Article 8.[43]

Section 403(1A) of the Education Act 1996, inserted by section 148 of the Learning and Skills Act 2000 as a replacement for section 28, requires the Secretary of State for Education to

> issue guidance designed to secure that when sex education is given to registered pupils at maintained schools ...
>
> (a)   they learn the nature of marriage and its importance for family life and the bringing up of children.

The resulting 'Sex and Relationship Education Guidance' states that: 'There should be no direct promotion of sexual orientation'.[44] The absence of a reference to 'homosexuality' appears to be an improvement on section 28. However, many people read 'sexual orientation' as meaning same-sex sexual orientation, because they do not see heterosexual individuals as having a sexual orientation. So it is possible that the harmful effects of section 28, and the hopelessly vague word 'promote', have been transferred from the statute book to the statutory guidance. The 'Report of the Working Group on Sex Education in Scottish Schools' is much better, and does not refer to 'promoting sexual orientation'. Instead, it says:

> All young people should be helped to understand, at an appropriate age, that different people can have different sexual orientations.[45]

Since 1988, the UK has gradually evolved from a position of rejecting and excluding lesbian and gay teachers and students ('no promotion of homosexuality'), to one of accepting and including them ('no discrimination based on sexual orientation'). On 1 December 2003, shortly after the repeal of Section 28, the Employment Equality (Sexual Orientation) Regulations 2003 came into force for Great Britain implementing Council Directive 2000/78/EC.[46] The Regulations prohibited sexual orientation discrimination in employment, which meant that lesbian and gay teachers at all levels of education (from primary school to university) were protected against refusals to hire or promote, and dismissals. The Regulations also prohibited such discrimination in vocational training, which includes almost all university or other education for persons aged 18 and over, if it improves their chances of employment.[47] This meant that students in educational institutions offering vocational training (as defined by EU law) were

---

[42]   *SL v Austria* (ECtHR, 9 January 2003).

[43]   *Schalk & Kopf v Austria* (ECtHR, 24 June 2010), para 94.

[44]   See www.education.gov.uk/publications/eOrderingDownload/DfES-0116–2000%20SRE.pdf.

[45]   See www.scotland.gov.uk/Publications/2000/06/6250/File-1 paras 5.25–5.29.

[46]   See also Employment Equality (Sexual Orientation) Regulations (Northern Ireland) 2003 (in force from 2 December 2003).

[47]   See Case 24/86 *Blaizot v University of Liège* [1988] ECR 379, para 20.

also protected against discrimination. However, students in primary and secondary education (from the age of six to the age of 16 or 18) were not covered by the Regulations, because the Regulations did not go beyond the material scope of the Directive.

This gap in protection existed both for religion[48] and sexual orientation. The UK Government decided to extend protection against both forms of discrimination beyond the minimum requirements of EU law (Directive 2000/78), by voluntarily introducing a bill in the UK Parliament which became the Equality Act 2006. Part 2 of the Act prohibited discrimination based on religion or belief, in access to goods and services, including education. Section 81 of the 2006 Act authorised the making of regulations that would prohibit discrimination based on sexual orientation in the same areas as for religion or belief. The power in section 81 was exercised through the making of the Equality Act (Sexual Orientation) Regulations 2007 (for England, Wales and Scotland), which applied to educational establishments (schools) and local education authorities (boards administering groups of schools).[49]

The 2003 Regulations on employment and vocational training, and the 2007 Regulations dealing with other areas, have now both been replaced by the Equality Act 2010, which for the first time deals with all prohibited grounds of discrimination, and all areas in which discrimination is prohibited, in a single Act. Lesbian and gay teachers and lesbian and gay applicants for teaching jobs, are protected against discrimination and harassment in employment by sections 39 and 40. Lesbian and gay students, and lesbian and gay applicants to educational establishments, are protected against discrimination by section 85 in the case of schools, and by sections 91 to 93 in the case of universities and other institutions of further or higher education. For example, section 85 provides:

(1) The responsible body of a school … must not discriminate against a person:
  (a) in the arrangements it makes for deciding who is offered admission as a pupil,
  (b) as to the terms on which it offers to admit the person as a pupil,
  (c) by not admitting the person as a pupil.
(2) The responsible body of such a school must not discriminate against a pupil:
  (a) in the way it provides education for the pupil,
  (b) in the way it affords the pupil access to a benefit, facility or service, …
  (e) by excluding the pupil from the school,
  (f) by subjecting the pupil to any other detriment.
(3) The responsible body of such a school must not harass:
  (a) a pupil,
  (b) a person who has applied for admission as a pupil.

---

[48] The Employment Equality (Religion or Belief) Regulations 2003 implemented the Directive with regard to discrimination based on religion or belief.

[49] Reg 7 of the 2007 Regulations. See also the Equality Act (Sexual Orientation) Regulations (Northern Ireland) 2006.

The Act defines 'direct discrimination' (section 13), 'indirect discrimination' (section 19) and harassment (section 26).

A strange feature of the Act is that harassment on the ground of sexual orientation is prohibited in relation to employment (section 40), and further and higher education (sections 91(5), 92(3), 93(3)), because these areas fall within the material scope of Directive 2000/78, and the Directive requires a prohibition of harassment. Yet, because EU law does not require protection against harassment outside these areas (in the cases of religion or belief, disability, age and sexual orientation), the UK Government decided to include exceptions in the Act. These exceptions state that general prohibitions of harassment do not apply to harassment on grounds of religion or belief or sexual orientation, if the harassment occurs in the area of services (sections 29(3), 29(6), 29(8)), 'premises' including housing (sections 33(3), 33(6), 34(2), 34(4), 35(2), 35(4)), and schools (sections 85(3), 85(10)). These exceptions do not affect harassment on other grounds, such as sex, race, age, disability and 'gender reassignment'.[50] The Act seeks to limit any harm caused by these exceptions through section 212(5), which states:

> Where this Act disapplies a prohibition on harassment in relation to a specified protected characteristic, the disapplication does not prevent conduct relating to that characteristic from amounting to a detriment for the purposes of [direct] discrimination within section 13 because of that characteristic.

This provision provides some consolation to victims of harassment barred from bringing claims. But the whole point of including express prohibitions of harassment in EU and national anti-discrimination legislation is to avoid the need to analyse the treatment the victim has suffered as 'direct discrimination'.

One possible explanation of why these exceptions were written into the Act is that the UK Government feared claims that homophobic statements by teachers, or homophobic statements by students left unchallenged by teachers, could amount to harassment on the ground of sexual orientation. Conversely, some students or their parents might claim that positive statements about lesbian and gay individuals, or about same-sex couples, amount to harassment on the ground of religion or belief.[51] The definition of harassment (section 26(1)) includes conduct that:

---

[50] An exception applies to 'gender reassignment' only in the case of schools (section 85(10)), presumably because schools fall outside the material scope of Council Directive 2004/113/EC (prohibiting sex discrimination in access to goods and services). This rationale would have supported extending the same exceptions to age and disability, and to sex in relation to schools.

[51] Unlike the Regulations for England, Wales and Scotland, the Equality Act (Sexual Orientation) Regulations 2006 (Northern Ireland) contained definitions and prohibitions of harassment in regs 3(3)–(4), 5(2), 6(4), 9(2), 10 and 12(1). These provisions were quashed on procedural grounds (absence of proper consultation) in *Christian Institute & Others, Re Judicial Review*, [2007] NIQB 66, paras 28–43 (11 September 2007), available at www.bailii.org/nie/cases/NIHC/QB/2007/66.html. Justice Weatherup observed, at para 42, that 'in outlawing

has the purpose or effect of

(i)   violating [the victim's] dignity, or

(ii) creating an intimidating, hostile, degrading, humiliating or offensive environment for [the victim].

This explanation would also account for the inclusion of another exception (section 89), which provides, with regard to schools, that '[n]othing in this Chapter applies to anything done in connection with the content of the curriculum'. This exception precludes claims that the content of the curriculum (as opposed to the conduct of a specific teacher or another student) discriminates on the ground of sexual orientation.

The National Curriculum 2007, which is currently under review, includes a non-statutory programme of study for 'key stage 3' (ages 11 to 14) entitled 'Personal wellbeing'. One of its 'key concepts' is 'diversity':[52]

(a) Appreciating that, in our communities, there are similarities as well as differences between people of different race, religion, culture, ability or disability, gender, age or sexual orientation.

(b) Understanding that all forms of prejudice and discrimination must be challenged at every level in our lives.

The programme states that teaching should cover:

(j) different types of relationships, including those within families and between older and young people, boys and girls, and people of the same sex, including civil partnerships,

(k) the nature and importance of marriage and of stable relationships for family life and bringing up children, ... (m) the impact of prejudice, bullying, discrimination and racism on individuals and communities [note: Links should be made with the school's anti-bullying policy, including the importance of challenging homophobic bullying].[53]

Although the word 'homophobic' is used, the National Curriculum website does not include the words 'heterosexual', 'bisexual', 'homosexual', 'gay' and 'lesbian'.[54] The absence of the word 'gay' is especially surprising, given the social fact that, in British schools, it has come to mean 'rubbish' or 'lame' (that is, 'worthless' or 'weak'), as in 'that is so gay'.[55]

---

harassment on the ground of sexual orientation the competing right may not only be the right to freedom of speech but [also] ... the right to manifest a religious belief'.

[52] See '1.5 Diversity', 245, available at www.curriculum.qcda.gov.uk/uploads/QCA-07–3348-p_PSHE_Pers_KS3_tcm8–409.pdf.

[53] Ibid, 249.

[54] See curriculum.qcda.gov.uk/Search/index.aspx.

[55] See eg, www.news.bbc.co.uk/1/hi/entertainment/5049566.stm.

Guidance on homophobic bullying published by the UK Government's Department for Education in September 2007[56] does give names to different sexual orientations. The 'Executive summary' notes that:

3.   Homophobic bullying occurs when bullying is motivated by a prejudice against lesbian, gay or bisexual people.
4.   Who experiences homophobic bullying?
      —   Young people who are lesbian, gay or bisexual (LGB),
      —   Young people who are thought to be lesbian, gay or bisexual …,
      —   Young people who have gay friends, … or their parents … are gay,
      —   Teachers, who may or may not be lesbian, gay or bisexual.

      …

6.   Schools have a legal duty to ensure homophobic bullying is dealt with in schools. Under the Education and Inspections Act 2006, head teachers … must … implement measures … to prevent all forms of bullying. This includes the prevention of homophobic bullying.
7.   Homophobic bullying can have a negative impact on young people:
      —   Bullying can … be linked to poor attendance … ,
      —   Seven out of ten young lesbian and gay people say homophobic bullying affects their work,

Bullying can cause low self-esteem, including the increased likelihood of self-harm and the contemplation of suicide.[57]

The guidance also notes that:

homophobic language can be used … [t]o describe an inanimate object or item that is thought to be inferior or laughable—'that pencil case is so gay'.[58]

The 2007 guidance was replaced in July 2011 by a much briefer, general document, 'Preventing and Tackling Bullying', which does not use the word 'homophobic', and says only that:

Successful schools … openly discuss differences between people that could motivate bullying, such as religion, ethnicity, disability, gender or sexuality. Also children with different family situations … Schools can also teach children that using any prejudice based language is unacceptable … [Successful schools] provide effective staff training. Anti-bullying policies are most effective when all school staff understand the principles and purpose of the school's policy … Schools can invest in specialised skills to help

[56]   'Homophobic bullying' (part of 'Safe to Learn: Embedding anti-bullying work in schools'), available at www.schools-out.org.uk/classroom/wp-content/uploads/2011/06/DCSF-Homophobic-Bullying.pdf.
[57]   Ibid, at 4–5.
[58]   Ibid, at 17. See also separate guidance in the same series: 'Guidance for schools on preventing and responding to sexist, sexual and transphobic bullying' available at /www.gires.org.uk/assets/Schools/DCSF-01136–2009.pdf.

their staff understand the needs of their pupils, including ... Lesbian, Gay, Bisexual and Transgender (LGB&T) pupils.[59]

The UK Government's efforts in this area are supplemented by those of the non-governmental organisation Stonewall. Its 'Education for all' campaign is 'against homophobic bullying and for an inclusive learning environment for all'.[60] The Equality and Human Rights Commission has also published a study on 'identity-based bullying'.[61]

Measures against homophobic bullying are, to a certain extent, reactive. It is possible that homophobic bullying could be reduced if the school curriculum included more information about the positive contributions that lesbian and gay individuals have made to society, that is, by explaining to students why they should value and respect lesbian and gay teachers and students in their schools.[62] However, a government-funded plan to assist teachers, who wish to introduce references to the existence of lesbian and gay individuals and same-sex couples into their mathematics, geography and science lessons, generated controversy (including the article referring to 'the all-powerful gay rights lobby' cited above)[63] when it received media attention in January 2011.[64] The plan is being implemented by the non-governmental organisation 'Schools Out', which is developing a website classroom, scheduled to 'go live' in May 2011, and intended to serve as 'a one-stop-shop of resources for teachers who want to cover LGBT issues'.[65] It is interesting to note that, on 13 July 2011, the Governor of California signed a bill passed by the California legislature, which amends California's Education Code as follows:

Instruction in social sciences shall include ... a study of the role and contributions of both men and women, Native Americans, African Americans, Mexican Americans, Asian Americans, Pacific Islanders, European Americans, lesbian, gay, bisexual, and transgender Americans, persons with disabilities, and members of other ethnic and cultural groups, to the economic, political, and social development of California

---

[59] See https://www.education.gov.uk/publications/eOrderingDownload/preventing%20and %20tackling%20bullying.pdf, 4–5.

[60] See www.stonewall.org.uk/at_school/education_for_all/default.asp. See also 'Teachers' perspective on homophobic bullying in Britain's primary and secondary schools' (2009), www.stonewall.org.uk/education_for_all/research/2731.asp; Rainbow Project (Northern Ireland), 'Left Out of the Equation: A Report on the Experiences of Lesbian, Gay and Bisexual Young People at School' (Oct 2011), www.rainbow-project.org/assets/publications/left% 20out%20of%20the%20equation.pdf.

[61] See Equality and Human Rights Commission, Research report 64, 'Prevention and response to identity-based bullying among local authorities in England, Scotland and Wales' (2010), available at www.equalityhumanrights.com/uploaded_files/research/64_identity_ based_bullying.pdf.

[62] See eg, www.independent.co.uk/news/education/education-news/school-highlights-achievements-of-worlds-leading-gay-figures-2128029.html.

[63] See, text accompanying n 38 above.

[64] See www.bbc.co.uk/news/uk-politics-12282413.

[65] See www.schools-out.org.uk/help-with-classroom.htm.

and the United States of America, with particular emphasis on portraying the role of these groups in contemporary society.[66]

On 6 April 2011, section 149(1) of the Equality Act 2010 on the 'public sector equality duty' came into force. It requires all public authorities in England, Wales and Scotland to

> have due regard to the need to … eliminate discrimination … that is prohibited by … this Act … [and] advance equality of opportunity … [and] foster good relations between [lesbian and gay] persons … and [heterosexual] persons … .

The UK Government's March 2011 action plan 'Working for Lesbian, Gay, Bisexual and Transgender Equality: Moving Forward' notes that section 149 'make[s] it a statutory duty for schools to consider how to advance equality for LGB&T people'.[67]

3. Free Movement, Immigration and Asylum

3.1. UK Residence for Same-sex Partners of Citizens of Other EU Member States

The requirements of 'Directive 2004/38/EC of the European Parliament and of the Council on the right of citizens of the Union and their family members to move and reside freely within the territory of the Member States' have been interpreted differently by different EU Member States. If a particular EU citizen is entitled to residence, Article 2(2) of the Directive requires the host Member State to treat as a 'family member' of the citizen:

(a) the spouse,
(b) the partner with whom the Union citizen has contracted a registered partnership, on the basis of the legislation of a Member State, if the legislation of the host Member State treats registered partnerships as equivalent to marriage … .

Article 3(2) of the Directive also requires the host Member State to

> facilitate entry and residence for … the partner with whom the Union citizen has a durable relationship, duly attested … .

This includes an obligation to

> undertake an extensive examination of the personal circumstances and … justify any denial of entry or residence to [the partner].

---

[66] 2011 California Statutes ch 81, sn 1, amending Education Code, s 51204.5, www.leginfo.ca.gov/pub/11–12/bill/sen/sb_0001–0050/sb_48_bill_20110714_chaptered.pdf.

[67] See www.homeoffice.gov.uk/publications/equalities/lgbt-equality-publications/lgbt-action-plan (p 2).

A Member State that is hostile to same-sex couples is likely to interpret the Directive in the narrowest possible way. The Member State could argue that the only spouses it recognises are different-sex spouses, that its legislation does not provide for registered partnerships for same-sex couples (let alone treat registered partnerships as equivalent to marriage), and that its tradition of recognising only married different-sex spouses for immigration purposes justifies denial of residence to all unmarried partners, different-sex or same-sex.

The UK has implemented the Directive in a generous way, through the Immigration (European Economic Area) Regulations 2006,[68] which make minor distinctions between the obligation to admit spouses and registered partners, and the obligation to 'facilitate' the residence of cohabiting partners, or justify a denial of residence. The Regulations apply to 'EEA nationals', which means nationals of any EU Member State other than the UK, and nationals of Norway, Iceland, Liechtenstein and Switzerland.[69] If an EEA national is in the UK as a jobseeker, a worker, a self-employed person, a self-sufficient person, or a student, he or she is a 'qualified person' entitled to reside in the UK for more than 90 days, and for as long as he or she remains a 'qualified person'.[70] A 'family member' of a 'qualified person' enjoys the same right as long as he or she remains a 'family member'.[71]

'Family member' is defined as including the spouse or civil partner of the EEA national and the children aged under 21, dependent children, or dependent parents of the spouse or civil partner of the EEA national,[72] as long as the marriage or civil partnership is not one 'of convenience' (that is, a fraudulent one contracted solely for the purpose of obtaining immigration benefits).[73] A person who qualifies as an 'extended family member' and has been issued an 'EEA family permit' is treated as a 'family member' for as long as he or she continues to qualify as an 'extended family member' and the permit remains valid.[74] The unmarried/unregistered partner of the EEA national qualifies as an 'extended family member' if he or she can prove that he or she is in 'a durable relationship' with the EEA national.[75] The same-sex spouse or registered partner of the EEA national will be deemed to be the 'civil partner' of the EEA national,[76] even if he or she is legally married to the EEA national under the law of another country

---

[68] Statutory Instrument 2006 no 1003.
[69] Reg 2(1).
[70] Regs 6(1), 14(1).
[71] Reg 14(2).
[72] Reg 7(1).
[73] Reg 2.
[74] Reg 7(3).
[75] Reg 8(5).
[76] Civil Partnership Act 2004, ss 212–18 and Sch 20 (as amended). It is not clear how UK immigration officials treat the different-sex registered partner of an EEA national, because no provision of UK law seems to provide for foreign different-sex registered partnerships to be deemed to be marriages. However, such a partner would certainly qualify as in a 'durable relationship', if not as a 'spouse' or a 'civil partner'.

because, under current UK law, marriage is only for different-sex couples and civil partnership is only for same-sex couples.[77]

The only difference between a same-sex civil partner (who is married or registered to the EEA national) and a same-sex cohabiting partner (who is not married or registered to the EEA national) is that the decision to grant an 'EEA family permit' to the partner is mandatory in the case of a civil partner ('An entry clearance officer must issue an EEA family permit'),[78] and discretionary in the case of a cohabiting partner ('An entry clearance officer may issue an EEA family permit ... if ... in all the circumstances, it appears to the entry clearance officer appropriate to issue the ... permit').[79] In exercising his or her discretion, the entry clearance officer

> shall undertake an extensive examination of the personal circumstances of the applicant and if he [or she] refuses the application shall give reasons justifying the refusal unless this is contrary to the interests of national security.[80]

Despite this difference in the application procedure, there is no evidence to suggest that EEA family permits are not routinely granted to cohabiting same-sex partners who have provided sufficient proof of their 'durable relationship'. Any applicant whose application is rejected could compare the treatment received with the way the UK Border Agency would treat the cohabiting same-sex partner of a UK citizen under the Immigration Rules (see below). The principle of non-discrimination on the ground of nationality of another member state (Article 18, Treaty on the Functioning of the EU) prevents the UK from granting more favourable treatment to its own citizens in its immigration law, even if the more favourable treatment goes beyond the minimum requirements of Directive 2004/38.[81]

A same-sex partner (married, registered or cohabiting) acquires the right to reside permanently in the UK after 'resid[ing] in the [UK] with the EEA national in accordance with these Regulations for a continuous period of five years'.[82] In the UK, the right to reside implicitly includes the right to work, as Article 23 of the Directive expressly requires:

---

[77] Under section 11(c) of the Matrimonial Causes Act 1973 (England and Wales), '[a] marriage ... shall be void [if] ... the parties are not respectively male and female'. Equivalent rules can be found in the Marriage (Scotland) Act 1977, s 5(4)(e), and the Marriage (Northern Ireland) Order 2003, Art 6(6)(e). Under s 3(1) of the Civil Partnership Act 2004 (UK), '[t]wo people are not eligible to register as civil partners ... if they are not of the same sex'. This system of segregating couples into two separate, but virtually identical, legal institutions is being challenged before the ECtHR: *Ferguson & Others v UK* (Application no 8254/11).

[78] Reg 12(1).

[79] Reg 12(2).

[80] Reg 12(3).

[81] See Case 59/85, *Netherlands v Reed*, [1986] ECR 1283.

[82] Reg 15(1)(b).

Irrespective of nationality, the family members of a Union citizen who have the right of residence or the right of permanent residence in a Member State shall be entitled to take up employment or self-employment there.

The case of *Roberto Taddeucci & Douglas McCall v Italy*, pending before the ECtHR,[83] provides an interesting example of how disparities in national legislation limit the choices of EU citizens, as to where they may live with their same-sex partners from outside the EU (see also Gasparini et al, chapter eight in this volume). Mr Taddeucci is an Italian national. His partner since 1999, Mr McCall, is a New Zealand national. After the refusal of a family-member residence permit for Mr McCall was upheld by Italy's highest civil court (the *Corte Suprema di Cassazione*) on 17 March 2009, Mr Taddeucci and Mr McCall were forced to leave Mr Taddeucci's Italian relatives and move to the Netherlands. If they had chosen to move to the UK, Mr McCall would have qualified for an EEA family permit under the 2006 Regulations, as an 'extended family member' of Mr Taddeucci (the EEA national), because of their 'durable relationship'.

3.2. UK Residence for Same-sex Partners of UK Citizens

A UK citizen may rely on the 2006 Regulations, as if he or she were an EEA national, if he or she is residing in an EEA Member State (other than the UK) or Switzerland, as a worker or self-employed person, 'or was so residing before returning to the [UK]', if the family member is his or her spouse or civil partner, and if they are or were living together in the EEA Member State or Switzerland.[84] If a UK citizen is living in the UK, and their same-sex partner is a citizen of a country outside the EEA and Switzerland, they fall outside of the 2006 Regulations. Instead, they are in an 'internal situation' not governed by EU law, that is, the admission of third-country nationals from outside the EU into the UK, which is not part of the Schengen Zone. The UK citizen may still apply for a residence permit for their same-sex partner, but they must do so under the older provisions of the Immigration Rules, which were adopted voluntarily before Directive 2004/38.

Under the Immigration Rules,[85] or concessions outside the Rules, UK citizens and permanent residents have been permitted to sponsor same-sex partners for immigration since October 1997.[86] Initially, the 'unmarried partner' category mainly covered same-sex partners, because of the requirement that 'the parties

[83] Application No 51362/09.

[84] Reg 9(1)–(2).

[85] See www.ukba.homeoffice.gov.uk/policyandlaw/immigrationlaw/immigrationrules. The Rules are not an Act of the UK Parliament, but must be approved by the UK Parliament.

[86] 'Concession Outside the Immigration Rules for Unmarried Partners of ... ', announced by Mike O'Brien MP on 10 October 1997. From 2 October 2000, see Immigration Rules, paras 295A–295O.

are legally unable to marry under [UK] law (other than by reason of consanguineous relationships or age)'.[87] That requirement was removed on 1 April 2003,
which meant that unmarried different-sex partners legally able to marry each
other also qualified. The category is now known as 'unmarried and same-sex
partners', on the understanding that 'unmarried' means different-sex partners
who have chosen not to marry, and 'same-sex' means same-sex partners who are
not eligible to marry in the UK (and many other countries). An example of the
requirements for this category is paragraph 295A of the Immigration Rules:

(i)   the applicant is the unmarried or same-sex partner of a person present and settled
      in the [UK] … and the parties have been living together in a relationship akin to
      marriage or civil partnership which has subsisted for two years or more[88] … ;
(ii) any previous marriage or civil partnership (or similar relationship) by either
      partner has permanently broken down; and
(iii) the parties are not involved in a consanguineous relationship with one another;
      and …
(v)   there will be adequate accommodation for the parties and any dependants
      without recourse to public funds in accommodation which they own or occupy
      exclusively; and
(vi) the parties will be able to maintain themselves and any dependants adequately
      without recourse to public funds; and
(vii) the parties intend to live together permanently

The existence of this 'unmarried and same-sex partners' category made it easy for
the UK to be generous in the way it included 'durable relationships' in the 2006
Regulations.

Since the Civil Partnership Act 2004 came into force on 5 December 2005,
same-sex partners no longer have to demonstrate two years of cohabitation as a
couple. Like different-sex couples who marry after a whirlwind romance, same-
sex couples may apply for a residence permit for the partner who is not an EU
citizen immediately after registering their civil partnership, under the 'spouses
and civil partners' category. The rules are the same as in the case of 'unmarried
and same-sex partners', except that no period of cohabitation is required. The
civil partnership certificate serves as sufficient evidence of commitment, as long
as 'each of the parties intends to live permanently with the other as his or her
spouse or civil partner and the marriage or civil partnership is subsisting'.[89] Since
2005, the UK Government has attempted to prevent marriages and civil partnerships 'of convenience' by prohibiting them from being celebrated in the UK
without a 'certificate of approval' from the UK Border Agency. However, the
ECtHR recently held that this system violates Article 12 (right to marry) of the
ECHR.[90]

---

[87] Immigration Rules, para 295A(iii).
[88] Reduced from 4 years in 2000.
[89] Immigration Rules, para 281.
[90] *O'Donoghue v UK* (14 December 2010).

If a UK citizen and his or her same-sex partner from outside the EU are living in France (for example), and decide to move to the UK, should they apply under the 2006 Regulations or the Immigration Rules? Each option has advantages and disadvantages. Under the 2006 Regulations, no fee may be charged for the EEA family permit,[91] and the permit includes the right to visa-free travel throughout all EU Member States.[92] Under the Immigration Rules, the combined fees for a 'proposed civil partner visa' to allow the same-sex partner to enter the UK, and the initial two-year residence permit after the civil partnership, are at least £1,250. If the same-sex partner is from a country whose nationals require a Schengen Visa, he or she will have to apply for one every time he or she wishes to travel from the UK to a country inside the Schengen Zone. It can take up to one month to book an appointment to apply for the visa, and another month for the visa to be processed. This is a major obstacle to the freedom of the UK citizen to travel spontaneously within the EU with his family member. On the other hand, under the Immigration Rules, the UK citizen may pay extra for same-day, in-person processing of applications, and their same-sex partner qualifies for permanent residence after only two years of residence in the UK, instead of five.[93]

3.3. Asylum-seekers

Since 1999, UK case law has provided solid support for granting refugee status to lesbian and gay asylum-seekers from outside the EU (including from 75 to 80 countries in which same-sex sexual activity is a criminal offence). In the joined cases *R (on the application of Shah) v Immigration Appeal Tribunal,* and *Islam v Secretary of State for the Home Department*,[94] judicial members of the House of Lords (who became the UK Supreme Court in October 2009) had to interpret the phrase 'membership of a particular social group' in Article 1A(2) of the 1951 Convention Relating to the Status of Refugees. Lord Steyn said:

> I agree with La Forest J in the *Ward* case [Supreme Court of Canada, 1993] when he said … that 'social group' could include individuals fearing persecution on 'such bases as gender, linguistic background and sexual orientation'.

Yet, despite this solid legal basis for claiming a 'well-founded fear of being persecuted for reasons of … membership of a particular social group', a 2010 study reported that:

---

[91] Reg 12(4).

[92] Directive 2004/38, Articles 5(2), 10. See also 2006 Regulations, reg 17 (issuance of the 'residence card' mentioned in the Directive).

[93] Immigration Rules, para 287. *Netherlands v Reed*, above n 79, might require that the two-year period be extended to nationals of other EU Member States.

[94] Joined cases *R (on the application of Shah) v Immigration Appeal Tribunal* and *Islam v Secretary of State for the Home Department* [1999] UKHL 20.

In claims brought to the attention of the UK Lesbian and Gay Immigration Group[95] ... between 2005–2009 over 98 per cent were refused [by the UK Border Agency] at [the] initial stage [before appeals]. Between 2005 and 2008 the percentage of all asylum applicants refused at [the] initial stage was [only] 76.5%.[96]

One of the main reasons for the extremely high rejection rate was the policy of the UK Border Agency, generally upheld by appellate tribunals, of finding that the applicant's fear of being persecuted was not well-founded, because he or she could avoid persecution in his or her home country simply by being 'discreet', that is, not discussing his or her sexual orientation with anyone other than trusted friends, and not doing or saying anything in public that might suggest that he is gay or she is lesbian. This was true even if the home country was Iran, where same-sex sexual activity can, in certain circumstances, attract the death penalty. In 2004, the ECtHR ruled that the rejection of the asylum claim of a gay man from Iran did not violate the ECHR.[97] The ECtHR declared his application inadmissible because he had not shown that he faced a real risk of being executed, flogged, or imprisoned for private, same-sex sexual activity:

> The Court observes ... that the materials ... do not disclose a situation of active prosecution by the authorities of adults involved in consensual and private homosexual relationships ... The majority of sources refer to a certain toleration in practice, with known meeting places for homosexuals in Tehran .... Although it must be acknowledged that the general situation in Iran does not foster the protection of human rights and that homosexuals may be vulnerable to abuse, the applicant has not established ... that there are substantial grounds for believing that he will be exposed to a real risk of ... treatment contrary to ... Articles [2, right to life, and 3, freedom from inhuman and degrading treatment] ... there is no concrete indication that [he] would face arrest or trial on any particular charge. A possible future unspecified problem with the authorities is too remote and hypothetical basis for attracting the protection of the Convention ... . Insofar as ... he would live under a ban against homosexual adult consensual relations, which would in Contracting States disclose a violation of Article 8 [respect for private life, see *Dudgeon v UK*][98] ... it cannot be required that an expelling Contracting State only return an alien to a country which is in full and effective enforcement of all the rights and freedoms set out in the Convention.

The ECtHR implicitly accepted the UK Border Agency's policy of requiring lesbian and gay asylum-seekers to remain 'discreet', to avoid bringing themselves to the attention of the police, thereby reducing the risk of a criminal prosecution and punishment.

The legal situation in the UK changed dramatically on 7 July 2010, when the UK Supreme Court ruled unanimously (5–0), in *HJ (Iran) & HT (Cameroon) v*

---

[95] See www.uklgig.org.uk.
[96] Stonewall, 'No Going Back: Lesbian and Gay People and the Asylum System' (2010), www.stonewall.org.uk/what_we_do/research_and_policy/2874.asp, p 18.
[97] *F v UK* (Application No 17341/03) (ECtHR, 22 June 2004).
[98] ECtHR, 22 October 1981.

Secretary of State for the Home Department,[99] that the assessment of the risk of persecution of lesbian and gay asylum-seekers, if they were returned to their home countries, should assume 'open' rather than 'discreet' behaviour. Lord Rodger (with the express support of three other judges) summarised the new interpretation of the Refugee Convention as follows:[100]

> (1) the tribunal must first ask itself whether it is satisfied on the evidence that [the applicant] is gay, or ... would be treated as gay by potential persecutors ... (2) If so, the tribunal must then ask itself whether ... gay people who lived openly would be liable to persecution in the applicant's country of nationality. (3) If so, the tribunal must go on to consider what the ... applicant would do if he were returned to that country. (a) If [he] would in fact live openly and thereby be exposed to a real risk of persecution, then he has a well-founded fear of persecution—even if he could avoid the risk by living 'discreetly'. (b) If ... [he] would in fact live discreetly and so avoid persecution, [the tribunal] must go on to ask itself *why* he would do so .... (i) If ... [he] would choose to live discreetly simply because that was how he himself would wish to live, or because of social pressures, e.g., not wanting to distress his parents or embarrass his friends, then his application should be rejected. Social pressures of that kind do not amount to persecution and the [Refugee] Convention does not offer protection against them [nor against discrimination that falls short of persecution; persecution often involves imprisonment, or physical violence committed by state or private actors] ... (ii) If ... the tribunal concludes that a material reason for the applicant living discreetly on his return would be a fear of the persecution which would follow if he were to live openly as a gay man, then, other things being equal, his application should be accepted. Such a person has a well-founded fear of persecution. To reject his application on the ground that he could avoid the persecution by living discreetly would be to defeat the very right which the [Refugee] Convention exists to protect—his right to live freely and openly as a gay man without fear of persecution.

By recognising the right of lesbian and gay refugees to live openly in their home countries, the UK Supreme Court removed the inconsistency between asylum claims based on sexual orientation, and those based on race, religion, or political opinion. Members of ethnic or religious minorities, and pro-democracy political dissidents, have never been asked to hide their ethnicity, religion, or political beliefs. Lord Rodger made this clear:

> No-one would proceed on the basis that a straight [heterosexual] man or woman could find it reasonably tolerable to conceal his or her sexual identity indefinitely to avoid suffering persecution. Nor ... that a man or woman could find it reasonably tolerable to conceal his or her race indefinitely ... Such an assumption about gay men and lesbian women is equally unacceptable.[101]

[99] *HJ (Iran) & HT (Cameroon) v Secretary of State for the Home Department* [2010] UKSC 31, available at www.bailii.org/uk/cases/UKSC/2010/31.html.
[100] See para 82.
[101] See para 76.

The fact that the lesbian or gay refugee, if returned to their home country, would for practical reasons be forced to live 'discreetly' to avoid persecution is irrelevant: 'discreet' behaviour that is coerced, even partly, by fear of persecution does not count. As Lord Rodger said:

> Unless he were minded to swell the ranks of gay martyrs, when faced with a real threat of persecution, the applicant would have no real choice: he would be compelled to act discreetly.[102]

Several judges reinforced this point by citing the case of Anne Frank. Lord Collins described as 'absurd and unreal' the argument that

> had it been found that on return to Holland [from the UK] she would successfully avoid detection by hiding in the attic, then she would not be at real risk of persecution by the Nazis ... It is plain that it [was] the threat to Jews [who lived openly] of the concentration camp and the gas chamber which constitute[d] the persecution.[103]

What did the UK Supreme Court mean by being 'open' about being lesbian or gay? Lord Rodger described living 'discreetly' as

> avoid[ing] any open expression of affection for another man which went beyond what would be acceptable behaviour on the part of a straight man[,] ... be[ing] cautious about the ... the places where he socialised[,] ... constantly ... restrain[ing] himself in an area of life where powerful emotions and physical attraction are involved and a straight man could be spontaneous, impulsive even. Not only would he not be able to indulge openly in the mild flirtations which are an enjoyable part of heterosexual life, but he would have to think twice before revealing that he was attracted to another man.[104]

He then illustrated living openly by citing

> trivial stereotypical examples from British society: just as male heterosexuals are free to enjoy themselves playing rugby, drinking beer and talking about girls with their mates, so male homosexuals are ... free to enjoy themselves going to Kylie [Minogue] concerts, drinking exotically coloured cocktails and talking about boys with their straight female mates. Mutatis mutandis—and in many cases [for example, Iran and Cameroon] the adaptations would obviously be great—the same must apply to other societies. In other words, gay men are to be as free as their straight equivalents in the society concerned to live their lives in the way that is natural to them as gay men, without the fear of persecution.[105]

---

[102] See para 59.
[103] See para 107.
[104] See para 77.
[105] See para 78.

However, he added that 'an applicant for asylum does not need to show that his homosexuality plays a particularly prominent part in his life'.[106]

Sir John Dyson stressed that the hypothetical 'right to be open back home' is based on 'objective human rights standards', not 'the social mores of the home country'. He disagreed with Lord Justice Pill's statement, in the decision of the England and Wales Court of Appeal that the UK Supreme Court reversed,[107] that

> a degree of respect for social norms and religious beliefs in other states is ... appropriate. Both in Muslim Iran and Roman Catholic Cameroon, strong views are genuinely held about homosexual practices. In considering what is reasonably tolerable [by a lesbian or gay person] in a particular society, the fact-finding Tribunal is ... entitled to have regard to the beliefs held [by the majority] there.[108]

Unlike in the case of HIV-positive persons who cannot access or afford medications in their home countries,[109] none of the judges expressed any concern about 'opening the floodgates', that is, about millions of lesbian and gay individuals leaving countries where they would risk persecution if they lived openly, and travelling to the UK to seek asylum. On the contrary, Lord Hope said

> a huge gulf has opened up in attitudes to and understanding of gay persons between societies [for example, EU countries *versus* Iran, Uganda and Malawi] ... It is one of the most demanding social issues of our time. Our own government has pledged to do what it can to resolve the problem [of persecution in other countries], but it seems likely to grow and to remain with us for many years. In the meantime more and more gays and lesbians are likely to have to seek protection here ... It is crucially important that they are provided with the protection that they are entitled to under the [Refugee] Convention.[110]

Now that the highest court of one of the larger EU Member States has adopted this interpretation of the Refugee Convention, it is important to present the UK Supreme Court's reasoning to the two European Courts, and attempt to persuade them to apply it to all EU Member States, or all Council of Europe Member States. One opportunity arose in *Khavand v Germany*,[111] a reference for a preliminary ruling lodged with the Court of Justice of the EU (CJEU) on 1 December 2010. A German administrative court referred the following questions to the CJEU:

> Is homosexuality to be considered a sexual orientation within the meaning ... of Article 10(1)(d) of Directive 2004/83/EC and can it be adequate reason for persecution?

> If Question 1 is to be answered in the affirmative:

---

[106] See para 79.
[107] [2009] EWCA Civ 172.
[108] See *HJ (Iran)*, paras 128–30.
[109] *N v UK* (ECtHR, 27 May 2008).
[110] See *HJ (Iran)* para 3.
[111] *Khavand v Germany* Case C-563/10.

(a) To what extent is homosexual activity protected?
(b) Can a homosexual person be told to live with his or her sexual orientation in his or her home country in secret and not allow it to become known to others?
(c) Are specific prohibitions for the protection of public order and morals relevant when interpreting and applying Article 10(1)(d) ... or should homosexual activity be protected in the same way as for heterosexual people?

Article 10 ('Reasons for persecution') is similar to the reasoning in *Shah and Islam*:

1. Member States shall take the following elements into account when assessing the reasons for persecution: ...

(d) ... depending on the circumstances in the country of origin, a particular social group might include a group based on a common characteristic of sexual orientation. Sexual orientation cannot be understood to include acts considered to be criminal in accordance with national law of the Member States.

Unfortunately, it would appear that Mr Khavand (whose name suggests that he might be a gay man from Iran) has been granted asylum, and that the case will not be heard by the CJEU.

On 27 January 2011, the ECtHR decided to communicate to the UK Government the application in *DBN v UK*,[112] in which the applicant was denied aslyum despite claiming that she risked ill-treatment in Zimbabwe as 'a "butch" lesbian who dresses like a man', and because she could not demonstrate support for President Mugabe's political party. The application was lodged with the ECtHR on 11 May 2010, before the UK Supreme Court's decision in *HJ (Iran)*. It is not clear whether the ECtHR will eventually rule on the merits of this case. Nor is it clear whether *HJ (Iran)* is being implemented, because of a lack of information about how many pending asylum claims involve sexual orientation.[113]

4. Cross-border Reproductive Services

4.1. UK Legislation on Donor Insemination and Surrogacy

The UK probably has the most advanced and detailed legislation in the EU on access to donor insemination and surrogacy, and on establishing legal parenthood of children born as a result of these techniques in the UK or another country. The UK's first comprehensive regulation of assisted reproduction, the

---

[112] Application No 26550/10.
[113] See 'Gay asylum claims not being counted despite pledge, admit ministers', www.guardian.co.uk/uk/2011/may/01/gay-asylum-claims-not-being-counted?CMP=EMCGT_020511&.

Human Fertilisation and Embryology Act 1990, contained three discriminatory provisions. First, section 13(5) of the 1990 Act prohibited any form of fertility treatment, including donor insemination at a clinic

> unless account has been taken of the welfare of any child who may be born as a result of the treatment (including the need of that child for a father).

This provision did not prohibit donor insemination of lesbian women (or unmarried heterosexual women with no male partner), but appeared to discourage it, making some clinics reluctant to treat lesbian women.

Secondly, sections 28(2) to (3) of the 1990 Act provided that the husband or male partner of a heterosexual woman receiving donor insemination was automatically the child's father, and did not have to adopt the child to become its second legal parent. These provisions did not apply to the female partner of a lesbian woman receiving donor insemination.

Thirdly, when a child was born to a surrogate mother, after being commissioned by parents who supplied the egg, the sperm or both, section 30(1) of the 1990 Act only permitted the commissioning parents to apply for a court order, designating them as the child's legal parents, if they were a married different-sex couple. No same-sex couple was eligible to apply for such an order.

The 1990 Act has been amended and supplemented by the Human Fertilisation and Embryology Act 2008, the cited provisions of which had all come into force by 6 April 2010. This Act has removed all three forms of discrimination, as well as the remaining differences between a different-sex marriage and a same-sex civil partnership, in terms of the substantive rights of the couple.

First, the reference in section 13(5) of the 1990 Act to 'the need of that child for a father' has been replaced by a reference to 'the need of that child for supportive parenting'. Additional conditions a licensed clinic must satisfy are found in new sections 13(6) and 13(6C) of the 1990 Act (inserted by the 2008 Act).[114]

> (6)   A woman shall not be provided with treatment services [including donor insemination] ... unless she and any man or woman who is to be treated together with her have been given a suitable opportunity to receive proper counselling about the implications of her being provided with treatment services of that kind, and have been provided with such relevant information as is proper ...
>
> (6C) ... the information provided ... must include such information as is proper about:
>
> (a)   the importance of informing any resulting child at an early age that the child results from the gametes of a person who is not a parent of the child, and
>
> (b)   suitable methods of informing such a child of that fact.

---

[114]   2008 Act, s 14.

Secondly, sections 42 to 45 of the 2008 Act regulate 'Cases in which woman to be the other parent'. The first case is where the female partner of the woman receiving donor insemination is her civil partner:

42(1)If at the time ... of her artificial insemination, W. [the woman receiving treatment] was a party to a civil partnership, then ... the other party to the civil partnership is to be treated as a parent of the child unless it is shown that she did not consent ... to her artificial insemination ... .

(2) This section applies whether W. was in the United Kingdom or elsewhere at the time mentioned in subsection 1.

The second case is where the female partner of the woman receiving donor insemination is her cohabiting partner, not her (legally registered) civil partner, and she agrees that her partner will be the child's second legal parent:

43. If no man is treated by virtue of section 35 as the father of the child and no woman is treated by virtue of section 42 as a parent of the child but:
(a) ... W. was artificially inseminated, in the course of treatment services provided in the United Kingdom by a person to whom a licence applies,
(b) at the time when ... W. was artificially inseminated, the agreed female parenthood conditions (as set out in section 44) were met in relation to another woman ... and
(c) the other woman remained alive at that time, then ... the other woman is to be treated as a parent of the child.

The 'agreed female parenthood conditions' are set out in section 44 of the 2008 Act:

44(1)The agreed female parenthood conditions ... are met in relation to another woman ('P.') ... if, but only if:

(a) P. has given ... a notice stating that P consents to P being treated as a parent of any child resulting from treatment provided to W. ... ,
(b) W. has given ... a notice stating that W. agrees to P. being so treated,
...
(e) W. and P. are not within prohibited degrees of relationship in relation to each other [they could register a civil partnership].

If either section 42 or section 43 applies, then the effect of the 2008 Act is that the child has two legal mothers, and no legal father:

45(1)Where a woman is treated by virtue of section 42 or 43 as a parent of the child, no man is to be treated as the father of the child. ...
53(1)Subsection 2 ... ha[s] effect, ... for the interpretation of any enactment, deed or any other instrument or document (whenever passed or made).
(2) Any reference (however expressed) to the father of a child who has a parent by virtue of section 42 or 43 is to be read as a reference to the woman who is a parent of the child by virtue of that section.

However, the legislation carefully avoids calling the lesbian woman's female partner 'the second mother' of the child. In Schedule 6 of the 2008 Act, she is described in several places as 'the second female parent'.

The third form of discrimination in the 1990 Act has been removed by section 54 of the 2008 Act. It permits any couple, whether different-sex or same-sex, whether married or in a civil partnership or cohabiting, to commission a surrogate mother and apply for a court order (a 'parental order') designating the commissioning parents as the legal parents of the child:

54(1) On an application made by two people ('the applicants'), the court may make an order providing for a child to be treated in law as the child of the applicants if:
- (a) the child has been carried by a woman who is not one of the applicants, as a result of the placing in her of an embryo or sperm and eggs or her artificial insemination,
- (b) the gametes of at least one of the applicants were used to bring about the creation of the embryo, and
- (c) the conditions in subsections 2 to 8 are satisfied.

(2) The applicants must be:
- (a) husband and wife,
- (b) civil partners of each other, or
- (c) two persons who are living as partners in an enduring family relationship and are not within prohibited degrees of relationship in relation to each other [they could marry or register a civil partnership]

(…).

(6) The court must be satisfied that both:
- (a) the woman who carried the child, and
- (b) any other person who is a parent of the child but is not one of the applicants

… ,

have freely, and with full understanding of what is involved, agreed unconditionally to the making of the order.

(7) (…) the agreement of the woman who carried the child is ineffective for the purpose of that subsection if given by her less than six weeks after the child's birth.

(8) The court must be satisfied that no money or other benefit (other than for expenses reasonably incurred) has been given or received by either of the applicants for or in consideration of:
- (a) the making of the order,
- (b) any agreement required by subsection 6,
- (c) the handing over of the child to the applicants, or
- (d) the making of arrangements with a view to the making of the order, unless authorised by the court. …

(10) Subsection 1a applies whether the woman was in the United Kingdom or elsewhere at the time of the placing in her of the embryo or the sperm and eggs or her artificial insemination.

In practice, surrogacy rarely takes place in the UK, because the Surrogacy Arrangements Act 1985 provides that '[n]o surrogacy arrangement is enforceable by or against any of the persons making it' (section 1A); prohibits negotiating surrogacy arrangements on a commercial basis (section 2); and prohibits advertising that any person is willing to facilitate the making of a surrogacy arrangement, or that any person is looking for a woman willing to become a surrogate mother (section 3). Commissioning parents tend to seek surrogate mothers either in the USA (especially California), or India. The combination of the 1985 Act (surrogacy is legal but strongly discouraged in the UK) and the 2008 Act (detailed rules provide secure legal parentage for the children of couples who commission surrogate mothers outside the UK) could be described as reflecting 'British pragmatism'. In the face of social reality (the existence of UK couples desperate for a child with a genetic connection to one or both of them, and the existence of different laws in other countries that permit commercial agencies to arrange surrogacy), UK legislation prefers not to punish the child for the decision of its parents, and instead to provide a mechanism for giving the child two legal parents.[115]

4.2. Application of this Legislation to Cross-border Situations involving the UK

With regard to donor insemination, the UK is likely to attract lesbian women from other EU Member States, even though they would probably have to pay for treatment at a private clinic. The legal parents of a child born to a lesbian woman who is inseminated in the UK, and then gives birth in another EU Member State, will be determined by the family law of the country of birth (for practical purposes, given the difficulty of asserting any rights under UK law outside the UK).

If a lesbian woman seeks donor insemination in another EU Member State (for example, Belgium), and then returns to the UK, her female partner is automatically the child's second legal parent under section 42 of the 2008 Act, if they were parties to a civil partnership at the time of the insemination. If they were cohabiting partners, not in a civil partnership, then section 43 does not apply (because the treatment was provided outside the UK). However, the genetic and legal mother's female partner would be able to apply to adopt the child (become

---

[115] See Convention on the Rights of the Child, Art 2(2): 'States Parties shall take all appropriate measures to ensure that the child is protected against all forms of discrimination or punishment on the basis of the status, activities, expressed opinions, or beliefs of the child's parents'.

its second parent) under sections 50, 51 and 144 of the Adoption and Children Act 2002 (England and Wales),[116] either as part of 'a couple' or as 'one person':

50(2) An adoption order may be made on the application of a couple where:
    (a)   one of the couple is the mother or the father of the person to be adopted and has attained the age of 18 years, and
    (b)   the other has attained the age of 21 years.

. . .

51(2) An adoption order may be made on the application of one person who has attained the age of 21 years if the court is satisfied that the person is the partner of a parent of the person to be adopted.

. . .

144(4) In this Act, a couple means:
    (a)   a married couple, or
    (b)   two people (whether of different sexes or the same sex) living as partners in an enduring family relationship.

The legal situation in the UK contrasts sharply with that in France, as illustrated by the pending case of *Valérie Gas and Nathalie Dubois v France*, heard by a Chamber of the ECtHR on 12 April 2011. The applicants are a lesbian couple who sought donor insemination in Belgium, because they were not legally permitted to receive it in France. Their daughter was born in France in 2000, but has only one legal parent (her genetic and birth mother, Ms Dubois), because Ms Gas is legally unable to adopt her. Article 365 of the French Civil Code only allows married different-sex couples to adopt each other's children. In all other cases, an adoption transfers the genetic and legal parent's parental authority to their partner. A 'second-parent adoption' is intended to add the partner as a second legal parent, without affecting the rights of the child's genetic and legal parent. If Ms Gas and Ms Dubois lived in the UK, they would not have had to travel to Belgium to seek insemination, and Ms Gas could have become their child's second mother, either through second-parent adoption, or (if the insemination took place in 2011) through automatic parenthood from the moment of the child's birth.

In the case of surrogacy, it is unlikely that a couple in another EU Member State would commission a surrogate mother in the UK, in view of the strong discouragement of the practice by UK legislation. Nor is a UK couple likely to commission a surrogate mother in another EU Member State, given that there do not seem to be any EU Member States that permit commercial agencies to arrange surrogacy. However, a parental order under section 54 of the 2008 Act is

---

[116] See also Adoption and Children (Scotland) Act 2007. In Northern Ireland, same-sex couples probably have access to joint or second-parent adoption because of *In re P*, [2008] UKHL 38 (18 June 2008) (unmarried different-sex couples must be allowed to adopt jointly), read with *Karner v Austria* (ECtHR, 24 July 2003) (the rights of same-sex and unmarried different-sex couples must be equal).

available to UK couples who arrange surrogacy in countries outside the EU. A recent celebrity example is provided by Elton John and David Furnish, who registered their civil partnership at Windsor, England, on 21 December 2005, and whose son Zachary was born to a surrogate mother in Los Angeles, California on 25 December 2010.[117] They were eligible to apply for a parental order in 2011.

---

[117] See www.bbc.co.uk/news/entertainment-arts-12084650; www.bbc.co.uk/news/entertainment-arts-12085179.

12

Legal Comparison, Conclusions and Recommendations

ROBERT WINTEMUTE

A.   whereas homophobia can be defined as an irrational fear of and aversion to homosexuality and to lesbian, gay, bisexual and transgender (LGBT) people based on prejudice and similar to racism, xenophobia, anti-semitism and sexism,

B.   whereas homophobia manifests itself in the private and public spheres in different forms, such as hate speech and incitement to discrimination, ridicule and … physical violence, persecution and murder, [and] discrimination in violation of the principle of equality

European Parliament resolution on 'Homophobia in Europe', 18 January 2006[1]

There is a prize-winning photograph which provides an excellent illustration of the social phenomenon of homophobia, and the need for a stronger legal response at the European Union level.[2] It was taken in Budapest (Hungary, one of the four EU Member States studied) on 7 July 2007, after the Lesbian and Gay Pride Parade. The photographer describes the scene of two men, both with blood on them, as follows:

Having been beaten up, [a] gay couple is waiting for the emergency car. A few ultraright groups organized demonstrations against the Lesbian and Gay Parade in Budapest, however, [they] did not succeed in disturbing it. When the festival ended and the police ensuring the security left, the gay people leaving for home were injured in a few spots. The [G]erman couple in the photo [tourists exercising their EU freedom to receive

---

[1] See text RC-B6- 0025/2006. This book employs the term 'homophobia' because it is commonly used in academic, legal and political debates, and is well understood. However, given that many lesbian women and gay men do not like to be described as 'homosexuals' or 'homos', it might make sense at some stage to consider replacing 'homophobia' with 'LGBphobia' and 'transphobia'.

[2] See, eg Dr Christine Loudes and Evelyne Paradis, 'Handbook on monitoring and reporting homophobic and transphobic incidents' available at www.ilga-europe.org/home/publications/reports_and_other_materials/handbook_on_monitoring_and_reporting_homophobic_and_transphobic_incidents_august_2008.

services?] entered a pub, where they were asked if they were gays. After answering yes, they were attacked and hit by the customers, and then bounced to the street.[3]

This chapter will begin with a comparison of the legal situations in Italy, Slovenia, Hungary and the United Kingdom (analysed in chapters eight to eleven), before setting out the Conclusions and Recommendations of the study.

1. Legal Comparison

1.1 Hate Crimes and Hate Speech

With regard to hate crimes, there is no legislation in Italy which makes hostility towards the sexual orientation of the victim of a crime of a violence an aggravating circumstance or an element of a separate, more serious offence. Legislation of this kind exists in Slovenia, Hungary and the UK, but gaps can be identified in the legislation of each of those countries.

In Slovenia, sexual orientation appears in the Criminal Code's definition of the crime of violation of equality, and both murder and torture linked to a violation of equality are separate criminal offences with higher potential sentences. In addition, under the Protection of Public Order Act, higher fines are prescribed for certain offences, if they are committed with discriminatory motives. However, the Criminal Code's sentencing provision states only that the convicted person's motive may be an aggravating circumstance, without mentioning discriminatory motives, the crime of violation of equality or a list of grounds of discrimination.

Similarly, in Hungary, the sentencing provision contains no reference to discriminatory motives or sexual orientation. However, the crime of assaulting a person because they belong to a national, ethnic, racial or religious group has been amended by adding 'any other group of society', which was intended to cover sexual orientation and gender identity, according to the Ministry of Justice.

In the UK, the position is the opposite of that in Slovenia. Legislation in England and Wales, Scotland and Northern Ireland expressly requires courts to treat hostility, malice or ill-will based on sexual orientation as an aggravating circumstance when sentencing the convicted person, but there are no separate crimes motivated by such hostility (unlike in the case of race and religion).

With regard to hate speech, there is no legislation in Italy prohibiting incitement to hatred based on sexual orientation (unlike in the case of 'racial, ethnic, national or religious grounds'). Legislation against homophobic hate speech

---

[3] See 'After the party' by Zsolt Szigetváry, available at www.flickr.com/photos/31100956@N06/4035696707/meta and www.archive.worldpressphoto.org/search/layout/result/indeling/detailwpp/form/wpp/start/34/q/ishoofdafbeelding/true/trefwoord/year/2007 (World Press Photo, 2nd prize, Contemporary Issues).

exists in Slovenia, Hungary and the UK, with Slovenia having what appears to be the strongest protection.

In Slovenia, the Criminal Code expressly prohibits incitement to intolerance based on sexual orientation, which has a symbolic value on its own, and is not weakened by a broad defence. In Hungary, the Criminal Code prohibits incitement to hatred against 'any group of society', which includes minorities defined by sexual orientation, but lacks the symbolic value of an express reference to sexual orientation. To protect freedom of expression, the Constitutional Court has blocked any extension of this prohibition beyond incitement to hatred to, for example, 'offensive or denigrating expression'.

In the UK, the strongest protection is found in Northern Ireland, which expressly prohibits incitement to hatred based on sexual orientation, in the same way as for race and religion. In England and Wales, there is less protection than for race, and the same as for religion, especially because of an exception for 'criticism of sexual conduct or practices or ... urging ... persons to refrain from or modify such conduct or practices'. In Scotland, there is no protection at all.

1.2 Education at all Levels

With regard to sexual orientation, Italy's anti-discrimination legislation does not go beyond the minimum requirements of Council Directive 2000/78/EC. It therefore prohibits discrimination only in university education and other forms of vocational training, but does not cover primary and secondary education (which are covered in the case of race). Slovenia, Hungary and the UK have all gone beyond the minimum EU standard, by extending their legislation to cover discrimination based on sexual orientation at all levels of their educational systems.

In Slovenia, the Act Implementing the Principle of Equal Treatment prohibits direct and indirect discrimination, as well as harassment, based on a number of personal circumstances ('sexual orientation' is expressly mentioned) in a number of fields of social life (including 'education', in addition to 'vocational training'). In Hungary, the Equal Treatment Act also prohibits both direct and indirect discrimination and harassment based on sexual orientation, at all levels of the educational system. However, in the UK, the anti-discrimination legislation of Great Britain and Northern Ireland covers only direct and indirect discrimination based on sexual orientation in education, and does not extend to harassment. This exception (which also applies to religion, but not to sex, race and other grounds) forces lesbian and gay students suffering homophobic harassment to argue that the harassment constitutes direct discrimination based on sexual orientation.

As for combating homophobic bullying in schools, which requires non-legislative measures in addition to legislation, Italy has yet to develop any national policies or programmes. Nor does Italy have a national policy on sexual education in state schools. In Slovenia, the learning plan for elementary schools includes sexual orientation under the topic of diversity in the fifth grade, but the textbooks that teachers and students use do not mention the existence of lesbian and gay individuals and same-sex couples. In Hungary, the Ministry of Education's decree concerning framework curricula mentions same-sex sexual orientation in the tenth and eleventh grades, but there is no national programme to combat homophobic bullying. In the UK, the national curriculum for England includes 'differences between people of different … sexual orientation' under the topic of 'diversity', for students aged 11 to 14. In 2007, the UK Government issued detailed guidance for schools and teachers on how to combat homophobic bullying.

1.3   Free Movement, Immigration and Asylum

With regard to immigration of same-sex partners, Italian law generally recognises only different-sex spouses as family members. Italian citizens living in Italy and sponsoring non-EU same-sex partners cannot rely on EU law, and must instead invoke the European Convention on Human Rights.[4] Citizens of other EU Member States moving to Italy (and Italian citizens returning to Italy) with their non-EU same-sex partners cannot rely on the category 'registered partner' in Article 2(2)(b) of Directive 2004/38/EC, because Italy does not have a registered partnership law for same-sex couples, and neither the case law of the European Court of Human Rights[5] nor EU law currently obliges Italy to adopt one. Same-sex couples who have married (especially in another EU Member State) can rely on the category 'spouse' in Article 2(2)(a), but this might require a reference to the Court of Justice of the EU. Alternatively, they can rely on the category 'durable relationship partner' in Article 3(2)(b), but this triggers only an undefined obligation to 'facilitate entry and residence' and to 'justify any denial of entry or residence'. Once again, a reference to the Court of Justice might be necessary.

Because Slovenia, Hungary and the UK have all passed registered partnership laws for same-sex couples, and 'treat[] registered partnerships as equivalent to marriage', Article 2(2)(b) does apply. In Slovenia, any doubt as to whether or not registered partnerships are treated as sufficiently equivalent to marriage will be removed by the Family Code adopted in 2011 (if it enters into force despite a proposed referendum). The combination of the Family Code, which recognises registered and cohabiting same-sex partners and equalises the rights of spouses and registered partners (except with regard to joint adoption and donor insemination), and the new Aliens Act (also adopted in 2011), will ensure that registered and cohabiting same-sex partners are recognised in immigration law. This will

---

[4]   See *Roberto Taddeucci & Douglas McCall v Italy* (App no 51362/09) pending ECtHR.
[5]   See *Horst Schalk & Johann Kopf v Austria* (24 June 2010) ECtHR (4–3).

avoid discrimination contrary to the principle of *Karner v Austria*,[6] because cohabiting different-sex partners are already recognised.

In Hungary, the Registered Partnership Act extends all of the rights of different-sex spouses to same-sex registered partners, unless an exception is made, and there is no exception for immigration. It is thus clear that the non-EU registered same-sex partner of a Hungarian or other EU citizen has a right to reside in Hungary. In the case of cohabiting partners (different-sex or same-sex), Hungarian immigration has no category for them, but a general discretion to recognise any other person as a family member could be invoked, along with Article 3(2)(b) of the Directive (if it applies).

In the UK, cohabiting same-sex partners have been recognised for the purpose of immigration since 1997, ie for much longer than in Slovenia or Hungary. This equal treatment now extends to registered same-sex partners, who are treated as 'civil partners' under UK law even if they are spouses in their own country.

With regard to asylum, the common obstacle in all four countries is persuading a court that a lesbian or gay individual has a well-founded fear of persecution in their country of origin because of their sexual orientation. Apart from being reluctant to believe that the individual is lesbian or gay, or has already suffered harm in their country of origin, courts either set a very high standard in defining the harm that would amount to 'persecution', or conclude that the individual can easily avoid the potential harm by being 'discreet'.

In Italy, the Court of Cassation takes an extremely narrow view of the kind of harm the individual would risk if they were returned. Even though private, consensual, adult, same-sex sexual activity is protected by Article 8 of the European Convention on Human Rights,[7] for the Italian Court, a risk of criminal prosecution for such activity is not enough. Instead, the prosecution must be based solely on 'being' lesbian or gay (having same-sex attractions without acting on them), rather than on same-sex sexual behaviour. Similarly, the Supreme Court of Slovenia thought it relevant to ask whether, in Iran, the death penalty is 'only for persons with homosexual orientation or also for persons who do not have such orientation but are apprehended while engaging in homosexual activity'. The Slovenian Court implies that even the death penalty is not enough, if it would also be applied to a heterosexual person engaging in same-sex sexual activity. In Hungary, the courts seem to expect lesbian and gay asylum-seekers to 'live a closeted life and keep their affection from the public', so as not to 'attract[ ] the attention of homophobes' and thereby avoid persecution.

The reasoning seen in the Italian, Slovenian and Hungarian cases was rejected by the UK Supreme Court in July 2010. Lesbian and gay individuals have the same right to be open about their sexual orientation in their home countries as members of religious minorities have to be open about their religious beliefs, and

---

[6] *Karner v Austria* (24 July 2003) ECtHR.
[7] *Dudgeon v United Kingdom* (22 October 1981) ECtHR.

as political dissidents have to be open about their political opinions. If hypothetical openness would trigger persecution, whether in the form of physical violence at the hands of state or private actors, or a criminal prosecution for same-sex sexual activity, then the lesbian or gay individual is eligible for asylum, even if they would be forced to be 'discreet' to avoid persecution if they were sent back.

1.4   Cross-Border Reproductive Services

In Italy, Slovenia and Hungary, restrictions on access to donor insemination create incentives for lesbian women to travel to other EU Member States with different legislation. Italy's legislation is the most restrictive because it bans 'heterologous insemination': the use of donor sperm, as opposed to the husband or male partner's sperm. If this restriction is lifted, perhaps as a result of *SH & Others v Austria*,[8] unmarried different-sex couples would have access to donor insemination, which would raise the question of discrimination contrary to the principle of *Karner v Austria*.[9] The same question can already be raised in Slovenia and Hungary, where unmarried male–female couples have access to donor insemination, but unmarried female–female couples do not. In Hungary, lesbian women with no partner have access to donor insemination. If they have a female partner (registered or cohabiting), they must pretend to be single when they request donor insemination, or travel to another EU Member State. Granting donor insemination to a heterosexual woman (with or without a male partner), but not to a lesbian woman with a female partner, is contrary to the principle of *EB v France*.[10] If a lesbian couple in Italy, Slovenia or Hungary seeks donor insemination in another EU Member State, the non-genetic mother may adopt the child and become its second legal parent only in Slovenia, and not in Italy or Hungary.

In the UK, legislation passed in 2008 fully equalised access to donor insemination for lesbian women, as individuals and as couples (in civil partnerships or cohabiting). Second-parent adoption for the non-genetic mother became available in 2005, but is no longer necessary. Under the 2008 law, the birth mother's civil partner or cohabiting partner will generally be treated as the child's second legal parent from the moment of its birth.

---

[8]   *SH & Others v Austria* (1 April 2010) ECtHR (reversed by Grand Chamber on 3 November 2011).

[9]   *Karner v Austria* (24 July 2003) ECtHR.

[10]   *EB v France* (22 January 2008) ECtHR.

Table 1: Summary of Legal Comparison

	Italy	Slovenia	Hungary	UK
'Sexual orientation' included in hate crimes legislation	No (cf race)	Yes	No (but 'any group in society')	Yes
'Sexual orientation' included in hate speech legislation	No (cf race)	Yes	No (but 'any group in society')	Yes, except in Scotland
'Sexual orientation' included in legislation on discrimination in primary/secondary education	No (cf race)	Yes	Yes	Yes
Immigration law recognises same-sex partners	No (unless EU law requires)	Yes	Yes	Yes
Lesbian women have access, as individuals or couples, to donor insemination (no need to travel to another Member State)	No	No	Yes (only lesbian women with no partner)	Yes
Same-sex couples have access to second-parent adoption (eg after insemination in another Member State)	No	Yes	No	Yes

2. Conclusions

This book has investigated homophobia, and efforts to confront homophobia, in the societies and laws of four EU Member States. Chapters three to five examined evidence of homophobic attitudes among students training to teach in schools or to educate teachers, while chapter six focused on homophobia in ethnic minority communities. Chapters eight to eleven considered evidence of homophobia in the national legal system (including government ministries, legislatures, and courts), as well as legal measures taken to combat homophobia in four specific areas: hate crimes and hate speech; education at all levels; free movement, immigration and asylum; and cross-border reproductive services.

One general conclusion from the sociological and legal research is that the content of statements or acts that are socially condemned as homophobic, or legally prohibited as discrimination based on sexual orientation, will vary over time. The same is true of the content of statements or acts that are socially condemned as racist or sexist, or legally prohibited as discrimination based on race or sex. In the case of racial minorities in the United States, there was an evolution from the constitutional prohibition of slavery in 1865[11] to the consti-tutional freedom to marry a person of a different race in 1967[12] (despite continuing social disapproval of different-race marriages). In the case of women in Europe, there was an evolution from the right to vote (first granted in Finland in 1906) to the right to equal pay under EU law (1957)[13] and the right to equal access to employment under EU law (1976).[14]

A similar evolution is occurring in Europe with regard to homophobia and discrimination based on sexual orientation. In England and Wales (as in most if not all European countries), the starting point for the treatment of same-sex couples was the death penalty for 'buggery' (anal intercourse), which was repealed only in 1861. Potential prison sentences for male–male sexual activity remained until 1967, and the UK Parliament described same-sex couples as 'pretended families' in 1988. However, social and legal change has been so rapid over the last two decades that, by 2011, the UK's prime minister could announce support for equal access to legal marriage for same-sex couples. This rapid evolution shows that objections to applying the term 'homophobia', not only to violence and discrimination against lesbian and gay individuals, but also to discrimination against same-sex couples, including in access to parental rights, are likely to decline over time.

Can homophobia (in the broad sense of rejecting equal opportunities for lesbian and gay persons) ever be completely eliminated from society and the law? Judging from programmes seeking to eliminate sexism and racism, which have existed in most European countries for much longer than action against homo-phobia, the answer is almost certainly no. Perfection cannot be achieved, espe-cially with regard to the attitudes and decisions of the huge variety of individuals working in the public and private sectors, or living in urban and rural settings, and coming from different religious, cultural and economic backgrounds. How-ever, all traces of discrimination based on sexual orientation can be removed from legislation, as in the case of discrimination based on sex, race or religion. Legal reforms, combined with public education and greater visibility on the part of lesbian and gay individuals and same-sex couples, can also gradually reduce

---

[11] Thirteenth Amendment to the United States Constitution.
[12] *Loving v Virginia*, 388 US 1 (1967).
[13] Art 119 TEEC, now Art 157 TFEU.
[14] Directive 76/207/EEC, now Directive 2006/54/EC.

homophobic attitudes until they become marginal, exceptional and socially unacceptable, as in the case of sexism and racism.

What would a country without homophobia look like? In its law, there would be no direct or indirect discrimination based on sexual orientation, and the strongest possible constitutional and legislative prohibitions of such discrimination by public and private actors would have been adopted. Of the four Member States studied in this book, the UK comes closest to the description of a country that has removed discrimination from its legislation. The main exception is the exclusion of same-sex couples from the right to marry, as opposed to the right to register a civil partnership. However, on 5 October 2011, an historic speech by Prime Minister David Cameron to the annual conference of the Conservative Party signalled the likelihood of change in the next few years, which could prove very influential in other EU Member States:

> I once stood before a Conservative conference and said it shouldn't matter whether commitment was between a man and a woman, a woman and a woman, or a man and another man. You applauded me for that. Five years on, we're consulting on legalising gay marriage.[15]

> And to anyone who has reservations, I say: Yes, it's about equality, but it's also about something else: commitment. Conservatives believe in the ties that bind us; that society is stronger when we make vows to each other and support each other. So I don't support gay marriage despite being a Conservative. I support gay marriage because I'm a Conservative.[16]

Legislation free of homophobia is one thing. But what would a *society* free of homophobia look like? Many different 'tests' can be imagined. One might be whether or not same-sex couples generally feel safe expressing affection in public places, in exactly the same way as different-sex couples, without fearing homophobic violence. Another might be whether or not most lesbian and gay adolescents, when they first become aware of their sexual orientation, feel comfortable discussing it with their parents, friends and teachers, because they can expect acceptance, respect and support, rather than homophobic hostility, ridicule or rejection.

---

[15] See 17 September 2011 speech of Lynne Featherstone, Minister for Equalities (Liberal Democrat), available at www.telegraph.co.uk/news/politics/liberaldemocrats/8770920/Liberal-Democrat-Conference-2011-Lynne-Featherstones-speech-in-full.html. See also www.home office.gov.uk/equalities/lgbt.

[16] See www.telegraph.co.uk/news/politics/conservative/8808521/Conservative-Party-conference-2011-David-Camerons-speech-in-full.html.

3. Recommendations

Based on the social and legal evidence analysed in this book, the sociological research team and the legal research team would like to make the following recommendations to the institutions of the EU, regarding action that should be taken at the EU level to help combat homophobia throughout the Member States.[17]

(1) Hate Crimes and Hate Speech

A measure should be adopted (through the appropriate post-Lisbon procedure) that would be similar in content to Council Framework Decision 2008/913/JHA of 28 November 2008 on combating certain forms and expressions of racism and xenophobia by means of criminal law.[18] This measure would require all Member States to adopt a criminal offence of 'publicly inciting to violence or hatred directed against a group of persons or a member of such a group defined by reference to [sexual orientation]' and, with regard to crimes of violence, 'to ensure that [homophobic] motivation is considered an aggravating circumstance, or, alternatively, that such motivation may be taken into consideration by the courts in the determination of the penalties'.[19]

(2) Education at all Levels

The extension to discrimination based on sexual orientation of the same protection that EU law provides with regard to discrimination based on racial or ethnic origin,[20] through the speedy adoption of COM (2008) 426 final: Commission Proposal (2 July 2008) for a Council Directive on implementing the principle of equal treatment between persons irrespective of religion or belief, disability, age

---

[17] See also the recommendations and studies of the Council of Europe, especially with regard to hate crimes, hate speech, education, and asylum: Recommendation CM/Rec(2010)5 of the Committee of Ministers to Member States on measures to combat discrimination on grounds of sexual orientation or gender identity (31 March 2010), available at wcd.coe.int/ViewDoc.jsp?id=1606669; Commissioner for Human Rights, 'Discrimination on grounds of sexual orientation and gender identity in Europe', 2nd edn (September 2011), available at www.coe.int/t/Commissioner/Source/LGBT/LGBTStudy2011_en.pdf.

[18] OJ L328/55 (6 December 2008), Arts 1(1) and 4.

[19] According to the EU's Fundamental Rights Agency, 13 of 27 Member States include sexual orientation in their hate speech legislation, and 12 of 27 do so in their hate crimes legislation. See 'Homophobia, transphobia and discrimination on grounds of sexual orientation and gender identity: 2010 Update', 42–43, available at fra.europa.eu/fraWebsite/attachments/FRA-2011-Homophobia-Update-Report_EN.pdf.

[20] Council Directive 2000/43/EC of 29 June 2000 implementing the principle of equal treatment between persons irrespective of racial or ethnic origin, OJ L180/22 (19 July 2000), Art 3(1).

or sexual orientation. This Directive would prohibit discrimination and harassment based on sexual orientation in education at all levels, as well as in access to social protection, social security, healthcare, social advantages, goods and services,[21] and housing.

EU institutions should support programmes at the national level seeking to educate teachers and students about diversity in the area of sexual orientation, and to combat homophobic bullying in educational institutions.

(3)   Free Movement, Immigration and Asylum

The definition of 'family member' in Article 2(2) of Directive 2004/38/EC should be amended as follows:

(a)   the spouse of the Union citizen, whether of different sex or of the same sex;

(b)   the partner with whom the Union citizen has contracted a registered partnership, whether of different sex or of the same sex ...

Directive 2004/83/EC should be amended to incorporate the principles of the UK Supreme Court's 2010 judgment,[22] in particular the principle that lesbian and gay asylum-seekers should not be expected to be 'discreet' in their home countries to avoid persecution.[23]

(4)   Cross-border Reproductive Services

EU institutions should study the problems caused by the conflicting legislation of Member States with regard to access to reproductive services for lesbian and gay individuals and same-sex couples, and with regard to legal recognition of the second parent of a child born after reproductive services are used, whether in another Member State or outside the EU.[24]

---

[21]   EU law is currently silent regarding the violent expulsion of a same-sex couple from a bar (a venue offering services to the public), as depicted in the photograph discussed in the introduction to this chapter. See n 3 above. See also the FRA's '2010 Update', n 19 above, p 7 (11 of 27 Member States have extended protection beyond employment to prohibit sexual orientation discrimination in all areas covered by the Racial Equality Directive, ibid).

[22]   *HJ (Iran) & HT (Cameroon) v Secretary of State for the Home Department* (7 July 2010) [2010] UKSC 31, available at www.bailii.org/uk/cases/UKSC/2010/31.html.

[23]   For more detailed recommendations, see Sabine Jansen and Thomas Spijkerboer, 'Fleeing Homophobia: Asylum Claims Related to Sexual Orientation and Gender Identity in Europe' (2011), 79–81, available at www.rechten.vu.nl/nl/Images/Fleeing%20Homophobia%20report% 20EN_tcm22–232205.pdf.

[24]   See '*25.000 europeas viajan cada año a otro país para tratarse la infertilidad*' ('25,000 European women travel every year to another country for treatment for infertility'), *El País* (Madrid), 20 August 2011, 30.

Bibliography

ACIERNO, M (2009) 'Ricongiungimento familiare per le coppie di fatto: la pronuncia della Cassazione' *Famiglia e diritto*, 5, 454–65.

ADAM, BD, DUYVENDAK, JW and KROUWEL, A (eds) (1999) *The Global Emergence of Gay and Lesbian Politics. National Imprints of a Worldwide Movement* (Philadelphia, Temple University Press).

ADAM, BD (1998) 'Theorizing Homophobia' *Sexualities*, 1(4), 387–404.

ALTIERI, L and FACCIOLI, P (2002) 'Percezione delle norme sociali, trasgressione e devianza' in C Buzzi, A Cavalli and A De Lillo (eds), *Giovani del nuovo secolo: quinto rapporto IARD sulla condizione giovanile in Italia* (Bologna, Il Mulino) 297–334.

AMATO, G and BARBERA, A (1997) *Manuale di diritto pubblico* (Bologna, Il Mulino).

BALKIN, RS, SCHLOSSER, LZ and LEVITT, DH (2009) 'Religious Identity and Cultural Diversity: Exploring the Relationships between Religious Identity, Sexism, Homophobia, and Multicultural Competence' *Journal of Counseling and Development*, 87, 420–27.

BARBAGLI, M and COLOMBO, A (2007) *Omosessuali moderni. Gay e lesbiche in Italia* (Bologna, Il Mulino).

BILOTTA, F (2005) 'Diritto e omosessualità', in P Cendon (ed) *I diritti della persona. Tutela civile, penale e amministrativa, I* (Torino, UTET).

—(ed) (2008) *Le unioni tra persone dello stesso sesso. Profili di diritto civile, comunitario e comparato* (Milano e Udine, Mimesis).

BIMBI, F (2009) 'Parola chiave "Genere. Donna/donne". Un approccio eurocentrico e transculturale' *Italian Journal of Social Policy*, 2, 261–97.

BINI, G (1975) 'Punto primo: educazione sessuale' *Donne e politica*, 31, 22–24.

BONI, S (2008), 'Stereotipi, valore, discriminazione: considerazioni socio-antropologiche', in T Casadei (ed), *Lessico delle discriminazioni tra società, diritto e istituzioni* (Reggio Emilia, Diabasis) 23–41.

BONINI BARALDI, M (2005) 'Il matrimonio fra cittadini italiani dello stesso sesso contratto all'estero non è trascrivibile: inesistente, invalido o contrario all'ordine pubblico?' *Famiglia e diritto*, 4, 418–26.

—(2010) *La famiglia de-genere. Matrimonio, omosessualità e Costituzione* (Milano e Udine, MIMESIS).

BORGOS, A (2007) 'Getting to Know Gays and Lesbians in Hungary: Lessons from a Gender-Informed Educational Program' in J Sempruch, K Willems and L Shook (eds), *Multiple Marginalities: An Intercultural Dialogue on Gender in Education* (Königstein/Taunus, Ulrike Helmer Verlag) 425–36.

BORRILLO, D (2009) *Omofobia. Storia e critica di un pregiudizio* (Bari, Edizioni Dedalo).

BOURDIEU, P (1998) *La domination masculine* (Paris, Editions du Seuil).

BRITTON, DM (1990) 'Homophobia and Homosociality: An Analysis of Boundary Maintenance' *Sociological Quarterly*, 31(3), 423–39.

BROWN, MJ and GROSCUP, JL (2009) 'Homophobia and Acceptance of Stereotypes about Gays and Lesbians' *Individual Differences Research*, 7(3), 159–67.

Bibliography

BRYANT, K and VIDAL-ORTIZ, S (2008) 'Introduction to Retheorizing Homophobia' *Sexualities* 11(4), 387–96.

BUTLER, J (1990) *Gender Trouble: Feminism and the Subversion of Identity* (New York, Routledge).

—(1991) 'Imitation and Gender Insubordination' in D Fuss (ed), *Inside/Out: Lesbian Theories, Gay Theories* (New York, Routledge) 13–31.

BUZZI, C (1998) *Giovani, affettività, sessualità. L'amore tra i giovani in una indagine IARD* (Bologna, Il Mulino).

CAPPELLO, F and GASPERONI, G (2003) 'Religione e morale: un carico di peso variabile' in F Garelli, G Guizzardi and E Pace (eds), *Un singolare pluralismo. Indagine sul pluralismo morale e religioso degli italiani* (Bologna, Il Mulino) 49–76.

CAVANA, P (2005) 'Sulla intrascrivibilità dell'atto di matrimonio validamente contratto all'estero tra persone dello stesso sesso' *Il Diritto di famiglia e delle persone*, 4, 1268–78.

COUNCIL OF THE EUROPEAN UNION (2009) *The Stockholm Programme: An Open and Secure Europe Serving and Protecting the Citizen* (Brussels, European Commission).

DANISH INSTITUTE FOR HUMAN RIGHTS (2009) *The Social Situation Concerning Homophobia and Discrimination on the Grounds of Sexual Orientation in the United Kingdom* (Copenhagen, Danish Institute for Human Rights).

DANOVI, AG (2006) 'Sull'inesistenza e non trascrivibilità del matrimonio per identità di sesso' *Diritto di famiglia e delle persone*, 2(1), 633–37.

DI CORI, P (2000) 'Genere e/o gender? Controversie storiche e teorie femministe', in A Bellagamba, P Di Cori and M Pustianaz (eds), *Generi di traverso. Culture, storie e narrazioni attraverso i confini delle discipline* (Vercelli, Mercurio) 17–70.

DOSI, G (2005) 'La Spagna è lontana: niente nozze gay. Quel sì è contrario all'ordine pubblico' *Diritto e giustizia*, 30–35.

DYNES, W (ed) (1990) *Encyclopedia of Homosexuality* (New York and London, Garland Publishing).

ENYEDI, ZS, FÁBIÁN, Z and SIK, E (2004) 'Is Prejudice Growing in Hungary? Changes in Anti-Semitism, Anti-Roma Feeling and Xenophobia over the Last Decade' in T Kolosi, Gy Vukovich and I Gy Tóth (eds), *Social Report 2004* (Budapest, TÁRKI) 363–85.

ERZEN, T (2006) *Straight to Jesus: Sexual and Christian Conversions in the Ex-Gay Movement* (Berkeley, University of California Press).

EURISPES (2003) *Gli italiani e i gay: il diritto alla differenza* (Roma, Eurispes).

—(2009), *Rapporto Italia 2009* (Roma, Eurispes).

EUROPEAN COMMISSION (2007) *Discrimination in the European Union: Eurobarometer 263* (Brussels, European Commission).

—(2008) *Discrimination in the European Union: Perceptions, Experiences and Attitudes. Eurobarometer 296* (Brussels, European Commission).

—(2009) *Discrimination in the EU in 2009: Perceptions, Experiences and Attitudes. Eurobarometer 317* (Brussels, European Commission).

EUROPEAN UNION AGENCY OF FUNDAMENTAL RIGHTS (2009) *Homophobia and Discrimination on Grounds of Sexual Orientation in the EU Members States: Part 1—Legal Analysis* (Brussels, European Commission).

—(2010) *Homophobia, Transphobia and Discrimination on Grounds of Sexual Orientation and Gender Identity: Comparative Legal Analysis* (Brussels, European Commission).

FAIRCLOUGH, N (1992) *Discourse and Social Change* (London, Polity).

Bibliography

FAIRCLOUGH, N and RUTH, W (1997) 'Critical Discourse Analysis' in TA van Dijk (ed), *Discourse as Social Interaction* (London, Sage) 158–83.

FALLETTI, E (2007) 'La filiazione. Questioni processuali sostanziali internazionali nell'analisi della giurisprudenza', 75.

FONE, B (2000) *Homophobia: A History* (New York, Picador).

FORTIN, J (2011) 'Sensitization to Homophobia for Professionals Working with Adolescents' in M Groneberg and C Funke (eds), *Combating Homophobia: Experiences and Analyses Pertinent to Education* (Berlin, Lit Verlang) 27–38.

FRASER, N (2002) 'Recognition without Ethics?' in S Lash and M Featherstone (eds), *Recognition and Difference: Politics, Identity, Multiculture* (London, Sage) 21–42.

FREDMAN, S (2002), *Discrimination Law* (Oxford, Oxford University Press).

FUNKE, M (2011) 'Non-Discrimination as a Value of Citizenship' in M Groneberg and C Funke (eds), *Combating Homophobia: Experiences and Analyses Pertinent to Education* (Berlin, Lit Verlang) 255–45.

GALLETTO, T (1982) 'Identità di sesso e rifiuto delle pubblicazioni per la celebrazione del matrimonio' *Giurisprudenza italiana*, 2, 169–72.

GALLI, N (1979) 'L'educazione sessuale nella scuola italiana?' *Vita e pensiero*, 9, 28–38.

GARFINKEL, H (1955) 'Conditions of Successful Degradation Ceremonies' *American Journal of Sociology* 61, 420–42.

GERBER, L (2008) 'The Opposite of Gay: Nature, Creation, and Queerish ex-Gay Experiments' *Nova Religio*, 11(4), 8–30.

GERHARDS, J (2010) 'Non-Discrimination towards Homosexuality: The European Union's Policy and Citizens' Attitudes Towards Homosexuality in 27 European Countries' *International Sociology*, 25(5), 5–28.

GOFFMAN, E (1963) *Stigma: Notes On The Management of Spoiled Identity* (Englewood Cliffs, Prentice-Hall).

GOODMAN, MB and MORADI, B (2008) 'Attitudes and Behaviours toward Lesbian and Gay Persons: Critical Correlates and Mediated Relations' *Journal of Counseling Psychology*, 55(3), 371–84.

GREENBERG, DF (1988) *The Construction of Homosexuality* (Chicago and London, University of Chicago Press).

GUASP, A (2009) *The Teachers' Report: Homophobic Bullying in Britain's Schools* (London, Stonewall).

GUSMANO, B and BERTONE, C (2011) 'Partnership e legittimazione nelle politiche locali LBGT' in Cirsde e Servizio LGBT della Città di Torino (eds), *Politiche locali LGBT: L'Italia e il caso Piemonte* (Torino, Città di Torino) 13–62.

GUTMANN, A (1987) *Democratic Education* (Princeton, Princeton University Press).

GUZMÁN, M (2006) *Gay Hegemony/Latino Homosexualities* (New York and London, Routledge).

HAMILTON, L (2007) 'Trading on Heterosexuality: College Women's Gender Strategies and Homophobia' *Gender & Society*, 21(2), 145–72.

HEREK, GM (1984), 'Beyond "Homophobia": A Social Psychological Perspective on Attitudes toward Lesbians and Gay Men' *Journal of Homosexuality*, vol 10, (1–2), 1–21.

—(1986) 'The Instrumentality of Attitudes: Towards a Neofunctionalist Theory' *Journal of Social Issues* 42 (2), 99–114.

—(1987) 'Can Functions be Measured? A New Perspective on the Functional Approach to Attitudes' *Social Psychology Quarterly* 50 (4), 285–303.

—(1990) 'The Context of Anti-Gay Violence: Notes on Cultural and Psychological Heterosexism' *Journal of Interpersonal Violence* 5(3), 316–33.

—(1991) 'Stigma, Prejudice, and Violence Against Lesbians and Gay Men' in JC Gonsiorek and JD Weinrich (eds), *Homosexuality: Research Implications for Public Policy* (Newbury Park, Sage) 60–80.

—(2004) 'Beyond 'Homophobia': Thinking About Sexual Prejudice and Stigma in the Twenty-First Century' *Sexuality Research and Social Policy* 1(2), 6–24.

—(2011) 'Anti-Equality Marriage Amendments and Sexual Stigma' *Journal of Social Issues*, 67(2), 413–26.

HEREK, GM, GILLIS, JR and COGAN, JC (2009) 'Internalized Stigma Among Sexual Minority Adults: Insights From a Social Psychological Perspective' *Journal of Counseling Psychology*, 56, 32–43.

HOCKEY, J, MEAH, A and ROBINSON, V (2007) *Mundane Heterosexualities: From Theory to Practices* (Basingstoke, Palgrave MacMillan).

HONNETH, A (1992), *Kampf und Anerkennung. Grammatik sozialer Konflikte* (Frankfurt, Suhrkamp).

HUDSON, WH and RICKETTS, WA (1980) 'A Strategy for the Measurement of Homophobia' *Journal of Homosexuality*, 5(4), 357–72.

HUNT, R and DICK, S (2008) *Serves You Right: Lesbian and Gay People's Expectations of Discrimination* (London, Stonewall).

HUNT, R and JENSEN, J (2007) *The School Report: The Experiences of Young Gay People in Britain's Schools* (London, Stonewall).

ISPES (1991) *Il sorriso di Afrodite. Rapporto sulla condizione omosessuale italiana* (Firenze, Vallecchi).

JENNESS, V and BROAD KL (1994) 'Antiviolence Activism and the (In)Visibility of Gender in the Gay/Lesbian and Women's Movements' *Gender & Society* 8(3), 402–23.

JULESZ, M (2008) 'A tojásdobálás jogi, társadalmi és etikai megközelítése' *Ügyészek Lapja*, 15(6), 19–34.

KÁRPÁTI, J (2005) 'Az utolsó próbatétel. Ítélet a Háttér Társaság kontra Károli Egyetem ügyben' *Fundamentum* 9(3), 105–08.

KÁRPÁTI, J et al (2006) *Az egyenlö bánásmódról és az esélyegyenlöség elömozdításáról szóló 2003. évi CXXV. törvény magyarázata.* (Budapest, Másság Alapítvány).

KIMMEL, MS (2000) *The Gendered Society* (Oxford, Oxford University Press).

—(2005) 'Masculinity as Homophobia. Fear, Shame, and Silence in the Construction of Gender Identity' in MS Kimmel (ed), *The Gender of Desire. Essays on Male Sexuality* (Albany, State University of New York Press) 25–44.

KITZINGER, C (1987) *The Social Construction of Lesbianism* (London, Sage).

KOMIDAR, K and MANDELJC S (2009) 'Homoseksualnost skozi analizo učnih načrtov, šolskih učbenikov in šolske prakse' *Sodobna pedagogika* 60(4), 164–81.

KOVAC ŠEBART, M and KREK, J (2009) *Vzgojna zasnova javne šole* (Ljubljana, Pedagoška fakulteta Univerze v Ljubljani).

KOVAC ŠEBART, M and KUHAR, R (2009) 'Breaking the Wall of Silence' *Sodobna pedagogika* 60(4), 16–25.

KRAMBERGER ŠKERL, J (2008) *Evropeizacija javnega reda v mednarodnem zasebnem pravu* (Ljubljana, Inštitut za primerjalno pravo).

KUHAR, R (2001a) *Mi, drugi* (Ljubljana, Škuc).

— (2001b) 'Geji in lezbijke vam želijo lep dan: Poročanje slovenskih medijev o homofobiji' *Medijska preža* (12), 17.

Bibliography

—(2006) 'Homophobija: kultura stahu pred homoseksualnostjo' *Teorija in praksa* 43(3/4), 540–56.

—(2007) 'The Family Secret: Parents of Homosexual Sons and Daughters' in R Kuhar and J Takács (eds), *Beyond the Pink Curtain: Everyday Life of LGBT People in Eastern Europe* (Ljubljana, Peace Institute), 35–47.

—(2009) *At the Crossroads of Discrimination: Multiple and Intersectional Discrimination* (Ljubljana, Peace Institute).

—(2010) *Intimno državljanstvo* (Ljubljana, Škuc).

—(2011) 'Heteronormative Panopticon and the Transparent Closet of the Public Space in Slovenia' in R Kulpa and J Mizielinska (eds), *De-centring Western Sexualities: Central and Eastern European Perspectives* (Burlington, Ashgate) 149–65.

KUHAR, R and MAGIC, J (2008) 'Izkušnje in percepcije homofobičnega nasilja in diskriminacije' in J Magić, R Kuhar and N Kogovšek (eds), *Povej naprej: Raziskovanje, spremljanje in beleženje primerov diskriminacije, kršitev pravic in nasilja nad istospolno usmerjenimi v Sloveniji v obdobju med novembrom 2007 in novembrom 2008 (Raziskovalno poročilo)* (Ljubljana, Legebitra).

KUHAR, R, MALJEVAC, S, KOLETNIK, A and MAGIC, J (2008) *Vsakdanje življenje istospolno usmerjenih mladih v Sloveniji (Raziskovalno poročilo)* (Ljubljana, Legebitra).

KUHAR, R and TAKÁCS, J (eds) (2007), *Beyond the Pink Curtain: Everyday Life of LGBT People in Eastern Europe* (Ljubljana, Peace Institute).

LELLERI, R (ed) (2007) *Schoolmates. Report finale della ricerca transnazionale sul bullismo di stampo omofobico nelle scuole superiori di quattro Paesi europei* (Bologna, Arcigay).

LELLERI, R *et al* (2005) *Modidi: sesso e salute di lesbiche, gay e bisessuali oggi in Italia. Principali risultati sociosanitari* (Bologna, Arcigay).

LENER, S (1977) 'L'educazione sessuale e la scuola' *Civiltà cattolica*, fascicolo 30056.

LEŠNIK, B (2006) 'Melting the Iron Curtain: The Beginnings of the LGBT Movement in Slovenia' in M Chateauvert (ed), *New Social Movements and Sexuality* (Sophia, Bilitis Resource Center) 86–96.

LIPKIN, A (1999) *Understanding Homosexuality, Changing Schools* (Colorado, Westview Press).

LOCATI, G (2009) 'Il ruolo pubblico della religione nell'enciclica *Caritas in Veritate*' *Diritto pubblico*, 3, 855–94.

LOFTUS, J (2001) 'America's Liberalization in Attitudes toward Homosexuality' *American Sociological Review*, 66(5), 762–82.

LONG, S (1999) 'Gay and Lesbian Movements in Eastern Europe: Romania, Hungary, and the Czech Republic', in BD Adam, JW Duyvendak and A Krouwel (eds) *The Global Emergence of Gay and Lesbian Politics. National Imprints of a Worldwide Movement* (Philadelphia, Temple University Press) 242–65.

MAGIC, J and JANJEVAK, A (2011) *Oprostite, gospa učiteljica, ste lezbijka? (Raziskovalno poročilo)* (Ljubljana, Legebitra).

MAGIC, J, KUHAR R and KOGOVŠEK, N (eds) (2008), *Povej naprej: Raziskovanje, spremljanje in beleženje primerov diskriminacije, kršitev pravic in nasilja nad istospolno usmerjenimi v Sloveniji v obdobju med novembrom 2007 in novembrom 2008 (Raziskovalno poročilo)* (Ljubljana, Legebitra).

MALJEVAC, S and MAGIC, J (2009) 'Pedri raus!: Homofobično nasilje v šolah' *Sodobna pedagogika* 60(4), 90–119.

Bibliography

MANALANSAN IV, MF (2009) 'Homophobia at New York's Gay Central', in DAB Murray (ed) *Homophobias: Lust and Loathing across Time and Space* (Durham, Duke University Press).

MASON, G (2002) *The Spectacle of Violence. Homophobia, Gender and Knowledge* (London and New York, Routledge).

MELUCCI, A (1996) *Challenging Codes. Collective Action in the Information Age* (Cambridge, Cambridge University Press).

MENCIN ČEPLAK, M and KUHAR, R (2010) 'Boji za enakost. Od diskriminacije homoseksualnosti do redefinicije družine' *Socialno delo* (49/5–6), 283–98.

MEYER, IH (1995) 'Minority Stress and Mental Health of Gay Men' *Journal of Health and Social Behaviour* 36(1), 38–56.

MONTELL, F (1999) 'Focus Group Interviews: A New Feminist Method' *NWSA Journal* 11(1), 44–71.

MORIN, SF and GARFINKLE, EM (1978) 'Male Homophobia' *Journal of Social Issues* 34(1), 29–47.

MOSCONI, F and CAMPIGLIO, C (2006) *Diritto internazionale privato e processuale. Parte speciale* (Torino, UTET).

MURRAY, DAB (ed) (2009) *Homophobias: Lust and Loathing across Time and Space* (Durham, Duke University Press).

NARDI, P (1998) 'The Globalization of the Gay and Lesbian Socio-Political Movement. Some Observation about Europe with a Focus on Italy' *Sociological Perspectives*, 41(3), 567–86.

NEGY, C and EISENMAN, R (2005) 'A Comparison of African American and White College Students' Affective and Attitudinal Reactions to Lesbian, Gay, and Bisexual Individuals: An Exploratory Study' *Journal of Sex Research*, 42(4), 291–98.

NOVAK, B (2007) 'Pravna ureditev istospolne partnerske skupnosti—nova slovenska pravna ureditev' *Pravnik*, 6–8, 313–41.

O'DONOHUE, W and CASELLES, CE (1993) 'Homophobia: Conceptual, Definitional, and Value Issues' *Journal of Psychopathology and Behavioral Assessment*, 15(3), 177–95.

OBERTO, G (2010) 'Problemi di coppia, omosessualità e filiazione' *Il diritto della famiglia e delle persone* 2, 802–33.

OLEKSY, EH (ed) (2009) *Intimate Citizenships* (London, Routledge).

ORLANDI, M (2005) 'Matrimonio contratto all'estero da cittadini italiani dello stesso sesso e sua efficacia giuridica in Italia' *Giurisprudenza di merito*, 11(1), 2292–304.

PACE, A (1992) *La problematica delle libertà costituzionali. Parte speciale 2* (Padova, CEDAM).

PACE, A and MANETTI, M (2006) *Rapporti civili. Art. 21: la libertà di manifestazione del proprio pensiero* (Bologna, Zanichelli).

PASCOE, CJ (2007) *Dude, You're a Fag. Masculinity and Sexuality in High School* (Berkeley, University of California Press).

PERICO, G (1972) 'Educazione sessuale scolastica' *Problemi minorili*, 6, 677–90.

PIERACCIONI, DD (1981) 'I rischi dell'educazione sessuale' *Idea*, fascicoli 8–10, 39–42.

PILE, S and KEITH, M (eds) (1997) *Geographies of Resistance* (New York, Routledge).

PLUMMER, D (1999) *One of the Boys. Masculinity, Homophobia and Modern Manhood* (New York, Haworth Press).

PLUMMER, K (1975) *Sexual Stigma: An Interactionist Account* (London, Routledge and Kegan Paul).

—(1981) 'Homosexual Categories: Some Research Problems in the Labelling Perspective of Homosexuality' in K Plummer (ed) *The Making of the Modern Homosexual* (London, Hutchinson) 53–75.

POON, MK and HO, PT (2008) 'Negotiating Social Stigma among Gay Asian Men' *Sexualities*, 11(1/2), 245–68.

PRATI, G (ed) (2010) *Report finale della ricerca sul bullismo omofobico nelle scuole superiori italiane* (Bologna, Arcigay).

PROSDOCIMI, S (2006) 'I rapporti tra Stato e Chiesa oggi in Italia: osservazioni su alcuni problemi di contenuto e di metodo' *Rivista italiana di diritto e procedura penale*, 2, 752–60.

PUTNAM, RD (2000) *Bowling Alone: The Collapse and Revival of American Community* (New York, Simon & Schuster).

QUARENGHI, V (1983) 'L'introduzione dell'educazione sessuale nella scuola statale' *Studi sociali*, 5, 77–83.

QUINLIVAN, K and TOWN, S (1999) 'Queer pedagogy, Educational Practice and Lesbian and Gay Youth' *Qualitative Studies in Education*, 12(5), 509–24.

RAHMAN, M and JACKSON, S (2010) *Gender and Sexuality* (Cambridge, Polity Press).

RASMUSSEN, ML (2010) 'Secularism, Religion and "Progressive" Sex Education' *Sexualities*, 13(6), 699–712.

RAYMOND, JG (2006) 'Sappho by Surgery. The Transsexually Constructed Lesbian-Feminist' in S Stryker and S Whittle (eds), *The Transgender Studies Reader* (New York and London, Routledge) 131–43.

RENER, T (2008) 'O življenju med filozofi in plemenskim govedom' *Narobe* 3(7), 24–25.

—(2009) 'Homoseksualnost in šola: stališča študentk in študentov do obravnave homo-seksualnosti pri pouku' *Sodobna pedagogika* 60 (126), 106–20.

RICHARDSON, D (2000) 'Constructing Sexual Citizenship' *Critical Social Policy* 20(1), 105–35.

RIVERS, I and CARRAGHER, DJ (2003) 'Social-Developmental Factors Affecting Lesbian and Gay Youth: A Review of Cross-National Research Findings' *Children and Society* 17(5), 374–85.

RODERICK, T *et al* (1998) 'Behavioral Aspects of Homonegativity' *Journal of Homosexuality*, 36(1), 79–88.

ROFFMAN, DM (2000) 'A Model for Helping Schools Address Policy Options Regarding Gay and Lesbian Youth' *Journal of Sex Education and Therapy*, 2–3(25), 130–36.

ROSIK, CH (2007) 'Ideological Concerns in the Operationalization of Homophobia, Part 1: An Analysis of Herek's ATLG-R Scale' *Journal of Psychology and Theology*, 35(2), 132–44.

RYE, BJ and MEANEY, GJ (2009) 'Impact of a Homonegativity Awareness Workshop on Attitudes towards Homosexuality' *Journal of Homosexuality*, 56(1), 31–55.

SÁNDOR, B (ed) (2010) *Mi vagyunk a család, a biztonság, az otthona. Leszbikus anyák, meleg apák és 'pótapák'* (Budapest, Inter Alia Alapítvány).

SARACENO, C (ed) (2003) *Diversi da chi? Gay, lesbiche, transessuali in un'area metropolitana* (Milano, Guerini).

SCHLESINGER, P (2005) 'Matrimonio tra individui dello stesso sesso contratto all'estero' *Famiglia e diritto*, 4, 415–18.

SCHOPE, RD and ELIASON, MJ (2003) '"Sissies and Tomboys": Gender Role Behaviours and Homophobia' *Journal of Gay and Lesbian Social Services*, 16(2), 73–97.

Bibliography

SCHUSTER, A (ed) (2011) *Omogenitorialità. filiazione, orientamento sessuale e diritto* (Milano e Udine, Mimesis).

SCHÜTZ, A (1971–73) *Collected Papers*, (The Hague, M Nijhoff).

SEARS, JT (1997) 'Thinking Critically. Intervening Effectively about Homophobia and Heterosexism' in JT Sears and WL Williams (eds), *Overcoming Heterosexism and Homophobia* (New York, Columbia University Press), 13–48.

SEDGWICK, EK (1990) *Epistemology of the Closet* (Berkeley, University of California Press).

SEIDMAN, S (2002) *Beyond the Closet. The Transformation of Gay and Lesbian Life* (London and New York, Routledge).

SEIDMAN, S, MEEKS, C and TRASCHEN F (1999) 'Beyond the Closet? The Changing Social Meaning of Homosexuality in the United States' *Sexualities* 2(1), 9–34.

SELL, RL (1997) 'Defining and Measuring Sexual Orientation: A Review' *Archives of Sexual Behavior*, 26(6), 643–58.

SESTA, M (2007) 'Il matrimonio estero tra due cittadini italiani dello stesso sesso è trascrivibile in Italia?' *Famiglia e diritto*, 2, 169–72.

SHIPLEY, H (forthcoming) 'Connected Identities: Challenging Narrative Scripts about Identity Construction' in P Dickey Young, H Shipley and T Trothen (eds), *Sexual Diversity and Religious Diversity* (Vancouver, University of British Columbia Press).

SIMMEL, G (1908) *Soziologie* (Berlin, Humbolt)

SIRAJ, A (2009) 'The Construction of the Homosexual "Other" by British Muslim Heterosexuals' *Contemporary Islam*, 3, 41–57.

SMITH, AM (1997) 'The Good Homosexual and the Dangerous Queer: Resisting the "New Homophobia"' in L Segal (ed), *New Sexual Agendas* (Houndmills, MacMillan Press).

SMITH, C (2010) 'British Sexual Cultures' in H Higgins, C Smith and J Storey (eds) *The Cambridge Companion to Modern British Culture* (Cambridge, Cambridge University Press) 244–61.

SOLYMÁR, B and TAKÁCS, J (2007) 'Wrong Bodies and Real Selves. Transsexual People in the Hungarian Social and Health Care System' in R Kuhar and J Takács (eds), *Beyond the Pink Curtain. Everyday Life of LGBT People in Eastern Europe* (Ljubljana, Mirovni Institut) 143–68.

SONEGO, A, PODIO, C, BENEDETTI, L et al (2005) *Cocktail d'amore. 700 e più modi di essere lesbica* (Milano, DeriveApprodi).

STANKO, EA and CURRY, P (1997) 'Homophobic Violence and the Self "at Risk": Interrogating the Boundaries' *Social & Legal Studies*, 6(4), 513–32.

ŠTULHOFER, A and RIMAC, I (2009) 'Determinants of Homonegativity in Europe' *Journal of Sex Research* 46(1), 24–32.

ŠVAB, A and KUHAR, R (2005) *The Unbearable Comfort of Privacy. The Everyday Life of Gays and Lesbians* (Ljubljana, Mirovni Institut).

SZYMANSKI, DM and GUPTA, A (2009) 'Examining the Relationship Between Multiple Internalized Oppressions and African American Lesbian, Gay, Bisexual, and Questioning Persons' Self-Esteem and Psychological Distress' *Journal of Counselling Psychology*, 56(1), 110–18.

TAKÁCS, J (2004) *Homoszexualitás és társadalom* (Budapest, Új Mandátum Kiadó).

—(2006) *Social Exclusion of Young Lesbian, Gay, Bisexual and Transgender (LGBT) People in Europe* (Brussels, ILGA-Europe and IGLYO).

—(2007) 'It Is Only Extra Information. Social Representation and Value Preferences of Gay Men in Hungary' in R Kuhar and J Takács (eds), *Beyond the Pink Curtain. Everyday Life of LGBT People in Eastern Europe* (Ljubljana, Mirovni Institut) 185–97.

—(2009) 'LGBT Youth at School: Being Threatened by Heteronormative Oppression' *Journal of Contemporary Educational Studies*, 60(4), 68–88.

TAKÁCS, J and KUHAR, R (2007) 'Introduction: What Is Beyond the Pink Curtain?' in R Kuhar ad J Takács (eds), *Beyond the Pink Curtain. Everyday Life of LGBT People in Eastern Europe* (Ljubljana, Mirovni Institut), 11–12.

TAKÁCS, J and SZALMA, I (2008) *Slovenian Public Opinion Survey 2008/1: European Values Study* [database] (Ljubljana, Faculty of Social Sciences).

—(2011) 'Homophobia and Same-Sex Partnership Legislation in Europe', *Equality, Diversity and Inclusion: An International Journal*, 30(5), 356–78.

TAKÁCS, J, MOCSONAKI, L and P TÓTH, T (2008) *Social Exclusion of Lesbian, Gay, Bisexual and Transgender (LGBT) People in Hungary. Research Report* (Budapest, Institute of Sociology, HAS—Háttér Support Society for LGBT People in Hungary. Report available at www.mek.oszk.hu/06600/06641/index.phtml).

TOMSEN, S (2006) 'Homophobic Violence, Cultural Essentialism and Shifting Sexual Attitudes' *Social & Legal Studies* 15(3), 389–407.

TOMSEN, S and MASON, G (2001) 'Engendering Homophobia: Violence, Sexuality and Gender Conformity' *Journal of Sociology* 37(3), 257–73.

TOŠ, N, MALNAR, B *et al* (2005) *Slovenian Public Opinion Survey 2005/3+4: World Values Survey* [database] (Ljubljana, Faculty of Social Sciences).

TRAPPOLIN, L (2004) *Identità in azione. Mobilitazione omosessuale e sfera pubblica* (Roma, Carocci).

—(2011a) 'L'homoparentalité et l'horizon de la modernité. Mères lesbiennes, péres gays dans les discours de la presse italienne' in E Ruspini (ed), *Monoparentalité, Homoparentalité, Transparentalité en France et en Italie* (Paris, L'Harmattan) 123–42.

—(2011b) 'Narrare l'orientamento omosessuale' in E Ruspini and M Inghilleri (eds), *Sessualità narrate. Esperienze di intimità a confronto* (Milano, Franco Angeli) 143–64.

—(ed) (2007) *Gli altri e noi. Giovani, pluralismo culturale e diversità* (Milano, Guerini).

ULE, M (ed) (2005) *Predsodki in disrkiminacije* (Ljubljana, Znanstevno in publicistično središče).

VAN DIJK, TA (1991) *Racism and the Press* (London and New York, Routledge).

VELIKONJA, N and GREIF, T (2001) 'Anketa o diskriminaciji na osnovi spolne usmerjenosti' *Lesbo* (11/12), 15–23.

VIDAL-ORTIZ, S (2008) '"The Puerto Rican Way is More Tolerant": Constructions and Uses of "Homophobia" among *Santeria* Practitioners Across Ethno-Racial and National Identification' *Sexualities*, 11(4), 476–95.

WARNER, M (2001) *The Trouble With Normal: Sex, Politics, and the Ethics of Queer Life* (Cambridge, Harvard University Press).

WEEKS, J (1979) *Coming Out: Homosexual Politics in Britain, from the Nineteenth Century to the Present* (London, Quartet Books).

—(2007) *The World We Have Won* (London, Routledge).

WEINBERG, G (1972) *Society and the Healthy Homosexual* (New York, St Martin's Press).

WILCHINS, R (2004) *Queer Theory, Gender Theory* (Los Angeles, Alyson Books).

WINTEMUTE, R (1994) 'Sexual Orientation Discrimination', in C McCrudden and G Chambers (eds), *Individual Rights and the Law in Britain* (Oxford, Oxford University Press, 1994).

—(2005) 'Sexual Orientation and Gender Identity', in C Harvey (ed), *Human Rights in the Community* (Oxford, Hart Publishing).

YIP, AKT (2004) 'Embracing Allah and Sexuality?: South Asian non-Heterosexual Muslims in Britain' in P Kumar and K Jacobsen (eds) *South Asians in the Diaspora: Histories and Religious Traditions* (Leiden, EJ Brill).

—(forthcoming) 'When Religion Meets Sexuality: Two Tales of Intersection' in P Dickey Young, H Shipley and T Trothen (eds), *Sexual Diversity and Religious Diversity* (Vancouver, University of British Columbia Press).

YIP, AKT with KHALID, A (2010) 'Looking for Allah: Spiritual Quests of Queer Muslims' in K Browne, SR Munt and AKT Yip (eds), *Queer Spiritual Spaces: Sexuality and Sacred Places* (Farnham, Ashgate).

YIP, AKT, KEENAN, M and PAGE, S (2011) *Religion, Youth and Sexuality: Selected Key Findings from a Multi-Faith Exploration* (Nottingham, University of Nottingham).

YOUNG, IM (1990), *Justice and the Politics of Difference* (Princeton, Princeton University Press).

ZANUTTO, A (2007) 'Comportamenti giovanili tra rappresentazione degli adulti e gruppo dei pari: la moralità situata', in C Buzzi, A Cavalli and A De Lillo (eds), *Rapporto giovani: sesta indagine dell'istituto IARD sulla condizione giovanile in Italia* (Bologna, Il Mulino) 209–24.

Index

Note: individual countries referred to are Hungary, Italy, Slovenia and the United Kingdom

Index

surrogacy 199–201
conclusions 201–2
cross-border reproductive services 197–201
donor insemination 197–9
education/schools
  enforceability 182–4
  generality issues 182
  legislation 183–4
  Proud of my Sex/Proud of my Pole
    campaign 185–7
  school curricula 184–5
equality violation 175–7
family reunification
  same-sex partners, EU citizens 187–90
  third-country nationals/refugees 190–3
free movement/immigration/asylum 187–97
hate crime
  Black Hoods case 177–9
  equality violation 175–7
  homophobia, as term 171
  incitement 173
  other crimes and 173–4
  personal harassment 174–5
  sexual orientation issues 171–5
hate speech 174–5
  personal harassment 174–5
  prosecution 179
  web portals, Code for regulation 181
Human Rights Ombudsman 180–1
international protection 193–7
refugees 190–3
Same-Sex Civil Partnership Act 2005 75
same-sex partners, EU citizens 187–90
sexual orientation issues 171–5
surrogacy 199–201
third-country nationals/refugees 190–3
web portals, Code for regulation 181
see also Slovenia, sociological case studies
Slovenia, sociological case studies
  case studies 54–5, 57, 76
  compensation 74–6
  conclusions 76–7
  definitions 56
  discrimination/violence 58
  education/schools discussion 62–71
    background 62–3
    coming out 68–9
    in curriculum 65–7
    means/timing 63–5
    parental fears 70–1
  Family Code debates 53, 55, 61–2, 75–6
  humanistic aspect 64–5
  integration 58–9
  meanings 57–60
  media responses 60–1
  medium-homonegative background 51–2
  new homophobia 52–4
  normalisation 59–60, 64–5

political correctness 61
prejudice 57
public discourse 60–2
resignation 74
self-censorship 72–3
sensitisation 73
strategies 71–6
see also Slovenia, legal case studies
Smith, AM 54
sociological case studies (*Citizens in Diversity: A
  Four Nation Study on Homophobia and
  Fundamental Rights*)
  by country *see under* individual countries
  education students/training 13, 14, 17–19
  ethnic minorities 13, 14, 19
  heteronormativity 15, 16–17
  heterosexual and lesbian/gay perspectives 13
  methodology 13–14
  publication details 1
  secrecy/resignation 19–20
  social/cultural norms 15–16
  thematic areas 14–15
  see also legal case studies
stigmatisation 71–2, 123
  by country *see under* Hungary; Italy
  sexual stigma 110
students *see* education/schools
surrogacy 161
  see also under individual countries
symbolic violence 22

Takács, J 66
third-country nationals
  Hungary 225–6
  Slovenia 190–3
transsexual/transgender issues 85–6

United Kingdom, homophobia, ethnic minority
  communities
  male-male decriminalisation 107
  sexual equality legislation 107–8, 124–5,
    126–8, 129
United Kingdom, legal case studies
  asylum seekers
    discretion requirement 254–8
    rejection rate 253–4
  cross-border reproductive services 259–64
  discrimination 273
  donor insemination 259–61
  education/schools 241–8
    equality legislation 243–5, 248
    exclusion of teachers/students 242–3
    fostering positive attitudes 247–8
    homophobic bullying 246–7
    National Curriculum 245
    section 28 241–2
    statutory guidance 242
  equality legislation 243–5, 248